CONTINENTAL!
ITS MOTORS
AND ITS PEOPLE

by

WILLIAM WAGNER

in cooperation with

AERO PUBLISHERS, INC.
Fallbrook, CA 92028

Copyright © 1983 by William Wagner. All Rights Reserved. Printed in the United States of America. No part of this publication may be reproduced, stored in a retrieval system, or transmitted, in any form or by any means, electronic, mechanical, photocopying, recording, or otherwise, without prior written permission.

Library of Congress Cataloging in Publication Data
Wagner, William, 1909–
Continental! Its Motors and Its People
Includes index.
1. Continental Motors Corporation—History.
2. Internal combustion engine industry—United States—
History. I. Title.
HD9710.U54C658   1983   338.7'62143'0973   83-3878
ISBN 0-8168-4506-9 (Aero)

Published by
Armed Forces Journal International
in cooperation with
Aero Publishers, Inc.
329 West Aviation Road, Fallbrook, CA 92028

PRINTED AND BOUND IN THE UNITED STATES OF AMERICA

To Carl, Jim and Art
>who reached back in time to bring to life the pre-Ryan/Teledyne days of Continental Motors

FOREWORD

Few are privileged, as the Ferry family has been, to be both participant in and witness to the birth, growth — even the survival — and ultimate success, of a great American industrial company.

Here was a story waiting to be told; the 80 years history of a company at the very center of the development of the internal combustion engine in its many forms.

The year was 1904 when my father, James H. Ferry, Sr., risked his savings to become a major investor in a small company trying to get started as a supplier of internal combustion engines for horseless carriages.

An enterprising young engineer, Ross W. Judson, had come back from an after-college European trip to extol the virtues of an automobile engine he had seen and examined while in France.

On his return to Chicago, young Judson and his brother-in-law, Arthur W. Tobin, formed Autocar Equipment Co. with $2000 to build "Continental Motors," the designs of which were based in part on what knowledge Judson had brought back from the Continent. Other members of the Tobin family, and of the Yeoman family (father's mother was Mary Jane Yeoman), supplied additional capital to get the company on its way.

Success followed success as the company, now Continental Motor Manufacturing Co., moved from Chicago to Muskegon, Michigan; then built an additional plant in Detroit.

My father was part of the venture from the beginning and therefore I was privileged to know the players in this drama which William Wagner has so carefully and accurately reconstructed for the serious student of American industrial development. Only two of the principals in the firm were not known to me personally. One was co-founder Arthur W. Tobin; the other, his brother Benjamin Franklin Tobin, who served as company president during many of its early years.

The company's initial success was in building engines for early car makers who were actually assemblers of parts bought from specialty suppliers. During the first World War they also made engines for Army trucks, the forerunner of later military business.

But, by the early 1920s, the 'big three' (General Motors, Ford and Chrysler, which built their own engines) dominated the market. To survive, Continental branched out into also supplying engines for industrial, agricultural, construction and marine equipment manufacturers.

After the death of Benj. F. Tobin in 1920 and the departure ten years later of flamboyant co-founder Ross Judson, management leadership was assumed by attorney William R. Angell, who had started with Continental in 1917 as corporate secretary.

At that time, as the Depression of the '30s began to drag the economy down, my father reluctantly had to take a more active role in management. Angell had earlier been responsible for Continental acquiring rights to single-sleeve-valve engines and, with Ross Judson, played an important role in the company moving into aircraft engines, a field in which it has been a major factor for over half a century.

Mr. Angell (he was always 'Mister' to me) wanted very much to manufacture an automobile; it was almost a hang-up with him. So Continental built the Beacon, Flyer and Ace cars in the thirties — and almost went broke after losing $14 million.

The company had hired a new purchasing agent during the car building years — a hard driving dedicated man by the name of Clarence J. Reese. By 1939 the company was in such serious straits that my father saw to it that Angell was replaced by the steadier "Jack" Reese.

In 1930, Angell could not have chosen a less opportune time to assume the company presidency. Ten years later, at the start of World War II, Reese could not have chosen a more propitious time to assume management responsibility.

During the war the ingenious people at Continental came up with the idea of installing an *aircraft engine* in a combat tank. The idea, though improvised, was successful and ever since Continental has been a world leader in the design and production of engines for military vehicles.

A single decision by my father, not to sell the Detroit plant in 1939, may have been the company's salvation. Within months that factory was urgently needed for the production of airplane engines for use in British and American tanks. From that point on the company got back on its feet, but within a year my father had passed away.

In the jet age, Carl Bachle, Continental's engineering innovator, returned to the Continent and came back with a contract which later resulted in a subsidiary company becoming a major producer of gas turbines for missiles, unmanned aircraft and trainer planes.

But I am already telling the reader too much of the fascinating story of Continental, its motors and its people. You will find it a vibrant history of the eight decades of the growth of an American enterprise in the 20th century.

With the decline in Jack Reese's health, and an aging Continental management, Ryan Aeronautical stepped in and became the controlling stockholder in 1965. Four years later, Teledyne, Inc. acquired Ryan and with it the Continental companies. A new team assembled by Ryan's G. Williams Rutherford, now a Teledyne vice-president, provided a smooth transition from Continental to Ryan to Teledyne.

Throughout, this volume has been generously illustrated in a manner to chronologically re-create the events the author relates so completely. Unlike many authors of corporate histories, Bill Wagner has given the reader insights into the key personalities at Continental rather than merely citing their academic training and business backgrounds.

He has done extensive research as well as conducted many interviews with many of the principals; men like master salesman Art Wild and engineer Bachle, both of whom obviously made major contributions to this fine account.

Air-cooled piston engines for aircraft; gas turbines for missiles; huge air-cooled diesels for tanks; heavy-duty engines for industrial use. Continental, through five separate companies, and backed by 80 years experience, builds them all.

Through my father's early connection with Continental Motors, and my own business association with the company for much of the period recalled in these pages, I know what a fascinating story there is to be told. I hope the reader finds the same interest I did when first reading the manuscript.

James H. Ferry, Jr.

Glencoe, Illinois   December 21, 1982

PREFACE

Every conveyance requires a propulsion system, but it's the vehicle, not the engine, that gets the recognition!

Not a very astute observation perhaps, but it's the rationale for this book which directs its attention to pioneering, robust Continental Motors and its modern successor companies. Too, we will see how Continental built a business, in part by subordinating recognition of its engines to the vehicles they powered.

There's an old saying that everyone remembers Paul Revere but nobody remembers the name of his horse. But, when you've finished the last page of this book, we think you'll remember Continental's *horse*power.

A New York business executive books a flight to Frankfurt, West Germany, on a Boeing 747. He knows his transport plane has four huge jet engines, but is likely oblivious of the fact that they are made by a United Technologies company. The honeymoon couple flies to Hawaii, well aware they are in a Douglas DC-10, but the engines of the tri-jet? General Electric.

The public, whether traveling by air, land or sea, knows that it can depend on the vehicle manufacturer to select a suitable and reliable power system. No need to worry who builds the engine as long as you get to your designation safely.

When TIME magazine did a cover story several years ago on Boeing it brought the usual number of letters-to-the-editor. One, by Californian Rolly Curtis, spoke to the point we have been making:

> "Boeing surely deserves credit for excellence in aircraft design, but don't forget the contribution made by the jet-engine companies, including Pratt & Whitney [United Technologies], General Electric and Rolls-Royce. The plane is designed around the engine. Recent advances in [engine] technology far surpass those of the air-frame makers. The principal reason that Boeing and the other companies are venturing into new models is that these [engine] advances cut fuel costs while improving thrust and reliability."

By contrast, the owner of a modern Chevrolet, Buick, Oldsmobile, or Cadillac, knows that General Motors furnishes its own engines, though there was consternation some years ago about Chevrolet engines in Oldsmobile cars. Other major manufacturers like Ford and Chrysler also generally design and produce their own engines.

But in the infancy of the automobile industry, many early motor car manufacturers (they were really 'assemblers' of purchased parts) bought their engines from companies whose sole business was making motors.

Thus it was that in the 'teens, '20s and early '30s, over a hundred automobile manufacturers depended on Continental Motors for their engines, making the company America's largest independent supplier of automotive power plants.

Airplanes and cars have a tendency to be named after people — Dodge, Lockheed, Chrysler, Cessna, Douglas, Ryan, Chevrolet, Beech. Engines are more likely to have inanimate identification — General Electric, Avco [Lycoming], Continental. There was, to be sure, no 'Christopher Continental' who founded Continental Motors. Ross W. Judson deserves that honor, but who today ever heard of him?

The engine business has vastly changed since the first Continental engine, designed by Judson, made its debut in 1902. Yet one student of engine technology insists that new development has usually been but a rediscovery of old ideas in need of perfection.

In some ways the airplane has followed the early tradition of the auto industry in that plane makers today do not supply their own engines. Instead Continental aircraft engines, in production since 1928, are being supplied as the chosen power plants of plane manufacturers — Cessna, Beech, Piper, Mooney and others.

As more and more auto builders provided their own engines, Continental Motors after World War I began to adapt its power plants to industrial applications and to sell them to special vehicle and equipment manufacturers such as makers of material handling, farm, highway and construction equipment and scores of similar labor-saving applications.

A pilotless jet plane flies over Hanoi on a reconnaissance mission during the Viet Nam war.

At the controls of his own plane, a business executive visits branch offices in three states and is home for dinner with his family that evening.

Across the trackless desert of the Sinai a huge tank lumbers toward Egypt in yet another phase of yet another Middle East conflict.

Water from an aquifer underground 'lake' is pumped to the surface to irrigate an otherwise unproductive farm.

In each case, and countless thousands more like them, the vehicle or equipment is powered by a Continental engine.

We'll learn more about Continental Motors' 80 years as a leading producer of power plants in the pages which follow.

So, join us as we start the story in the 'Gay Nineties.'

vii

IN THE BEGINNING...

Somewhere in the 1890s a number of ingenious experimenters began marrying the horse-drawn buggy and the gasoline-fueled internal combustion engine. The end product was the "horseless carriage" which, in time, evolved into the modern automobile.

Those in this country most often credited with the invention of the motor car and the beginnings of America's leading industry were the Duryea brothers.

America's first workable gasoline-engine vehicle was designed by Charles E. Duryea, and built and driven by his brother J. Frank Duryea. Their single-cylinder horseless carriage first appeared in 1892 on the streets of Springfield, Massachusetts, where they opened the country's first automobile factory.

That same year, the first import arrived — a Benz from Germany, shown at the Chicago World's Fair. And, in 1894, Elwood G. Haynes joined the ranks of embryo auto makers when he designed a single-cylinder engine which was installed in a car built for him by the Apperson brothers — Elmer and Edgar — at Kokomo, Indiana.

THE HORSELESS AGE magazine made its debut in 1895, spreading the word of the coming transportation revolution. The next year Henry Ford began operating his two-cylinder, four-cycle "Quadricycle," a tiller-steered motorized carriage. It was, an early Ford Motor Company advertisement said, "the first Gasoline Automobile in Detroit and the third in the United States."

Some early builders offered gasoline, steam and electric models of their cars. The Olds Motor Works of Detroit advertised "Electric Vehicles mounted on the same running gear as the Vapor [gasoline] Automobiles." But the steam- and electric-powered vehicles were soon left behind by those with gasoline engines.

The U.S. Patent Office in November, 1895 had issued a patent to George S. Selden of Rochester, New York. In 1879 he had filed to protect a claim which appeared to cover any self-propelled gasoline-powered vehicle which might be built. The pioneer auto makers — Packard, Olds, Haynes-Apperson, Cadillac and many others — began paying royalties to Selden for licenses to build cars under his patent. All except Henry Ford . . . and a few others.

In 1903 the Ford Motor Company was organized in Detroit and that year Henry Ford brought out his two-cylinder Model A "Fordmobile," the first "auto carriage" to be a commercial success. Then came the four-cylinder Model B, with engine located under the hood. The Model C followed in 1905; then came the $500 Model N for 1906 and the famed Model T "Tin Lizzie" in 1908 for the 1909 model year.

At that time, the Association of Licensed Automobile Manufacturers controlled the Selden patent and arranged for most early companies to build cars under license. "No other manufacturers," they said, "are authorized to make or sell gasoline automobiles." But Ford did not buy that argument.

A court decision against Ford in 1909 upheld the Selden patent, but two years later a U.S. Court of Appeals reversed that decision.

The Selden patent stranglehold on the industry had been broken. Unburdened by patent disputes, the motor car business shifted into high gear. The public's love affair with the automobile had begun.

It has been said of the automobile that it was invented by the Germans; made practical by the French; mass produced by the Americans.

While no one person truly invented the automobile it is generally acknowledged that Carl Benz and Gottlieb Daimler, working separately in Germany in 1885, were first in the field.

Because cars with German names were difficult to sell in France, an enterprising merchandiser adopted the name of his daughter, Mercedes, for French cars powered by the Daimler engine. However, the Daimler car eventually became a British product and Mercedes-Benz became a household word.

It was in the United States, of course, that mass production of automobiles was perfected. Ross Whitcomb Judson, co-founder of Continental Motors, had a major role in that achievement.

In its Silver Anniversary Issue, AUTOMOBILE TRADE JOURNAL noted that "Ross W. Judson has made commercially possible the high-class motor. In June [1924] he okayed the order for castings for engine No. 2,000,000."

Teledyne Continental Motors

SYNOPSIS

A "JACKRABBIT" START *(1902-1916)*
A "two-lunger" embryo develops into a full-blown industrial leader when Chicago motor pioneers move their new company to Muskegon and on to Detroit in the automotive State of Michigan.

Pages 5 to 19

IT'S CONTINENTAL MOTORS CORPORATION *(1917-1929)*
The new corporation imports the single-sleeve valve principle — and makes its first aircraft engine. But the market for its automobile engines shrinks as the independents lose out to the "big three" integrated auto makers.

Pages 23 to 47

AN ANGELL IN CHARGE *(1930-1939)*
Continental's own car and $14 million in losses nearly bankrupt the company as William R. Angell struggles to keep the firm afloat during the Depression. Then an *aircraft* engine is tried in a combat tank!

Pages 51 to 81

THE WAR YEARS *(1940-1945)*
With the aid of huge World War II orders for aircraft engines to provide power for combat tanks, Jack Reese and his "team" get the company back on its feet.

Pages 85 to 113

POST-WAR TO KOREA *(1946-1953)*
A new family of military engines developed for the Ordnance Corps opens the door to a long-range program for the company. So, too, does an agreement under which Continental Aviation and Engineering makes a strong entry into the jet engine business.

Pages 117 to 143

ON THE HIGH PLATEAU *(1954-1961)*
Business holds at a strong level but as senior management gets along in years there is too little room for new ideas and new people.

Pages 147 to 165

THE RYAN AND TELEDYNE ERAS *(1962-1975)*
Aggressive, profit-oriented Ryan Aeronautical Company of San Diego makes a stock investment in old-line Continental Motors and in four years gains control of the company. Then, Teledyne, Inc. buys out the Ryan-Continental group of companies.

Pages 169 to 204

THE FIVE COMPANIES . . . in the '80s
Precisely eighty years ago — 1902 — Ross W. Judson built the first Continental engine. Now the ninth decade opens with five companies carrying on the Continental Motors tradition.

Pages 206 to 230

A "JACKRABBIT" START
(1902-1916)

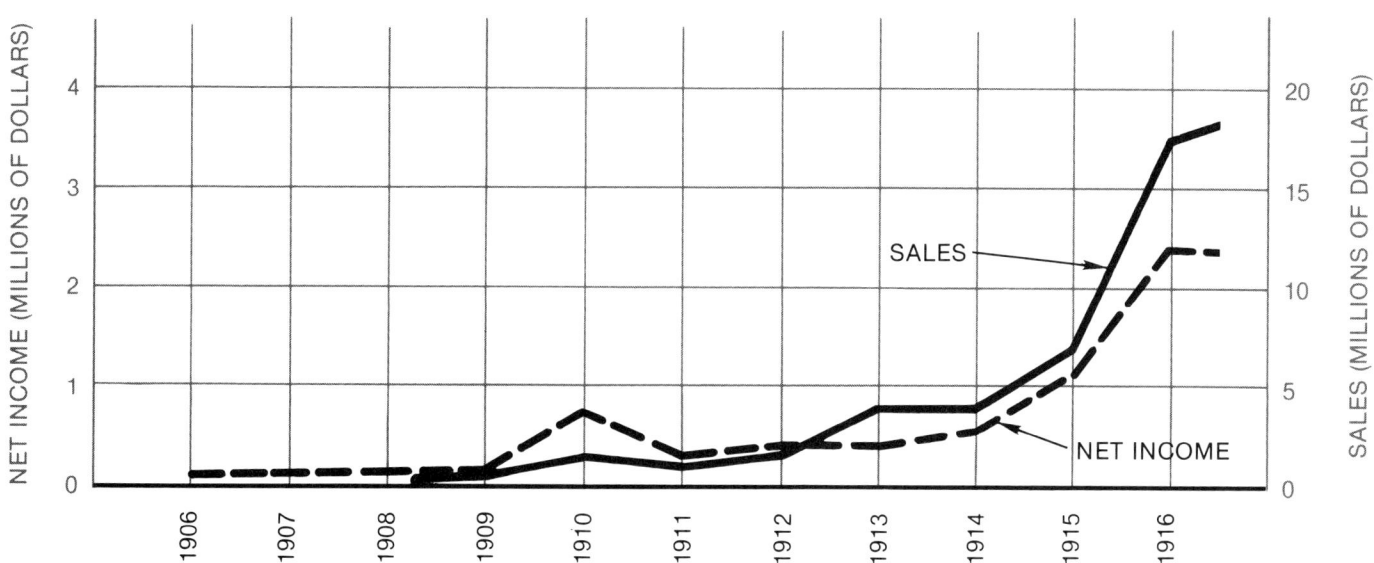

A "two-lunger" embryo develops into a full-blown industrial leader when Chicago motor pioneers move their new company to Muskegon and on to Detroit in the automotive State of Michigan.

Pages 5 to 19

1902-1916

Continental Design Features	Page 5
The Investors	6
Build Engines; Not Cars	6
The Motor Manufacturing Company	7
Move to Muskegon, Michigan	8
Company Co-Founder Dies	9
Detroit Beckons Continental	10
Winning the Races	11
Interchangeable Parts	11
Frederick and the Sixes	12
Three 'Fours' — Three 'Sixes'	13
Back Seat for Women	15
Financial Success	16
"Manufacturing" Dropped from Name	17

Off and Running

Early American cars were "one-lungers," powered by a single-cylinder, or at most by a double-cylinder horizontally opposed two- or four-cycle gasoline motor. In Europe, however, advanced engineering and experiments were then under way looking toward development of four-cylinder, four-cycle motors for installation in automobiles.*

Continental Design Features

While a student at the Armour Institute of Technology in Chicago from 1898 to 1902, Ross W. Judson designed his first multi-cylinder gasoline engine, a primitive two-cylinder model. Perhaps he inherited his engineering talent from his inventor father who lived in Mankato, Minnesota, where Ross was born in 1881. When his son was 14, Judson's father installed a hand lathe, a makeshift punch press and other tools in the family barn so young Ross might experiment.

Many of the youthful engineer's ideas undoubtedly came from mechanical experience he had gained while working on the 1901 Mercedes car owned by John W. Gates. The noted steel tycoon's car had broken down while on a trip to Chicago and Judson was asked to look it over. When Ross tore the engine down he was surprised to find many of the features were nearly identical with those on which he had already been working.

For two days and nights Judson worked on the Mercedes and when he had it in running order again he also had a complete set of drawings. He had castings made of some of the parts and incorporated many of his own ideas in other mechanical details.

Whether from a trip to Europe in 1901 or from earlier glowing reports of the 1899 Paris Salon de l'Automobile, young Judson had been tremendously impressed and influenced by the classic pattern of the European cars and engines introduced by "continental" designers.

On graduation from Armour where he had been assisted and encouraged by Dr. H. M. Raymond and Prof. G. F. Gebhardt, 20-year-old Judson decided to build a career around his interest in engines, starting by himself in a small machine shop at 202 South Clinton Street in Chicago. His first "production" engine, designed along lines of the French Renault, was completed in June 1902. It was a four-cylinder, four-cycle L-head motor with all valves on one side, operated by a single camshaft. In design it was well ahead of contemporary American engineering and gained immediate recognition.

If he was going to grasp the opportunity the new industry offered, Judson would need additional capital and facilities. His sister, Ione, was married to Arthur W. Tobin and together the Tobins invested $2,000 in the venture in September 1902, with his brother-in-law becoming Judson's partner. Prospects were bright. After all, they had sold three engines by Christmas Day.

In January 1903, additional manufacturing facilities were required and they moved to 160 Bunker Street, Chicago, where a building with a total of 912 feet of space became their manufacturing plant. Machine equipment was crude, representing an investment of less than $900. In its first full year, the partnership's seven employees produced 25 engines for use in light touring cars, runabouts and motor boats.

While moving into the new plant — it was actually the loft of a barn — Judson and Tobin carted the first four-cylinder engine off the "production line" for display at the 1903 Chicago Automobile Show, where its advanced design attracted wide and favorable attention. However, it was nearly upstaged by a new automobile, the three-cylinder Pope-Toledo, the "nickel-chrome car."

Orders for Judson's engine began coming in. The first motor he built in 1902 had been sold to Henry T. Truby of Joliet, Illinois, who installed the engine in a Marvel-Swift chassis. Truby ran the car until it fell apart, then took the motor out and used it for years to run a portable sawmill.

*See chapter Technical Notes, Page 18.

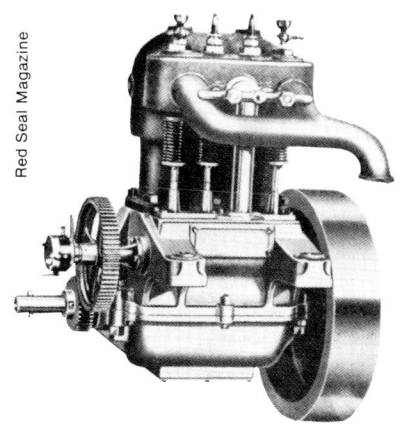

... a primitive two-cylinder model. Note petcock priming cups on top of cylinder block

As the business grew, it was decided to change the partnership to a corporation and extend its activities. On May 3, 1904 the members of the co-partnership incorporated the Autocar Equipment Company, an Illinois corporation, with an authorized capital of $6000.

The Investors

Judson became President of Autocar; his sister, Ione J. Tobin, Vice-President; and her husband, Arthur W. Tobin, was named Secretary and Treasurer. Additional capital, $2,600, was invested in the new corporation by Tobin's mother (Mrs. Cornelia O. Curtis) and by his brother, Benjamin F. Tobin, Chicago real estate investor and builder. With a total investment of $4600, Autocar Equipment Company was on its way.

At this time, other Chicago area investors including members of the Yeoman family became financially interested. To accommodate their interest, the authorized capital was increased to $25,000.

Most important was the investment of James H. Ferry of Glencoe, Illinois, whose mother was Mary Jane Yeoman before her marriage. Another significant shareholder buying into the fledgling engine company was George W. Yeoman and, like members of the Ferry family, was related to the Tobins by marriage. Yet another was Ferry's friend, Roger Sherman of nearby Winnetka.

Spanning more than seven decades, the longest continuity in the affairs of what was to become Continental Motors came from early investor Ferry and his engineer/investor son, James H. Ferry, Jr.

Born with the instincts of a true entrepreneur, the senior Ferry as a young man held a three-days-a-week job as railway mail clerk for the U.S. Mail Service. That gave him an assured income and the spare time necessary to tackle various business ventures on his own.

Sitting in her living room in Glencoe, Mrs. Ferry, Senior — she was Mary Shaw before her marriage — told us on a summer afternoon in 1980 that, "My husband looked the engine over, had confidence in it and thought it would work.

"He was willing to invest $8,000 or $10,000 of the first money that he'd ever saved, and became the company's largest stockholder. Because of that we had Continental Motors as a viable company, and later on I'll tell you why."

Three generations of Tobins — Benjamin F. Tobin, Sr. (who always signed as Benj. F. Tobin); B. F. (Ben) Tobin, Jr.; and Benjamin III — were also involved in company affairs but not over as long a time span as the Ferrys, father and son.

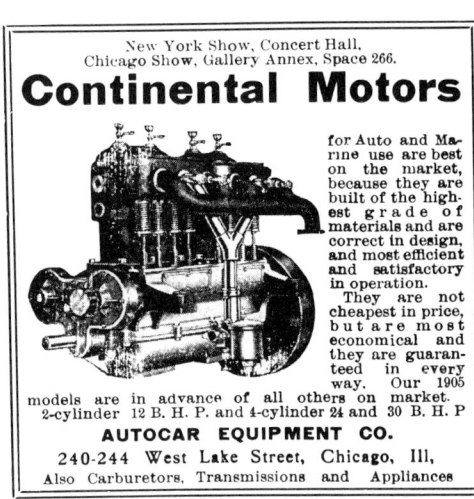

When the first Autocar Equipment Company advertisements began appearing in THE HORSELESS AGE in 1904 they offered both two-cylinder, 12-horsepower and four-cylinder, 24-horsepower models. "'Continental' Motors," they said, "are handsome in design, economical in operation, durable in wear and every part accessible. They are of latest foreign design and at one-half their price. The four-cylinder motor will drive a 2000-pound car at 45 miles per hour."

Build Engines; Not Cars

An early brochure pointed out additional advantages: "Motor can be placed under hood... when so placed it is not necessary for all persons riding in car to get out in the street while floor is removed from vehicle, should motor or accessories need attention."

Business volume continued to grow; a new, still larger location had to be found. Again the plant had to move, this time to facilities ten times larger — an entire floor of 9900 square feet in the Lakeside Power Building at 240-244 West Lake Street, Chicago.

Arthur W. Tobin, company co-founder and brother-in-law of Ross W. Judson

Continental engine "suggestive of Renault construction." — The Automobile

The Automobile/Harrah's

"CONTINENTAL MOTORS ARE STANDARD"

Continental Motor Manufacturing Co.

SOLE BUILDERS OF

Continental HIGH GRADE

Automobile and Marine Equipments

AUTOMOBILE MOTORS
TRANSMISSIONS, CLUTCHES
CARBURETORS AND
APPLIANCES

MARINE TYPE MOTORS
REVERSING GEARS, SHAFTS
PROPELLER WHEELS AND
ACCESSORIES

Judson attributed the company's early success to sticking to building engines rather than complete cars. "When times were hard with us," Judson said, "and people laughed at our ideas, it was pretty tough to stick it out, but we were convinced of the need for a company specializing just in engines.

"About the time we started supplying engines to the early automobile makers, other engineers were busy too. Henry Ford had brought out his two-cylinder car and was working with a four-cylinder design. Harry Stutz was busy down in Indianapolis and George Hupp was developing a motor car. Everyone realized there could be a great future for the automobile.

"When we saw the success others were having in the sale of autos, we were sorely tempted to enter the field with a complete machine instead of specializing in the power units. But we adhered to our original policy."

Cycle and Automobile Trade Journal/Harrah's

Vertical type Continental 4-cylinder 24 horsepower motor "will drive a 2000-pound car at 45 miles per hour."

Having long stressed the advantages of "continental" engine design and having used "Continental Motors" in advertising, Judson and the Tobins decided this should be reflected in the corporation's name. February 14, 1905 Autocar Equipment Company became Continental Motor Manufacturing Company, and capitalization was increased to $100,000.

The Motor Manufacturing Company

To head off competitors and imitators, the new company warned that, "Unscrupulous dealers and others offering for sale, imitations of our goods under the name 'Continental' will be prosecuted to the full extent of the law."

The new name also avoided possible confusion with the Autocar Company, which had been organized in 1899 in Ardmore, Pennsylvania, to build cars and trucks. While avoiding confusion with Autocar, the name change did the opposite with Continental Engine Company, also of Chicago, which had been established in 1896 and incorporated in 1901. *That* Continental firm continued in business for a decade without having made much impact on the industry.

For the 1905 sales year, the Judson-Tobin firm offered two "Continental" Vertical Engines; the 2-cylinder Type "B" developing 12-14 horsepower (hp) and the 4-cylinder Type "D", practically a doubling up of the 2-cylinder, developing 28-32 hp. At the same time the product line was expanded to include Continental transmissions, clutches, carburetors, timers and other accessories the company had developed. The Continental "XX" carburetor was described as of the Mercedes type. The four-cylinder timer carried the designation "AECO", short for the former Autocar Equipment Company.

Reporting on the 1905 Automobile Show at the Coliseum in Chicago, THE AUTOMOBILE furnished this description of Continental's exhibit:

"There is a suggestion of Renault construction in the four-cylinder vertical water-cooled engine. It has four cylinders.. cast in pairs, with water-packets and valve chambers on one side cast integral. The tops of the cylinder casings are dome shaped. At 1000 revolutions the motor is guaranteed for 28-30 horsepower, and its weight is 300 pounds."

"CONTINENTAL" MEANS QUALITY

THESE ARE SOME OF OUR 1905 MODELS

Third Year of successful manufacture of "Continental" Motors and Accessories.

We are the only Makers of Genuine "Continental" Products.

Unscrupulous dealers and others offering for sale, imitations of our goods under the name "Continental" will be prosecuted to the full extent of the law.

Continental Motor Mfg. Co.
Successors to Autocar Equipment Co.
General Office and Factory: 240-242-244 W. LAKE ST.
CHICAGO

The Automobile/Harrah's

Company name just changed from Autocar to Continental, the founders are ready to move from Chicago to Muskegon

By the middle of the first decade of the new century, the State of Michigan was becoming the center of the burgeoning automotive industry. Seeking a stake in the new industry, the Chamber of Commerce and city fathers of Muskegon, two hundred miles up the eastern shore of Lake Michigan from Chicago, sponsored voter passage of a $200,000 bond issue for industrial expansion. That led to a proposition for Continental Motor Manufacturing Company.

Move to Muskegon, Michigan

On July 25, 1905, Judson and the Tobins signed a contract with the Greater Muskegon Chamber of Commerce to move Continental to Muskegon under terms of a bonus contract. If Continental employed 125 men for six years, the young firm would collect a $12,500 bonus. A two-story brick factory of 16,000 square feet was then built for the engine company's use at the corner of Market and Water Streets.

Production at Continental's new factory and administrative offices got under way on May 15, 1906. The city's contract called for Continental to have its 125 employees by January 1, 1907, but employment soon far exceeded that target figure.

One of the first important engine contracts of 1906 was with Studebaker Wagon Company of nearby South Bend, Indiana, for 100 engines. Output was one motor a day.

Manufacturing continued at Chicago for some time, but having moved the company from Illinois, Judson and the Tobins formed a Michigan corporation of the same name on August 22, 1906. Its authorized capital was $125,000. The new stock was exchanged for the old share for share.

At the time, Benj. F. Tobin was named Secretary and Treasurer while his brother Arthur, was moved up to President. Judson served as Vice-President.

A 20 percent stock dividend payable in 1907 was declared September 29, 1906 on the $47,100 in common stock which had been issued up to June 30, 1906, bringing the total to a par value capitalization of $56,500.

To provide the additional capital necessary for the growing business, authorized capital was again increased: $200,000 in common stock and $25,000 in 6% preferred stock. The investment in plant and equipment in 1908 was listed as $122,333.

From 1907 to 1910 Continental bought property adjoining the original Muskegon plant and built additional factory space as the business grew. The first motor-driven trucks, powered of course by Continental engines, began making their appearance on the streets of Muskegon.

By the end of December 1912, the company had exceeded requirements of its bonus contract and was given a deed by the Chamber of Commerce to the original property.

Luring Continental from Chicago paid off handsomely. For over half a century the pioneer engine maker was to be the Muskegon area's largest employer.

Although early records are difficult to trace, auto makers who were early Continental customers included Auburn, Hudson, Jordan, Paige-Detroit, Studebaker, Saxon, Velie, Davis and Moon. Some also say the "one-eyed Briscoe"—which had a single headlamp, front and center on its radiator shell.

Automobile engines were the company's primary business, but Continental continued to supply such accessories as transmissions, clutches and carburetors, just as they had done in the Autocar Equipment days in Chicago. The company also retained "Autocar" as its cable address.

Marine type motors, including reversing gears, shafts, propeller wheels and other marine accessories were also offered.

In a relatively few years, perhaps half of the new American cars being assembled had Continental motors, whose reputation was enhanced when a Continental-powered racing car won the Indianapolis Speedway classic.

By 1908, some 515 companies had entered into assembly or manufacture of cars. That was the year Henry Ford introduced the Model T and General Motors was founded by William C. Durant.

Company Co-Founder Dies

The year 1908 was also when Ross Judson lost the services and counsel of his original partner and brother-in-law, Arthur W. Tobin. Early in December, Tobin had returned to Chicago to attend a social event, and while there had an operation to remove a growth of bone in his nose. Blood poisoning set in, and he passed away December 13.

Just four weeks before his death, A. W. Tobin had written James H. Ferry concerning a letter this important Chicago investor had sent to Tobin's mother.

"She wanted me," Tobin wrote, "to tell you we would like to have you begin your services with us just as soon as you can. We, of course, understand that you do not wish to leave the Mail Service except in good standing."

After his brother's death, Benj. F. Tobin became increasingly active in the

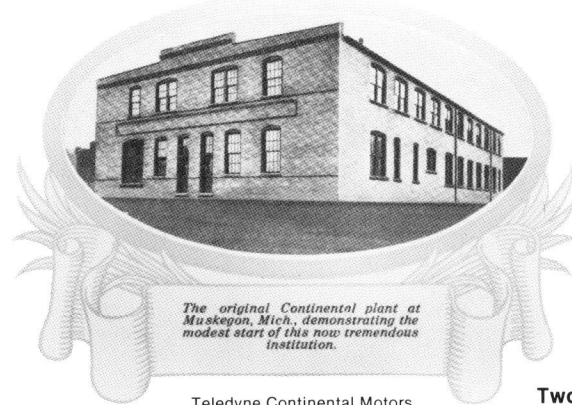

Teledyne Continental Motors

Two-story brick factory was first Muskegon plant, built in 1906 for "Continental Motor Man'f'g. Co."

company's business affairs while Judson spent his efforts principally on sales and engineering.

Judson, who had served Continental as both president and chief engineer, was among those leading the way toward automation of the industry. By 1908 he had installed a "conveyor" along which cylinder and other large castings were moved on rollers from station to station for machining.

Production continued to center around four-cylinder vertical engines. In 1906, when 350 engines were built, the high powered Type "O" 45 hp model was intro-

1910 Advertisement ▷   Largest plant in the world devoted exclusively to manufacturing gasoline automobile motors. Capacity 15,000 motors per annum

National Automotive History Collection, Detroit Public Library

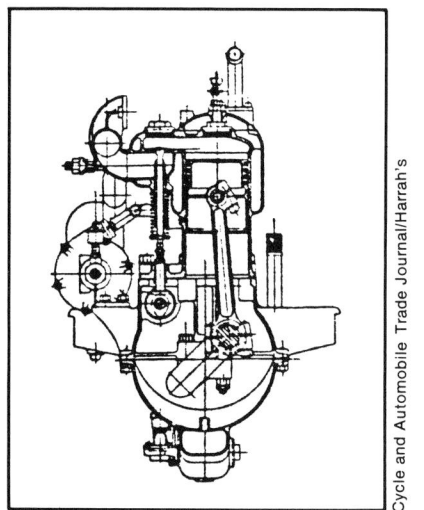

MODEL "K"

Continental Motor Manufacturing Co. trucks — with Continental engines — began appearing on Muskegon streets

duced. "Before shipment," Continental said, "each motor is given a thorough test and required to develop its rated power." A new test house permitted running 40 finished motors at the same time.

For 1907, Continental's marketing policy was changed from trying to meet the ideas of different purchasers for a multiplicity of power sizes to the production of only one size motor. It would, the company said, "permit tool making sufficient to obtain complete interchange of all parts of the motor, and so not only improve the product, but lower its cost."

Despite this earlier policy change, three sizes were available for the 1909 market: Model K, 24-28 hp; Model G, 38-42 hp and Model HB, 44-48 hp.

"We can meet your motor requirements," read an ad in THE AUTOMOBILE, "whether they be for taxicabs or light runabouts, heavy touring cars or commercial vehicles. These motors are manufactured in the largest and most completely equipped plant in the country devoted exclusively to the manufacture of Gasoline Automobile Motors."

After moving to Muskegon, Continental retained K. Franklin Peterson as direct factory representative in Chicago, later adding Thomas J. Wetzel as eastern representative in New York City. Then, in 1910, with the auto industry beginning to concentrate in Detroit, L. D. Bolton was appointed factory representative there.

By that time, engine horsepower was being stepped up and the three models offered for 1910 were the 28-30 hp Type R, the 45-50 hp Type J and the 55-60 hp Type T. Plant capacity at Muskegon was said to be 15,000 motors per annum.

The year 1910 was a significant turning point in Continental's success. For the first time, sales for a single year exceeded $1 million; they were in fact nearly $2 million. After that, yearly sales continued to soar.

Inlet Side

TYPE "T"

Exhaust Side

In 1911, Hudson Motor Car Company of Detroit placed an order with Continental for 10,000 engines, by far the largest production order the Muskegon firm had ever received. With Detroit increasingly recognized as the "motor city," Judson and Benj. F. Tobin, the latter now serving as president, felt it was time to take another step forward. Hudson sold Continental a site across the street from its own plant on Algonquin Avenue, and a long-term contract between the two firms was signed.

Detroit Beckons Continental

Continental built a huge factory there, between Kercheval and Jefferson, the plant fronting on the latter avenue. Its 225,000 square feet of manufacturing space was more than double the 110,000 square feet at the Muskegon factory which continued in operation.

POWER WAGON, the journal of the embryo trucking industry, noted that "Muskegon's annual output of 18,000 to 20,000 gasoline motors is far too small to satisfy the demand that has been created for 'Continental' products."

The new $1 million two-story Detroit factory, over 500 feet in length, covered 12 of the 30 acres at the plant site. When manufacturing operations began in April 1912, the company's administrative offices were moved to the new Detroit plant, where the first production run was the 10,000 engines for Hudson.

1912: A portion of the immense new plant (now building) of the Continental Motor Mfg. Co.

Two drivers in the November 1911 Vanderbilt Cup Races at Savannah, Georgia, had selected Continental's new 32-47 hp 4-cylinder L-head Model E engine for their racing cars. Of 14 starters in the 291-mile race, six cars, which were equipped with engines nearly double the horsepower of the stock model Continentals, dropped out for mechanical failures. Both Continentals finished the grueling race.

Winning the Races

Three days later, the 411-mile race for the Grand Prize was run over the same course. Sixteen cars started, but only seven including the two Continental-powered cars, finished.

Continental was not bashful in its subsequent advertising: "The Continentals stayed in," they boasted. "Though matched against the biggest and most powerful *racing* motors ever built, both cars finished both races, while over fifty percent of the big racing motors had to drop out. Furthermore, these Continental motors were from regular stock—not built merely to win a race, but exactly the same motors we are shipping every day to a lot of people who want endurance and dependability as well as speed.

"The motor is the heart of the car. Ten of the drivers in the big Savannah race realized to their cost the seriousness of automobile heart failure. It goes without argument that the source of power must be as nearly perfect as human skill can make it.

"The Continental motor is the *ONLY* product of a big factory. All the brains and intelligence and mechanical skill of twelve hundred trained workers are concentrated all the time upon one problem—how to make the Continental motor better, more efficient, more dependable than any automobile power plant ever before built."

Luther S. Watson of Cedar Rapids, Iowa, could testify years later to the reliability of the Continental E engine installed in his Abbott-Detroit touring car which, after five years' service, was stored for the duration of World War I.

"In 1946, after the car stood idle for 29 years," Watson wrote Continental, "I was getting ready to drive it to Los Angeles. The engine started very easily, and is A-1 from the standpoint of operating condition, but could you provide me with a service manual just in case?"

The engine was serial No. 2380 and was built January 25, 1912.

Interchangeable Parts

To demonstrate the precision of Continental-built engines, at a time when most motors had to be individually hand fitted to make them run properly, one of the company's key production executives decided on an experiment unique for its day.

Ten identical engines off the production line had just been put through their initial test runs. Employees were instructed to completely dismantle the motors; then all the parts were scrambled and the ten engines reassembled. All ran perfectly. Continental demonstrated that precision production had achieved standardization with perfect interchangeability of parts. It was, they said, a "first" in the industry.

1910 four-cylinder Hudson. Note the rumble seat

CONTINENTAL EQUIPPED CAR IN 1911 VANDERBILT RACE—MITCHELL DRIVING

Harrah's Automobile Collection

Six-Cylinder MODEL 6-C

Efficient, simple chain drive for electric starters and generators

Before long auto makers began paying more attention to early day "consumer advocates" and to customer wishes as to appointments and features. When Continental introduced its long-stroke, 30-42 hp Model C at the 1912 Chicago Auto Show, it put special emphasis in its sales pitch on having produced an engine that would run as noiselessly as possible without sacrificing power.

"The valve gears," Continental said, "are practically noiseless and the timing gear wholly so, the latter being very accurately cut and operated in oil.

"The Continental self-contained oiling system — a practice first introduced to this country by this company — has been improved until in the 1912 models it is guaranteed that lubrication will remain uniform even when climbing and descending hills."

An early associate of Judson's was Walter A. Frederick, a young engineer who had been graduated from Cornell in 1903. He first went to work for Autocar, the Pennsylvania truck manufacturer; then for Reo (Ransom E. Olds) in Lansing, Michigan.

Frederick and the Sixes

At Continental, Frederick pioneered the six-cylinder engine in 1911, expanding the standard four-cylinder C motor by casting extra cylinders in the same pairs and mounting them on a longer crankcase.

Owing to the interest shown by potential customers for a short, compact and accessible six-cylinder motor, Continental Motor Manufacturing Co. brought out its first such production engine in the new 45-60 hp Model 6-C in 1912. The cylinders of the refined 6-C sextuple motor were cast in threes, thereby bringing them closer together so that the small over-all dimension of the engine made it possible to place it under a 40-inch hood. This and other six-cylinder models continued in production for the next six years.

"Whatever the engine," Continental claimed, "it really establishes the standing of a motor vehicle. It is the first consideration in automobile specifications. In more than 60 makes of cars, Continental has been chosen to make the first appeal to the prospective buyer. During 1914, fully forty thousand men will buy motor vehicles largely because they are Continental-equipped."

Of the new six-cylinder engine, Frederick Othman wrote about the Auburn Beauty Six and its ideal motor: "Under its hood the car had a Continental Red Seal engine of 60 horsepower. It didn't use much gasoline, nor did it care what kind of gas. In an emergency, I once poured in a can of coal oil, and it worked fine after I'd pushed the spark lever down a little.

"The engine had a minimum of mysterious ganglia bolted on the outside, but it did have petcocks. These little brass funnels were screwed into the head near each spark plug. On bitter cold mornings when the machinery didn't want to start, I merely poured a small dollop of ether into each priming cup, waited a moment, and then touched the starter. Bang! I got action."

When introducing the first six-cylinder models at the 1912 Chicago Show, Continental also disclosed its production figures for the five prior years:

Year	Motors Built
1907	1,000
1908	2,010
1909	9,480
1910	15,000
1911	18,000

Factory capacity for the year 1912 was projected at 35,000 engines by which time the Detroit plant contained 240,000 square feet of space. The Muskegon plant, too, had continued to be enlarged.

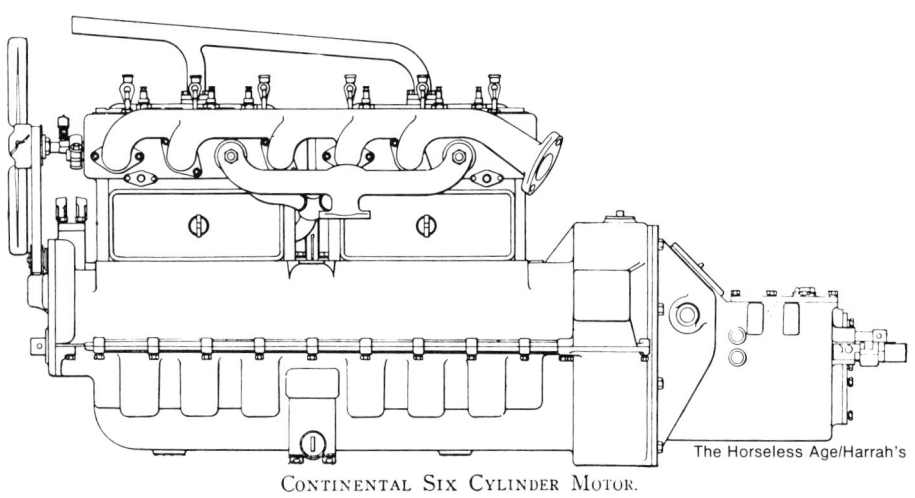

CONTINENTAL SIX CYLINDER MOTOR.

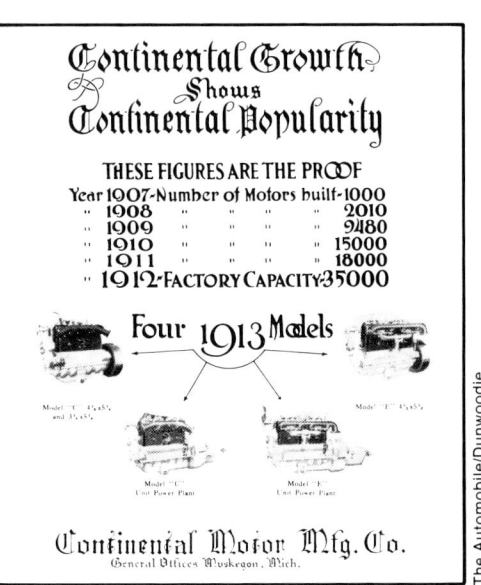

National Automotive History Collection

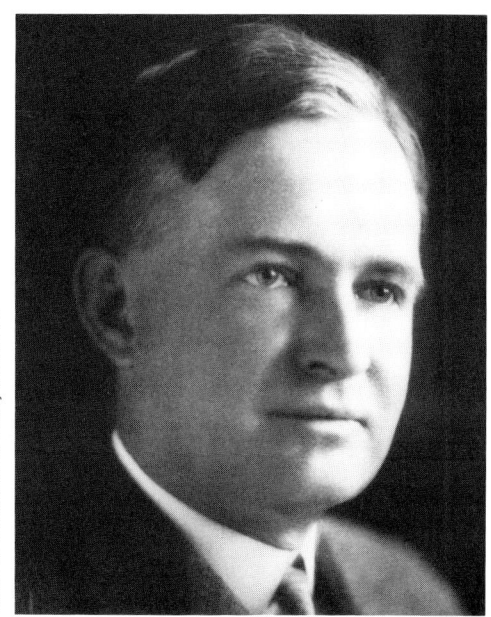

WALTER A. FREDERICK

One of the Continental's prized facilities at Detroit was its modern testing room where 70 new engines could be run-in at the same time. Anticipating production of 25,000 engines annually at Detroit, the fireproof test room was soon expanded with 55 more test stands. And, at Muskegon, another 15,000 automobile motors could be tested each year.

With successful launching of the six-cylinder engine, Frederick won the title of Chief Engineer in 1913 and began refinement of a new generation of 'fours' and 'sixes' which became very popular with auto assemblers. Soon he was also named a director of the corporation.

Meanwhile, George W. Yeoman, one of Continental's original investors who had become well-known in the industry as the company's sales and advertising manager, resigned to become manager of the Ames Motor Car Company of Owensboro, Kentucky. However, he retained his stock ownership in Continental and continued as a director.

Continental's best customers continued to be the makers of "assembled" cars—independent automakers who bought and assembled standard components from established suppliers. To be a motor car "manufacturer" in those days was, perhaps, too easy. Few survived.

Ford Motor Co. proved to be a healthy survivor, not as an assembler, but as an integrated manufacturer. In 1913 Henry Ford fired up the world's first moving assembly line in Highland Park, Michigan, to build Model T's and began paying workers the then unthinkable wage of $5 a day.

Saxon Motor Company of Detroit also came into the mass production picture. It ordered 10,000 four-cylinder L-head engines from Continental for its entire production of the small cars it was introducing for the 1914 model year.

Three 'Fours' — Three 'Sixes'

Each year Continental's product line of three 4-cylinder and three 6-cylinder models added new business, taxing the capacity of the Muskegon and Detroit plants and requiring the expansion of both until the production capability by 1919 was ten times that of 1912.

Large additions at Detroit were under construction in 1914 when the company

Red Seal Magazine

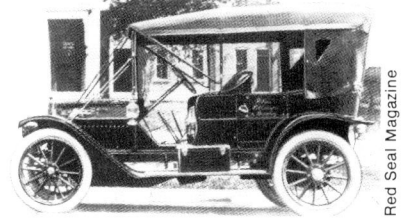

1910 Davis touring car. Davis was a Continental customer until auto maker retired from business in 1927

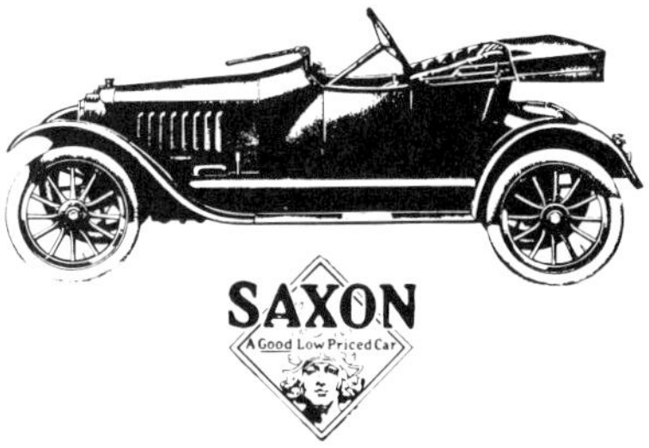

The Horseless Age/Dunwoodie

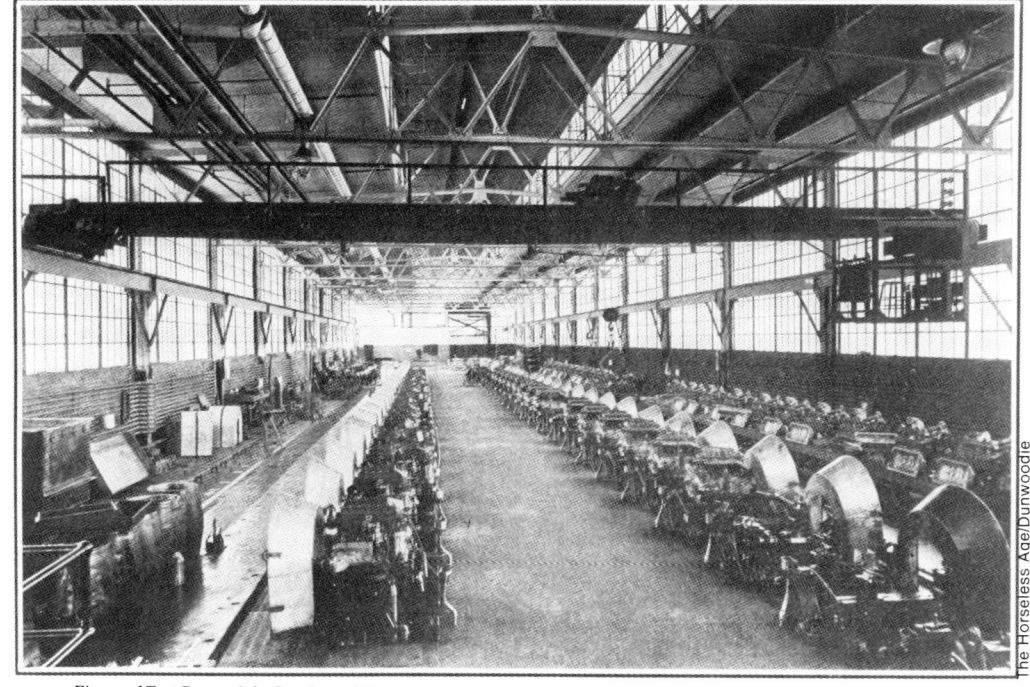

Fireproof Test Room of the Continental Motor Manufacturing Company, Detroit Mich., With Its Rows of Testing Stands

In nine years since moving to Muskegon, Continental plant had been doubled and redoubled in production capacity

announced that the rapid-growing but "almost unprecedented" popularity of the 'Six' required that "this enormous factory has been given over entirely to their manufacture."

The company had 600 employees in 1911. Twelve months later there were 750 workers and in 1913 employment reached 1000.

In 1916, to make things easier for its 2100 men at Muskegon, the company began to pay employees semi-monthly in cash "because the men sometimes had difficulty in cashing their checks, except at banks."

In mid-year 1915, Continental gave considerable attention to light, low-powered engines, introducing a new six-cylinder 35 hp motor with an unusually large crankshaft. This feature was claimed to overcome torsional vibrations, providing better passenger comfort and reduced noise in the timing gears.

The price, too, appealed to car makers for the engine was quoted as lower than that of any Continental engine, either four- or six-cylinder, of comparable piston displacement. THE AUTOMOBILE reported that "the Continental company has never made a neater looking job, nor one that runs more smoothly."

Early passenger buses like this Continental-powered Stewart were huge open air cars

STEWART BUS BUILT IN 1914

In marked contrast to the low-powered engine line was the huge 12-cylinder Continental engine developed for the 7-passenger Pathfinder automobile in which that Indianapolis company matched the new Packard line.

AUTOMOBILE TRADE JOURNAL called the announcement of the valve-in-head engine "startling both for Pathfinder and Continental, which latter concern has been adhering to the L-head type for many years."

Even in the days before consumer advocate Ralph Nadar, companies did make voluntary service adjustments. Willys-Overland, in 1915, offered an exchange or engine-rebuilt plan when Continental's engine for the Model 82 Overland showed excessive oil consumption and fouled spark plugs.

The Willys-Overland Company
Automobiles

JOHN N. WILLYS, PRESIDENT

Toledo, Ohio

Further additions to the Detroit plant, including a new three-story factory and two lines of test blocks to handle 100 more motors, were completed. The company's aim for the immediate future was to be able to produce 500 motors daily. Muskegon alone was building nearly 300 engines a day by mid-1916.

At Muskegon, facilities had been added year by year as production expanded. Property on Water Street across from the original factory building was acquired, giving Continental water frontage. On Western Avenue property was purchased and a drop forge plant installed.

Also in 1916 Continental acquired the Lee Ferry Dock which had supplied the bonus fund by which the company had its start in Muskegon.

Trade reports were that domestic business was so brisk Continental was unable to take substantial foreign orders being offered. However, for the Morris Motor Car Co. of England, Continental was able to supply the 4-cylinder Model U motor which was a high-speed, lightweight motor of small piston displacement producing 15-18 hp. The engine was designed to meet the European demand for small displacement high speed engines.

Service on Continental engines for 200,000 motorists was said to be available nation-wide since the 143 auto and truck manufacturers using the motors reported having 15,000 dealers and sub-agents in "almost every village and hamlet."

What, asks the 1982 motorist, was a World War I era automobile really like? AUTOMOBILE TRADE JOURNAL answered the question with its description of the new Lexington Minute Man Six in the parlance of February 1917:

Back Seat for Women

"The Lexington-Howard Co., Connersville, Ind., has concentrated its efforts on building a car which is produced by the co-operation of a group of parts makers operating under a single ownership and control.

"The Salon type of body with an aisleway between the front seats [the early 'two door'] is a feature of the Lexington Minute Man Six for 1917. High rolling sides, rakishly slanted windshield and the straight lines of the hood and cowl give the exterior of this car an appearance of refined elegance.

"The aisleway between the front seats facilitates lowering and raising the one-man top, permits the passengers to change seats while the car is in motion and affords ventilation for the driver's compartment. Ample doorways make it easy to enter or leave the car. Not only are the openings generously wide, but the doors themselves swing out at right angles to the running boards so as to give the passengers the advantage of every inch.

"In the upholstering the designers have been influenced by the requirements of feminine motorists. This is especially true of the rear seat which has been treated as the woman's seat primarily. The tilt of the cushion, the angle of the back and the height from the floor have been studied at length.

"A good deal of locker room have been provided. Under the rear cushion is the place where the dust boot is carried when the top is up. Under the front cushions are lockers for the tool equipment, jack set.

Lexington Minute Man Six Touring Car, $1185.
Upon the well-built chassis of the Minute Man Six is mounted an attractive and comfortable body.

Salient feature of the Minute Man Six is the Lexington-Continental engine

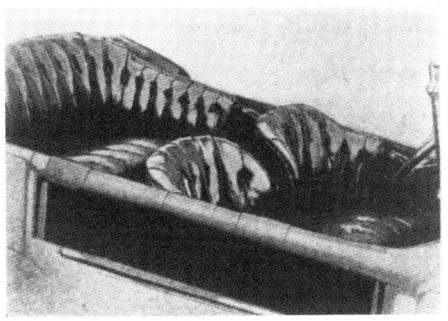

Seating Arrangement in the Minute Man Six.
Divided front seats and French pleated upholstery adds immeasurably to the car's appearance and increases the comfort of the passengers.

Driving Compartment of the Minute Man Six.
Accessibility is the keynote of the driving compartment. Instruments are located on the cowl-board and controls are within easy reach of the driver.

"The 'one-minute' storm curtains are suspended over the tonneau in a neat envelope that hangs from two bows of the tops. This arrangement permits a rapid adjustment without leaving the car in case of a very sudden shower.

"The touring model sells for $1185.

"The convertible sedan and convertible coupe round out the complete line of Lexington cars and provide a closed or open car for every purpose. The versatility of the convertible car is well known and requires no effort to recommend its excellent features. Both models sell for $1350.

"The salient features of the Lexington mechanism are the *Lexington-Continental engine*, Moore multiple exhaust system, cut steel starting gear, Independent ignition, lighting and starting circuits and the Wick-feed oil cups."

During the first decade after incorporation, earnings of Continental were such that plant expansion was financed almost entirely from these earnings. Then, as business expanded and profits piled up over the years, the Judson-Tobin management channeled the surplus funds into increased capitalization and declared generous stock dividends for themselves, James H. Ferry and 45 other early investors.

The Board of Directors as pictured in a sales brochure of the period

While Continental sped the day of mechanical power, its contractor for new Muskegon plant buildings still used horse-drawn wagons in Summer 1916

Financial Success

In the initial eleven years of operation, annual sales had increased—slowly at first, then steadily higher—from $200,000 in 1906 to $17.5 million in 1916. Profits kept pace, virtually exploding from $20,000 the first full year in Muskegon to $2.4 million a decade later.

Cash dividends were insignificant in the first ten years, but stockholders who were fortunate enough to acquire an early interest and stay with the company were richly rewarded. The stock dividends were of near staggering size, were paid frequently and established the capital structure for later, more liberal cash disbursements.

By 1912, when capital stock was increased from $500,000 to $2,400,000, there were outstanding $940,000 of common stock and $470,000 in preferred stock. This was increased to $2,000,000 authorized common shares and $900,000 authorized preferred in October 1915 at which time owners holding the $958,300 common shares then outstanding received a 100% stock dividend.

[Among those, in addition to Tobin and Judson, then serving on the Board of Directors were George W. Yeoman, engineer Walter A. Frederick, and C.O. Curtis. The latter was undoubtedly Mrs. Cornelia O. Curtis, mother of the Tobin brothers.]

More stock dividends and an issue of serial notes brought the outstanding capitalization late in 1916 to $3,840,860 of common stock, $472,320 of preferred and $1,000,000 in gold notes.

Following is the record of stock disbursements paid from 1907 through 1917. The par value of these dividends, including the large ones in 1916 and 1917, totaled $11,870,380 for the 11-year period.

	Per Cent	Stock Dividends Par Value Distributed
1907	20	$9,400
1908	50	39,900
1910	60	87,960
1911	100	234,000
1913	*200	940,000
1916	200	2,877,400
1917	†200	7,681,720

*100% dividend in common stock and 100% in preferred stock.
†Includes the exchange of 3 shares of common stock of new corporation and $5 in cash for 1 share common stock of old company.

Generous cash payments were also paid stockholders during the same period, amounting to $7 million on common stock and $1¼ million on preferred shares.

For years, Continental had stressed "Motor Manufacturing" in its corporate name but its products were always referred to as "Continental Motors." So, on February 14, 1916, the Board of Directors shortened the corporate name to Continental Motors Company. At the same time, common stock was increased to $5,000,000, bringing the total authorized capital, including $900,000 in preferred stock, to $5,900,000.

"Manufacturing" Dropped from Name

To further strengthen product identification, Continental pointed out that several hundred car makers compete actively for the auto market. "Many of them," officials said, "build their own motors, each with entire confidence that his motor is superior to the others.

"But more than 150 [independent] automobile and motor truck manufacturers agree that among all present-day engines, Continental Motors stand foremost. They express that conviction by using Continental Motors in their own products."

The Automobile/Harrah's

A track 350 ft. long was used for progressive assembly of engines in Continental's Detroit plant

Teledyne Continental Motors

New corporate name, "Continental Motors Co.," appears for the first time on company's Acme chain-driven truck, left; and on expanding Detroit factory, below

National Automotive History Collection

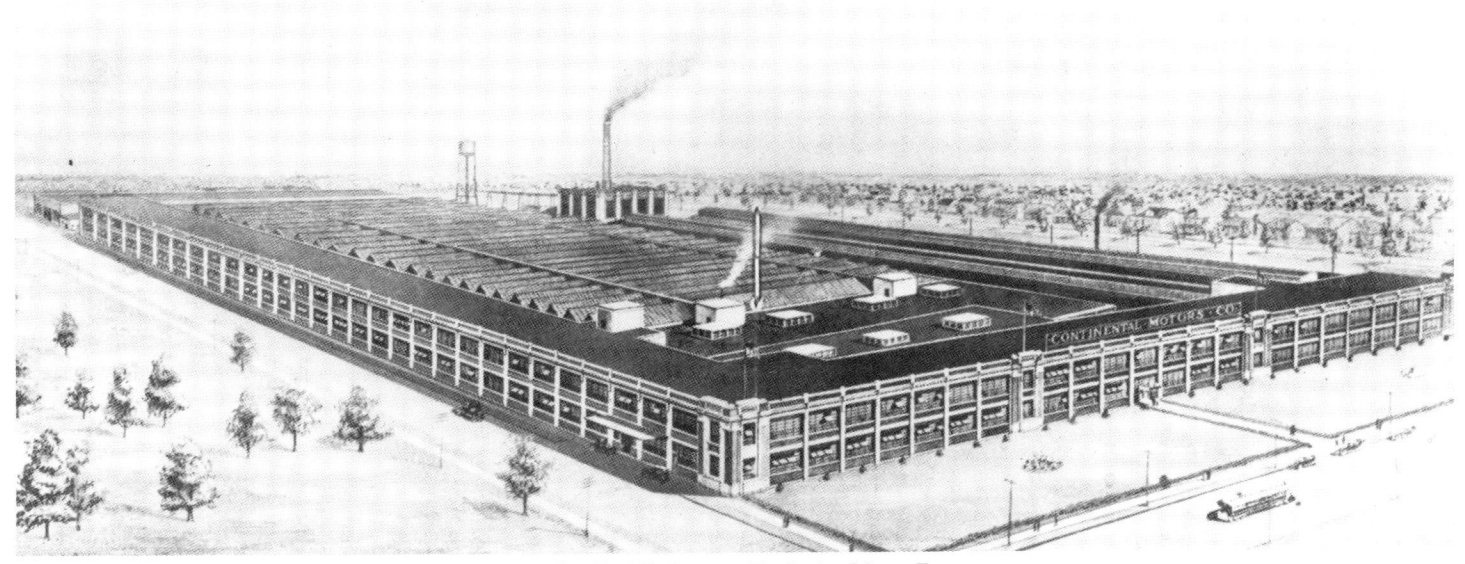

View of the World's Largest Exclusive Motor Factory

17

Technical Notes

Prior to about 1930, the terminology 'motor' was generally used; after that, 'engine.'

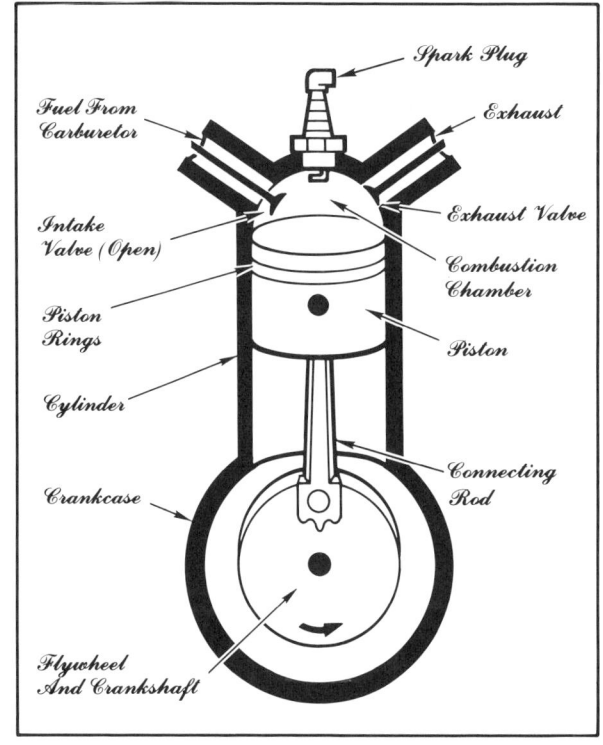

Typical Gasoline Engine (Overhead Engine)

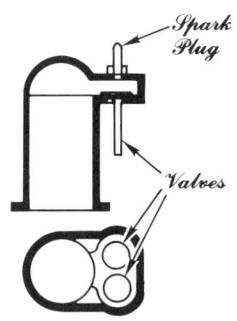

L-Head Valves Side By Side

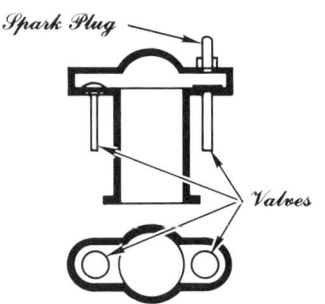

T-Head Valves On Opposite Sides

In a two-cycle motor, all four operations which must take place within the cylinder (fuel intake, compression, combustion, exhaust) are completed in two strokes or cycles of the piston (one revolution of the crankshaft). Fuel enters, and exhaust gases leave, the cylinder through ports in its wall.

In a four-cycle engine, each of the four operations is performed on one stroke of the piston; thus the complete operation requires four strokes or cycles. Ports in the cylinder wall are replaced by valves, usually of the poppet type, in the combustion chamber. The four-cycle engine is now universally used in automobiles.

Engines are also classified according to type of valves used and their location in the cylinder head. In an "L" head, inlet and exhaust valves are located side by side on either the left or right side of the cylinders. In a "T" head, valves are on opposite sides of the cylinders. In a "valve-in-head" engine (also called "overhead" valve engine), all valves are located in the cylinder head.

The single-cylinder motor is of the simplest possible construction. However, though it uses a heavy flywheel to help smooth out its mechanical imbalance, it still has excessive vibration.

On two- and four-cylinder engines, the reciprocating masses are so arranged that one affects the forces of the other, reducing vibration. This advantage increases as the number of cylinders is increased.

The cylinders are castings provided with water jackets or fins for cooling. Cylinders have an open end and a closed end; the latter forms the combustion chamber and houses the valves. Cylinders may be cast single, in pairs or in block (en-bloc) of three, four or more cylinders.

CONTINENTAL ENGINE TYPES (Typical) 1904-1918

Year	Model	Cyl./Valves	h.p.	@rpm	*Bore & Stroke	†c.i.d.	Typical User
1904		2 L	12				
		4 L	24				
1905	B	2 L	12-14		4.25 x 4.75	134.7	
	D	4 L	28-32		4.25 x 4.75	269.5	
1906	O	4 L	45		4.88 x 5.00	373.3	
1908	K	4 L	28-24		4.25 x 4.50	255.3	Davis
1909	G	4	38-42				
	HB	4	44-48		5.00 x 5.00	392.7	
1910	R	4 L	28-30		4.25 x 4.50	255.3	
	J	4 L	45-50		5.00 x 5.00	392.7	Speedwell
	T	4 T	55-60		5.00 x 5.75	451.9	
1912	C	4 L	30-42		3.75 x 5.00	220.5	Hudson, Davis
	E	4 L	32-47		4.50 x 5.50	349.9	Abbott-Detroit Colby, Davis
	6-C	6 L	45-60	1500	4.13 x 5.25	421.0	Pathfinder, Howard, Hudson
1914	6-P	6 L	48	1500	3.75 x 5.25	347.9	Saxon, Velie Moon
1915	U	4 L	15-18	2000	2.75 x 4.00	283.5	Saxon
	N	4 L	32-38	2200	3.75 x 5.00	220.9	Moon, Hudson Davis, Kent
	6-N	6 L	50	1600	3.50 x 5.00	288.6	Lexington, Moon Auburn, Westcott
1916	7-W	6 L	36	1600	3.25 x 4.50	224.0	Elcar, Columbia Abbott, Anderson
1917	7-N	6 L	50	1900	3.50 x 5.25	303.1	Overland, Roamer Willys, Paige Velie, Abbott
1918	9-N	6 L	55	2200	3.50 x 5.25	303.1	Case, Comet Anderson

Note: ***Bore** is the **cylinder's** inside diameter
Stroke is the distance the **piston** travels up and down
†Cubic Inch Displacement

The new corporation imports the single-sleeve valve principle — and makes its first aircraft engine. But the market for its automobile engines shrinks as the independents lose out to the "big three" integrated auto makers.

Pages 23 to 47

IT'S CONTINENTAL MOTORS CORPORATION
(1917-1929)

1917-1929

The New Corporation	Page 23
World War I Slump	24
Engines for Army Trucks	24
First Annual Report	26
Red Seal Engines	26
Benjamin F. Tobin Dies	27
The Industrial Engine Market	28
Meeting Customer Needs	29
Engines for Car Assemblers	30
Business Revives in Mid-Twenties	31
Single-Sleeve-Valve Engines	33
"Straight Eights"	35
A Fifth Grouping?	36
More Financial Success	37
Continental's Company Plane	39
Claude Ryan at Continental	41
The A-70 Radial Aircraft Engine	42
Building to Customers' Designs	43
Depression Days Ahead	45

Continental's new corporate name was short lived. The need for additional capital for expansion, so as to take advantage of business opportunities, was responsible for yet another reorganization and refinancing plan.

The New Corporation

To assist in that task Judson and Benj. F. Tobin sought the counsel of Chicago attorney William R. Angell, a Continental stockholder who had grown up in Muskegon before going to law school. In late 1916, Angell became a Director and signed on as Corporate Secretary of Continental in June 1917, spending much of his time in Detroit. He subsequently became very closely associated with Judson and Tobin in management roles of ever-increasing responsibility.

Chartered under laws of the State of Virginia, the new Continental Motors Corporation, capitalized at $18,500,000, was incorporated on January 2, 1917 to take over the entire assets, business and goodwill of the former company. The old board of directors, with two new members added, was continued. The office of President was assumed by Tobin and Judson took the post of Vice-President.

The capital structure called for $15,000,000 in $10 par common stock and $3,500,000 in 7 percent preferred shares. Under the reorganization plan, stockholders were to receive $5 cash and three shares of the common capital stock (of which 1,452,258 were issued) in exchange for each common share of the old company.

From the sale of all the preferred stock and 300,000 shares of the common of the new corporation, additional working capital was obtained and the preferred stock and serial notes of the old company were retired. Control and management of the new corporation (frequently referred to as CMC) would remain in the same hands, officials said.

A total of $4,400,000 in cash was received from the investment banking firm of William P. Bonbright & Company for the shares they purchased for investment. Howard Bonbright of that firm became one of the new Continental directors.

A. H. Zimmerman, who had been Secretary and Treasurer for many years, continued as Treasurer after Angell was named Secretary of the new corporation.

Although having both business and family ties, correspondence between B. F. Tobin and James H. Ferry was on a "Dear Mister" basis.

No sooner had the new financing plan been settled than Tobin was writing Ferry about "subscribing to a block (of stock) in our new foundry organization. We will naturally favor it and thereby keep it full up with work at all times.

"We probably will be able to let you have ten to fifteen thousand dollars worth. It is an excellent opportunity for you to make a high class investment."

Continental had been operated very profitably for many years. In the four years ended October 31, 1916, net income totaled $4,676,894, of which nearly $2.5 million had been earned in 1916. By the fiscal year end the company had 3467 stockholders.

From $303,000 in 1909, net tangible assets had increased 2000% to $6.6 million in October 1916. From an output of 350 motors in 1906, deliveries of motors rose in ten years to a 150,000 annual rate. Six thousand workers were employed and unfilled orders exceeded $20 million in March 1917.

Only a few weeks later, the United States joined the war against Germany.

Along with prosperity and new stock issues came some quasi-legal implications for management. Continental Realty Co., a concern organized by Tobin and Judson, was involved in the sale of a block of Detroit industrial property to Continental Motors Corp. Had there been a conflict of interest? Later Continental Realty was also interested in real estate development and building in Muskegon.

150,000 Motors a Year

23

A month after reorganization of Continental as a new $18.5 million corporation, the Michigan Securities Commission issued an order forbidding the company from paying more than 6 percent on its common stock until the $10,265,000 representing the value of patents, trademarks, goodwill, etc., was reduced to $5,000,000.

The company asked the commission for a re-hearing on the ground that not all facts were previously presented. As a result the 1917 Annual Report to Stockholders showed assets as "not including any value for goodwill."

For the 1917-1918 commercial market, Continental continued its established strategy of offering three 4-cylinder and three 6-cylinder models. THE AUTOMOBILE noted that manufacturers casting about for engine equipment for their forthcoming 1918 cars would find that all Continental motors were refined continuations of the models which were on the market in prior years.

World War I Slump

"They are so designed," THE AUTOMOBILE wrote, "as to cover the entire field from the four-cylinder truck up to the high-powered, six-cylinder passenger car.

"These six engines are the result of more than 13 years of specialization in this particular field and show the result of the development through that time. As a result, the changes are few and those that have been made are more in the nature of minor details than alterations in fundamental practices."

The leader of the 1917-1918 product line was Continental's 7-W six-cylinder model developing 36 hp. Two larger sixes were the 6-P developing 48 hp at 1500 revolutions per minute (rpm) and the 7-N developing 50 hp at 1900 rpm.

The three four-cylinder engines offered were models C, E and N, the latter being particularly adaptable to truck use. Horsepowers were 30-42, 32-47 and 32-38, respectively.

Major customers during the period included Velie, Paige, Columbia, Moon, Hudson, Davis, Elcar, Lexington, Overland, Auburn, Willys and Westcott. Among the independent engine makers, Continental was out-producing its nearest rival, Lycoming, by better than two-to-one.

Most widely used of Continental engines of the period was the model 7-W. This popular six-cylinder 36 hp engine powered such lesser-known cars as the Abbott,

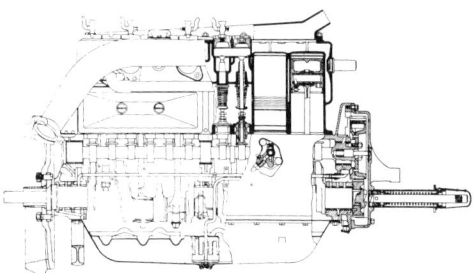

Continental six-cylinder 7-N engine favored for Overland, Paige and Velie cars

American, Beggs, Bush, Crawford, Detroiter, Economy, Empire, Halladay, Hanson, Howard, Huffman, and scores more.

But all was not well, as Benj. F. Tobin reported to the shareholders in January 1918 at the annual meeting in Richmond, Virginia:

"Curtailment of production schedules by our passenger car customers has been unusually frequent, especially since the declaration of war [April 5, 1917], owing to conditions which were beyond the control of both our customers and ourselves.

"Other unusual problems . . . have taxed the ingenuity . . . of your officers." Tobin went on to explain that the government had appropriated supplies for war purposes; that the cost of raw materials and labor had increased rapidly; that skilled workers were being drafted or had enlisted; and that income and excess profits taxes had eaten into the company's net income. Too, new engineering problems had arisen due largely to changes in the quality of available gasoline.

One of the early applications for the four-cylinder 32-38 hp Model N engine was as the power plant for the U.S. Army's standard truck. In 1916, however, motors for military vehicles were a minor consideration in Continental business decisions.

Engines for Army Trucks

All that changed when the United States entered the war against Germany in April 1917. Within three weeks, Congress appropriated the first $7 billion of the $35 billion spent for war purposes through June 1919.

Because it had designed and produced so many different engines for so many customers with varying requirements, Continental was able to draw on a reservoir of internal combustion engine know-how quite unique at the time the United States got into World War I.

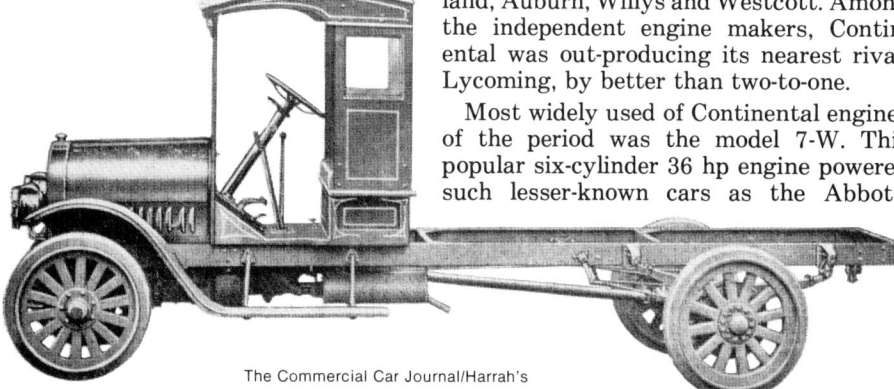

Type in adjacent column is stacked on 1918 flatbed Independent Truck, which is Continental-powered

Initially Continental began supplying its standard engines for customers who had secured large military orders from the War Department and the Allies for trucks and ambulances. Soon the Ordnance Department decided that standardization was necessary for the mass production of the huge number of trucks needed for the war effort.

Plans got underway to design and produce a so-called "Liberty" truck with cooperation of the Society of Automotive Engineers. For design of the standard engine to power the Liberty Class "B" 5-ton truck and other motorized vehicles, the Army called on Continental for assistance.

Under Ross Judson's leadership, twelve Continental designers and detailers went to Washington where they worked for several months assisting the government in engine design. After blueprints and specifications were received, Continental had the sample engine [probably based on an existing engine] running in the remarkable time of 19 days and 18 hours.

Subsequently all drawings and specifications for the Class "B" engine were turned over to the government so that war production might be augmented by the other manufacturers.

Contracts for the Class "B" Military Motors were placed by the Army directly with Continental and four other manufacturers. Continental's quota was 50 percent of the entire order. These orders amounted to approximately $21.5 million for Continental.

Later Continental produced all of the drawings for the Class "A" motor truck and assisted in the design of the Class "AA" engine. The sample Class "A" motor was of a new design, built completely from new drawings, new patterns and new dies. It was claimed to have been running 16 days and 20 hours after the drawings were started. Such were the pressures of wartime needs.

Of the War, Judson wrote that "The gasoline motor was undoubtedly the most important factor, its value conclusively proven in tanks, airplanes, trucks, tractors, passenger cars, ambulances and submarines.

"The broadening fields of usefulness of gasoline motors, promises an almost incalculable volume of business when conditions readjust themselves."

Beginning in May 1917, Continental's Muskegon plant was given over entirely to the production of two sizes of engines for military trucks. Daily engine output was soon tripled, and all production for passenger cars taken care of exclusively at the Detroit factory. Combined military and commercial production was 12,000 engines in a single month.

Concentration on military orders naturally created some consternation among Continental's regular commercial customers. In the automobile industry it was reported that "Continental cannot take any more business."

"Not so," said John G. Painter of the sales department. "This condition no longer exists. Completed factory additions at both plants enable us to offer our latest six-cylinder motors, Types 9V, 7W, 7N and 6P.

"You can sign up the best dealers in every locality because they know that with a Continental Motor in their cars, prospective buyers are already half sold."

Assembly of Class "B" military truck at Diamond T Motor Car plant

Forerunner of military tank was 1916 pre-war armored car by King company

Truck Train No. 314 composed of Continental-powered Class "B" military trucks built by Velie

25

First Annual Report

In the new corporation's first Annual Report, for the period ending October 31, 1917 (covering the 9¼ months since the new company began operations), Tobin reported earnings of $1.4 million. In addition, in the 6¾ months between the end of the 1916 fiscal year, June 30, and formation of the new corporation in January 1917, the company earned $1.1 million or a total of $2.5 million for the 16 months. Earnings in 1918 were nearly $2 million.

In November, Continental received additional orders calling for 360 engines for Model "B" standard Army trucks to be delivered in January, with increasing monthly production until 6400 engines had been delivered.

These WW I production orders set the stage for the "family concept" of military powerplants, a field in which Continental worked in close association with the Army Ordnance Corps in the decades — and wars — to follow.

After the War, Continental resumed full commercial production and further developed its established line of passenger car and truck engines. Business was brisk and profitable, with net income reaching $3.5 million annually in both 1919 and 1920.

Optimistic forecasts continued to be issued from the company's headquarters. In June 1919 the company announced plans for increased production and facilities at both Detroit and Muskegon. Already, Continental said, Detroit was manufacturing 300 engines daily, and the Muskegon plant 350 daily.

"... dealers know that with a Continental Motor in their cars, prospective buyers are already half sold."

Within two years the Muskegon plant was to be doubled in size. To finance this expansion, Ross Judson arranged to sell $5 million of five-year 7% gold notes to Chicago bankers. A thousand more men would be employed, giving Muskegon a capacity of 1000 engines daily. But within two years the company was operating at a loss.

With its new corporate name, Continental began in the early '20s to polish its image. It had graphically developed its "Powerful as the Nation" and "America's Standard" slogans with a modern logotype style some years earlier. Now it set out to fully promote these sales tools. At the same time Continental began to describe its engines in advertising as bearing the "Red Seal."

Red Seal Engines

The story of the origin of the Red Seal is perhaps apocryphal.

Seals used by Continental in its engines were said to have been blue. However, that supply ran out one day and a worker substituted red. An inspector at the Jordan Motor Car Co. of Cleveland noticed the change, as did Edward S. (Ned) Jordan, the company head. He asked his friends at Continental about it, and they explained what had happened.

Soon after that Jordan began advertising that their cars were powered by Red Seal engines, implying that the engines somehow were superior to other engines, including even those provided to other Continental customers.

Actually, very few automobile "assemblers" wanted to admit that they didn't build their own engines. Moon Motor Car Co. of St. Louis was an exception. They not only featured "Red Seal Continental motors" but also prominently listed Rayfield carburetors, Delco ignition and other major supplier-furnished equipment.

Columbia Motors Co. of Detroit was another "assembler" to feature Continental Red Seal and other supplier items — Timken axles, Stromberg carburetors and many others.

Only Continental, however, could fully promote its engine. This was done in ads such as one featuring the salesman in the automobile show-room whose "strongest selling point is the Red Seal Continental Motor." "The argument," said the advertising copy, "that most often clinches the sale of an automobile or truck is the Red Seal Continental Motor."

Various combinations of manufacturers, assemblers and suppliers began to develop in the industry. As an example, Hudson was approached in 1919 with a proposal to merge with Dodge, Continental Motors and Timken-Detroit Axle Co., the new combine to be under Dodge control. The plan, however, was never completed.

Ross Judson, founder and designer/engineer was also the company's principal promoter and salesman. Benj. F. Tobin was the less visible, steady business executive who served as President of the new corporation.

Benjamin F. Tobin Dies

In January 1920, Tobin became Chairman of the Board. Known for his sound, conservative business practices, he was a steadying influence in an industry noted for its often erratic leadership. Just short of his 55th birthday, Tobin had been lately bothered by indigestion attacks but continued his business activities. Then on November 23 he unexpectedly passed away in his suburban Detroit home in Grosse Pointe. He was one of the most widely known and respected executives in the automotive industry.

Judson, who had taken over the office of President in January, emphasized the company's and his personal loss: "I cannot say enough for the integrity and loyalty of Benjamin F. Tobin as a business associate." Of Tobin, another friend wrote, "He pushed forward the wheels of progress and Detroit stands as a greater city by reason of his activity."

William R. Angell, Secretary, chairman of the finance committee, and Director since 1918, became the firm's Vice-President in 1921, moving further up the executive ladder and more and more into what had been Tobin's business management role. The board of directors was strengthened later in the year by the election of James H. Ferry.

Four years had passed since Continental changed its legal structure from a Michigan to a Virginia corporation, including a major refinancing and reorganization of the 14 year old firm.

Believing that taxable profits had accrued to the stockholders as a result of a $5 per share cash payment and exchange of old shares for stock in the new corporation, the Internal Revenue Service sent inquiries to Continental offices in November 1920. Requested was detailed information on stockholders' individual holdings, including fair market values of shares in the former Michigan corporation both at the time of transfer and as of March 1, 1913.

The corporation's officers failed to respond fully and on a timely basis so that the matter dragged on for several years. Early in 1922, Ross Judson sent stockholders of record January 20, 1917 a lengthy explanation of the status of the IRS inquiry.

The controversy was still going on early in 1923 but since the IRS claims would have been against individual stockholders there seems to have been no corporate

BENJAMIN F. TOBIN, SR.
"He pushed forward the wheels of progress and Detroit stands as a greater city by reason of his activity."

Moon said it got the greatest engine value by having its engines built "by the finest engine specialists in the automobile industry."

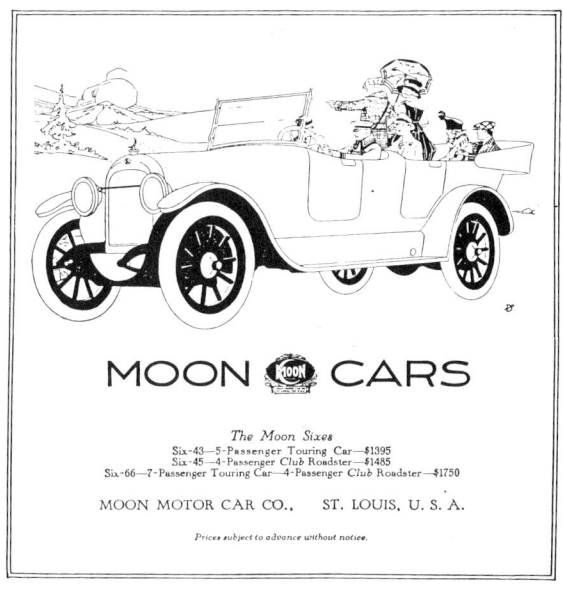

MOON CARS

The Moon Sixes
Six-43—5-Passenger Touring Car—$1395
Six-45—4-Passenger *Club* Roadster—$1485
Six-66—7-Passenger Touring Car—4-Passenger *Club* Roadster—$1750

MOON MOTOR CAR CO., ST. LOUIS, U.S.A.

Prices subject to advance without notice.

National Geographic/Bolan

LOUIS J. KANITZ
General Sales Manager

record of how the matter was finally settled.

A June 12, 1922 letter of W. R. Angell's to a major stockholder was, however, somewhat revealing:

"... the Peninsular Motor Company ... was organized in connection with the refinancing plan and in order to get around certain legal obstacles.

"To what extent the fact that the properties of the old company were first conveyed to Peninsular and then to the Virginia corporation will figure in the opinion, no one can say."

One who sensed the coming recession was Louis J. Kanitz, scion of the pioneer Von Kanitz family of Muskegon. As a high school boy in 1909, he had found summer employment in the plant of newly arrived Continental Motor Manufacturing Co., which had moved to Muskegon three years earlier.

The Industrial Engine Market

After graduation from the U.S. Naval Academy and wartime service at the Brooklyn Naval Yard, Kanitz returned to his home town to start a real estate business.

Continental was just starting a $3 million construction program including a power plant and production facilities and, on the basis of similar work with the Navy, secured a position from Angell in March 1920 as the company's construction coordinator.

Angell and James Ferry, Director and Vice President, were partners in Michigan Material Corp., a sand and gravel firm, which Kanitz managed for them for two years, finally liquidating the company, selling its tug boats, scows, dredges and cranes and returning the stockholders' investment 100 cents on the dollar.

Jim Ferry, Jr., recalls his father telling him that during the winter the lakes north of Muskegon froze so solidly that the gravel sledges could cross the ice. However, "all of a sudden Mr. Angell and I found ourselves completely out of business, because the whole works had sunk through the ice. The guy had gone a little bit too late in the season."

"After completion of the Michigan Material liquidation," Kanitz wrote, "I was given the task of operating and liquidating National Construction Co., another intercompany ally.

"It was during this time that I noted the transition from steam power to gasoline power on portable construction machinery so I interested Continental into going into the industrial and agricultural gasoline engine business. The first year we did $32,000 worth of business. It built up to approximately $5 million annually within four years.

"Our customers were Allis-Chalmers, Massey-Harris, Worthington Pump, even General Electric and Westinghouse, all of which purchased Continental gasoline engines for tractors, combines, road building and construction machines."

It was the beginning of Continental's diversification as its automobile engine business declined, and of Kanitz rise in the company's sales organization, for he soon became Industrial Engines Sales Manager.

Continental Motors was subject, as were many other industrial firms, to the serious deflation and post-WW I slump in business. For the first time Continental reported an operating loss — $1.2 million for the 1921 fiscal year. After reducing inventory values to cost, the year's net loss was reported at $371,534. In the four prior years, profits had averaged $2.5 million annually.

Business, however was soon looking up again as the country emerged from the post-war depression. In preparation for a production schedule of 20,000 cars monthly, Durant Motors placed an order in March 1922 with Continental for a quarter of a million engines. A record-breaker for the number of units ordered, the contract was for four-cylinder engines for the newly introduced Star car with a phenomenally low price tag of $348.

At the time of the large Durant orders, which were a continuation of previous business relations between the two companies, Continental had been working on a part-time basis at the Muskegon plant for nearly a year.

Despite selling merits of its engines for industrial use, Continental in 1920 still used horsedrawn wagons to carry cylinder blocks and crankcases to factory yard

Earlier, the Durant Corp. had offered a unique stock purchase plan. A limited number of Continental Motors shares, Durant announced, could be purchased through the automobile firm at $6 per share. No individual could purchase less than five shares nor more than 20 shares under the plan.

In October 1922, Continental's capital structure was again changed under its Virginia charter. Stockholders approved an increase in capital stock to 3,000,000 shares without nominal or par value. Of the authorized shares, 1,500,000 were issued share-for-share in exchange for the previous $10 par value shares and $3.5 million in 7 percent preferred stock authorized in 1917 was retired.

[For the first time, Continental's common shares were approved for trading on the New York Stock Exchange.]

Two years after his father's death, B.F. Tobin, Jr. became Secretary, succeeding W.R. Angell, who had been named Vice President.

Over the years Continental had built up a large "family" of engine models which could easily be customized to fit the specialized needs of virtually any "assembler" ready to challenge the already established, integrated manufacturers for the ever expanding automobile market.

Meeting Customer Needs

The company had a large, capable staff of salesmen and a product line broad enough for nearly every size and type of passenger car and commercial truck. Continental Red Seal engines were also very competitive in the market, usually being available at prices as low as or lower than its competitors.

Often new models of Continental engines were developed without a particular customer's requirements in mind. In various bore-and-stroke configurations and power ratings, they were put "on the shelf" ready to meet the needs of the automotive industry, and later those of industrial, construction and agricultural equipment manufacturers. Engines were available virtually from a catalog.

The sales brochure for the 1922 Model J-4 engine became effusively lyrical in describing Continental's manufacturing processes:

"... slowly but steadily the major units of the Red Seal Motor begin their trip down the long line of elevated rails, gathering in bulk as they come abreast of the various machinery lanes out of which the finished parts are flowing. You watch as rings are fitted to pistons by the dexterous hands of experts, while connecting rods and pistons are placed on sensitive scales and assorted into complete motor sets according to their weights.

"You note the precision with which bearing fits are made; you see the assembly of crankcase and cylinder block; you follow a hundred and one operations in which care is the guiding principle and in which tests are applied again and again to check up the work of men and machines and, finally, you come almost, but not quite to the end of your journey — the testing department."

Still, Continental admitted that "no booklet can re-create the smoke, heat, or all-pervading noise of foundry, machine shop or test room." The brochure continued . . .

Teledyne Continental Motors

Market Street Plant, Muskegon, in mid-twenties featured Model T cars and "Keystone" cop

Factory in 1922: smoke, heat and noise of foundry, machine shop and test room. Battery of drop-forge hammers making crankshafts

National Automotive History Collection

29

9-N six-cylinder L-head engine with longer pistons and heavier crankshaft than its 7-N predecessor

Motor World/Harrah's

Machine taps all bolt holes in a crankcase in one operation in Continental's Detroit plant

"Through a soft haze you can see long lines of completed motors. Marshalled in orderly rows that never diminish in length, for as motors are picked up at the head of the line the entire row moves forward leaving a space that is quickly filled by the steady flow from the Assembly Division. Like well-trained athletes they seem almost impatient for the final, crucial test.

"Before you, several hundred Red Seal Continental Motors are purring on the blocks — generating power that, properly applied, might have built the Pyramids in a day or made child's play of the task of up-ending an obelisk. The work of the thousands of units that you saw along the machining lanes has here been brought to the focal point. The one thing that they were designed to do has been done.

"But watch this overhead crane that is now picking a tested motor from its block. Follow it as it travels to the other end of the building, and deposits it on the inspection bench. Here it is taken down piece by piece, each bearing surface, every working part inspected. And when that is completed to the entire satisfaction of a corps of experts it will go on to the blocks once more for a final running test that will determine, for all time, its fitness to carry on its crankcase — The Continental Red Seal."

Motor/Dunwoodie

After World War I, many new companies tried to get into the lucrative auto industry as assemblers of motor cars. Fortunately there were scores of reliable manufacturers of the required components — engines, transmissions, radiators, brakes, bodies, axles, etc.

Engines for Car Assemblers

A Moon Motor Car ad of the mid-20's faced up to the scorn heaped on "assemblers" by the major, integrated manufacturers:

"Moon long ago freed itself from any false pride about making its own engines. What Moon is after is the greatest engine value. We get it by having our engines built by the finest engine specialists in the automobile industry today."

Continental was, of course, that specialist.

The back-to-normal transition period after the War caused high mortality among the countless small auto companies which had sprung up. More and more of the few that survived turned to producing their own engines.

To fill the increasing need for a lightweight six-cylinder car, especially the growing market for new cars classified as "$1,000 sixes," Continental offered the Model 6-Y engines. At that time Continental was building about 10% fours and 90% sixes.

Introduced at the February 1922 Chicago Auto Show, the 6-Y was standard equipment for the Moon, Columbia and Davis models, all priced close to $1,000. Somewhat smaller than any previous Continental six, the new monobloc engine gave excellent performance (a speed range from 3 to 60 mph in high gear; 38 mph in second speed). Horsepower ranged from 22 hp at 1000 rpm to 50 hp at 2600 rpm, later to be increased to 66 hp in the Paige-Detroit "6-66" automobile.

One of the classier installations of the 6-Y was in the $3400 Winton Roadster. This engine was followed by the 70 hp Model 6-B of 1925.

To its 1923 truck engine line, Continental added the 35 hp Type K-4 which had been developed earlier, but not previously produced in quantity. It was designed for 2- and 2½-ton trucks. The complete truck engine line, all of the same general design, included the J-4 for 1- and 1½-ton trucks; the L-4 for 3- and 3½-ton trucks; and Model B-5 for the 5-ton and larger truck market.

Commercial business had never been better. In 1923, output was 237,000 motors — more than twice the number sold in any previous year. Sales volume totaled $30 million, nearly equalling the wartime peak of 1920.

Teledyne Continental Motors

Aerial view of Muskegon plant in 1924 as shown in Annual Report to Stockholders

A number of companies — Checker and Yellow Cab were typical — maintained their long affiliation with Continental which had supplied the latter with four-cylinder engines since the beginning of cab production in 1915, through 1926.

In 1924 Yellow Cab produced its first Hertz cars, powered by Red Seal L-head sixes. Initially called the "Ambassador," the car name was changed to Hertz, and the last Hertz was built in 1926. Then the car was converted to a taxicab and sold under the Yellow Cab name through early 1929.

It was the cars of mixed ancestry (engine supplied by an independent manufacturer) which in time lost out to the industry leaders — Ford and General Motors, and then Chrysler as well, in the late twenties.

Business Revives in Mid-Twenties

Continental Motors remained confident but still was coming face to face with the realization that its hope for the future lay in developing additional markets to replace those being lost through the evolution of the motor industry into self-sufficient units.

Sporty 1922 Winton roadster was ideal car for sophisticated lady of the day

There were concerns in mid-1924 that a saturation in car and truck ownership was near at hand and the automobile industry in the throes of a slump. "Not so," declared Continental's Angell, who pointed out that there was no real foundation for the rumor, except perhaps it was a presidential election year.

"As far as I can see," he said, "the automobile business is establishing itself on a firm and permanent foundation. Probably 1.5 million cars will be required this year for replacement purposes alone, and this number will gradually increase each year.

"There are also tremendous trade possibilities abroad — Canada, Europe, Asia, Australia and South America."

Earlier in the year, Continental issued and sold $7.5 million in bonds secured by a mortgage on the company's fixed assets, to retire the Gold Notes issued in 1920 and to provide additional working capital.

In summer 1925, Ross Judson indicated that Continental was anticipating large increases in business volume and was expanding production rather than decreasing it, as was traditional for that time of year.

"Our customers," he said, "have materially increased their schedules and are contemplating still further increases. In addition, negotiations are nearing completion for two very large contracts, one with a major foreign manufacturer. These contracts will practically double our output of motors for commercial vehicles.

"Our Division of Industrial Engineering is making rapid strides, and the number of customers we have in the industrial field is steadily increasing. Our gasoline motors

Motor/Harrah's

Oil pan removed to show four-bearing crankshaft of six-cylinder model 6-Y engine

are now being used in agricultural implements, road building machinery, portable air compressors, hoisting machinery, excavating shovels and dredges, railway equipment, mining machinery and in the marine and motor bus fields."

Judson's confidence in the business was not misplaced. Profits rose from $1.5 million in 1922 to $2.5 million in 1924. For 1925 they were $2.8 million, third highest in the company's history.

The balance sheet again showed "patents, goodwill, trade name and other intangible values." This time they totaled $5.9 million.

Too, the company had excellent facilities; it could produce 360,000 motors per year. Floor area of the Detroit and Muskegon plants was approximately 2,000,000 square feet, located on 74 acres of plant property. More than 7,000 men were employed at an annual payroll exceeding $10 million. Stockholders, too, had increased; to 7,000 from the 48 owners a decade earlier.

There was, however, occasional attrition in the executive ranks. George W. Yeoman, one of the earliest investors had left the company in 1912 but later returned as assistant to the president, Secretary, Treasurer, and then Vice-President. However he again resigned, in 1925, and did not return.

Although the company had begun its first serious efforts at true product diversification, it did not back away from the automotive market but went ahead to exploit every possible opportunity to continue as a major factor in the industry.

As largest employer in Muskegon, Continental played a major role in community affairs. Good employee morale made an important contribution to company's success.

Strike up the band! Mid-twenties musical group featured colonial uniforms. Band played frequently during plant lunch hour and at local events

Dispensary at Market Street plant provided first aid. Heavy machinery and hard labor made medical facilities a necessity

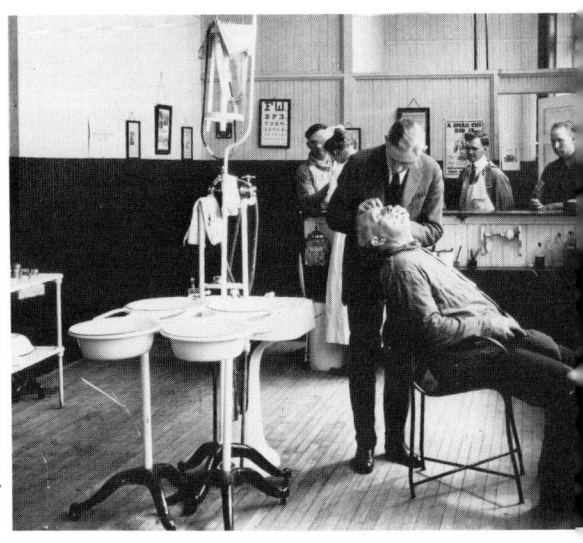

One of Continental's first steps toward maintaining its position in the automotive market was to look, as it had at the time of the company's founding a quarter century earlier, at technical advancements abroad. This time it was not to the Continent but to Scotland, that Continental's W. R. Angell turned.

Single-Sleeve-Valve Engines

From 1909 to 1914, Argylls, Ltd. of Alexandria, Scotland had produced the Argyll automobile, considered a leader in its class because the engine incorporated single-sleeve-valves which had been developed under Burt-McCollum patents. (The Knight double-sleeve-valve engine was in production at the Daimler Motor Co., Coventry, England.)

A month before the outbreak of World War I, the Argylls concern was placed in receivership and the patent rights reverted to Peter Burt, the inventor. After the Armistice in 1918 the patents were purchased outright by Wallace, Ltd. of Glasgow, which placed a series of stock automobile engines on the market. Licenses were also granted to other companies for industrial, marine and motorcycle engines, both air-and water-cooled. Thus it was not until 1919 that the single-sleeve-valve engine was placed on the open market.

By 1925, when Continental became interested, there were two passenger car companies and three motorcycle manufacturers in Great Britain and one automobile company in Switzerland building engines on the Burt-McCollum principle.

American patents for the single-sleeve engine were purchased by Continental from Wallace. A month later, May 19, 1926, Angell returned on the *S. S. Paris* to announce exclusive world patent rights as well as formation of British Continental Motors, Ltd., to which European manufacturers were required to begin royalty payments.

What prompted Continental to acquire the patents was the belief that the demand for single-sleeve-valve engines would gradually exceed that for poppet valve engines, and perhaps lead to the eventual elimination of the poppet entirely. [The poppet is a conventional valve as used universally today, consisting of a round disc lifting off a round hole.]

Along with the patents, Continental also acquired the services of A. M. Niven, one of the pioneers of Argyll engine development in Scotland and inventor of several features incorporated in the engines. At Detroit, Niven was placed in charge of the new project reporting to W. A. Frederick, Continental's Vice-President and Chief Engineer.

When both appeared before the Society of Automotive Engineers in Detroit, Nevin made clear "the fact that our firm manufactures poppet-valve engines is sufficient to indicate that we are not out to 'kill' the conventional type of valve."

The advantage of the Argyll design was said to be the simplified operation of the single-sleeve-valve engine which tends to be quieter, of greater durability and eventually lower production cost. Other claims for the engine were better fuel economy, decreased weight, higher speed and less vibration. For Continental, it was the first major change in 25 years from traditional engine design.

In this design, the sleeve valve not only moves up and down so that its ports match similar ports in the cylinder wall, but it also oscillates at the same time from side to side. It is this elliptical motion which permits use of a single sleeve. This motion gives the quick port opening and closing required in a high-speed internal combustion engine.

Outside of the sleeves, their operating mechanism and the cylinder heads, the design of the engine was conventional and embodied many features common to all Continental engines.

By late 1926, when it was hoped the first Continental-Argyll engines would become available to customers, Continental officers were hinting that the 2,750,000 poppet-valve engines they had already produced might eventually be replaced by single-sleeve models. "We have a yearly production capacity of half a million engines," Angell said, "and the cost would be very little more to switch our entire production to this type, which lends itself to air cooling."

Development work at the Detroit plant was concentrated on a six-cylinder auto-

Red Seal Magazine

Import from Scotland

Scottish Argyll car brought to Detroit by Continental was powered by 4-cylinder sleeve valve engine. At the wheel: Walter A. Frederick, chief engineer.

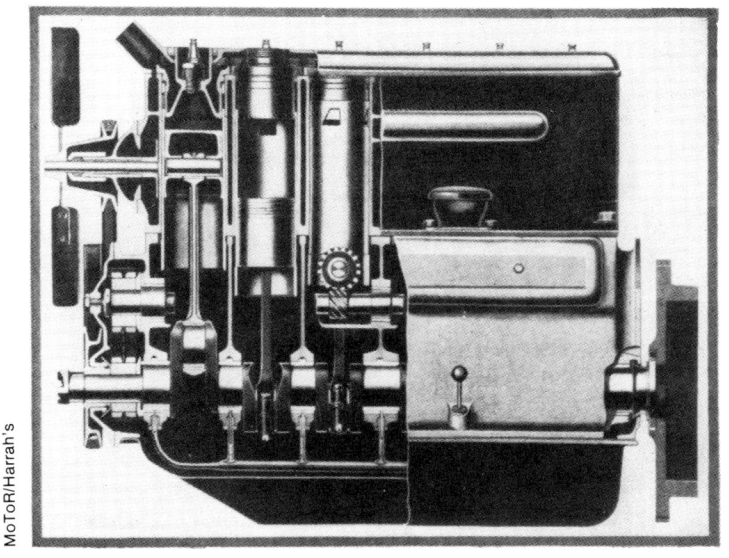

Cutaway and detailed drawings. MoToR magazine commented that it may be a bit wide of the mark to suggest that the single sleeve valve might forecast passing of the poppet valve engine

Promotional give-away for auto shows featured 'windows' which pictured various stages—*intake, compression, firing, power, exhaust*—*as dial was turned*

mobile engine developing 57 hp at 3000 rpm, but the company announced that Argyll-type engines would be built in the same sizes as the established line of poppet-valve engines.

Continental's ambitious plans called for a complete line including fours, sixes and eights for passenger cars; and fours and sixes for trucks, tractors and buses, as well as motorboat and motorcycle engines and air-cooled radial airplane engines. "Models for automotive use and for aeroplanes will be on display in January 1927," wrote Judson.

The extensive use of the single-sleeve engine abroad over a period of 14 years and the outstanding service it had given was regarded by Continental as ample proof of the soundness of the design.

MoToR Magazine wrote that "this is the first patent Continental has bought in the 25 years of its existence, notwithstanding . . . that inventions involving engine improvements have been brought to it at the rate of several a month.

"All these were examined . . . and thousands of dollars spent in experimental work, but . . . results . . . did not warrant the adoption of any inventions. In view of this record the announcement of the single-sleeve-value engine is most significant."

At the request of Anthony H. G. Fokker, the Americanized Dutch aircraft manufacturer, Continental included the aircraft application of the design in its long-range plans. They would develop an air-cooled radial engine of approximately 200 hp, using single-sleeve valves. While the Argyll engine in the long run did not work out for Continental on the automobile, the single-sleeve-valve principle was employed extensively in aircraft engines by Bristol in England until the advent of the gas turbine engine. Bristol, however, had difficulty competing with Rolls-Royce aircraft engines which used poppet valves.

Despite the overblown optimism and marketing efforts through 1927, there is little on the record today to indicate that the project met with any great success for Continental. Reportedly, General Motors had earlier tested—and rejected—the Argyll engine. Still, at the 1927 New York automobile show, Continental introduced a cut-away section model of an eight-cylinder single-sleeve automobile engine showing the up-and-down operation of the sleeves and port openings as each sleeve rotated in the cylinder.

On the lookout for new engineering talent, Walter Frederick, the company's top engineer, brought into the organization Carl F. Bachle, a recent mechanical engineering graduate from the University of Michigan, and son of a personal friend. Young Bachle started as a dynamometer operator and rapidly rose to project engineer. He was to become Continental's brightest engineering innovator during the next four decades.

"Straight Eights"

Although Continental engineers saw great potential in the single-sleeve engine, they continued development of more conventional power plants of increased performance for quality cars.

Up to the mid-20's nearly all auto engines were of either four or six cylinders, but Deusenberg helped change that by announcing a new engine design of eight cylinders "all in a row," later referred to as the "straight eight."

Continental joined the straight eight parade starting in 1925 with introduction of its overhead valve Type 8-P engine and the L-head 9-K, followed in 1926 by the popular 72 hp Model 12-Z.*

For the 1927 market, Jordan Motor offered a new "Airline Eight" which, it said, was developed jointly by Continental, Jordan and Stromberg Carburetor Co. Ned Jordan, President, described it as a revolutionary new engine with "characteristics strikingly similar to those of the finest airplane engines."

For this 14-S and similar L-head eights, Continental claimed a 33 percent increase in horsepower and 21 percent increase in torque. Mainly responsible for the high performance was use of a double (duplex) carburetor and of an inlet manifold supplying charge from one mixing tube to the four inner, and from the other to the four outer, cylinders.

The Continental eights were "top of the line" engines and were produced in the golden age of the company's role as sup-

*See chapter Technical Notes, Page 46.

Continental Shows New Sleeve Valve Engine

ONE of the features of the Continental Motors Corporation exhibit at the New York automobile show will be the initial showing of the Continental single sleeve valve engine.

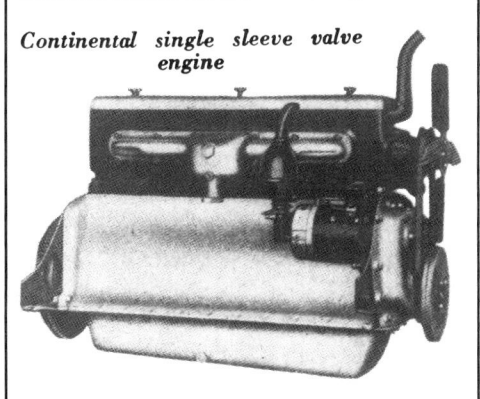

Continental single sleeve valve engine

The single sleeve valve engine to be displayed is an 8 cylinder cut-away sectional model showing the actual operation of the sleeves and port openings as well as the complete driving mechanism.

Motor Age/Dunwoodie

plier to the automobile industry. In all, Continental produced 18 models of L-head straight eights for auto builders.

The success of its eights was highlighted in late 1928 by W. R. Angell, Executive Vice-President, in announcing a "new order calling for 5,000 engines for well-known eight-cylinder car engines which, up to this time, have been produced in the buyer's own plant.

"Other orders placed with our Industrial Division by some of the country's leading agricultural implement houses call for

Continental's Model 14-S 'eight-in-line' 85 horsepower engine powered Jordan's "Airline Eight" luxury car

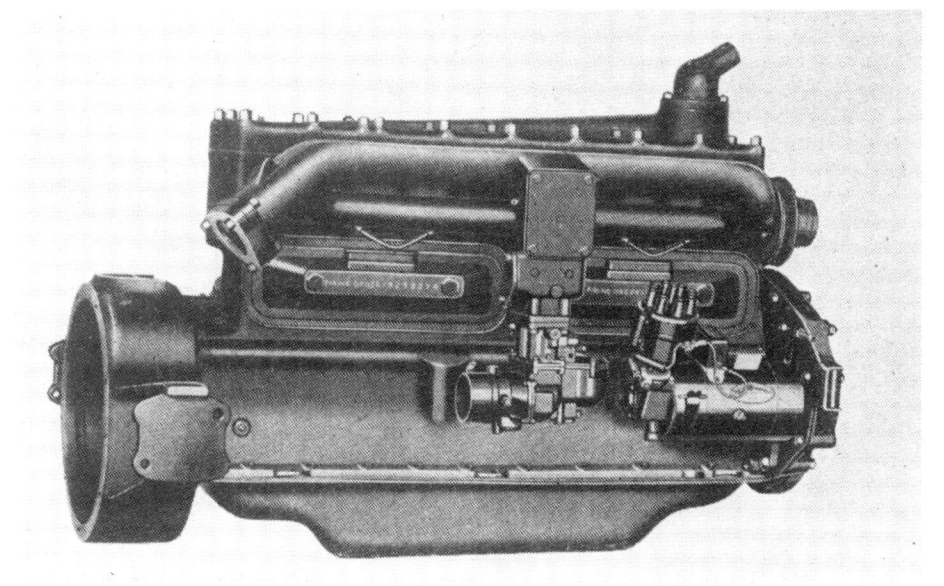

Motor Age/Dunwoodie

35

Few Changes in Star Line
Star Six Sport Coupe
Motor Age/Dunwoodie

For this forerunner of the modern motor home, built by Ray F. Kuns, editor of *Automotive Digest*, the Continental 6-B bus motor was selected

immediate production of between 20,000 and 30,000 heavy-duty engines. We anticipate a larger production than usual during the remainder of the year."

Little mention was made of it at the time, but in 1928, Continental worked out a mutually advantageous arrangement with well-established Gray Marine Motor Co., which also had started business in the early 1900s. Gray was granted the exclusive world-wide conversion and sales rights for boat propulsion purposes of the complete line of Continental Red Seal engines.

Within a decade, the "straight-eight" engine design had eliminated many of the V-8s—with a few exceptions, such as Cadillac and Lincoln. So popular were they that the industry, except for Ford in 1935, returned to V-8s only after World War II.

Since the straight-eight engine required a longer chassis than an equivalent V-8, designers were forced into building longer autos as well as longer hoods—a styling asset in those days—to accommodate the engines. Thus the straight-eights led the way for some of the classic car designs of the period.

The day of the assembled car—and the stock engine manufacturer—was nearly past its prime by the time the straight-eight became a factor in the U.S. automotive business.

Continental was the largest independent manufacturer of straight-eights (Lycoming was the other) and these motors were used principally by the smaller independent manufacturers whose financial resources and limited volume of business could not have supported an expensive engine-building facility.

Still, Continental's customer list from 1925 to 1931 was impressive: Jordan, Locomobile, Diana (an offshoot of Moon), Graham-Paige, Cole, Moon, duPont, Peerless, front-wheel-drive Ruxton, Windsor (another Moon offshoot) and Willys.

In the late 1920s there was, in addition to General Motors, Ford and Chrysler, a fourth major automotive grouping—Durant Motors, which included the Star, Flint, Locomobile and Durant cars. It was headed by William C. Durant who had founded General Motors in 1908 and had organized his new group after being ousted from the GM presidency.

A Fifth Grouping?

Since 1921, Continental had provided engines for Durant cars and at one time the majority of the company's annual output of engines went to fill Durant orders. There was, apparently, a close relationship between Bill Durant and Continental's Angell.

Angell had also developed close business ties with Ned Jordan of Jordan, and with Peerless Motors, serving since 1925 on the board of directors of the latter company.

A fifth grouping—Peerless, Continental and Jordan—appeared imminent. While a physical merger did not seem likely, rumor had it that an alliance including Peerless and Jordan would manufacture complete lines of cars powered with the Argyll single-sleeve-valve engine, controlled by Continental Motors.

Investment bankers, too, got into the act. Alfred W. Wallace, a Detroit investment banker, announced in March 1928 that a group he represented had obtained and would formally take control of the Peerless Motor Car Corp. at the April 3 annual stockholders meeting in Richmond, Virginia.

"Those associated with me," Wallace said, "comprise a comparatively small group of Detroit and Cleveland businessmen. Two of the Detroit men are connected with Continental Motors Corp. But that company, as such, has no part in activities of the group. It is equally true that W. C. Durant is not a member of this group.

"It is true, however, that negotiations are pending for the use eventually of the Argyll single-sleeve-valve engines in Peerless cars."

Ross Judson of Continental stated that "Aside from 500 shares of Peerless stock purchased more than six years ago, this company does not own any stock in that company. I am among those who have personally acquired a stock interest in Peerless because the stock constitutes an attractive investment.

"That a merger of Continental and Peerless or Jordan is contemplated is untrue. This company, as an independent engine manufacturer to the trade, is

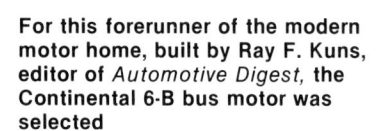

Red Seal Magazine

interested only in Peerless as a purchaser of Continental engines.

"W. R. Angell, Vice President of this company, has for several years been a director of Peerless. No doubt his active interest in the business affairs of the Peerless company will continue.

"We have not been advised that W. C. Durant has any interest in the Peerless company. Neither is he a stockholder of Continental Motors. Aside from our cordial relationship with him as a user of the engines we manufacture there is no connection between him and his company."

Subsequent records show that nothing came of the potential Continental-Peerless-Jordan combine.

Continental Motors' fiscal year ended October 31 and results for the 1927 period were available early in 1928. At that time, John C. Gourlie of AUTOMOTIVE INDUSTRIES wrote perhaps the first definitive financial analysis of the company's operations covering the two prior decades.

More Financial Success

Charts and text revealed that net worth, which exceeded $1 million for the first time in 1911, had grown to $28 million in 1927. Cash dividends had been paid in each of the 13 years from 1909 through 1921, but after 12 years of profitable operation, the company had sustained an operating loss of

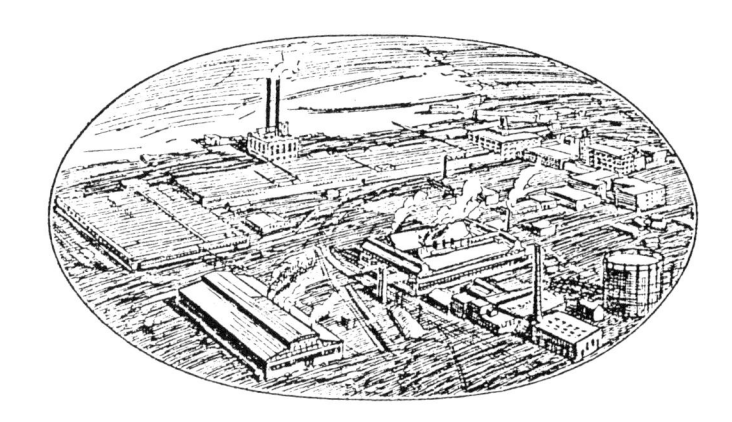

Financial Progress of Continental

Net Worth, 1909-1927

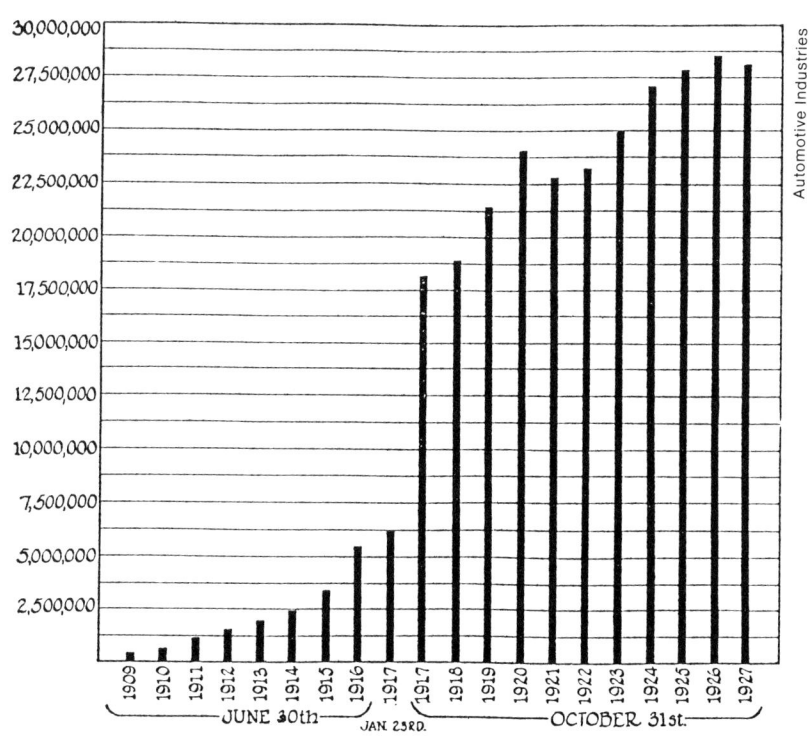

$1.1 million in fiscal 1921, reduced to $371,534 after subsequent adjustment by revaluing inventory at cost.

In the six years 1922-1927, net income averaged $2 million annually; and cash dividends were resumed in 1924.

Lacking "full disclosure" requirements later adopted by the Securities and Exchange Commission, it was the practice of industrial companies, for competitive business reasons, not to disclose sales figures. Thus, net income, rather than sales volume, was the primary index by which companies were judged as to their business success.

Beginning in 1935, however, Continental annual reports disclosed sales volume figures and, later, information on business done in previous years was disclosed.

Early investors in Continental had prospered handsomely. As AUTOMOTIVE INDUSTRIES pointed out, an original investment of $100 was worth $27,000 in 1928:

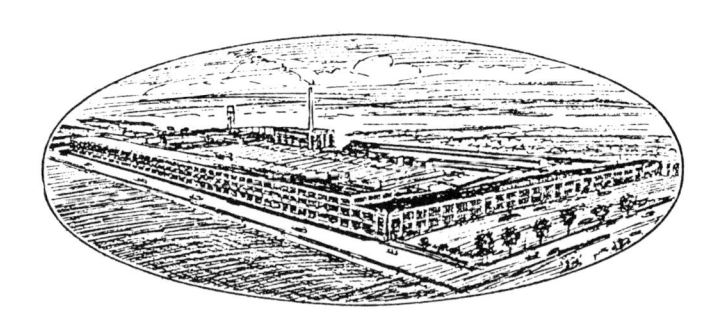

Original Investment of $100 Returns $27,039.86

ONE share of the stock of the Auto Car Equipment Co., par value $100, is represented today by 1382.4 shares of the Continental Motors Corp. This number of shares at the present quotation of about $11 would have a market value of $15,206.40.

In addition to this, cash dividends paid to date have meant a return of $11,833.46 on each share of the original $100 par stock.

Adding the cash dividends to the present market value of the stock, it is seen that each original $100 investment has returned the investor a total of $27,039.86, or a **270-time increase.**

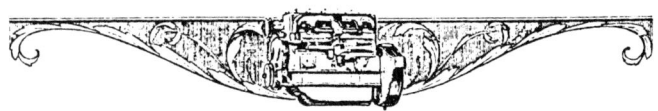

Net income for the period 1906 to 1927 totaled $28.3 million, while $12.5 million was paid to stockholders in cash dividends. This left $15.8 million available to implement the company's policy of financing expansion through reinvestment of the surplus in the business.

For the 1927 fiscal year Continental earned $1,248,831, or 71 cents per share on the 1,760,845 shares of no par value then outstanding. Cash dividends were 80 cents per share, providing a 7 percent yield on the quoted price of approximately $11 per share.

"Continental is largely dependent upon automotive business for satisfactory earnings," wrote Gourlie, "yet in recent years it has vigorously pursued a policy of diversification and now sells a good portion of its products for engine installations in non-automotive industries. This contributes to stability and to the support of business at times when car and truck manufacturers are retrenching."

Engineer Carl Bachle had his own explanation for diversification and for the decline in Continental's automobile engine business.

"In the mid-20s," he wrote, "it was evident that the survivor automobile companies would want to build their own engines and most other components. As a large share of the cost of the car was in the engine, the prime manufacturers wanted the profit on the engines for themselves.

"As these companies generated capital from profits they chose to put it into engine building capability. This also happened to such things as axles, bodies, steering gear, etc.

"Those companies that did not generate capital could not expand their manufacturing, except by borrowing, and soon became non-competitive."

There was a clear downtrend in business in 1927 when Henry Ford helped push the country's economy into a slump by halting all Ford output for five months, as he switched production from the Model T to the Model A.

Earlier in the year Continental had reported record production; April shipments were the largest in the company's 26-year history, according to Executive Vice-President Angell. More than 8000 workers were on the payroll. June production of 30,000 motors exceeded year earlier shipments by 10,000 units.

AUTOMOTIVE INDUSTRIES' analysis of Continental ended on the optimistic note that "In view of the prospect that the single-sleeve-valve engine will be installed in a new car . . . the outlook for Continental is particularly interesting at this time." That optimism was not fully justified.

Ross Judson was the type of outgoing executive who enjoyed the life style made possible by his company's success. He had estate homes in both Muskegon and Detroit and was always one of the first to acquire any new mechanical invention that enhanced his image.

Continental's Company Plane

The aeroplane, as it was then termed, was such an invention. In the summer of 1923 he acquired a flying boat—the company plane of its day—and made frequent trips to the Upper Great Lakes, hosting such guests as Ned Jordan, president of the motor car company of the same name.

To explore and fish the Heron Bay area, not readily accessible except by flying boat, Judson and Jordan flew some 1200 miles in less than 12 hours "running time." Judson's aeroplane was said "to have caused a sensation among the Indian inhabitants."

Other customers such as Durant Motors executives were afforded similar courtesies. Colin Campbell, Durant vice president, was in Muskegon in the Fall of 1924 looking over the manufacture of Continental engines for Star and Durant cars, and became so interested he and J. S. Hunt, Durant's production manager, missed their intended train.

So that Campbell and Hunt could keep to their intended schedule, AUTOMOBILE TOPICS reported that Judson made available "his private hydroplane to fly across Lake Michigan to Chicago, arriving in time for the meeting."

Judson and other Continental officials continued to develop their interest in aviation, perhaps because of Tony Fokker's suggestion regarding the application of the single-sleeve-valve to aircraft engines. Well over a year before Lindbergh's famed New York-Paris flight in May 1927, the company had purchased a 14-passenger tri-motored Fokker monoplane which executives planned to use for business travel.

The Muskegon Chamber of Commerce and Continental began looking for a local site suitable for an airport. Also, William B. Stout, designer of the Ford Tri-Motor, was trying to promote regular plane service between Detroit, Grand Rapids and Muskegon.

In March 1926, Judson and Angell, together with a Detroit pilot and an official of the Detroit Chamber of Commerce, flew to Muskegon in a Stinson-Detroiter plane to find the best location for the proposed airport. Continental then bought the land, a 160-acre site on a hill north of Getty Street, overlooking the Muskegon River. On July 23 the Continental airport was dedicated.

The next spring, Judson and Angell, accompanied by Harry D. Kline, Continental's advertising manager, made an 8000-mile business trip to St. Louis, Los Angeles, San Francisco, Portland and Seattle, calling on Continental customers. Pilots of the Fokker were Lieut. George Pond and Rene N. (Ray) La Badie.

A motion picture record of the week-long West Coast trip was made for promotion purposes. Afterward, Angell observed that "no trouble was encountered on the trip; and we believe it will not be long before such air-liners will be in regular service between the eastern and western sections of the nation."

Putting that forecast to practical use in Continental's business, the company's Fokker was soon being scheduled regularly for business trips between Detroit headquarters and the Muskegon plant. Before

Continental's early interest in aviation centered on tri-motor Fokker transport purchased in 1926 for executive travel

Airport at Muskegon, left, north of Getty Street, was developed by Continental as early contribution to regular air service

At Continental Airport dedication in July 1926 company executives pose with congressional and civic leaders. In center, W. R. Angell. On his left, also in dark suit and holding straw hat, is founder Ross W. Judson. On Angell's right, in golf knickers, is V. M. Smith, superintendent of Continental's Detroit plant

that executives had to either take two night trips on the train, or else spend a night at Muskegon, since the trip by rail took seven hours.

With the plane, executives could fly to Muskegon in the morning, transact business there and return to Detroit several hours before close of the business day. AUTOMOTIVE INDUSTRIES observed that "... operation of this plane will also prove of value to Continental in the development of its airplane engines."

Utility was not the only reason for the Fokker. "It was a very effective publicity getter," observed Carl Bachle, "because there was no other firm in Detroit which had a company plane at that time."

Later other automobile executives and companies took to the air in their own planes for business travel. They included L. P. Fisher of Cadillac, E. L. Cord of Auburn (who later started his own airline), Cliff Durant, Russell Boynge of Chevrolet, Henry DuPont and the Marmon Motor Car Co.

It was not lost on Judson and Angell that the market for airplane engines ought to be pursued as an important part of Continental's product diversification.

W ork on Continental's first aircraft engine had begun not long after the company had acquired rights to the single-sleeve-valve principle. First announcements of the new engine were appearing in Spring 1927 trade journals even as Judson and Angell were soaring west on their first long business trip in the company's Fokker plane.

Among other models of the Burt-McCollum single-sleeve type engine, Continental revealed its nine-cylinder radial air-cooled engine which was to produce 220 hp at 1800 rpm. Its development had been hastened because of a favorable report on single-sleeve-valve engines for aeronautical purposes by the British Aeronautical Research Committee.

"The United States Government," Ross Judson wrote stockholders in 1927, "has entered into a contract with us for development of aeroplane engines (R-790) of the single-sleeve-valve type."

Then, somewhat too optimistically as was later proved, Judson wrote, "Our

Nine-cylinder single-sleeve-valve radial aircraft engine was adapted by Continental from Wright poppet-valve engine

40

Continental's single-sleeve-valve nine-cylinder engine is displayed first time at New York and Chicago auto shows

engineers are now satisfied that it is in final shape for quantity production. A higher percentage of horsepower has been developed than in poppet-valve engines of the same size."

The sleeve-operating mechanism of the aircraft engine provided for two exhaust ports in each cylinder, located on the propeller side; and three inlet ports in the opposite side of each cylinder wall. The cylinders were cast aluminum with integral cooling fins.

Shown for the first time at both the New York and Chicago automobile shows, the single-sleeve aircraft engine was the first of its kind to be seen in the United States. Although this revolutionary engine did not make it into production, it did signal a new era for other general aviation power-plants.

The company's demonstration engine had been converted to a sleeve-valve type from a Wright nine-cylinder engine similar to the one in the company's Fokker trimotor plane and to the engine later used by Lindbergh.

That particular demonstration engine didn't really get off the ground. "It never came to fruition," said salesman Arthur W. Wild, who had joined Continental in 1924 as a draftsman. Bachle agreed: "That engine was never fully tested. The conversion parts were made, and then the project was put aside. I know that engine well because I was assigned to preserve it."

Similarly, the follow-on R-794 engine which was also tested did not reach the production stage.

It was only two months after Continental announced its new single-sleeve aircraft engine that Lindbergh made the historic trans-Atlantic flight in his "Spirit of St. Louis" Ryan monoplane. Interest in aviation skyrocketed throughout the world.

Continental had always been interested in new engine ideas from the Continent and so W. R. Angell particularly welcomed a European-bound visitor to his Detroit office in March 1928.

Claude Ryan at Continental

Angell's guest was pioneer aviator T. Claude Ryan, founder of Ryan Airlines, Inc., which had built Lindbergh's plane. Ryan was en route to Germany with his bride on a honeymoon trip, and to confer there with officials of the Siemens-Halske company.

Like his counterparts at Continental, Ryan had looked to the Continent for ideas and had obtained the American distribution and manufacturing rights to the German company's line of five-, seven- and nine-cylinder radial air-cooled engines and was already selling them widely in the United States under the Ryan-Siemens trade name.

Although nothing came of Ryan's proposal to sell Continental the American manufacturing rights to the Siemens-Halske line of aircraft engines for $100,000, it did represent the first business contact between Continental and Ryan Aeronautical Corp., as Claude Ryan's San Diego firm was then known. (More about Ryan-Continental contacts later—three decades later, in fact.)

Aviation pioneer T. Claude Ryan and his Ryan M-2 monoplane powered with Ryan-Siemens aircraft engine. Ryan held American rights to German Siemens-Halske aircraft engines which already powered three American planes being built under Approved Type Certificates. Ryan offered to sell his rights to Continental's W. R. Angell

The meeting between the two executives was of additional interest to Angell because his sister's grandson, Paul E. Wilcox, had learned to fly the previous summer in San Diego at Ryan's Dutch Flats field where Lindbergh's plane had been assembled and test flown.

Angell had dismissed Ryan's proposal for rights to the Siemens-Halske German aircraft engines because Continental's own plans called for an almost identical line of power plants.

To head up its new aircraft engine projects Angell had been able to hire away from the Army Air Service one of its top engineers, Robert Insley. When he graduated from Massachusetts Institute of Technology in 1920, Bob Insley went to McCook Field, Dayton, Ohio, as assistant chief of the Power Plant Branch, a post he held for eight years.

"Insley had good connections," recalls Art Wild, "not only at Dayton but also in Washington. He was the main influence on the aircraft engine side of the business and tried to steer us into a course that would lead to production."

Also involved early in the program was Carl Bachle who was "extracted from the 'cast iron engine' part of the company" to work on aircraft engines, which were to be his whole occupation for many years.

In September 1928, Angell disclosed that formation of the new Continental "Aeronautical Division" was in keeping with the company's policy of diversification. The unit, headed by Insley, would offer three popular sized radial engines—a five-cylinder, a seven and a nine—the same power grouping which Ryan had offered.

After release the following spring of information on a seven-cylinder 165 hp radial—first in the projected series—Judson announced organization in August 1929 of the Continental Aircraft Engine Co., a Delaware corporation, as a subsidiary.

Air-cooled A-70 radial 165 horsepower aircraft engines made debut at National Air Races, Cleveland

President of the aircraft engine company was Angell, and Bob Insley served as Vice-President. Beside its officers, directors of the new subsidiary included W. A. Frederick, the parent company's engineering Vice-President.

All of the 250,000 shares of no par common stock of the Aircraft Company were issued to and held by the parent company. The engine subsidiary would continue to use the production facilities of the parent company in Detroit so as to have ready access to Detroit City Airport for flight testing.

The A-70 Radial Aircraft Engine

First public display of the 165 hp Model A-70 air-cooled poppet-valve radial engine was scheduled for the aeronautical exposition held in connection with the Cleveland National Air Races at Cleveland.

Meanwhile, Continental test pilot Ray LaBadie, accompanied by Angell, was running trial flights in the company's four-place Stinson Junior between Detroit and Muskegon, with an occasional after-business-lunch extension from Muskegon on to Angell's hideaway retreat on North Manitou Island in upper Michigan.

Then, on October 5, 1929, the A-70 engine received Approved Type Certificate No. 32 from the Department of Commerce. In its design, major attention was given to a high safety factor for all parts and to reliability of operation, rather than to high power output. Eleven aircraft manufacturers promptly placed orders for Continental's new radial engine.

Just as Continental provided engines to independent auto makers rather than building complete automobiles, the company made it clear to the embryo airplane

Basic layout for seven-cylinder air-cooled poppet-valve radial aircraft engine offered by Continental Aircraft Engine Co.

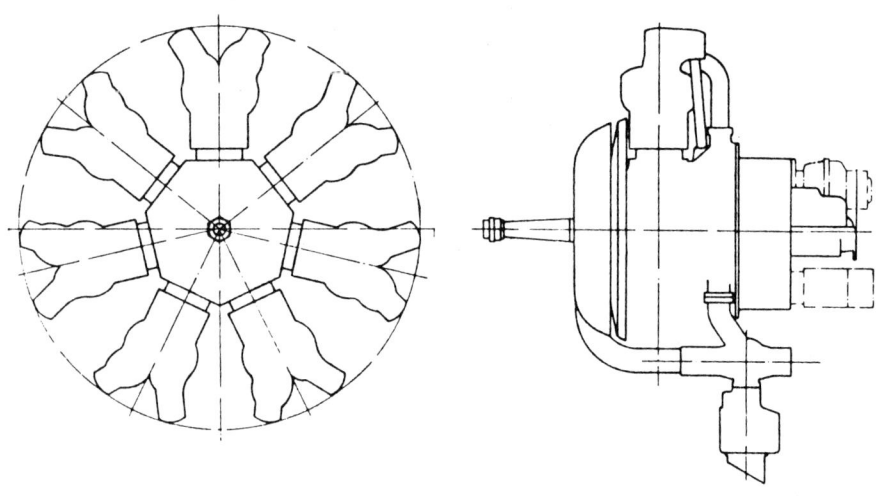

industry, pioneered by men like Clyde Cessna and Walter Beech, that "We have no intention of entering into the manufacture of complete aircraft, as we do not believe it fair to compete with our customers." That policy has remained in force in the aircraft segment of Continental's engine business for half a century.

Continental was clearly on the right course in its thinking on aircraft engines. In November the National Advisory Committee for Aeronautics issued a technical report stating that "in the active competition between air-cooled and water-cooled engines, it can be confidently stated that, up to 600 hp, the advantage lies with the radial air-cooled engine." That advantage would one day put Continental into a new field—aircraft engines for military tanks.

Angell, who was playing an ever-larger role in Continental management, also began to investigate the possibilities of expanding foreign business. In summer 1927, following the world-wide interest created by Lindbergh's flight, Angell made a two months' business tour of Europe.

Building to Customers' Designs

"We have quite a substantial volume of business lined up in Europe and most of it is on the Continent," Angell said on his return. "While most of the business has been negotiated on purchase orders and has not developed great volume, we are now negotiating for several regular contracts." Continental, Angell reported, had already filled one foreign order for 5000 automobile engines.

Under the leadership of Louis Kanitz who had been promoted to General Sales Manager, Continental continued to broaden its market for specialized applications in commercial trucks, buses, taxicabs, rental cars and similar fields, offering an ever increasing number of engine models so alike that it is unnecessary to describe each.

Typical was the Model R series consisting of five overhead valve six-cylinder engines introduced in 1928 for bus and truck service and produced at both the Detroit and Muskegon plants. The outstanding features of the engines were their overhead valve construction and the use of a comparatively short stroke, making for smoothness in operation and improved accessibility. The Model 20-R developed 87 hp.

For light trucks, the company offered the 18-E model, a 61 hp six-cylinder of L-head design with valves on the right side of the engine. A similar model, 18-U, powered the 1927 "sedan type" Yellow Cab.

Dodge came through with a substantial contract for Continental to build the engine for the Dodge "Senior Six". This engine was produced to Dodge's own specifications because Continental, as the long-established independent engine builder, was a less costly producer than the car company's own factory.

Continental did expand its product line into accessories with purchase of the business of the Hydro Check Shock Absorber Corp. Based on hydraulic and pneumatic principles, the units incorporated high and low pressure chambers so that on smooth roads the action of the shock absorber was against air, permitting free spring and tire action. But over rough roads the action was against oil.

The company also became a parts manufacturer, or sub-contractor, to other manufacturers. For the Ford Motor Co., Continental began production at Muskegon in 1929 of 300 to 400 engine blocks (and their pistons) daily for the Ford Model T, which was then being replaced by the Model A.

A spirit of optimism permeated the automotive industry. The company's promotional brochure for the January 1928 National Shows stated that "Never before has Continental Motors occupied so commanding a position in industry as it does today."

But nothing stemmed the tide as independent engine makers lost out to the integrated automobile companies producing their own engines.

Independent auto makers, too, fell by the way even as new companies were formed to introduce more stylish models. One attractive new offering was the reliable 1928 "Rickenbacker" with Continental straight six-cylinder Red Seal engine.

Even the four-door, seven-passenger Rickenbacker with its wooden spoke wheels and luxurious interior featuring lap-robe rails and fold-down jump seats in the rear didn't find an adequate market.

Like Dodge, Willys-Overland, whose Knight sleeve-valve engine had chronic oil consumption problems, turned to Continental for production of a poppet valve engine to their own design. It was an 80 hp conventional straight eight L-head type for a "senior" companion car to the Willys six.

Aware that the future of the independent automobile engine supplier was at stake, Continental had begun in summer 1929 an

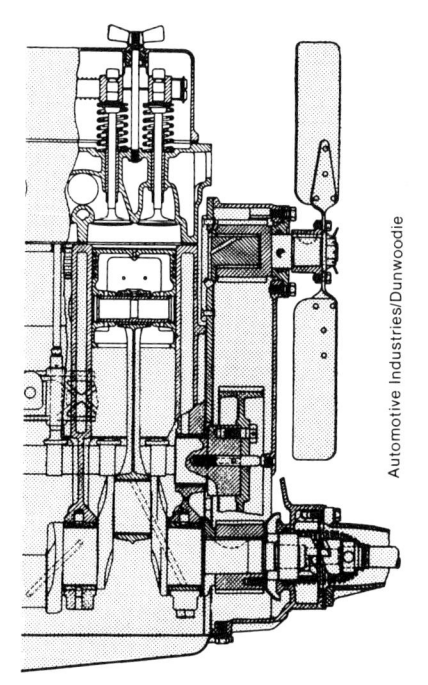

Carburetor side of Continental overhead valve engine

Detail of one of the Model R Series of Continental six-cylinder overhead valve (OHV) automotive engines

"Every motor which comes from the assembly line is tailor made to individual specifications..."

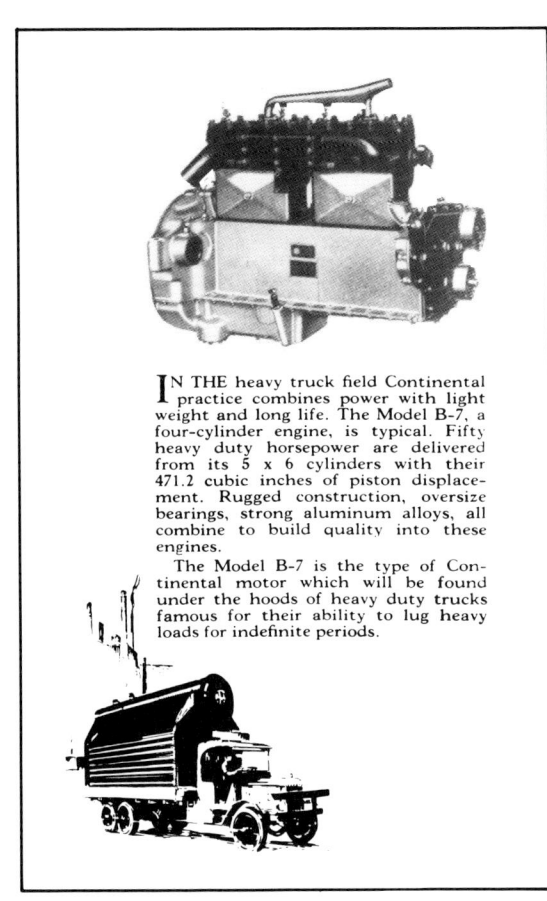

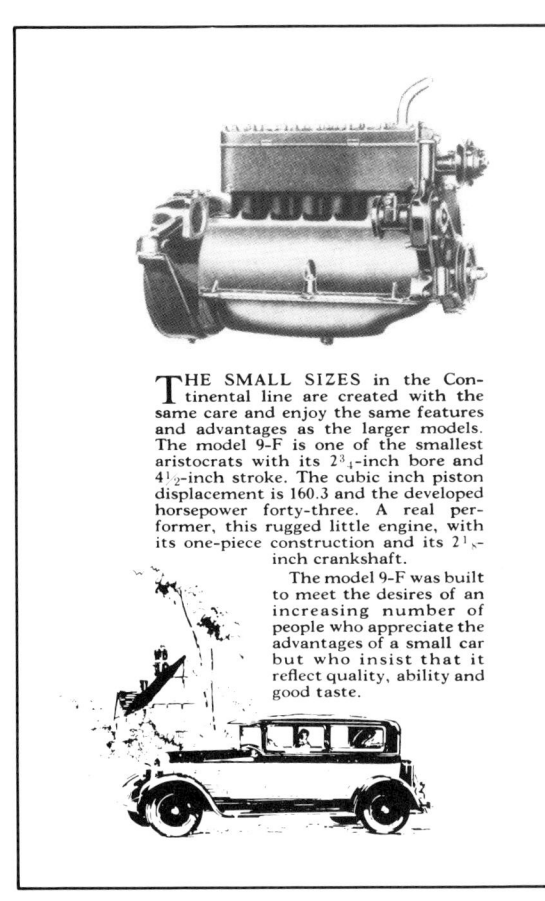

IN THE heavy truck field Continental practice combines power with light weight and long life. The Model B-7, a four-cylinder engine, is typical. Fifty heavy duty horsepower are delivered from its 5 x 6 cylinders with their 471.2 cubic inches of piston displacement. Rugged construction, oversize bearings, strong aluminum alloys, all combine to build quality into these engines.

The Model B-7 is the type of Continental motor which will be found under the hoods of heavy duty trucks famous for their ability to lug heavy loads for indefinite periods.

THE SMALL SIZES in the Continental line are created with the same care and enjoy the same features and advantages as the larger models. The model 9-F is one of the smallest aristocrats with its 2¾-inch bore and 4½-inch stroke. The cubic inch piston displacement is 160.3 and the developed horsepower forty-three. A real performer, this rugged little engine, with its one-piece construction and its 2⅛-inch crankshaft.

The model 9-F was built to meet the desires of an increasing number of people who appreciate the advantages of a small car but who insist that it reflect quality, ability and good taste.

Even with excellent promotion of Continental's capabilities, nothing stemmed the tide as independent engine makers lost out to the integrated companies producing their own motors.

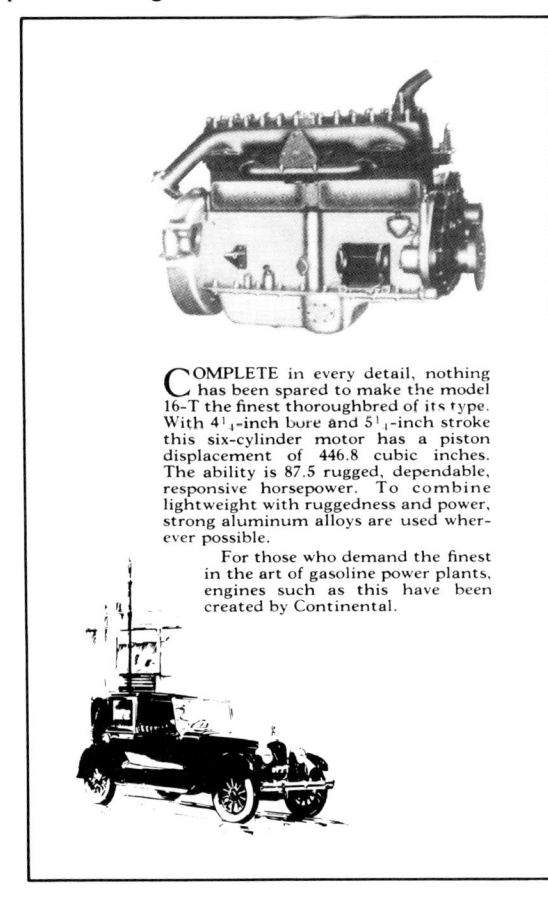

COMPLETE in every detail, nothing has been spared to make the model 16-T the finest thoroughbred of its type. With 4¼-inch bore and 5¼-inch stroke this six-cylinder motor has a piston displacement of 446.8 cubic inches. The ability is 87.5 rugged, dependable, responsive horsepower. To combine lightweight with ruggedness and power, strong aluminum alloys are used wherever possible.

For those who demand the finest in the art of gasoline power plants, engines such as this have been created by Continental.

BUS SERVICE, the most severe demand yet made on gasoline power plants, is fully covered by a complete line of Continental bus motors. The model 15-H, a six cylinder masterpiece, is 4½-inch bore by 5½-inch stroke. The piston displacement is 548.7 cubic inches. Its 109 horsepower at the low engine speed of 2000 R. P. M. speaks for its efficiency and ruggedness. Nickel iron, aluminum alloy, three-inch seven-bearing crankshaft, heat treated nickel steel, silchrome, vibration dampener, oil filtration are but a few of the specifications which reflect the excellence of these bus motors.

Charles L. Betts, Jr./The Society of Automotive Historians Inc.

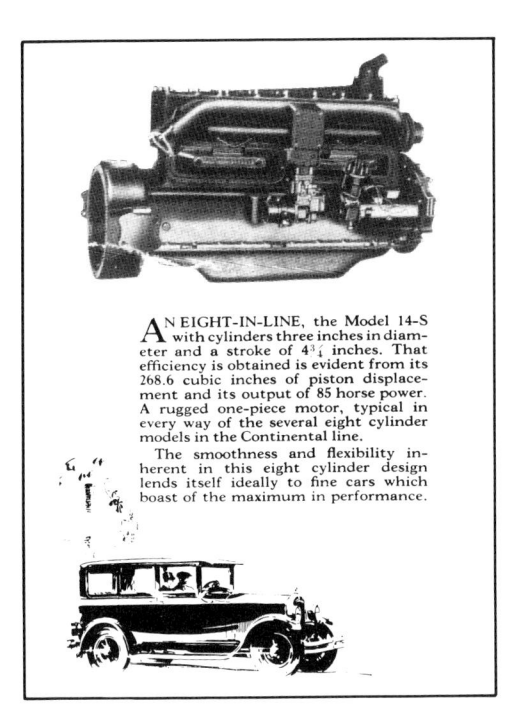

AN EIGHT-IN-LINE, the Model 14-S with cylinders three inches in diameter and a stroke of 4¾ inches. That efficiency is obtained is evident from its 268.6 cubic inches of piston displacement and its output of 85 horse power. A rugged one-piece motor, typical in every way of the several eight cylinder models in the Continental line.

The smoothness and flexibility inherent in this eight cylinder design lends itself ideally to fine cars which boast of the maximum in performance.

aggressive trade magazine advertising program directed to its automotive industry customers:

"The Continental assembly line can be, in reality, yours to function as smoothly, as expertly, as consistently as though it were under your own roof.

"Every motor which comes from the assembly line is tailor made to individual specifications whether for passenger car, bus, truck, industrial, motorboat, airplane or agricultural machinery.

"All of Continental's skills are developed to creating specific types of gasoline engines, either to your design or our own."

Continental was then making 21 distinct engine models to the specifications of 78 different customers. It presented a truly complex problem in manufacturing and planning not to mention quality control and customer satisfaction.

Depression Days Ahead

That was the summer of 1929. Not only had the day of the independent engine manufacturer passed its zenith; the stock market crash of October and the Great Depression of the 30s were just ahead.

To retire $6,215,300 of outstanding 6½% gold bonds, Continental in February 1929 offered stockholders the right to subscribe to 352,169 shares of new common stock, on the basis of one new share for each five held, at $17.50 per share.

The company said it would save $122,000 annually in interest charges on the bonds even allowing for dividends of 80 cents annually per share on the new stock. After issuance of the new shares, there were then 2,113,014 shares outstanding.

In August, the company had organized its new Delaware corporation, Continental Aircraft Engine Co., and opened a West Coast headquarters to take care of its rapidly growing business west of the Mississippi.

Despite the decline of the independents, the future for Continental and for American industry still looked rosy; and the stock market reflected this aura of confidence. Even after the stock market crash in October, Ross Judson was optimistic.

"More and more have the careful people of the nation come to regard the going units of the automotive industry an attractive and safe investment," Judson said.

"By this I do not mean from the speculative angle, but purely as a means of making savings earn money for them. A concrete evidence of this is the remarkable increase in the number of stockholders in the Continental Motors Corp., which amounted to more than 100 percent in one year."

"In October 1928, there were 11,336 stockholders in this corporation." On October 31, 1929, the number was reported to have grown to 23,750.

Judson's optimism was short lived. A general slowing in the automotive plants had begun in late summer. Then, in October, the stock market collapsed. Chaos reigned on Wall Street. Continental's earnings for 1929 dropped to $710,535 from the year-earlier net income of $1,802,835.

To help stem the tide and restore confidence, Judson spoke up. "The automotive industry," he said in November, "belongs to America. Millions of dollars worth of its securities repose in strong boxes throughout the nation. A comparatively small percentage changing hands day by day may fluctuate in price. However, the great majority, safely held, represents a value as fundamentally sound as our national existence."

Within two months, Continental omitted its regular quarterly dividend of 20 cents per share. "Reflecting the unsettled conditions in the motor car industry," Judson explained, "the directors have decided to omit the dividend due at this time because of the policy that dividends are not to be paid unless earned.

"Our policy is to preserve the strong cash and asset position of the corporation which keeps it in a position to take care of all future business.

"Continental enters its new fiscal year [1930] with no preferred stock, no bank loans, no funded debt and an improved outlook for its future."

But the Depression had begun.

In two months, Continental had a new president.

ROSS WHITCOMB JUDSON
Founder, engineer, promoter, salesman, extrovert,
Ross Judson saw his $2000 firm expand for 27 years
and become an industrial giant—then faded out of the
Continental Motors picture

Technical Notes

In early automobiles the engines were firmly bolted to the frame so that the shake forces from the engine were keenly felt by the riders. These shaking forces are of two kinds:

    a) that which comes from the uneven driving force of the engine (torque reaction)

    b) the unbalanced forces due to the weight of the pistons moving up and down in the bore (inertia force).

The torque reaction force can be greatly reduced by adding cylinders so that automobile engines of the early era went from one cylinder all the way to 16 cylinders.

The shaking force due to the piston weight, however, is small at low revolutions per minute and therefore was of small consequence as long as rpm was low (under 1500 rpm). As engine speeds were increased, the piston inertia force became predominate as shakers of the car.

Engine cylinder numbers of 6, 8, 12, and 16 are free of piston inertia fault while all others are objectionable. From the trade-off of car shake versus extra cost of more cylinders there evolved the 6-cylinder predominance to 1933 and the 8-cylinder after 1933.

Both the torque reaction shaking force and the inertia shaking force were reduced to almost zero consequence by the introduction of "Floating Power" by Chrysler about 1930. With Floating Power the engine is insulated from the riders by extremely soft rubber mounting of the engine in the automobile frame with the result that today practically any number of cylinders can be used.

—Carl F. Bachle, 1982.

CONTINENTAL ENGINE TYPES (Typical) 1920-1931

Year Introduced	Model Type	Configuration	Horsepower
1920	7-R	6-cyl.	55 hp
1922	6-Y	6-cyl.	50 hp
	J-4	4-cyl.	32 hp
1923	K-4	4-cyl.	35 hp
	L-4	4-cyl.	
	B-5		
	9-F	4-cyl.	43 hp
1925	B-6	6-cyl.	70 hp
	15-L	6-cyl.	44 hp
	8-P	8-cyl.	57 hp
	B-7	4-cyl.	50 hp
	9-K	8-cyl.	69 hp
	S-4	4-cyl.	50 hp
	15-S	8-cyl.	85 hp
1926	12-M	6-cyl.	64 hp
	12-Z	8-cyl.	72 hp
	14-S	8-cyl.	85 hp
	16-E	6-cyl.	61 hp
	8-S	8-cyl.	64 hp
	8-U		61 hp
	17-S	8-cyl.	73 hp
	15-H	6-cyl.	109 hp
	8-T	bus engines	
	16-T	6-cyl.	88 hp
1927	15-K	8-cyl.	114 hp
	18-U	6-cyl.	35 hp
1928	10-S	8-cyl.	64 hp
	20-R	6-cyl. ohv	87 hp
	18-E	6-cyl. L-head	61 hp
1929	12-K	8-cyl.	114 hp
	13-K	8-cyl.	120 hp
	16-S	8-cyl.	85 hp
	18-S	8-cyl.	85 hp
	21-S	8-cyl.	85 hp
	50-L	8-cyl.	
1931	14-W	8-cyl.	78 hp

AN ANGELL IN CHARGE
(1930-1939)

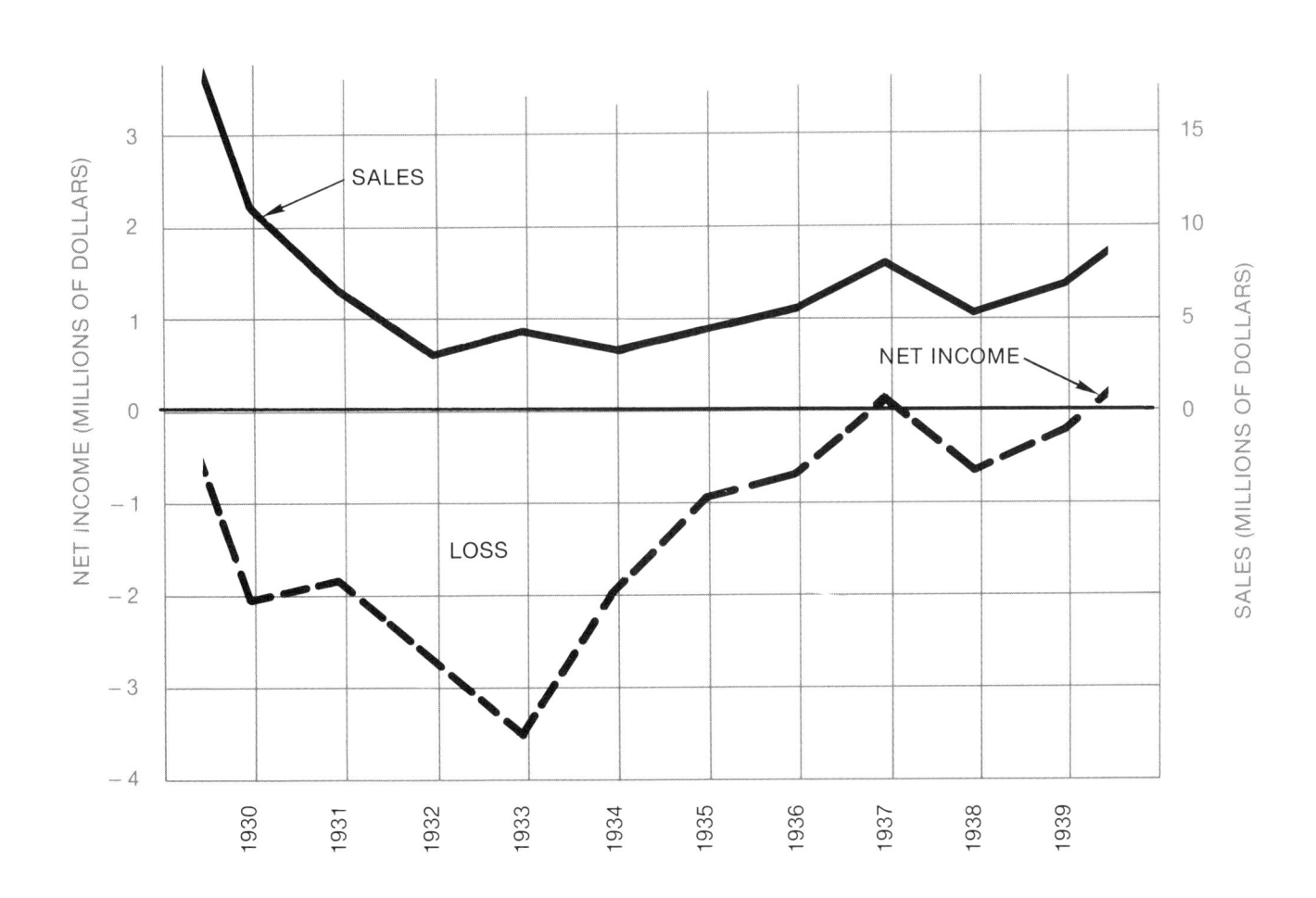

Continental's own car and $14 million in losses nearly bankrupt the company as William R. Angell struggles to keep the firm afloat during the Depression. Then an *aircraft* engine is tried in a combat tank!

Pages 51 to 81

1930-1939

Judson Out; Angell In 51
The Red Ink Flows 51
A-70 Air-Cooled Aircraft Engine 52
R-670 Air-Cooled Radials 52
Horizontally-Opposed A-40 54
Service Testing the A-40 55
Taylor and Piper's Cub 56
More Power for the Flat Fours 57
The DeVaux-Hall Deal 58
Continental-DeVaux Co. 58
Continental Automobile Co. 59
New Way to Sell Cars 60
Beacon, Flyer and Ace 60
The End of the Road 62
Sputtering Engine Sales 63
"Bad Times are Good Times" 64
The Engine Development Field 64
Getting Into Diesels 66
Oil-Carbureted Engines 66
Trading in Continental Shares Suspended 67
Stockholders' Protective Committee 70
$1,000,000 Loan from RFC 72
"Hyper" Cylinder and Engine 73
Product Diversification 74
Jack Reese Moves Up 75
Aircraft Engines for Tanks 76
Nothing Seemed to Work 78
Angell Out; Reese In 79

The Founder's Departure

Precisely what had transpired between Ross W. Judson, the company's President and founder, and William R. Angell, Executive Vice-President, is not now clear, some half-century after the events of 1930.

Judson Out; Angell In

At the February 27, 1930 meeting of the board of directors, Angell, then 49, was elected President and Judson, 52, "promoted" to Chairman of the Board. Other new officers included investor James H. Ferry of Chicago, related by marriage to B. F. Tobin, Sr., who had been an early partner of Judson's. Ferry was named Vice-President and B. F. Tobin, Jr. was elected Treasurer.

Two theories have been advanced. "Just before the stock market crash in late 1929," we were told, "Judson was advising everyone to hold their stock, but he was selling his. When this was learned, he was booted out, and Angell took over."

And a second source: "Angell was active in organizing a coalition of stockholders which included James Ferry, Sr. and Ben Tobin, Jr. The three of them could vote enough stock to get Judson out; and they did."

Perhaps the management change also reflected the conflict which often arises between two strong personalities—one oriented more to engineering and sales, the other to financial matters.

In any case, Angell could not have taken over the presidency at a less opportune time.

In automotive trade circles it was merely said that Judson lost control and was eased out. He disposed of all his Continental holdings, believed to have been in excess of $4 million. By October he was completely out of the firm he had founded 28 years earlier. He also gave up his Michigan estates; one on Spring Lake near Muskegon, the other at Grosse Pointe, near Detroit.

What sort of a leader was Continental's founder?

"He was the big wheeler-dealer," said Carl Bachle, "Judson was the major influence, the principal salesman, the big and flashy kind of executive. He was a flamboyant character and had some unfavorable publicity of various kinds."

"Judson was a remarkable man in many ways," recalled Art Wild. "He had the ability—when the company needed a big order—to go out and get it. He was his own salesman. It was he who got the orders from Willys-Overland, for the Dodge Senior, and earlier those from Jordan, Stutz and Moon . . . dozens."

Judson continued in industry as director of Bath Ironworks in Maine, but moved to his winter estate at Miami, Florida. Separated from her husband since 1920, Mrs. Judson charged he was "too much concerned with his business and airplanes." After nineteen years estrangement they were divorced in 1939. Judson remarried, but died in Miami in 1946 at age 65.

Soon after Judson left Continental, so did his engineering Vice-President, Walter A. Frederick, "a very talented fellow," who had been Continental's design expert and top engineer since the earliest days of the company. Several other longtime management people also left.

Even as old-timers left, new talent came aboard. A new recruit in the purchasing department at Muskegon, with similar experience at Chevrolet, was Clarence J. (Jack) Reese, who like Angell would move up to ever increasing responsibility at Continental.

The Red Ink Flows

Between the deepening Depression and the declining share of the engine market for independent motor builders, Continental went down fast. But Angell either had no inkling of what was ahead or was whistling in the dark when accepting the presidency.

"Never before in the history of the automobile industry," Angell said, "has there been a better opportunity for the independent engine builder. Our company is certain to have its full share of the new business which is developing so rapidly, particularly in the industrial field. And, our airplane engine is proving a great asset to the industry."

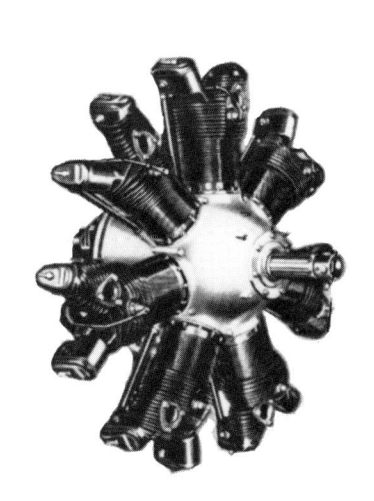

For competitive reasons, sales figures pre-1930 seem to have been unavailable to the public at the time; perhaps even to stockholders. But, assuming a reasonable 7 percent profit on sales, Continental's 1928 profit of $1,802,835 translated to an annual gross business of $26.6 million. In 1929, business volume was still strong, but profit fell to $710,535. Then the red ink began to flow as volume dropped precipitously.

Continental reported one disastrous loss after another: $2.0 million in 1930; $1.9 million in 1931; $2.7 million in 1932. That brought the three-year loss to over $6.6 million. And the quoted price per share on stock exchanges had fallen to 1¼ in December 1931 from the $17.50 which stockholders had paid to purchase additional shares in February 1929.

More red ink was to follow. The company was bleeding to death.

Continental had started its 1929 fiscal year with a surplus of $11,247,767. By October 31, 1931 it had melted to $360,179; a year later, the "surplus" was a $2,394,100 deficit.

"In 1929 we sold 330,000 automobile engines," recalls salesman Art Wild. Two years later we sold about 13,000. That's when the decision was made to really start diversification, not necessarily into other lines of business but to cover all of the engine requirements in as many areas as we could."

Continental did what it could to stop the hemorrhaging. There were new projects in aircraft engines, industrial engines, military vehicle engines, the single-sleeve-valve program, diesel engines, engines for agricultural use and more. Even its own car—which also proved a disaster.

Times were tough indeed. The Depression deepened. What Continental, the industry and the country lacked were buyers.

General business conditions were far from sanguine in the early 30s, but Continental's Bob Insley pressed forward on aircraft engine projects which had been started in 1927.

A-70 Air-Cooled Aircraft Engine

The Model A-70 seven-cylinder air-cooled engine found quick acceptance after receiving its Approved Type Certificate in October 1929. Its 165 h.p. rating was ideal for early cabin planes of the post-Lindbergh era.

The first production A-70 engine went to General Aircraft Corp. of Buffalo, N.Y., then starting to sell its four-place cantilever-wing "Aristocrat" cabin plane. The company's vice president and sales manager-pilot was Allen E. (Pat) Patterson,

Col. Frank E. Hoffman

First use of A-70 radial engine was in General's "Aristocrat"

Joseph Juptner

Verville AT "Sportsman" biplane with Continental A-70 radial engine. Military trainer version was YPT-10

a pioneer west coast flier, later Far East representative in Hong Kong for many American aircraft manufacturers.

Pat flew the Continental-powered Aristocrat on sales demonstration flights from Roosevelt Field, New York, throughout the Atlantic states and South, but by the time the Depression of the 30s set in only a dozen Aristocrats had been sold and the company had to close. About the A-70, Pat recalls that "it threw a couple of cylinder heads, made some noise, but kept on running. Anyway, Continental soon corrected that trouble."

Using a Continental A-70 engine, Detroit-based Verville tried to get an Army contract for military training planes, but Waco of Troy, Ohio, was Continental's prime user of the radial engine. Other installations were in the Travelair, Verville Aircoach and American Eagle.

Over a hundred A-70 engines had been sold by 1931, "exceeding," Continental boasted, "the combined sales of all its competitors in their respective power classes." And, for possible military sales, the A-70 was given the designation R-540.

R-670 Air-Cooled Radials

Soon Continental upgraded the existing design by increasing displacement from 540 cubic inches to 670 cid (cubic inch displacement). Engine bore was increased from 4-5/8" to 5-1/8"; stroke remained 4-5/8". Some parts were used from the A-70 (R-540) which was continued in production. Power output of the new models—R-670 and W-670—was increased from the A-70's 165 hp to 220-240 hp.

The first flight with the R-670 engine was made December 14, 1931 by test pilot Paul Wilcox in the company's Waco F-2, a three-place open cockpit job. In February, the same type engine was installed in the company's Waco cabin plane.

"During qualification flights for the R-670's Approved Type Certificate," Wilcox recalls, "I would take the plane on cross-country flights, running the engine wide-open for hours on end, trying to discover some weakness. I remember one trip from the factory to New York, then down to Florida and across the Gulf to San

Antonio; up through St. Louis and back to Detroit. I flew it wide-open, virtually the whole trip, and finally managed to have some engine trouble.

"An oil pump shaft broke and I had to set the plane down in a farmer's field, climbed through the fence and walked into a small town nearby. There I waited for a new part to be shipped to me via the local "milk train" from the factory in Detroit. That was the only mechanical failure I ever had with an R-670 engine."

After Approved Type Certificate No. 80 was issued on February 11, 1932, the -670 engine was placed in production, but general business conditions throughout the country remained so poor that few were built for the commercial market. Even the sale of 15 engines for 1933 model Waco cabin planes rated a story in the Wall Street Journal.

Four years later as business conditions somewhat recovered, the company improved the engines by pioneering in the W-670 model development of fuel injection systems for the general aircraft market.

While Bob Insley was busy developing poppet-valve aircraft engines, Angell continued to press for single-sleeve-valve projects. In October, 1931, engineer Andre Meyer and Continental sales people interested the U.S. Navy in underwriting for $20,000 development of a radial aircraft engine using the single-sleeve-valve principle.

Wacos with Continental R-670 engines. At left, Model UKC cabin plane. At right, Waco XJW-1 with trapeze to permit mid-air retrieval by dirigible "Macon"

Because Continental felt the design of this seven-cylinder engine represented the ultimate in performance and might lead to major production contracts, the company underwrote all expenses above the Navy's minimum financial support.

Development costs were very heavy, not only for this aircraft engine, but also for other single-sleeve engines for submarines, for electric generators, and of course, for automobiles.

"We Americans", reported Bachle, "could never make a success of the single-sleeve engine. It was later tried by Pratt & Whitney and by Wright Aeronautical without success. But the British succeeded where we did not."

In 1929 Continental Aircraft Engine Co. inaugurated company's half-century promotional campaign to sell public on general aviation. This ad featured A-70 engine

Connecting rods are subject to great stress. Failure of these parts is safeguarded by securing each articulated rod to the master.

THERE is no quivering of the fabric or quaking of the fuselage when the Continental Red Seal Airplane Engine takes the air. Vibration has been reduced and the plane itself is as steady as the hum of the engine that carries it along.

CONTINENTAL AIRCRAFT ENGINE CO.
Office and Factory: Detroit, Michigan

53

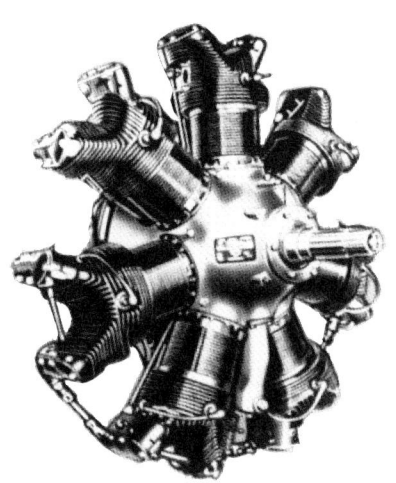

Teledyne Continental Motors

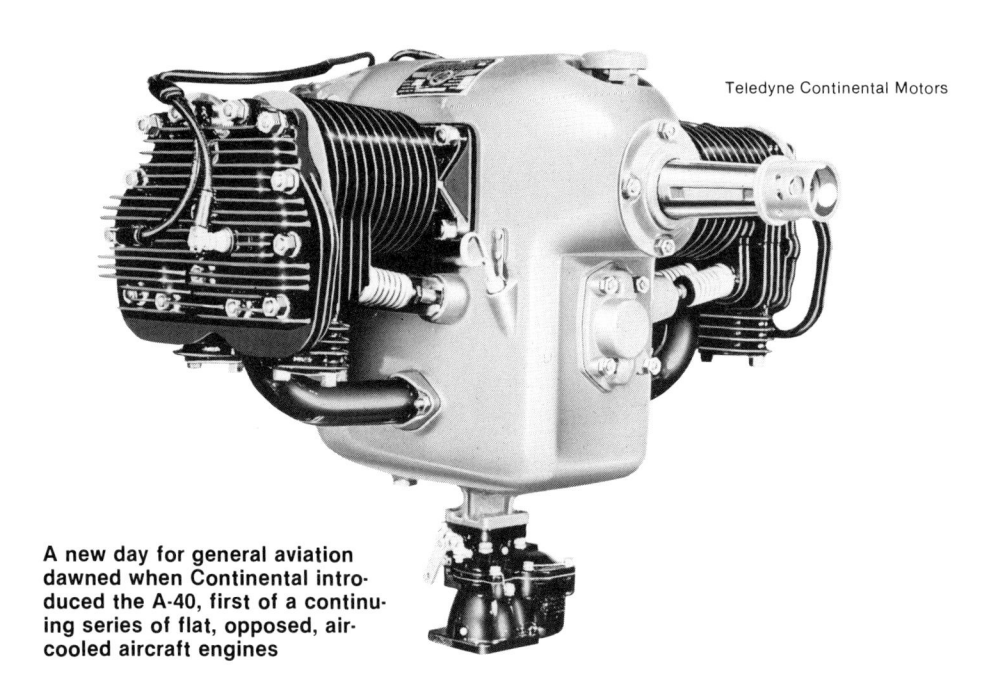

A new day for general aviation dawned when Continental introduced the A-40, first of a continuing series of flat, opposed, air-cooled aircraft engines

Although the market for the medium-size, single-engine cabin plane was being serviced by the seven-cylinder radial engine, Continental did not neglect the needs of smaller aircraft.

Horizontally-Opposed A-40

Development started in 1930 on a small four-cylinder air-cooled L-head engine in which the cylinders were positioned to make them horizontally opposed, a design which was to come into wide use in the general aviation field for many decades. Unlike the "cast iron" automobile engines, the aircraft power plants would make extensive use of aluminum to reduce weight.

Continental Aircraft Engine Company's sales and engineering executives were convinced there was a vast market for an aircraft power plant priced within reach of many more users than could afford the costly radials.

Until the appearance of the Continental Model A-40, it was economically impossible for a new engine design to compete with the thousands of World War surplus Curtiss OX-5 engines which were so inexpensive they were considered virtually disposable as soon as they needed overhaul. Thus, for years, the OX-5 was the standard power plant for private aircraft such as Travelair, Waco, Eagle Rock and even Curtiss in their smaller craft like the Curtiss Robin monoplane. By contrast, Lindbergh had paid $4,580 for his Wright Whirlwind J-5C radial engine.

The technical advantage of the flat, horizontally-opposed engine was that it provided better forward visibility than did the radial engine or an upright design with vertical cylinders. It also afforded much better aerodynamic streamlining. Fins were cast on cylinders and heads for air cooling the same as in radial engine design.

By mid-summer, craftsmen started dynamometer testing of the A-40. Running the flight test program was Carl Bachle's principal assignment. Ray LaBadie was still piloting Continental's A-70 powered Waco and Verville planes, but hardly had the qualifications of an engineering test pilot.

"Ray was my good friend," recalls Bachle, "and he was a fine pilot in the days when pilots were considered supermen. But he knew nothing about engines; he knew nothing about airplanes. He just knew how to fly."

A pilot with extensive aircraft engine experience would have to be hired.

Angell had a suggestion, "Why not contact my grand-nephew, Paul Wilcox, out in San Diego. He's a flight instructor for the Ryan School of Aeronautics. Paul has a transport pilot license and lots of aircraft engine experience. He's a licensed mechanic as well as a fine pilot."

As soon as Wilcox and his young wife, Alma, arrived in Detroit, Paul began flying the company's A-70-powered planes on business trips between Detroit and the company's plant at Muskegon.

Wilcox recalls that "I also worked on the A-40 dynamometer testing for several months. We were having trouble with crankcases and finally got a design that would hold.

"From another Michigan company, Buhl Aircraft Co., we bought one of the 'Bull Pup' models, a wire-braced, shoulder-wing single-place plane with a two-cylinder 'Aeronca' 26 hp engine. After one 15-minute flight in the Bull Pup, we took out the Aeronca engine and installed our 38 hp A-40. I made the first flight with our new power plant on November 10, 1930.

"In a few months I had put in the necessary 50 flight hours to qualify the A-40 for its Approved Type Certificate— No. 72—which was awarded May 19, 1931. Our primary test tools were potentiometer leads to various parts of the engine to record heat and ribbon tufts outside the engine cowling to check air flow.

"The main problem we had initially with the A-40 was burning valves and blowing head gaskets. We were using 'steelbestos' head gaskets made of steel and asbestos but this did not permit transfer of heat from the cylinders into the engine block. The cylinders got so hot the head gaskets kept blowing out.

"With the help of a draftsman I designed

"... we took out the engine which was in the 'Bull Pup' and installed our 38 hp. Model A-40. First flight with the new power plant was in November 1930"

aluminum fins for the exhaust ports to help cool the valves, and this cured that trouble. Also, we came up with an O-ring attachment, where the intake manifold went into the crankcase, which was used for many years. Later I designed the first carburetor heater and built it in our maintenance shop, doing the welding myself. After testing it in flight, we had the engineering department detail the heater for production.

"While putting in the 50 hours of air time on the engine—much of it in the dead of winter—I either flew within range of Detroit City Airport or out around Lake St. Claire. Occasionally I had to make forced landings on the ice, but I carried spare head gaskets and a wrench so I could make my own repairs, taking the head off and putting new gaskets on. As an engineering test pilot I had the advantage of also being able to do my own mechanical work.

"Fishing through the ice was a winter pastime for local fishermen and they had shanties all around on the ice. They often gave me fish—they were frozen, just like a board—which I put in the Bull Pup's little luggage compartment. I'd take them home to thaw out and Alma and I would make a meal of them."

Service Testing the A-40

Design improvements came from a number of sources as Wilcox recalls. "The company told me about a customer in Upper Michigan who was having cooling problems with his A-40, so I flew up to see if I could help. This young fellow was trying to build a helicopter and had installed one of our new engines.

"By the time I got there he didn't need any help. He was ahead of us in tackling and apparently solving the head gasket problem. He showed me how he used a sheet of aluminum sandwiched between two sheets of copper to make a head gasket which permitted the heat from the cast iron cylinders to come up into the heads where it was dissipated.

"I couldn't get back to the factory fast enough to report to our engineers. We hand-made some new gaskets which I installed in the engine in our little test plane. I abused the engine all I could by climbing at as steep an angle as possible and at low speed for long periods of time—thus heating up the heads. The gaskets held and from that day on we had little head gasket trouble."

Cooling an engine inside the cowling of an aircraft has always been a major headache for designers. When the A-40 first appeared on the market, its nickel iron cylinders were cast in pairs and the heat was dissipated poorly. There weren't sufficient cooling fins, and they were thick, whereas radial engine cylinders were machined with many thin fins. Later on, A-40 cylinders were individually cast and machined, making a big difference in engine serviceability.

"What we learned in our engineering test flights went first to the engineers," Wilcox continued, "then to production and finally in improved service through liaison with the companies which were buying the A-40 engine.

"Taylor Aircraft [later Piper] with its line of 'Cub' light planes, was the primary user of the A-40 and I spent a lot of time at Bradford, Pennsylvania, where Alma and I became close friends of the Piper family."

Although his great uncle was president of Continental, Paul seldom saw Angell on the job. "The only times I recall," Wilcox says, "was when I would fly him and guests in the company's Continental-powered Waco cabin plane to North Manitou Island near Travers City in the Straits of Mackinaw. He and a group from Chicago owned the island with its lodge, dirt air strip and cherry orchard. While they played I waited for two or three days and flew them home."

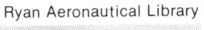

Continental's first engineering test pilot was Paul Wilcox, grand-nephew of W. R. Angell. Wilcox later returned to Ryan Aeronautical Company as Chief Pilot

Wilcox left Continental in 1932 and returned to San Diego where he eventually became Chief Pilot of Ryan Aeronautical Company.

Pioneer light plane builders C. G. Taylor and W. T. Piper fathered the famed Cub in 1931. But the Cub, powered by a two-cylinder 20-horsepower Brownbach Tiger Kitten engine, could barely struggle into the air. "Needs a bigger engine," said Piper, after the first test flight.

Taylor and Piper's Cub

Taylor installed a French-made Salmson radial of 45 hp. The Cub flew far better but the engine cost too much for their flying flivver concept.

"Piper and I," recalled Taylor, "chased around looking for a suitable engine, then heard of the Continental A-40 up in Detroit, so went there to look it over. R. C. (Bud) Havens was our test pilot and when we got the Continental engine installed in our first model E-2 Cub, we had 26 forced landings between us in the first 30 days. It kept blowing gaskets and the single magneto would occasionally fail. Continental, however, got the engine refined to operate reliably."

One of the first airplanes ATC'd with an A-40 was the Alexander "Flyabout," built by the makers of the Eaglerock series of planes. Earlier, on June 15, 1931, the Continental-powered Taylor E-2 was granted an Approved Type Certificate for the first 14 airplanes and the $1325 Cub was on its way to fame.

Still no product is ever perfect and, with increasing service, the Continental continued to have problems, crankshafts being added to the head gasket and magneto difficulties. Using automobile design principles to handle the strains imposed by engine torque, the crankshaft thrust bearing was at the rear. But mounted in the nose of an airplane, the engine was subjected to the pull of the propeller, putting a strain on the front of the crankshaft, resulting in too-frequent failures and forced landings.

Pilots reported that the crankshaft would break in the rear rod journal at almost exactly the 100 hour mark. "It wasn't a particularly dangerous problem," said one pilot, "since the engine would run for several hours with the shaft broken. The back rod bearing held the parts in place."

Taylor Aircraft Company's business was at a near standstill in the middle of the Depression. Continental began to feel that the light plane business was too small to bother with. After all, the engines sold for only $400 each.

C. G. Taylor, in desperation, tried a three-cylinder Szekley 30 hp radial engine, but it "had every known mechanical defect that could be built into a reciprocating, internal combustion engine plus some that were truly exotic."

Then Taylor, with his uncanny gift in mechanics, designed and built his company's own four-cylinder, air-cooled engine. It, too, had problems, not the least of which was broken crankshafts.

To help out, Continental agreed to make design changes in the A-40 engine. The addition of a thrust bearing at the front end solved the crankshaft problem. A second magneto was added as was a second spark plug to each cylinder. And the head gaskets no longer blew out.

Attention to customer needs paid off. The Continental A-40, according to Piper historian Devon Francis, "became classic in light planes." Between 1931 and 1938, some 3,000 engines were produced with about 70 percent going into Cubs. Other installations were in the Alexander Flyabout and various Heath, Porterfield

Famed Taylor E-2, first of the long line of "Cub" aircraft in which thousands of pilots got their introduction to flying

and Aeronca models. Another user was Taylorcraft, a new company formed after C. G. Taylor and W. T. Piper went their separate ways. Its order was for 1,050 engines.

The engine was inexpensive, light, simple and went 500 hours between overhauls. Dr. Chester L. Peek of Oklahoma City University has written that "development of the horizontally opposed, air-cooled aircraft engine was perhaps the single most important factor in the growth of our modern private aircraft industry."

Peek knows whereof he speaks. He wrote us in 1980 that he has a "mid-30s A-40 engine in my antique E-2 Cub and fly it frequently. It is really a fine engine".

Perhaps more intellectually honest than his sales counterparts, Carl Bachle took a rather dim view of the A-40 even though he was deeply involved in its development.

More Power for the Flat Fours

"It was a terrible engine", Bachle conceded. "But it was famous and it was used a lot. It was my job to fix it, and I couldn't fix it.

"I became so enraged that I said we ought to scrap it; do it over, and do it right. Bob Angell—William R. Angell, Jr.—was in authority then and he made a survey to see what the aircraft companies wanted. What they wanted was something like the A-40 with more power and a little cheaper.

"I made an impassioned speech, that you can never make the A-40 work right, and forget it. 'The crankcase is lousy, the cylinder head is lousy, everything is lousy on it. We all agree it's 10 horsepower short. Let's start all over.'

Warren D. Shipp

"That viewpoint finally prevailed, but it took a lot of in-house selling. I killed the A-40 but was the principal influence in development of the A-50 which was a great success because it had the reliability the A-40 lacked."

Following introduction of the A-40, W. R. Angell, Sr. and Bob Insley, in the early 30s brought into the Continental organization Harold A. Morehouse, an associate of Samuel D. Heron, pioneer engine designer at the Army Air Service Engineering Division at McCook Field. (Bob Insley left Continental in 1933 to head research at Pratt & Whitney Aircraft. He returned to Continental in 1941.)

One of Morehouse's first tasks was to do the preliminary layout of the A-40's successor, the 50 hp Model A-50, which went into production in 1938. Later, the fuel-injected A-65, A-75 and A-80 models of corresponding horsepower ratings were added to the four-cylinder line. Of these, the A-65 became the star performer for Piper, Aeronca, Luscombe, Taylorcraft, Stinson and other light planes.

Later manufactured by Piper Aircraft, the popular "Cub," in Model J-3, was also available as a seaplane powered by A-40 engine which had been uprated to a full 40 horsepower

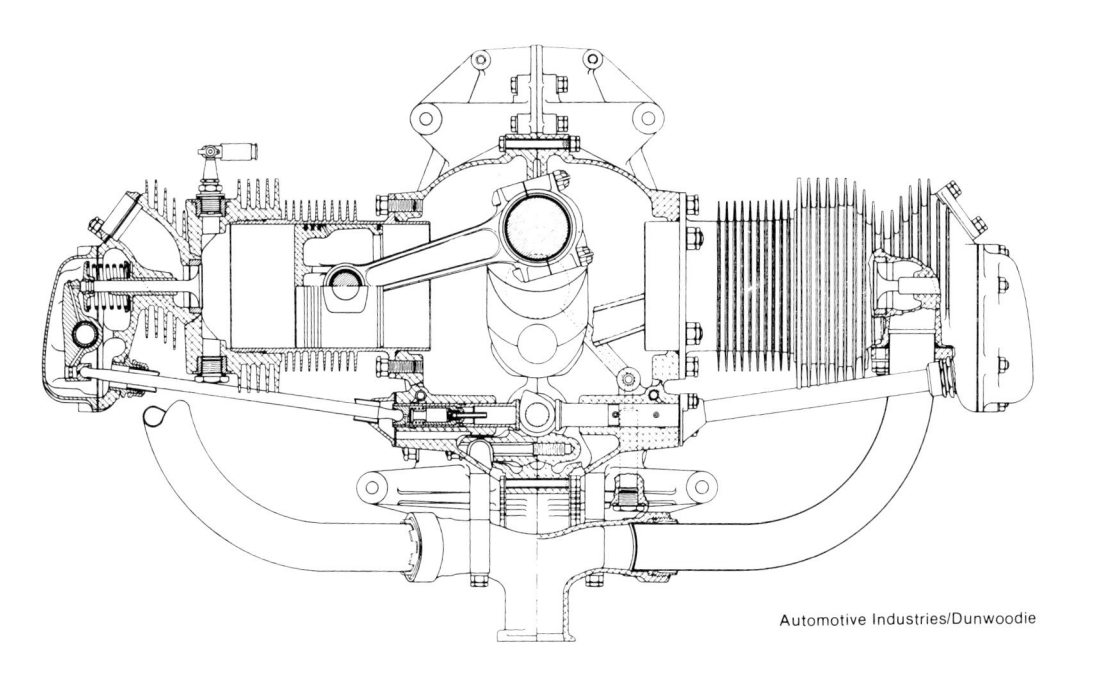

Automotive Industries/Dunwoodie

The improved Model A-50 four-cylinder opposed engine was the forerunner of more powerful, more efficient 'flat' engines

57

Continental's Car Runs Out of Gas

What to do about a creditor who, in the middle of the Depression, owes your company half a million dollars you are unable to collect? That was the dilemma Continental and Angell faced in 1932.

The DeVaux-Hall Deal

The creditor, DeVaux-Hall Motors Corp. of Oakland, California, and Grand Rapids, Michigan, had gone into receivership because of its failure to sell its Oakland factory to the Chrysler Corp. as a west coast assembly plant.

Norman DeVaux had been President of Durant Motors Corp. of California, and when Cliff Durant, W. C. Durant's son, decided in 1930 to close out his California operation, DeVaux purchased the company and announced plans to offer a car under his own name. He enlisted the help of Col. Elbert J. Hall, co-founder of Hall-Scott Motors Corp., whose reputation as an engineer was based on his work as co-designer of the famed Liberty aircraft engine. Hall had a new automobile engine design DeVaux wanted to use. It would be installed in the DeVaux model 6-75, nothing more than a Durant with different trim and the new Hall-Scott motor.

The DeVaux-Hall firm had selected Grand Rapids as its principal assembly plant because Hayes Body, builders of the cars' bodies, had a factory there. March 20, 1931 was a big day in Grand Rapids when civic leaders, politicians and the press turned out to welcome the new firm.

Among honored guests were "President W. R. Angell and Sales Manager L. J. Kanitz of Continental Motors." Principal speakers in addition to Norman DeVaux and Colonel Hall, were Michigan's U.S. Senator Arthur H. Vandenberg, a native son, and nationally famous business writer B. C. Forbes.

Delivery of the new DeVaux Six had not yet started, but the company's sales manager reported 8000 firm orders on the books. Production was scheduled to begin in April with the Grand Rapids plant building 1900 cars and Oakland a thousand that month. In May, 3500 cars were expected to be built at Grand Rapids.

Production of engines for the new DeVaux-Hall cars was contracted for with Continental Motors, but the new car manufacturer soon ran into financial difficulties and could not pay its suppliers.

Although Continental had a three-decades-long policy not to build cars and compete with its customers, Angell and Henry W. Vandeven, Assistant Treasurer, felt the only way they could recoup $487,118.26 owed by DeVaux-Hall was to take over the Michigan assets of that company and rights to its line of cars.

The plant at Grand Rapids which DeVaux-Hall leased was only 35 miles from Muskegon, where Continental, in an economy move, had concentrated all manufacturing operations in August 1931, maintaining only general offices and a few support departments at Detroit.

February 18, 1932, Continental paid $40,000 for DeVaux-Hall's Michigan assets and withdrew $250,000 in claims against its former customer, at the same time announcing that production of DeVaux cars would be continued. "It is our intention," Angell announced, "to popularize and aggressively merchandise the DeVaux automobile."

The Oakland, California, unit of DeVaux-Hall remained in the hands of the receiver.

Continental-DeVaux Co.

A new subsidiary, Continental-DeVaux Co., was formed March 4 with Angell as President and investor Roger Sherman as Vice-President. Authorized capital was 10,000 shares of preferred stock with a par value of $100 per share, and 300,000 shares of no-par common stock.

Production of the Continental-DeVaux was scheduled to start in mid-April with shipments going out to DeVaux's 700 dealers. Nearly 7000 DeVaux cars had been sold in nine months in 1931. Dominion Motors, Ltd., of Toronto, successor to

ENTERING manufacture of complete automobiles for the first time with its under-$400 Beacon, Continental faced formidable obstacles

Durant of Canada, would market the car in Canada under the Frontenac Six label.

AUTOMOTIVE TRADE JOURNAL reacted favorably to Angell's leadership in difficult times for the industry and particularly for Continental. Of him, they wrote:

> "The man who cut millions from overhead expense within a year after taking the reins of Continental and who has led that long-established company successfully through the worst depression the industry has known, is very forceful about his plans and hopes for his new venture.
>
> "Big in stature, slow in physical movement and keen in mental vision, Mr. Angell sees every chance for sound growth in manufacture and sales of the DeVaux car. There is clear determination on the part of executives with proved success to their credit to make for DeVaux a real place in the automotive sun."

Of his future plans, Angell told his interviewer, "We are going to manufacture automobiles and we are going to keep on manufacturing them. We did not make this decision merely with the idea of protecting our claim for products purchased from us." Angell forecast building 3200 DeVaux cars at Grand Rapids in the first 60 days of Continental ownership.

The new Continental-DeVaux "80" had an 80 hp six-cylinder Red Seal engine, the only passenger car still using an L-head motor. The body was styled by Count Alexis de Sakhnoffsky, a Russian nobleman who had earlier designed cars in Paris for French companies, and was four-time winner of the famed Monte Carlo Contest of Elegance.

To publicize its entry into the field, Continental set out to establish new world's records with a standard DeVaux coupe. In August, in the simmering heat of Muroc Dry Lake, California, driver Clint DuBois helped set a 1000-mile endurance record at an average speed of 65.9 miles per hour. At the 5 p.m. start, the temperature was 109 degrees; at the 8 a.m. finish it was 100 degrees.

In all, 22 world's records for Class "C" stock cars were established under A.A.A. observation. After the desert trials, DuBois negotiated the 8.65-mile mountain grade to Big Bear Lake in 14 minutes, 39 seconds.

In September, Angell announced appointment of two experienced auto industry sales executives. Henry Krohn, for 17 years Vice-President of sales at Paige Motor Car Co., became general sales manager of Continental-DeVaux.

Even more significant was the resignation of Fred L. Rockelman, President and general manager of Plymouth Motors Corp., to take a not yet identified role at

CONTINENTAL DE VAUX

establishes 22 World's Records

MoToR/Dunwoodie

Continental which Angell said, "we expect to announce shortly as part of our plan for enlarging our position in the automotive industry." Earlier, Rockelman had for many years been sales manager of the Ford Motor Co.

The news of Angell's grand strategy was broken by financial writer B. C. Forbes, who scooped his competition with the word that "I have learned authoritatively that Continental, which has built the motors for 90 percent of all the 600 automobile companies born in American during the past 30 years, is ready to enter the car manufacturing field on a big scale and with an entirely novel machine. The price will be lower than that of any full-size car now on the market.

"President Angell," Forbes wrote, "began planning a long time ago to launch a complete car in a price class by itself whenever the American people become properly endowed with a sense of thrift, economy, frugality."

Two days later Angell announced that "Within 90 days we will introduce a new line of low-priced passenger cars, while continuing the DeVaux line.

"We feel that there has never been a time so opportune as the present to develop and market a new conception of motor car values."

Continental Automobile Co.

To emphasize the new product line, the company's hyphenated subsidiary was renamed Continental Automobile Co., and F. L. Rockelman was appointed Vice-President in charge of sales.

Design and production of the new Continental cars would be under direction of F. F. Beall, Continental Vice-President,

Manufacturing and Engineering, who had held similar responsibilities for 14 years with Packard Motor Co.

For a market survey on which to base future plans, Angell turned to Continental's 30,000 shareholders, of whom five thousand replied.

The findings: Nine-tenths of motor buyers up to the $1000 car class prefer fours and sixes; 78% put gasoline economy ahead of high speed; for three-fourths, 60 miles an hour or less is fast enough. In the $400 and $450 brackets, the number who said they would purchase a new car exceeded those who would not. The lower the price class, the greater the popularity of the four-cylinder engine. From $500 up, the lead of the six-cylinder engine was overwhelming.

Angell had the answers on which to base his conviction that Continental's real opportunity lay in developing the industry's lowest-price, full-size cars. One report had it that the car would be offered for sale in the Montgomery Ward & Co. 1933 mail order catalog.

Angell turned to stockholders as potential customers as well as for a sampling of customer preference in automobiles. "We are giving you," he wrote, "the first opportunity to place your order for the Beacon model . . . as the universal interest already shown indicates a demand in excess of our early productive facilities.

"We are hopeful that each stockholder will own and drive a Continental car. It will be equal to a million dollars in advertising."

"It costs too much to distribute automobiles," Angell told B. C. Forbes, "We have plans to cut the cost. They include vigorous advertising. They also include things never before attempted. Just because a thing has always been done in one way is no reason for not adopting a better way."

No sooner had Continental announced its 1933 line as also including a light Six and medium Six, than Angell startled the automotive world with news that its anticipated Four would be sold direct to the buyer under a merchandising plan which, for that model only, would entirely eliminate dealers and agencies.

New Way to Sell Cars

"Since the early days of the motor car industry," Angell said, "there has been little or no change in the method of selling automobiles. Until now no serious attempt has been made to reduce retail purchase prices by eliminating the steps between the manufacturer and the purchaser.

"Continental is putting a large, full-size car within the reach of millions of incomes adjusted to a new scale of economic values. We are in a unique position to take this step since we have no established distribution precedents to overcome. Too, our low operating and plant overhead costs are ideally constituted for the present economic period."

Sales plans also included tested methods of mail order selling in small towns. Nine thousand car dealers received direct mail literature on the full line of Continental Sixes and Fours, and 58,000 independent garages were queried as to their interest in becoming a new form of associate franchise.

To distribute its four-cylinder car, Continental would establish a chain of "terminals"—independent garages and service stations—which would not stock cars, but would be required to have a demonstrator.

The terminals would depend on Continental distributors and dealers for stocking cars and parts. Only these regular distributors would handle Continental's two lines of Sixes in a normal factory-distributor relationship.

Grandiose plans to gain a foothold as an integrated automobile manufacturer at a time when all America was in economic trouble!

In his first announcement Angell stressed that "The big Six is to be a luxury car brought down to the bottom rung of the medium-price bracket. This completely new and beautiful car will replace the DeVaux models of the former Continental-DeVaux line." Engines for all models were to be built in Muskegon with car assembly in th Grand Rapids plant of Hayes Body Corp.

Beacon, Flyer and Ace

In a well-coordinated publicity blitz, Continental introduced its three cars at the 33rd National Automobile Show in New York's Grand Central Palace. Greatest interest was naturally shown in the low-priced Four—The Continental "Beacon"—selling in the unheard of $400 price range against the higher priced Willys.

The light Six "Flyer" was in the $500 price class, and the top-of-the-line luxury Six-cylinder "Ace" was priced in the $700 range. All three cars had "winged power", result of a patented three-point engine mounting.

The C-400 Beacon was described as a "well-finished car with pleasing lines and roomy bodies considering that the wheel base is 101½ inches. The L-head engine develops 40 hp and maximum speed is between 60 and 65 mph.

"Here is a really low-priced car of ample body size for comfort, and light weight for economy of operation. It is capable of 33 miles to a gallon of gasoline at 40 mph."

The Beacon offered four body styles. Completing the line-up were the light C-600 Six Flyer with 65 hp, 107-inch wheelbase and four body styles; and the big Six Ace, an 85 hp, 114-inch wheelbase car of high speed, with three body styles. The Ace was said to have been developed from the prior year's Continental-DeVaux.

One reviewer's comments: "The cars reveal an independence of thought in design as original in conception as the plan of direct merchandising. Continental has had no design of its own to change and no commitments to absorb. In starting from scratch, Continental has no precedents to handicap it. Therefore, its engineers have introduced many interesting and unique features."

Continental, however, did face other handicaps—competition from the major car makers; Ford, Chevrolet and Plymouth—and insufficient financial resources.

Wall Street properly evaluated the risks. Financial columnist Waldo Young in response to a reader request for "your opinion on the outlook for Continental Motors," warned:

". . . the company has been operating unprofitably and has been affected by the change in car manufacturer's policy, in making their own motors, as well as by the Depression in general.

"This new venture should be regarded as a highly speculative one. The situation is one verging on a battle of giants for supremacy. The position of a company of secondary size, entering this type of competition, and by no means as well fortified financially as the leaders presently engaged in it, is uncertain at best.

"We regard it as a situation that had as well be avoided because of the risks involved."

In other words, don't buy Continental shares at this time. [Continental stock had registered an 88% price gain in 1932. From 1-1/8 per share to 2-1/8].

Sales manager Fred L. Rockelman felt Continental was 'on the right track' but he was derailed after six months

The first day of the new year, 1933, Continental posted its prices: Beacon roadster, an unbelievably low $355. The four-door sedan, just under $400, at $395. Price range for the Flyer light Six, $450 to $535; and for the luxury Ace big Six, $725, to $815 for the DeLuxe custom sedan (with five wheels).

The Continental cars made their debut a week later at the New York Show. As befit his role as top salesman, Fred L. Rockelman, despite the "it won't work" caution of his industry friends, was ecstatic:

"I have never known of a single phase of the automobile business that has aroused such widespread comment and interest as Continental's program.

"Since the Auto Show's opening I have noticed that many of my doubting friends have changed their minds and now are

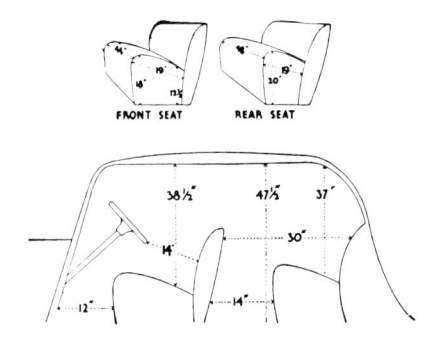

Five Passenger Two-Door Continental BEACON four cylinder Sedan. Price was raised for 1934 model "Red Seal Four" to $445

61

AT THESE PRICES CONTINENTAL IS A NATURAL

The 4-cylinder Beacon from . . . $355 to $395
The 6-cylinder Flyer from . . . . $450 to $535
The 6-cylinder Ace from . . . . $725 to $815

f. o. b. factory

Although many dealer points have been closed, some choice territories are still available. Visit Continental's Chicago Show Headquarters in the Stevens Hotel, or write or wire the factory direct.

Continental Automobile Company
Division of Continental Motors Corporation
General Offices: DETROIT, MICHIGAN • Manufacturing Plants: DETROIT, GRAND RAPIDS AND MUSKEGON

Automobile Topics/Dunwoodie

Six cylinder FLYER (above) priced from $450 to $535 when introduced. Top-of-the-line ACE (below) had 114 inch wheelbase; was sold as a Big Six priced from $725 to $815

Automobile Trade Journal/Dunwoodie

agreed that we're 'on the right track.' Perhaps not all of them, but many now admit that Continental is off to a flying start. I'm sure of that fact."

To show what the home town thought of Continental Motors, the Greater Muskegon Chamber of Commerce sponsored a two-day celebration to mark the company's entry into the passenger car field. At an employees dinner at the Armory, Rockelman outlined an "employees sale plan" which paid workers a commission of from $10 to $20 on every sale where they introduced the prospect to a local dealer.

High spot of the banquet was President Angell's statement that the program contemplated by the company would mean the employment of from 3000 to 5000 additional men in the Muskegon plants.

A month later, a similar program and banquet was held for a thousand employees in the Detroit area.

Despite such sanguine talk by Continental executives, matters were not going well with the new enterprise.

Early production difficulties were exacerbated by a strike in the Hayes Body factory and in addition the situation arising out of the national bank holiday was an unfavorable factor at the outset. Shipments of completed cars were resumed in April and from April first to June 30th, 1,324 autos were delivered.

Sales manager Rockelman left his post the end of April, just six months after signing on as Vice President of Continental's automobile subsidiary.

The End of the Road

The pace of activity in Continental's automobile project was slowing. For the 1934 market the line was greatly diminished with only one offering in that model year. It was billed as the 1934 Continental Red Seal Four and in reality was an updated and improved version of the 1933 Beacon.

Percy R. Gilbert, an automotive historian of Lakewood, New Jersey, some years ago corresponded with retired Continental executives in an effort to try and find answers to previously unanswered questions about the Continental cars.

Henry W. Vandeven, Treasurer, retired 11 years and then 82 years of age, informed Gilbert that "Continental Automobile Company, as a wholly-owned subsidiary, was carried on the parent company's books as just an account in the general ledger," inferring, Gilbert felt, that the basic reason for being in the business was to recoup, if possible, the indebtedness to DeVaux-Hall creditors.

"As near as can be ascertained," writes Gilbert, "1933 car production totalled about 6500 units. The C-400 Beacon accounted for most, with 4092 units; C-600 Flyer sales were 1764, and the Big Six Ace sold 651 units.

"Production for 1934 is completely unknown, but one can approximate the completed units of Red Seal Fours at less than 1200 because production ceased altogether around July 1934.

"The project died, almost taking the parent company with it."

Thus, the ill-starred Continental car venture drew to an end after one final gasp. Sales were estimated to be about one-half of one percent of the total market at a time when Chevrolet had 30 percent, Ford 25 percent and Plymouth 15 percent.

In an effort to liquidate the remaining inventory, Continental wrote in September to all car owners offering new parts at up to 60 percent discount. A new engine, $146.60. Completely upholstered bodies, $147.50. A stripped body, just $88.00. And free mechanical advice.

Then Norman DeVaux made a final gesture. He would take over the four-cylinder Beacon/Red Seal car. His Four-Forty-Four would be built in Oakland, California, " . . . for the motoring public of

Minimum dashboard gauges were typical of spartan BEACON appointments

the Pacific Coast and foreign lands." It was an idle gesture.

There was, however, a sequel according to many auto historians. In 1935, they claim, it became the Graham Crusader; in 1936, the Graham Series 80; and the Graham 85 of 1937.

"Apparently," wrote Jim Cwach of Tankton, South Dakota, "Graham got the rights to the Beacon-Flyer body which continued to be made by Hayes Body Corp. at Grand Rapids. The engines for all 'sixes' from 1936 through 1941 were built by Continental to Graham specs and this continued after the war when Graham-Paige was absorbed into Kaiser-Frazer.

"Continental did build good engines. I've sat behind them for many hours as an airplane pilot, in the Kaiser-Frazer cars I drove; also worked on many of them in Massey-Harris tractors."

DEPARTING, Continental's Beacon heads down the road for the last time in the middle of the Depression

Three months after acquiring the defunct DeVaux-Hall automobile business, Angell also moved the company into the light truck field. Seeking further diversification, Continental in May, 1932 purchased the assets and business of Divco (Detroit Industrial Vehicle Corp.), manufacturers of special-purpose milk delivery vehicles. To head the new Continental-Divco Co., Angell took the post of President, with Roger Sherman as Vice-President.

Sputtering Engine Sales

There, of course, had been other efforts to re-start the sputtering Continental engine business.

General Sales Manager Kanitz had been dispatched on several overseas ventures— to France, Germany, England and Austria. Most interesting was a four-week visit to Russia in 1931 negotiating a potential $5 million order for industrial motors and a contract, said Kanitz, "to build and equip a motor plant in Moscow. The deal had to be deferred, however, because of England going off the gold standard and upsetting the arrangements."

A new series of six-cylinder L-head truck and industrial engines, designated E-600, were introduced. All of the same stroke, but different bore, the series of four graduated engines filled the gap, Kanitz said, "between the well-known model 16-C and our heavier R-series of overhead valve type."

"We have been experiencing a slow but steady increase in payroll and production since the first of the year," announced T. M. Simpson, Secretary, who was then the chief executive of the Muskegon plant. "We are employing 1140 men at longer hours and more days than even a few weeks ago."

One significant order announced by Kanitz was for large production of 16-C Red Seal engines to be delivered to the manufacturer of trucks for the U. S. Mail Service.

At the beginning of 1932, Louis Kanitz and Wallace Zweiner of Detroit, Controller, had been added to the Continental board of directors. At the same time, Robert Insley, Vice President and General Manager of the subsidiary Continental Aircraft Engine Co. retired from the board of the parent company to devote full time to the aircraft division.

In an effort to improve sales of the Divco subsidiary, truck prices were reduced several hundred dollars on both the four- and six-cylinder house-to-house delivery trucks. Sales soon increased under Continental management. One observation by management was that "There is a large prospective market for beer delivery."

So that the delivery trucks could be

". . . our heavier R-series of overhead valve type engines."

Continental Divco milk delivery trucks. Management also noted "there is a large market for beer delivery."

Red Seal Magazine

operated from either a standing or sitting position, the Divco vehicles featured a patented low "aisle" or platform for the driver. To protect its market position and patents, Continental-Divco had to sue International Harvester Co. for alleged infringement of patent rights.

In addition to recently-acquired Divco, Continental noted in a 1933 Prospectus that it had four other wholly-owned subsidiaries: Continental Aircraft Engine Co., Continental Automobile Co., (and its subsidiary, Continental Auto Sales Corp.) Continental Gas and Oil Co., and British Continental Motors, Ltd. It also owned 35,000 shares of Lakey Foundry and Machine Co. of Muskegon, a major vendor to whom Continental had also made cash advances and on whose Board the company was well represented.

"Bad Times are Good Times"

Because of continued depressed business conditions throughout the country, none of the subsidiaries was able to better the parent company's business results.

Rather than giving up under pressure, Continental management was doing everything possible to improve the company's fortunes in the market place.

With the 1931 departure of Walter A. Frederick as Vice-President, Engineering, the top technical job was assumed by Lewis P. Kalb, who, like his predecessor, was an engineering graduate of Cornell. Kalb had joined the company in 1921 after having worked for Pierce-Arrow and Kelly-Springfield and soon was moving up through the ranks at Continental.

Under Kalb's leadership new developments were sponsored and the company's ideas given visibility by his frequent appearances before technical societies.

At the 1932 New York Auto Show, Kalb talked about his ideas. "Progress in engine design," he said, "is the outstanding achievement in the automobile industry. In any one year, progress is never as impressive as it deserves to be. But when measured over a period of years it cannot fail to impress even the most skeptical.

"In the past ten years specific power output has increased approximately 50 percent—so that an engine of any given displacement which developed 50 hp in 1922 will develop 75 hp in 1932."

Angell spoke up, too, on behalf of more research, holding that "bad times are good times for the development of new ideas. When things are slack, opportunity is afforded for work in the laboratory of the brain and in the laboratory of the factory.

"More new devices pertaining to engines and vehicles are being submitted to us than ever before. Everyone seems to appreciate the desirability of offering something radically different."

Lewis Kalb was called upon for his opinion on mixing grain alcohol with gasoline. In 1933 it was proposed as a farm relief measure by a University of Illinois professor. [In 1980 it was proposed as an energy conservation measure].

Kalb's answer: "Even the low proportion of 10 percent of grain alcohol would require a different type of carburetor, intake manifold and combustion chamber. It is too expensive to be used as a substitute for gasoline, or to be mixed with gasoline.

"It would be a more sensible solution of the problem of farm relief to put a 2-cent per gallon tax on all gasoline and hand it to the farmers. It would save them the trouble of raising corn for alcoholic production."

On another technical subject, AUTOMOBILE TOPICS in its June 17, 1933 issue brought up the matter of Continental's single-sleeve-valve Argyll engine.

The Engine Development Field

"A public announcement," it said, "revealing the results of six years of experimental work will be made shortly. Some rather startling claims for performance and economy are promised.

"Continental is amply protected by patents on this novel type motor; indeed, the company now holds 175 U.S. patents, with another 325 applications pending on this and other developments.

"This wide array of patents covers almost every phase of design of the passenger car and truck motor field, the Divco low-aisle delivery vehicle, aircraft, diesel and Argyll engines."

Patents, yes. But in the depth of the Depression they failed to bring in much new business. And the promised favorable report on the Argyll engine failed to appear in the later issue of AUTOMOBILE TOPICS.

The matter did come up, however, late in 1934 during a financial crisis when Angell reported that "several sizes and designs of these (single-sleeve) engines are now about ready for production. One of these is for use in the light new Diesel-electric bullet trains."

Nearly half a century later engineer Carl Bachle offered an evaluation of the single-sleeve-valve project and some philosophical observations on engine design:

"The engine development field is replete with examples of an innovative change leading the way, followed shortly by an improvement in the conventional which leads in turn to discard of the innovation. We often see inventions that are for the sake of being different, not for the sake of improving. The piston engine that we use in automobiles is no accident. Alternatives are awful hard to find and some, like the sleeve-valve engine, though they sound attractive, aren't.

"Before 1927 automobile engines suffered from knock of detonation which was (and still is) a sound like hammering, and very objectionable to people, both inside and outside the car. It was expected that the single-sleeve-valve would overcome this fault as well as be otherwise quieter because it eliminated the sound of the poppet valve cam and tappet. Ample test evidence justified these expectations.

"However, in 1927 a great improvement in understanding of what caused detonation in conventional poppet valve engines evolved and the establishment of Octane fuel rating and detonation suppression poppet valve combustion chambers reduced the sleeve-valve advantage to zero.

"Continental had concurrently under development a sleeve-valve and a conventional poppet valve aircraft engine of high output, and the result was no detonation advantage of either type. (I was in charge of this comparison and personally ran the tests.)

"Among others, the following single-sleeve-valve engines were developed at Continental:

An 8-cylinder in-line automobile engine

A 6-cylinder in-line automobile engine

A 7-cylinder radial air-cooled aircraft engine

A 6-cylinder radial air-cooled, two-cycle aircraft engine

A 10-cylinder radial water-cooled, two-cycle submarine diesel engine

A 5-cylinder radial water-cooled, two-cycle electric generator engine

"These engines were successful in a development sense but offered no real advantage over the poppet valve competitor of its day.

"They were all very expensive projects. All had virtues and faults—mainly excessive oil consumption. The faults finally overcame the virtues. But these projects were tremendous engineering educators for the crew and permitted our people to go on to other things that were successful.

"All the engines were acceptable, but none was outstanding or revolutionary. The 1936 submarine engine was probably the most successful.

"The main requirement was that the entire engine could be taken apart and moved into the submarine through the standard deck hatch. The engine was the only two-cycle sleeve-valve type of which I have knowledge. The sleeve-valve was a mistake, but remember in those days the party line was 'the future belongs to sleeve-valve.'

"Of course, we hoped each engine would be successful and that this would lead to production contracts. It didn't work out that way.

"The sleeve-valve campaign was such a great drain of the Continental financial reserves that it was almost fatal. The development of the sleeve-valve principle should have been discontinued early but was continued because of Angell's unwillingness to face up to the changes in engine design since the original purchase of the patents."

Perhaps the final gasp for the single-sleeve engine came in 1935 in connection with the Bureau of Air Commerce's campaign to develop safer, easier-operated, low-priced aircraft for the private owner. For this project, the Bureau awarded Continental a contract for a six-cylinder 90 hp radial air-cooled engine.

"We often see inventions that are for the sake of being different, not for the sake of improving"

Six-cylinder E-600 series truck engines

Model	E-600	E-601	E-602	E-603
Bore	3-11/16"	3-7/8"	4-1/8"	4-1/4"
Stroke	4-1/2"	4-1/2"	4-1/2"	4-1/2"
Displacement (cid)	288.3	318	360.7	382.9
Max. hp	75	81	89	97
at r.p.m.	3000	2600	2400	2400

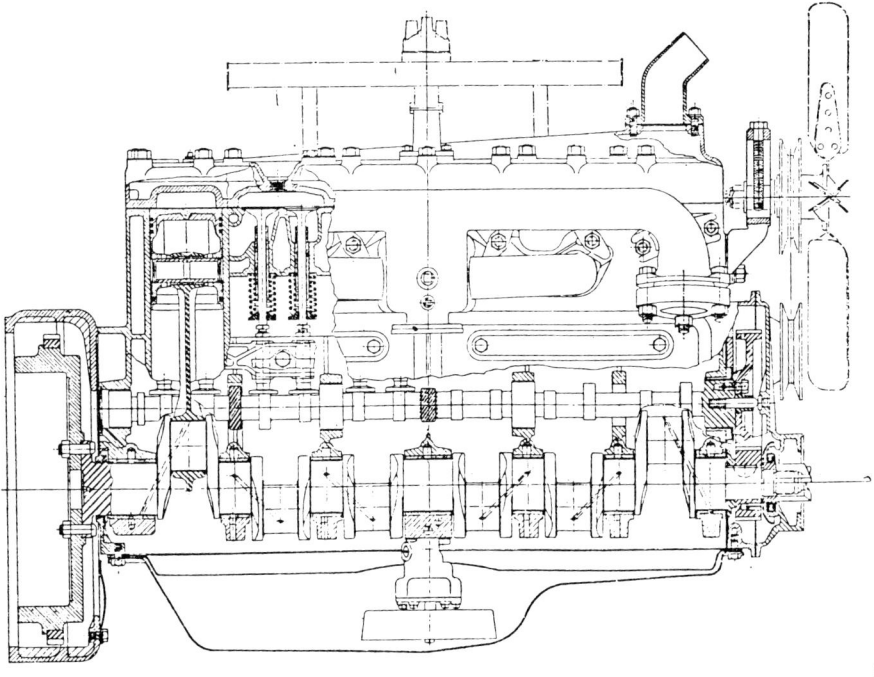

Designed to be only 20 inches in diameter, it was to operate on a two-stroke cycle, and to weigh not over two pounds per horsepower. But it was never produced.

It was ten years since Angell had gone to Scotland to obtain rights to the Argyll single-sleeve principle. He had little to show for that investment of time and money.

Early in 1937 letters went off from Continental's patent counsel to Glasgow, Scotland, birthplace of the S.S.V. (single sleeve valve). The company offered all of its British, German and French patents on the controversial sleeve valve design for a $25,000 fee "in order to obtain some revenue" from the project.

Along with other companies, Continental began to take a serious look at the potential for "heavy oil" diesel engines which offered simpler operation by elimination of carburetors and spark ignition, as well as lower fuel cost.*

Getting Into Diesels

Edward T. Vincent, Continental's diesel research engineer, stated that "a high-speed diesel engine suitable for a motor vehicle, need not weigh more than 10 to 15 percent more than a comparable gasoline engine of the same power and, as means are developed for more rapidly and completely mixing fuel and air, the diesel engine should weigh less than its gasoline competitor."

See chapter Technical Note, Page 81

Continental's 10-cylinder radial sleeve-valve diesel engine, first of its type built for rail car use

Automotive Industries/Dunwoodie

First success in the diesel field came in May 1933 when the company obtained a contract from the U.S. Navy for two engines to be installed in torpedo retriever boats at Newport, Rhode Island. The 200 hp engines were two-cycle, six-cylinder diesels. A feature of the design was the use of sleeve valves to control the exhaust and scavenging ports.

A year and a half later, Continental exhibited at the New York Automobile Show the country's first radial-type diesel engine for rail car trains. It was a two-stroke, ten-cylinder single-sleeve-valve type supercharged diesel developing 635 hp. It was felt the unit would be well adapted for all transportation and stationery powerplant purposes including small central stations, factories and large apartment buildings. It used No. 4 furnace oil.

Following introduction of its diesel locomotive engine, Continental announced availability of five-, eight-, and ten-cylinder radial diesel models.

Ten 450 hp engines were placed in production for use as industrial installations. "These diesels," Vincent said, "have been designed as heavy-duty engines where continuous operation is necessary. They are extremely light for the horsepower developed and are very smooth in operation. They will be available for marine purposes as well as stationery, industrial installations."

"None of these diesel efforts," Carl Bachle explained, "went on to production, but there were good accomplishments, among them a four-cylinder diesel truck engine built at the expense of the Russian government and delivered to them about 1938, and a fuel injection method known as the 'common rail system.'"

The Army was also beginning to consider diesels for armored vehicles and in 1935 awarded a contract to Guiberson Diesel Engine Co. for testing radial air-cooled diesels in combat cars and tanks. Thereafter the Armored Force favored all-out dieselization, but reversed that position seven years later.

Continental would capitalize on the full potential of diesel power plants even later, particularly as applied to military tracked vehicles.

Forecasting later development of sophisticated multifuel engines, Continental engineers sought to combine the advantages of spark-ignition gasoline engines and diesel power plants, the former using fuel more volatile than the heavy oils burned in diesel engines.

Oil-Carbureted Engines

Consequently, since some Continental engineers had an out-and-out aversion to diesel, someone suggested starting an engine on gasoline, then switching to oil.

Edward T. Vincent had been studying that potential since 1931. Economy of operation would be in proportion to the difference between the cost of ordinary fuel oil and gas station gasoline prices.

Four years later the company announced a line of spark ignition engines manifolded to burn No. 1 fuel oil. They used standard overhead valve gasoline engines with special attachments for conversion to oil burners. Continental referred to them as "oil-carbureted" engines and pointed out that "they will operate with equal facility on gasoline, distillate, furnace oil or approved types of kerosene, but operation must begin on gasoline."

In April 1935 the company closed a three-year half-million-dollar contract with an agricultural equipment manufacturer for oil-carbureted engines. At the same time a contract of similar value was signed with a large commercial truck firm for standard gasoline engines.

The multi-fuel, oil-carbureted version was also offered to truck companies in a series of engines having a weight and initial cost approximately the same as the conventional gasoline engine, yet operating on low-priced fuel oil to effect a saving in fuel cost of 35% to 40% over gasoline engine operation.

The oil-carbureted engines did burn diesel, "but very poorly," as Carl Bachle put it. "It never developed into a real product line and was regarded by some of us as more stunt than business."

Another technical field being investigated involved experiments with a standard gasoline engine with spark ignition, but using fuel injection instead of a carburetor. The reason for wanting fuel injection was because a carburetor does not supply fuel equally to all cylinders. With fuel injection, it mechanically goes equally to all cylinders. Gains of 5% to 10% power output were obtained with fuel injection.

Because of over $6 million in net losses in three years, Continental was in deep financial trouble. In Spring 1933 it was decided to raise additional working capital by selling authorized but unissued stock.

Trading in Continental Shares Suspended

At that time, there were outstanding 2,112,143 shares of no par value. Of these, 21,900 were held by the company as treasury stock. The rest were held by the company's 30,000 stockholders. The New York Stock Exchange ten years earlier had authorized listing 2,500,000 of the company's authorized 3,000,000 shares.

A public offering of Continental shares "as a speculation," priced at the market, was made through John J. Bergen, New York broker, of 40 Wall Street. Information in the Prospectus was prepared by W. R. Angell, President of Continental. Presumably, the company had permission to sell 387,857 shares. In addition, an application to list the remaining 500,000 shares was also pending.

On June 14, 1933, the New York Stock Exchange summarily suspended trading in Continental shares. The Detroit Stock Exchange did likewise. Between March 27 and June 8, the price had increased from $1 per share to $4 per share. (In 1932 the stock sold as low as 62½ cents a share).

What was the ruckus all about?

Several things caught the attention of Richard Whitney, President of the New York Stock Exchange. In his announcement temporarily delisting Continental shares, Whitney said it was done "pending investigation of circumstances surrounding the recent distribution of treasury stock of the company."

A pro forma statement dated March 31 showed that the company no longer carried on its books the 21,900 treasury shares held in October 31, 1932, then valued at $40,115.

The Exchange was also concerned about the rapid run-up in the price of Continental shares and the fact that 303,820 additional shares had been disposed of by the company between April 27 and June 13.

However, what must have caused the greatest consternation was Angell's statement on the company's future outlook as expressed in the Prospectus prepared for the Bergen Wall Street brokerage firm. Here is Angell's summary:

"The Corporation's forecast indicates that with an annual production of 36,000 Automobiles, 20,000 Motors for outside customers, 500 Divco

OIL CARBURETION
MEANS FUEL OIL ECONOMY WITH GASOLINE ENGINE SMOOTHNESS AND FLEXIBILITY

After losing $6 million, Angell "conservatively estimated (for 1934) that the corporation would earn a profit of $2,000,000"

Trucks and 200 Aircraft Engines, the Corporation would operate at a profit.

"It is conservatively estimated that the Corporation will produce and sell in 1934, 60,000 Automobiles, 35,000 Motors for outside customers, 1,000 Divco Trucks and 300 Aircraft Engines on which it is estimated the Corporation would earn a profit of $2,000,000.

With the business—particularly the Continental Automobile venture—collapsing about him, Angell's rosy forecast raised serious doubts in the minds of the Exchange and Wall Street.

Angell was quick to respond to the financial press when queried about delisting of Continental shares. "The company," he told Robert P. Vanderpoel, financial editor of THE CHICAGO AMERICAN, "has been selling its unissued or treasury stock previously listed, for the sole purpose of providing additional working capital. No officer or director has been financially interested in any transactions connected with the marketing activities incident to this stock."

At the same time, Angell announced a special meeting of stockholders to be held in two weeks to vote on a change in the capital stock to $1 par value from no par value, reducing the capital as of June 7, 1933 to $2,361,927 from $23,898,907 and transferring the difference of $21,536,980 to surplus.

Stockholders were also to vote on amending the charter to increase the authorized capital to 5,000,000 shares of common stock from 3,000,000 shares and to write down the stated value of goodwill from $5,908,317 to $1 as of June 17, 1933.

The July 6 special meeting of stockholders was postponed to August 9, then plans, which Angell said "involved compliance with the Federal Securities Act and the sale of common stock," were cancelled as "not possible nor desirable in the circumstances."

In the meantime, Angell had been meeting with officials of the New York Stock Exchange to thrash out what was, at least in part, a misunderstanding and failure of communications. Yet Angell could be difficult to deal with as reported by New York financial editor Ralph Hendershot:

"After having been suspended from trading on the New York Stock Exchange for a month, stock of the Continental Motors Co. has been welcomed back into the good graces of the institution. Many people contend that it never should have been suspended and would not have been had not a misunderstanding arisen between the Listing Committee members and the head of the company.

Continental had been traded in on the Big Board for a number of years. When it went into the manufacture of automobiles a few months ago, it was required to spend quite a little money. To reimburse the company for this expenditure and to improve its working capital position it sought to issue additional common stock. And it was over the proposed listing of this additional stock that the trouble arose.

It seems that the Continental head was not prepared to answer all the questions the committee members wanted to know concerning the company's operations and its position in the industry. He had assumed, so the story goes, that questioning would be along somewhat different lines. The Exchange authorities apparently thought he was trying to hide something, so they pressed their inquiries all the harder. The automobile man finally lost his head and made a few observations of his own which were not particularly flattering, with the result that this stock was tossed out the window for the time being.

The moral, if any, of the story is that you may think what you like about the Exchange, but you had better not say it unless you happen to be a Senator.

A month after suspension, shares of Continental were readmitted to trading on the New York and Detroit exchanges. The governing committee of the New York Stock Exchange issued an explanation:

"The committee felt that in certain particulars a circular used in connection with the sale of a part of its authorized but not issued stock was objectionable. The management of the corporation has recognized the views of the committee and has agreed to send to stockholders a communication which the committee recognizes as eliminating the features of the offering circular to which objection had been made."

In his new communication to stockbrokers, Angell modified many of the statements he made in the stock Prospectus, eliminating entirely production and profit estimates for 1934. He also revealed a 1933 first-half loss of $1,432,917. Angell also pointed out that "recent passage of the Federal Securities Act has created new and serious problems for corporations requiring additional financing."

Continental had been retrenching almost from the day Angell took over management of the company. In August 1931, it was decided to concentrate manufacturing in Muskegon, leaving only general offices, engineering, tooling and aircraft engine production at Detroit.

Retrenching to Muskegon

"The economies effected," Angell announced, "will be a decided advantage in

CONTINENTAL MOTORS CORPORATION

A VIRGINIA CORPORATION

COMMON CAPITAL STOCK

Listed on the New York Stock Exchange

Transfer Agents	*Registrars*
NEW YORK TRUST COMPANY New York	BANKERS TRUST COMPANY New York
CONTINENTAL MOTORS CORPORATION Detroit	DETROIT TRUST COMPANY Detroit

SALIENT POINTS

1. Continental has been a vital part of the automobile business for more than thirty years. Only five other manufacturers in the automotive field have this record.

2. Continental has produced more than 3,500,000 Red Seal engines. They have set new standards of dependable, economical performance in every field where gasoline power is employed.

3. Continental furnishes engines to 53 per cent of all the companies building trucks.

4. Continental has provided engines to almost 300 different manufactures of industrial machinery and to many makers of buses and boats.

5. Continental has powered more than 100 different makes of passenger cars. It is estimated that approximately one million cars with Continental engines are now in operation.

6. Continental in 1932, SOLD MORE AIRCRAFT ENGINES in its several power classes THAN ALL OTHER MANUFACTURERS COMBINED

THIS STOCK IS OFFERED AS A SPECULATION

Price at the Market

JOHN J. BERGEN

FORTY WALL STREET

NEW YORK

With 140 times as many shares as the outsiders' Stockholders' Protective Committee, officers and directors had the most to lose if there was any mismanagement of the company

meeting competition during this period of below normal demand for our products."

For a number of years Continental Annual Reports dealt almost entirely with financial matters rather than with product and sales information. "There is not an item of operating expense, including salaries," Angell wrote, "which has escaped searching scrutiny and decisive action."

In the stock Prospectus, Angell advised prospective shareholders that the company "in the past three years of subnormal business had definitely cleared the decks for action."

More action came in 1934 with further consolidation of sales, service and engineering activity at Muskegon and plans prepared to locate everything there. For the present, aircraft and engine production, manufacture of Divco delivery trucks and research on the single-sleeve-valve engine remained in Detroit, but a large portion of the Detroit plant was leased to Chrysler which built bodies there for its modernistic air flow car.

Nothing, however, could stanch the flow of red ink.

To 1930-32's three-year loss of $6.7 million, further losses of $3.5 million in 1933 and $2 million in 1934 brought the five-year total to a whopping $12 million loss.

Beset at every turn, Angell and his associates faced a multitude of problems. A loan application to the Reconstruction Finance Corporation was bogged down in bureaucratic red tape. Where to turn?

Stockholders' Protective Committee

L. N. Rosenbaum of Rosenbaum & Rosenbaum, New York City, was recommended as one who could obtain the required funds. But that avenue led only to a challenge to Continental management by a stockholders' protective committee.

Rosenbaum became a Director of Continental in July 1934 and was granted his request that two associates, Col. James H. Graham and Percy N. Booth, both of Louisville, Kentucky be named directors.

Also, Rosenbaum was named Chairman of the Finance Committee, replacing Roger Sherman in that post. Sherman, an early investor, prominent Chicago attorney, and legal counsel for the company, continued as a director.

The relationship between Continental and Rosenbaum was short lived. It was soon obvious that neither Rosenbaum nor those associated with him could make good on his claim they could procure adequate financing for the company. In August all three resigned.

Instead of coming up with financial assistance, Rosenbaum served an ultimatum demanding that Angell and other Continental directors resign and turn the management over to him. That demand was, of course, refused.

Owners of 625 shares of Continental stock, recently purchased, the Rosenbaum group in September formed a "committee for the protection of stockholders." Among its members was Rosenbaum and Walter A. Frederick, former Vice-President, Engineering during the Ross Judson regime, who had left soon after Angell took over. Committee chairman was A. W. Porter, New York investment banker; the committee secretary was a New York lawyer.

"The affairs of Continental Motors," the committee announced in soliciting irrevocable proxies, "have reached the point requiring concerted stockholder intervention and action in the interest of all stockholders."

Named as defendants were the officers and directors—Angell; B. F. Tobin, Jr., Treasurer; Craig Keith, Secretary; Roger Sherman, Vice President of the automobile subsidiary; and largest stockholder and director, James H. Ferry.

The suit asked restitution of some $16 million alleged to have been lost during the prior four years by officers and directors.

The plaintiffs' allegations and charges [never substantiated] were ridiculously sweeping and extreme:

"that Angell obtained control of the Corporation by procuring director's votes through promises of large salaries;

"that he maintained control by illegally casting the vote of an absent director;

"that by entering the motor car field ill-prepared the Company was made to lose more than $2,500,000;

"that in trying to raise a capital levy the officers acquired only $638,918 at the excessive rate of 15 per cent;

"that Angell negligently allowed the New York Stock Exchange to strike Continental shares from listing, leaving the company with a large amount of unissued stock which it could not sell;

"that officers and directors permitted waste of assets through complicated subsidiaries;

"that payroll and administrative costs were left adjusted to a $25,000,000 business although actual volume was only $2,500,000 to $3,500,000;

"that officers and directors sold a large amount of unnecessary real estate to the Company;

"that they permitted orders to be taken at a loss;

"and that Mr. Angell and Roger Sherman, vice-president of Continental Automobile, purchased Peerless stock for the sum of $375,000 and that 'thereafter, realizing the said stock was not worth that much money, caused Continental to assume such purchase'."

Responding to public knowledge of the stockholders' suit, Angell termed the charges "ridiculous on their face."

"We do not care to dignify them further than to say that we emphatically deny each and every one of them," Angell said, "and that we will take the first opportunity to definitely and positively disprove every misstatement made.

"This suit appears to be the outgrowth of an attempt made last summer by certain persons to gain control of the company's affairs. It is evidently brought as a continuation of those efforts by eastern stockholders who hold 625 out of a total of 2,448,652 shares.

"The company recently has booked substantial orders aggregating $2,000,000 and it appears that the persons behind this suit are seeking to gain control at a time when the Company's prospects are definitely on the upgrade and better than at any time during the past four years.

"At present we have on our books over $3,000,000 in unfilled orders for machine products and parts including motors for use in governmental, automotive, aviation, marine and industrial application."

In a letter to stockholders, the company pointed out that the few shares held by the Continental Stockholders Protective Committee contrasted sharply with the 89,136 shares held by the officers, directors and members of their immediate families. The latter, clearly, had the most at stake, the most to lose from any mismanagement of the company's affairs.

A group of substantial Muskegon, Detroit and Chicago businessmen and stockholders conducted their own investigations and came to management's aid, pledging their shares. Thus, the support of 121,895 shares was absolutely assured in any contest with the so-called stockholders protective committee which, it was pointed out, was formed not by stockholders but by *outsiders*. Opportunist Rosenbaum and his friends owned no stock to "protect" except the few shares recently purchased.

As to the Peerless Motor Car Corp. stock, management reported it had been traded for shares in the Lakey Foundry & Machine Co., a major supplier of castings for Continental engines.

When Rosenbaum and Continental came to a parting of the ways, the record shows the company retained a New York investigative firm to inquire about him and his associates. Correspondence to Craig Keith, Continental's corporate secretary, indicates that Graham and Booth were highly regarded in Louisville business circles. Rosenbaum, who "was known to cultivate the friendship of reputable people," apparently did not meet the same high standard.

In January 1935, Rosenbaum sought a court injunction to prevent the Annual Meeting scheduled for the 16th in Richmond, Virginia, from being held. The injunction was denied.

WILLIAM R. ANGELL
Described as "big in stature, slow in physical movement and keen in mental vision"—but, by others, as "austere and aloof," Angell was as much a victim of the Great Depression as he was of poor business judgment during his ten years as President of Continental Motors. He figured Continental's own car was the way out of his dilemma. It wasn't.

The meeting went off smoothly; all directors were reelected. And there was no contest between the management and the Rosenbaum committee since that group did not even appear.

Walter A. Frederick, who had joined Continental in 1911, spent the World War II years with Willys-Overland and played a large part in adapting the famous wartime Jeep for civilian use. He retired in 1950 and passed away in 1966 at the age of 86.

Roger Sherman resigned as a director soon after the 'Rosenbaum' incident. In later years, James H. Ferry, Jr. said it "frightened Sherman away. He was a very fine man. My father was extremely fond of him." Judge George M. Clark of Muskegon succeeded Sherman as a director.

[Yet another executive and director who left was Louis J. Kanitz who wrote: "I finally left in June 1934 because of great differences of opinion which eventually caused four of the nine members of the Board of Directors to resign within a period of four months."]

Because of huge financial losses, Continental was in desperate need of additional working capital but was having trouble obtaining it. The company had to abandon plans Angell had worked out for the June 1933 stock issue which would have somewhat relieved the problem.

$1,000,000 Loan from RFC

A year earlier, 1932, the administration of President Herbert Hoover had established the Reconstruction Finance Corp. with $2 billion in borrowing power to help revive the Depression-ridden economy.

Initial RFC loans reportedly went to huge companies and institutions, motivating Angell to write President-elect Franklin Roosevelt with suggestions for more financial "fertilizing" at the roots, rather than at the top.

"It would," wrote Angell, "increase employment, instill confidence that jobs will be permanent, promptly increase buying power through release of hoarded funds, give the banks courage they now lack, increase railway tonnage, help the farmer and accomplish the greatest good for the greatest number."

To which suggestion, financial writer B. C. Forbes, added this comment: "That sounds more sensible than do most 'plans,' doesn't it?"

In January 1934, Continental stockholders approved Angell's plan to seek a $5 million loan for three years at 6 percent interest from the Reconstruction Finance Corp.

In a letter to stockholders seeking their approval, Angell had written:

"The continued Depression, the lack of sufficient volume of motor business during the past four years and the expense of launching the new Continental automobile have reduced the company's funds to the point where a loan is indicated as essential. New money is required to meet current obligations and to supply the necessary working capital for operations."

An application for the loan was filed with the RFC and the Federal Reserve Bank, but it was not until June 21, 1935 that a loan for $1 million was approved; the loan being for five years at 5 percent interest and secured by a first mortgage on plant, equipment, patents and trade-marks.

Of the $1 million, $650,000 was made available immediately to settle all back taxes and provide some working capital. In September, the balance of $350,000 was paid to Continental after stockholders approved complete terms of the mortgage.

As part of the understanding with stockholders and the RFC, the company capital structure was revamped. The no-par stock was changed to shares of $1 par value, the effect of which was to write down the capital structure from $24 million to $2,448,652, including 11,900 shares held in the corporate treasury. (There were still 51,348 shares unissued of the 2,500,000 authorized for listing by the New York Stock Exchange).

The capital write down was accompanied by elimination of Good Will in the amount of $5,908,317, which had appeared on the balance sheet for many years. Patents and development costs of the single-sleeve motor totaling $753,336 were also written off. Total employment was down to only 1,100 workers.

As a further measure, the Board of Directors initiated a study of the book value of plant, property and equipment to determine how much represented excess capacity not being used, and what was the fair value of that needed in current operations.

There were political overtones to getting the loan, according to one in a position to have known. "Jesse Jones, Chairman of the RFC," he said, "insisted that the company take on a relative of President Roosevelt's. He was closer to high living than he was to Continental's work. But that's just the way he was."

In September 1934 when Continental was looking into L. N. Rosenbaum's background, an investigative report was also received on G. Hall Roosevelt, brother of Mrs. Eleanor Roosevelt, wife of the President.

This Roosevelt seems to have gone from job to job in executive capacities usually "secured due to the influence . . . of the Roosevelt family." The report continued:

"The subject resigned as Controller (of

the City of Detroit under Mayor Frank Murphy) and went to Cleveland to become general manager of the Lubrigraph Company which was acquired in the spring of this year by the Continental Motors Corp. of Detroit with whom the subject is now connected."

The hemorrhaging of company resources continued after the RFC loan, but the red ink flowed more slowly. The combined loss in fiscal years 1935 and 1936 dropped to $1.5 million and in 1937, with an upswing in business volume to $8.2 million, there was, after seven years of losses, a small profit—$71,335.

A further recession in general business nationally took place in late 1937 and continued into 1938, in which year Continental reported a further loss of half a million dollars. Angell was able to report that "The RFC graciously has extended to 1940 the payment of mortgage installments falling due in 1937 and 1938."

In the decade of the 30s, Continental had nine years of losses with only one year's operations in the black. Little wonder that the Reconstruction Finance Corp. indicated that unless a drastic course of action was taken it would foreclose the mortgage on all Continental assets.

Although Continental radial and horizontally-opposed air-cooled engines were being built for commercial aircraft, the company was not neglecting the military market for large liquid cooled aircraft engines. Bob Insley with his Army Air Corps contacts at Wright Field saw to that.

"Hyper" Cylinder and Engine

In the early thirties, Pratt & Whitney and Wright Aeronautical were developing high-horsepower radial engines and Curtiss-Wright was supplying its large, liquid-cooled, 600 hp "Conqueror" military engine for pursuit planes.

Army experiments under the direction of British-born Sam Heron, a world-renowned consultant on engine design, convinced the Army that the power they had obtained from a single liquid-cooled test cylinder was much greater than then being realized in other engines.

Separately, English engineer H. R. Ricardo contended that the poppet valve had already reached its limits and should be replaced by sleeve valves (to which Continental had world rights). The Army wanted to investigate that possibility.

Some of the Army experiments involved an air-cooled cylinder, developed by Heron in 1923-24 for the converted Liberty aircraft engine, modified to water cooling by use of a complete water jacket. Results were so encouraging the Army wanted to proceed with development of a "Hyper" cylinder using it as the basis for development of a new liquid-cooled V-type 1000 hp 12-cylinder engine.

Army designers also decided that the ethylene glycol coolant should operate at the very high temperature of 300° F in order to minimize weight and drag of the radiator. This would require that the engine be built of individual cylinders instead of standard monobloc construction.

In 1932 an arrangement was reached between the Army and Continental for the engineering and development of the Hyper cylinder and the engine employing that technique. Continental received the contract, in part, because of the Navy contract it had obtained in October 1931 for a radial air-cooled engine with single-sleeve valves.

Continental's role in the Hyper project was to be confined to routine engineering and testing. The Army had already decided on the basic design and cylinder size, and also laid down the lines of the complete proposed engine. Harold Morehouse, now with Continental, was assigned to the project.

The company set up a special office in Dayton to work on the cylinder with Heron and a very competent assistant named Prescott. Carl Bachle recalls that "the cylinder was built in Detroit, and it was my job to test both the 'Hyper' and the competing single-sleeve-valve cylinder.

"There was a race on, and I was the conductor of the tests on both the single-sleeve in one room, and the hyper-cycle in the other. We got to the point the single-sleeve performed the highest horsepower per cubic inch of anything of that era. Following that—six months later—we made the Hyper do the same thing.

"The Hyper was a relatively conventional cylinder except for the spherical combustion chamber and sodium-cooled exhaust valve. Of course everything in the way of material and construction was of the very finest so that you could reach the highest possible power output. It had conventional liquid cooling but with ethylene glycol as the coolant."

In 1934 the Army instructed Continental to proceed with Hyper No. 2, a cylinder of somewhat larger size and reduced performance.

Originally the Army expected that the Hyper engine could get into production and service in a few years, but various difficulties including funding, technical problems and contract changes slowed progress. For supporting the development of the Hyper and other liquid-cooled engines, the Army had available only about $150,000 a year in the first half of the 1930s.

If Continental could get the engine in production quickly, the Army hoped the company would use the profits from

> "We tested the Single-Sleeve in one room, and the Hyper-Cycle in the other"

Flat, opposed arrangement of Hyper engine's cylinders was to provide for installation within fighter plane's wings

Teledyne Continental Motors

quantity sales to build up its development resources and to finance further development. But that simply was not possible during the Depression years.

Progress was necessarily slow. Six years were spent in trying to obtain a cylinder which would meet the very tight Army specifications.

Further complicating the matter was an Army decision to use a flat, opposed cylinder arrangement, instead of a V layout, so the flat engine could be installed within the wing of a combat plane. The first complete 0-1430 opposed engine was built in 1938 and passed its 50-hour development test at 1000 hp in 1939.

One design requirement, solved by Morehouse, was to provide an easy method of changing the direction of propeller rotation so that opposite-rotating propellers could be used on twin-engined planes. This was accomplished by an adjustment outside the gear case, without opening up the engine or substituting any parts.

By the time 0-1430 engine was ready for further tests, this type of installation was considered as impractical because fighter aircraft wings were too thin for a submerged installation. The engine was again redesigned—model IV-1430—back to a V configuration but this time as an inverted vee (Λ) engine rather than upright V. This would provide better visibility for the pilot but the design created new and unexpected technical problems. Total investment in the '1430' engine by 1939 was less than half a million dollars, nearly all paid under Army contract.

The Army meanwhile, though its financial resources were minimal, placed similar development contracts with Allison and still later with Lycoming and Pratt & Whitney. Heron later agreed that the Army's insistence on its original coolant temperature put the entire Continental development behind its competitors. And, in the long run, Allison was more successful because it was able to invest more of its own money for development and plant facilities than it received from the Army.

Probably because of Continental's critical financial condition, Angell insisted on a signed contract for every expense, however small. Work virtually stopped during the intervals between the negotiation of contracts for the next phase of work.

Art Wild recalls that "Mr. Angell, [he was always 'Mister'] with his legal background, would drive us absolutely nuts. I was then working in government sales and was down at Wright Field quite a bit. We'd bring a contract back and he would nit-pick it to death and insist that we go back and ask them to make changes that didn't amount to a damn. The Army began to think that we weren't really interested."

The need to supplement the company's line of automobile engines with power plants for all types of industrial and agricultural applications was nothing new to Continental. Early in 1927, founder Ross W. Judson, then President, had described how this diversified and stabilized production.

Product Diversification

"Today our products, in addition to their use in automobiles," he wrote, "are used in boats, tractors, trucks and busses, in ore-crushers, hoists, elevators and air compressors; for electric generators, milkers, pumps, threshing machines, churns, vacuum cleaners, dredges, shovels, cranes, concrete mixers, railroad locomotives and cars.

"Such diversification spells stabilization as against seasonable demands and against depression in any given industry and furnishes one of the most substantial, permanent and satisfactory assets a manufacturer of gasoline engines can have."

Red Seal Magazine

Inverted V configuration was feature of IV version of 1430 Hyper engine but created new technical problems

But in the thirties, what Continental faced was not "depression in any given industry" but Depression, with a capital D, in all industry.

Having picked up the Divco delivery truck product line in 1932, Angell sought out other items three years later which Continental might advantageously manufacture and market.

Noting that "approximately 18 percent of all new automobiles are being equipped with radios," Angell purchased rights to the "Perm-O-Flux" speaker which "draws 80 percent less current from the car's battery as it operates on a 'permanent' magnet in combination with other features covered by patent applications controlled by us."

Another article which Continental manufactured under contract with a distributing organization was the "Health Air Junior" portable air conditioner and humidifier. The manufacture of even 100 units daily, which retailed at $19.50, would clearly make only a small contribution to Continental's problem of keeping its huge plants in Detroit and Muskegon busy.

Then, in March 1936, Continental acquired the farm lighting division of Westinghouse Electric and Manufacturing Co. and moved it to Muskegon. Continental would build the power plants for the lighting equipment but would continue to use Westinghouse generating and control units.

None of these projects worked out advantageously for Continental. In all the Depression years, business volume did not exceed one-fourth of what it had been in the previous decade. Thus, the huge losses, because it was simply impossible to productively utilize the company's unoccupied manufacturing facilities.

The entire stock of Continental Divco was sold by Continental in April 1936 for $175,000 to a firm which merged that subsidiary with a similar delivery truck business of Twin Coach Co. However, all Divco trucks continued to be powered exclusively by Continental-built engines.

Also, a new contract was negotiated with H. E. Wilber for the manufacturing and selling rights of a portable battery charging and lighting set with the trade name "Tiny Tim." At the same time, the Health Air Junior activity was renamed "Continental Clean Air."

A property which Angell described as non-productive and involving carrying charges—the company's guest lodge and lake at Bitely, near Muskegon—was offered for sale, but there were no buyers.

Continental's guest lodge at Bitely in the wooded Michigan lake country was placed on the block but there were no takers

Foreshadowing future developments in the corporation's front office, Clarence J. Reese was slowly working his way up in the management structure. His progress was due mainly to just plain hard work.

Jack Reese Moves Up

"When Jack arrived here in 1927 to take a job as Continental's purchasing agent," said W. Earl Lakey, Muskegon civic leader and industrialist, "he was a square-jawed, determined fellow with the firm conviction, then unpopular in the roaring '20s, that the way to get ahead was to work, work, work."

In 1936, Jack Reese was named Vice-President and Assistant General Manager and made a member of the slimmed-down five-man Board of Directors. He shared that distinction with W. R. Angell, James H. Ferry, B. F. Tobin, Jr. and new Corporate Secretary, Judge George M. Clark.

Angell took on the post of Treasurer as well as President. Tobin gave up the Treasurer position to become Vice-President, Sales. Ferry was Vice President and Lewis P. Kalb, not a member of the board, continued as Vice President of Engineering and Manufacturing. H. W. Vandeven retained the post of Assistant Treasurer.

Executive salaries in Depression days were modest indeed. In 1938, Angell received $18,000 and Reese $12,000. Next highest paid was engineering-manufacturing executive Kalb at $8,550.

Shares of stock held by each of the Directors were: Ferry, 57,631; Angell, 19,000; Tobin, Jr., 8,700; Reese, 500; Judge Clark, none.

Continental owned 35,125 shares of Lakey Foundry & Machine Co. Angell, who owned 49,170 Lakey shares, and Reese with 4,000 shares, were on the Lakey board of directors. Ferry owned 23,698 shares of Lakey and Tobin, Jr. 2,201 shares.

To eliminate unprofitable manufacturing activities which Angell said were "most foreign to our regular engine business," he announced discontinuance in 1938 of the Clean Air and Perm-O-Flux Magnetic

Teledyne Continental Motors

Speaker divisions and the combination of the Farm Light division with the Tiny Tim division in a new Power and Light division.

In 1939, the sale of automobile engines and parts represented only 16% of Continental's total business, which nonetheless increased 27% over 1938 to $7¼ million for the 12 months ended October 31, 1939. Agricultural engines accounted for 30% of business volume, truck and commercial engines, 18%; aircraft engines, 13%.

ROBERT INSLEY
He brought a lot of aircraft engine know-how to Continental, then applied it to power plants for military track-laying vehicles

Though it would appear all was gloom and doom, there was one bright spot in the thirties which, more than any other, was to contribute over the years of Continental's promising future.

Refinements of the radial air-cooled gasoline engine—and other engines which grew out of an unusual application of that engine—were destined to become the largest revenue producers in the company's 80-year history.

Aircraft Engines for Tanks

Engineer Carl Bachle and salesman Art Wild were in on the project almost from the start. Bachle recalls that "When it was evident, as early as 1931, that the commercial aircraft market for the R-670 engine was not going to materialize into large production, Bob Insley suggested renewed efforts with the Army Ordnance Department to convince them they ought to have that engine in a military tank.

"He fastened onto an officer by the name of Capt. John K. Christmas, Chief of the Automotive Section of the Artillery Division, who came out to Detroit nearly every month to see what we had. I was assigned to be his technical contact and tried to instill in him the enthusiasm I felt for an air-cooled engine in a tank."

By the time the United States had entered the World War in 1917 only a few tank projects had been designed and most were agricultural caterpillar tractors covered by armor plate.

Later, Ford Motor Company was given a contract for 15,000 three-ton tanks but only 15 were built before the Armistice of 1918 led to cancellation of the order. This was followed by the Mark VIII Liberty but only a hundred were built. Next came the M1917, some 950 of which were built after the war.

The Tank Corps was disbanded in 1920 and it was decided the future role of the tank would be confined to support of the infantry. To continue development of light tanks it was necessary to use the cover name of "Combat Cars" because of service rivalry between the Infantry and the Cavalry.

From 1920 to 1935, only 35 new tanks were produced in the U.S. Such was the state of combat armor.

More background on early Continental/Ordnance Department cooperation came recently from Lt. Gen. Jean E. Engler, USA (Ret.), who was deeply involved in WWII tank production for the Army.

"Modern tank development," he wrote, "really began in the middle 1930s when the need for mobile armor was recognized in the changing doctrine of the Army cavalry and the specifications for a combat car were drawn up. The Ordnance Corps was assigned the design and manufacturing responsibility because of the gun mounting and armor protection which was prescribed.

"A suitable engine was a problem. Funds were scarce and no truck or tractor power plant had the capability to propel an armored vehicle with the speed and mobility desired. A start from scratch development could not be financed. The nearest thing was the adaptation of an aircraft engine. It had the horsepower, light weight, and relatively small package which were characteristics sought for. The air-cooled feature was also considered advantageous in reduced weight and vulnerability.

"Continental Motors with experience in the radial engine and in power plants for large vehicles accepted the responsibility of converting the radial aircraft engine for tank application. As a result Continental became the engine development and manufacturing agency for the Ordnance Corps throughout the 1930s. Their radial engines in a 7-cylinder version for the lighter combat vehicles (and later in a 9-cylinder

Legacy of World War I: From left—Ford 3-ton tank; the 6-ton M1917; the 40-ton Mark VIII

version from another aircraft engine design for the heavier tanks) became the power source for all United States armored vehicles until the Lend-Lease build up just before World War II".

In September 1934, the Army Ordnance Corps awarded Continental's aircraft engine division an initial $290,000 contract for engines suitable for use in combat cars and tanks but no tank models went into volume production until the outbreak of World War II.

But before the engine project got to production tank installations, the Continental R-670 aircraft engine was first tried in the Army's M1 Combat Car in 1932.* Instead of driving a propeller to pull the airplane forward, the same radial aircraft engine turned a driveshaft geared to the ground vehicle's tracks.

"The major technical problem," Bachle continued, "was how to cool the engine in the very confined area inside a tank or combat car. I thought I knew the way; and, as it turned out, it was relatively easy.

"Capt. Christmas, and there were others, saw to it that our R-670 aircraft engine was put into the new T2 and similar tank test vehicles of 1932-36. First of all, however, you had to get the cooling air inside the tank, and that was done with a fan.

"The first tank engine had a fan installed by the Army. It took 70 hp of the engine's 250 hp to drive the fan, and that was a scandal. So they turned over the whole fan idea to us.

"The point is, you've just got to have a very efficient fan. We hired a famous Harvard professor named Marks, of Marks Engineering Handbook fame, an expert on fans. I got the idea to hire him right out of his handbook.

"Any fan blade is really a wing — an aerodynamic foil just like an airplane wing. By carefully adjusting the wing and measuring the air flow we got a fan which required only 7 hp. Having done that, all of the other air-cooled engines could use a similar design. They all turned out wonderfully. That's how the air-cooled aircraft engine became a practical engine for tanks and other combat vehicles."

*NOTE:
A word about combat vehicle designations:
T stands for test vehicle; a numeral stands for the chronological design. Standardized models are designated M followed by the design number and description (as for M1 Combat Car).
Other examples: T2 means test unit of the second design. M3 Medium Tank describes the third medium tank standard model. There can also be an M3 *Light* Tank designation since its design and mission is different than that of the M3 Medium Tank.
Additional letters and numbers after M3, for example, would describe further refinements in detailed components used in the basic type.

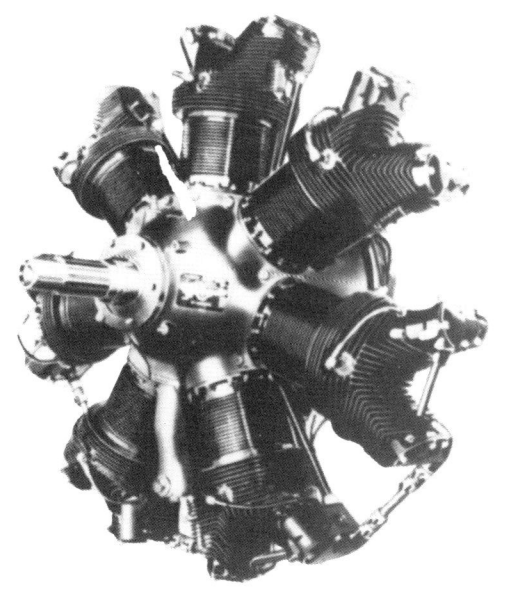

Teledyne Continental Motors

"Continental became the engine development and manufacturing agency for the Ordnance Corps"

The Continental radial engine, now designated W-670 for military use, was installed experimentally at the Army's Rock Island Arsenal in a number of combat vehicles used to test a variety of components for future tanks.

During tests at Rock Island, a column of W-670-powered light tanks stalled, all within a few hundred feet of each other. They got them started again, but next day the same thing happened. Carl Bachle was called in and diagnosed the problem as 'vapor lock,' for he saw that the fuel line between the gasoline tank and carburetor was heating up because it was too near the exhaust.

"As an experiment," he advised, "let's put in some aviation grade fuel." After that there was no trouble at all, so the Army specified that aviation grade must be used.

For tracked vehicle use, Continental's R-670 radial aircraft engine was first tried in 1932 in the Army's M1 Combat Car

National Archieves

"That wasn't necessary at all as a permanent fix," Bachle says. "All they had to do was relocate the fuel line away from the exhaust heat."

Typical of tracked vehicles with the W-670 aircraft engine was the T4 Medium Tank which was based on design of its combat car counterpart, but with the chassis strengthened to carry increased armor. Sixteen of this model, convertible to run on either wheels or tracks, were produced in 1935 and 1936. At 13½ tons, the T4 could do 38 mph on wheels; 24 mph on its tracks.

Other W-670 installations were in the T5 Medium Tank (Phase I), an enlarged version of the M2 Light Tank. (The Ordnance Corps rated the T4's Continental 7-cylinder aircraft engine at 268 hp.) In Phase III tests of this larger tank, the Wright 9-cylinder aircraft engine, then rated at 346 hp, was installed and this became the M2 Medium Tank in production. Its 9-cylinder engine was subsequently built, uprated to 400 hp and further developed by Continental for the M2A1 tank.

It was from these early light and medium tanks, many powered by Continental seven- and nine-cylinder aircraft engines, that America's World War II combat tanks were developed.

"Tank engine production in the late thirties," recalls Bachle, "was for about 100 tanks a year. Not large, but in those days every dollar of revenue was very important.

"At that time I was in charge of production as well as engineering aspects of the tank engines. Every Friday afternoon Jack Reese would come into the factory and stand beside me much of the afternoon to check how many engines we had delivered.

"That was the day the Navy inspector, assigned by the Army, came in to inspect the engines we had produced during the week. If we didn't build—and have accepted—the requisite number, the payroll for the men assigned to the job could not be met."

Installation of the Continental radial engine in lightweight tanks had been such a success, according to Bachle, that "the Army decided to have the next larger size tank also powered with a radial aircraft engine."

That decision and gathering war clouds in Europe opened up a new and still larger market for Continental's special talents.

By summer 1939, Continental was on the brink of bankruptcy and the Reconstruction Finance Corp. was snapping at Angell's heels.

There were other problems, too. The Army Air Corps was critical of Continental's slow progress with the 12-cylinder 1430 Hyper engine, which was to have been its stellar combat power plant.

Nothing Seemed to Work

Continental had plans to develop six-cylinder horizontally-opposed aircraft engines for the civilian market to complement its highly regarded four-cylinder 'flat' models but was unable to complete the development work at the time.

A series of new four-cylinder F-4124 engines for agricultural tractors was introduced and new emphasis was placed on diversification.

Continuing its role as the power plant specialist willing to customize its engines for the end uses in which they would be employed, Continental redesigned and modernized its product line to suit the needs of industrial and agricultural equipment manufacturers.

Starting with eight basic engine sizes, the line was expanded to include some 21 models of heavy duty engines, primarily for industrial use. Among these were several models for motor trucks, one marine job, and even one passenger car engine.

The company also became a subcontractor to other manufacturers to whom they supplied machined parts including crankshafts, camshafts, cylinder blocks, pistons, connecting rods, flywheels, cylinder heads, etc.

But nothing pulled the company out of the economic paralysis into which it had sunk. Sales of all products had dipped to unprecedented low levels and the company had sustained great financial losses for a whole decade.

The tremendous plants at Detroit and Muskegon were largely idle and the overhead costs were dragging the company's finances farther and farther down.

It was a time for decisive action.

James H. Ferry, Sr., primarily an investor and the company's largest stockholder found he had to assume a more active role in management decisions. Formerly a Director, he had earlier agreed

Teledyne Continental Motors

Twin-turreted M1 Combat Car which for obvious reasons was known as the "Mae West"

Larger version of the M2 Light Tank with Continental-supplied 9-cylinder aircraft engine became the M2A1 Medium Tank

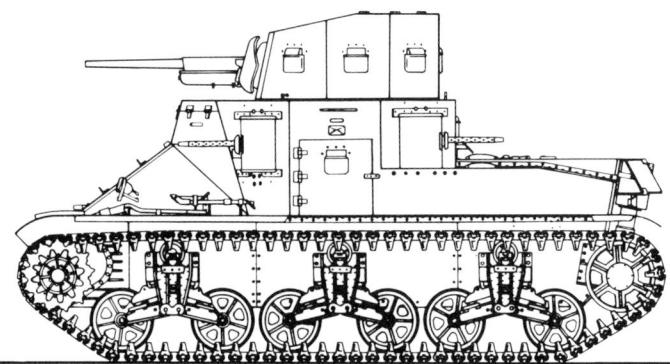

Richard P. Hunnicutt

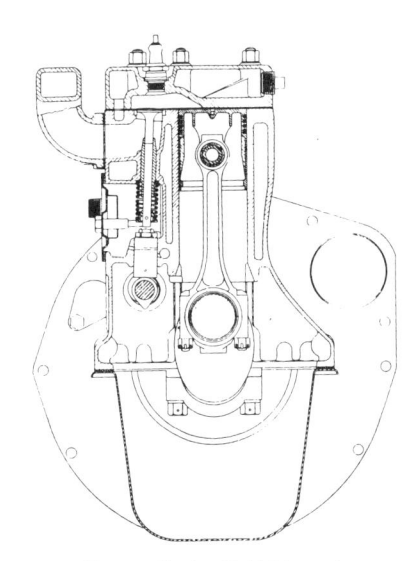

Four-cylinder F-4124 engine for agricultural tractors

Factory areas were dark and dingy as Continental turned to sub-contract work to keep plants going during the Great Depression

to also serve as Vice-President. His son, Jim Ferry, Jr., mentioned that "Father got to the age where he should have been able to take life a bit easier, but the Depression came along so he had to take a more active part than he wanted to."

Young Ferry's mother, Mrs. Mary Ferry, recalled that Roger Sherman, also an early investor, "was selling some of his stock as were some of the other directors—just taking what they could and getting out because they thought the company was going to fall apart.

"My husband said, 'I suppose I could sell everything I have and get out too, but I can't do that. There are the other stockholders to think about; people who put their hard earned savings into the company.'

"His unselfish thought in not selling at that time helped save Continental Motors."

That, and some hard decisions which had to be made about how the company was being managed, saw Continental through the crisis.

As an alternative to foreclosure, the RFC came up with a multi-point plan which offered—

* *To extend maturity of the $1,000,000 loan 4½ years to December 1944*
* *Make an additional loan of $300,000 toward $225,000 in delinquent taxes and the expense of moving machinery and equipment from Detroit to Muskegon*

The RFC's plan was contingent upon—

* *Registering and listing an additional 201,348 shares of capital stock on the New York and Detroit Stock Exchanges, of which 75,000 shares would be sold to officers, directors and key employees at $2 per share. [This left 350,000 shares unissued of the 3,000,000 authorized].*
* *Handling other sales at $2 per share through the underwriting firm of Van Alstyne, Noel & Co.*
* *Taking definite steps to close the Detroit plant and consolidate all operations at Muskegon*
* *Obtaining a $45,000 loan from the Greater Muskegon Industrial Foundation for erecting an aircraft engine test house.*

There were further stipulations from the New York Stock Exchange: The 52,875 shares purchased in those very critical times by six members of management with their personal funds could not be sold for a period of six months.

The deadline for accomplishment was set at July 28, 1939.

Angell Out; Reese In

Four days later, W. R. Angell, Sr. was out, tendering his resignation as President, Treasurer and Director, effective August 1, 1939 at a special meeting of the Board of Directors. Jack Reese, who had served as General Manager since the first of the year, was named to fill the top executive post.

James Ferry, Sr. and Angell had long been at loggerheads over the double overhead caused by maintaining both the Detroit and Muskegon plants. "It got to the point," Jim Ferry, Jr. said, "where father had to insist they close Detroit. He supported Jack Reese against Angell. That's when father put Jack in as President."

At the August first board meeting Reese saw to it that long-term employment contracts were entered into between the corporation and the executive heads of the sales, engineering and manufacturing and treasury divisions. Of five years duration, the contracts had the approval of the RFC and were, Reese said, "designed to provide stability of management."

To assist the new management in its program of increasing its operating efficiency, the consultative services of the Trundle Engineering Company of Cleveland were employed.

The board retained Angell temporarily as technical advisor, but there is no record of his further participation in company matters. In October, his son Bob—William R. Angell, Jr.—resigned as Assistant Secretary, a post which for him had been more honorary than administrative.

Bob Angell went out to the west coast where earlier in the year he and his father had organized Continental Aeronautic Corp. with father as president and son as vice president. There was no public offering of shares in the $500,000 corporation.

The Angells indicated their Burbank, California, plant would make parts for local aircraft companies and perhaps build Continental aircraft engines. After a few months ownership of the manufacturing plant, the Angells sold the facility to nearby Lockheed Aircraft Corp.

During his tenure with Continental, Angell senior served on the boards of several other companies in the automotive industry—Peerless, Lakey Foundry & Machine Co., Evans Products Corp. and others. He was also a Vice President of Hackley Union National Bank, Muskegon.

Angell remained in the Detroit area for the next decade. On a cold, rainy night in January 1950, huddled against the storm, he stepped off the sidewalk and walked in front of a transit bus in downtown Detroit. Four hours later, Angell died of a fractured skull at the age of 72.

In 1949 he had established the William R. Angell Foundation which has made many charitable contributions, often in the name of his adopted son, Lieut. Chester Angell, who was killed on a bombing mission in the Mediterranean during WW II.

One of the Foundation's holdings was title to most of North Manitou Island where Angell and other executives maintained a hunting lodge. The island had only 12 permanent residents, but boasted 1200 deer and 5000 cherry trees. The lodge burned to the ground in 1953.

Angell was described as austere, aloof, reserved, non-communicative. Carl Bachle, as a then junior member of the firm, said "I knew him and his son very well but it was always 'Mister' Angell for senior but 'Bob' for junior."

Jim Ferry, Jr., recalls that "Mister Angell wanted very much to manufacture an automobile: it was almost like a hang-up with him. He could see the vertical integration through which the industry was going and figured that its own car was

C. REESE

Reese Heads Continental

Continental Motors Corp. last week announced the election of C. Reese as president of the company succeeding W. R. Angell, who resigned as president, treasurer and director.

perhaps the way out for Continental. It wasn't."

In large measure, Angell was a victim of the Depression and of physical plant facilities of far larger capacity than any business volume which could reasonably be expected under those economic conditions.

In February 1930, W. R. Angell could not have chosen a less opportune time to assume the presidency of Continental Motors. In August 1939, Jack Reese could not have chosen a more propitious time to assume management responsibility.

A month to the day after Reese was named President, Germany invaded Poland igniting the flames of World War II. On September 3, Britain and France declared war on Germany.

After declaring that the United States was not neutral in thought, President Franklin D. Roosevelt did remind the country that it must remain neutral in policy. But to facilitate action if necessary, the President on September 8 declared a limited emergency.

Two months later the Arms Embargo Act was repealed, authorizing trade with belligerents friendly to the U.S.

The unprecedented requirement for huge military production by the "arsenal of democracy" would soon push Continental to the limit of its capacity to build engines. And Jack Reese was at the helm.

Technical Note

In a **spark-ignition engine,** fuel and air are injected into the cylinders through a carburetor. As the piston comes up in compression it heats the mixture, but not enough to ignite the fuel. A spark plug has to start the explosion and continue to provide ignition.

In a **diesel compression-ignition engine,** you drag nothing but air into the cylinder. The piston comes up and compresses the air that's trapped. Then fuel is injected under high pressure through a fuel injection nozzle. The air is now so hot from compression that once combustion starts the fuel burns as fast as it is squirted in. It's not the flash point that counts, but the temperature of the air.

With spark-ignition, the fuel-air mixture is compressed, say, eight-to-one. That gets you a temperature of around 500 degrees Fahrenheit; not enough to cause an explosion. In the diesel, however, compression is 14-to-one. That gets you up around 900 degrees. You squirt some fuel into that temperature and it's going to burn right away. But because of the high pressure in the cylinders, diesel engines require heavier construction than spark-ignition engines.

In starting a diesel auto engine, heated fuel or a glow plug that gets red hot in the combustion chamber gives the initial push to ignite the fuel. After that, the engine is on its own.

The basic difference between diesel and gasoline is volatility. Gasoline is more volatile. Any fuel you burn is a combination of light and heavy. Gasoline is mostly light; diesel is mostly heavy.

—Carl F. Bachle, 1982

THE WAR YEARS
(1940-1945)

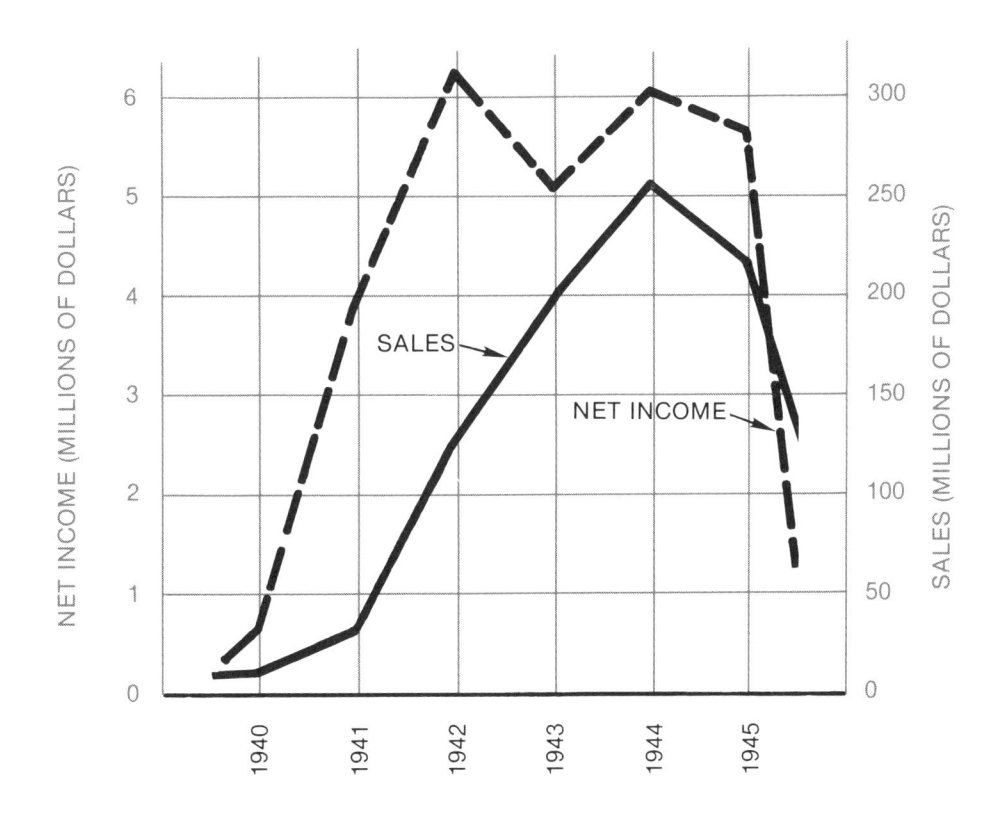

With the aid of huge World War II orders for aircraft engines to provide power for combat tanks, Jack Reese and his "team" get the company back on its feet.

Pages 85 to 113

1940-1945

A Self-Made Man	85
The Turn Around	86
Continental Aviation & Engineering	86
British Orders for Tank Engines	87
Detroit Production Capability 'Saved'	88
Germans, Too, Liked W-670 Engines	89
Arsenal of Democracy	90
Wartime Tank Production	91
Overseas Tech Reps	92
Salt Water Solution	94
Aircraft Engines for Aircraft	96
Record-Setting Flights	96
Wartime Piper Cubs	98
Powering the Invasion Fleet	98
Getty Street Plant	100
Hyper Engine for Pursuit Planes	101
P&W R-1340 Engines	102
Rolls-Royce Merlins	102
Relations With Employees	104
Young Ferry Gets Involved	105
Sales Hit Peak in '44	106
Post-War Planning	107
Wisconsin Motor Corp. Acquisition	108
Gray Marine Motor Acquisition	109
Wisconsin Since 1909	110
Gray Marine Since 1906	112

A Remarkable Fellow

If any man put his own stamp on Continental Motors, that man was Clarence J. (Jack) Reese. For the quarter-century which included WW II and the Korean War, Jack and his "team" were the dominant factors in the company's growth and acceptance as a leading supplier of highly sophisticated engines to the government, to industry and to agriculture.

A Self-Made Man

One who knew Jack well was Jim Ferry, Jr., still in his twenties at the time his father insisted that Reese replace Angell as president and try to improve the company's dismal prospects. Reese, then 38, was only 15 years young Ferry's senior.

"Jack grew up in Muncie, Indiana, where he was born August 25, 1900 and attended public schools. He was orphaned by an accident or epidemic and was raised by an uncle who farmed there. He was a natural leader, putting himself through Muncie Normal School with the proceeds of a few acres of pop-corn he farmed.

"When it came time for Jack to leave and make his way in life, his uncle slipped him $50 on the railroad platform as he left for Pittsburgh looking for work in the steel mills. He came up from that."

Reese's earliest jobs were in Youngstown, Ohio, first as a stockkeeper and machine shop apprentice in a rubber company; then later with Youngstown Sheet and Tube Company as a production planner. For four years, 1917-1921, he was with the Glascock Body Co. of Muncie as a salesman.

For the next two years he was with Chevrolet Motor Co. in the production and plant engineering departments. Meanwhile Jack was taking correspondence courses in industrial management. Soon he was purchasing agent for Hayes-Hunt Body Co., of Elizabeth, New Jersey. It was there that future Continental top sales executive Art Wild first met him.

Having been close to the Durant organization, Reese moved to Michigan in 1927 after it folded and later became purchasing agent of the successor DeVaux-Hall Motor Co. in Grand Rapids. When DeVaux-Hall owed Continental so much money it was literally forced into the automobile business in 1932, Reese was part of the "package" and became Continental's purchasing agent. While still with DeVaux-Hall, Reese married Bessie Eberly.

"My father," Jim Ferry remembers, "always marveled that a man without a college education would be so well educated. Jack had a broad comprehension of all aspects of every problem and could evaluate all factors out of his own knowledge.

"He could sense and use the meaning of words as well as anyone I've ever seen or met. He was a remarkable fellow. I never met a more educated man than Jack. And in Bessie (Pat) he had a perfectly swell wife who balanced everything right along."

While coming up through the ranks at Continental, recalls Art Wild, "Jack was a hell raiser. We'd go out at night with our wives and we'd probably end up with half the nightclub chorus at our table.

"But after Jack became president, things changed. He shut off everything—booze, cigars, carousing around—and applied himself exclusively to work.

"After he gave up drinking and smoking, he became a total workaholic. He had no home life. He had no social life. Just work. But he did become addicted to flying.

"We were all at our house one night playing poker. Jim Fornasero, one of our pilots was there, because he was supposed to take Jack the next day to North Manitou Island to negotiate for hunting rights.

"Jack had never flown before, and we were needling the hell out of him. Well, you'd have had to flown a lot and landed at the Manitou strip in the cherry orchard to understand why none of us felt really comfortable landing there. And this was to be Jack's first flight.

"Believe it or not, after that trip Jack got addicted to flying. He just loved it. Weather didn't bother him a bit although our pilots often had to override him. His enthusiasm was the most radical change from not wanting to fly to being the most avid aviation person you ever saw.

"But later it was utterly impossible to get him to fly to Europe. He just would not fly over the ocean."

It was a rare occasion to find Jack Reese not wearing his hat. It didn't matter whether it was indoors or out. "He always wore a hat" Jim Ferry told us, "at every meeting where I was, and the reason was that in the steel mills at Youngstown and elsewhere the foreman always wore a hat. It was the custom in those days, and he kept to it all his life."

Carl Bachle observed that "the hat became such a trademark that soon Jack kept it on on purpose."

By 1939, as the national economy was getting back on its feet, Jack Reese and his sales people went to work trying to get some orders back on the company's books. Meanwhile, only the Muskegon plant was in production, and there employment had dwindled to 700 men working a six-hour shift five days a week.

The Turn Around

By vigorous cost cutting and aggressive selling, Reese was developing a lean, hard-working group. Within three months of taking over—and before the impact of defense production—the "Reese team" had drummed up $5 million worth of new engine contracts. But before those orders could begin to produce income, there were payrolls to be met.

Employees were paid bi-weekly and there often was not enough cash on hand to meet the payroll. Reese took the matter into his own hands.

"Every other Friday," Jim Ferry, Jr. related, "Jack would gather all the accounts receivable billings together and drive the six hours to Chicago, some two-hundred-plus miles from Muskegon. In Chicago he would visit the factoring firm of Walter E. Heller & Company which would lend Continental funds to meet the payroll, accepting the accounts receivable as security for the loan.

"That's how tough things were when Jack took over."

The company's 1939 fiscal year ended just three months after Reese was named president. On 12-months sales of $7,256,648, the company had a net loss of $215,165. The company's cash position had also improved through recent sale for $566,542 of 152,651 shares in an issue of 350,000 shares authorized by the Securities and Exchange Commission.

As a result of the RFC's requirement that officers and directors increase their proprietary interest in the company by purchasing additional shares, the following ownerships by nominees for directors in 1940 were reported: J. H. Ferry, 71,631 shares; B. F. Tobin, Jr., 25,888; Clarence Reese, 19,187; L. P. Kalb, 2,000; and Leslie L. Vivian, a partner in the Fenner & Beane brokerage firm of New York, 1,000 shares.

In the first quarter of the new fiscal year, Reese got operations into the black at long last. For the three months ended January 31, 1940, Continental Motors reported a net profit of $94,875. For the full year, fiscal 1940, earnings were $663,814 on sales which had increased 50 percent to $10,908,460. And the backlog of unfilled orders was a very substantial $60 million.

Things were beginning to turn around.

Continental faced a serious problem in its relations with the Army because of slow progress of the IV-1430 liquid-cooled Hyper engine which it needed for new pursuit planes then in the design stage. Much of the problem was caused by W. R. Angell's foot-dragging as explained by Art Wild:

Continental Aviation & Engineering

"The Air Corps was very unhappy with our progress and felt—and I think with some justice—that Angell wasn't particularly interested in it because the project certainly wasn't getting the kind of push it really needed.

"That was a key situation Reese had to face when he came in as president.

"Jack's solution was to separate the project entirely from other company operations and set it up as a separate entity in a subsidiary company."

On May 13, 1940, Continental Aviation and Engineering Corp. was incorporated for the purpose of acquiring all of Continental Motors' business in connection with the development of aircraft-type engines of over 500 horsepower. That description fit the '1430' engine.

From the parent company, the new corporation—soon to be identified as CAE—acquired property, plant and equipment at the Kercheval Avenue plant in Detroit plus patents and engineering data required for its operations.

In exchange for these assets, Continental Motors acquired 270,000 CAE shares valued in excess of their $1 par value. Through an underwriter, the public purchased 260,000 CAE shares. Thus, Continental Motors had controlling interest in CAE, had raised additional working capital

ARTHUR WILD
Key contact with the military services, Art Wild was also a central figure in the new Continental Aviation and Engineering subsidiary

of approximately $425,000 for its subsidiary through sale of shares to the public, and had given the '1430' engine project priority attention by setting it up in a separate entity.

The public offering of CAE stock was handled through the New York investment firm of Van Alstyne, Noel & Co., and David Van Alstyne, Jr. became a member of the CAE board of directors. According to Jim Ferry, Jr., Dave Van Alstyne placed most of the public stock with Armin Schlesinger, a Milwaukee investor.

Jack Reese made clear the company's position. "It is intended," he wrote, "that Continental Motors Corp. will remain at all times the controlling stockholder."

Art Wild was placed on the CAE board of directors. He also served the subsidiary as a Vice-President, as did Carl Bachle and James W. Kinnucan.

"Jimmie" Kinnucan had joined Continental Motors in 1930 as a research engineer, moving to the Aircraft Division's Dayton office three years later to work on the 'Hyper' cylinder and '1430' engine. When named Engineering Vice President of CAE, Kinnucan was serving as Chief Engineer of the Aircraft Division.

The Continental W-670 radial aircraft engine having been proven satisfactory for use in light tanks, Army Ordnance decided as Bachle reported, "to also make the next larger size tank with a radial engine.

British Orders for Tank Engines

"But we didn't have one of enough power. The most likely engine for that tank was being made by Wright Aeronautical, so the Army installed one of Wright's R-975 nine-cylinder aircraft engines in the T5 tank during its Phase III testing.

"It worked just like the W-670 we had pioneered in the light tanks. Later when it came to production for installation in M3 Medium Tanks, Wright Aeronautical had other fish to fry, so the R-975 was farmed out to Continental under contracts direct with the Army."

When Congress repealed the Arms Embargo Act in November 1939, Great Britain was able to open negotiations with American defense firms for war material. One of their urgent needs was combat tanks, and the engines to power them.

Art Wild was Continental's principal contact with Defense Department officials in Washington. "They suggested," he recalls, "that we go and talk to the British Purchasing Commission which was interested in the R-975 engine. Michael Dewar headed tank procurement for that Commission and was assisted by Ian MacGregor." Through him contracts between Continental and the British Purchasing Commission for production of the engines were negotiated by a third party.

"That order," Jim Ferry, Jr. reported, "was for $44 million. I remember the amount because we were all sitting around wondering how much 5% of $44 million was—that was what the agent who put the deal together was to get. That's the way the initial business with the British was done." [This was probably the same export agent referred to in the 1942 Annual Report as suing Continental for sales commissions allegedly due on business obtained by the Corporation after expiration of his contract.]

With war conditions abroad worsening, President Roosevelt in May 1940 proposed production of 50,000 airplanes annually by American industry. To speed the total war production effort, William S. Knudsen, President of General Motors, was asked in August to head the National Defense Advisory Commission.

America was arming for defense, not war; but the British were already at war, so coordination of the war materiel needs of the two countries was essential.

Nazi Panzer tactics in Poland and elsewhere in Europe had upset traditional concepts of tank warfare. Medium tanks, especially, had to be completely redesigned to provide more armor and firepower.

Knudsen immediately called U.S. and British representatives to meet with him

For Army Ordnance, Continental installed the R-975 radial aircraft engine in the T5 tank, then went into mass production of the engine for British tanks

Continental-powered M3 Medium Tanks in production at Chrysler-operated Detroit Tank Arsenal in November 1941 before U.S. entered the war.

In honor of Michael Dewar, head of the British Tank Mission, this Continental-powered M4A1 Sherman was among hundreds built at Lima Locomotive Works under British contracts.

and key production experts of the auto and other major American industries. The British certainly needed help, but the U.S. also needed more equipment for its own armored divisions.

Ordnance experts from both countries came to agreement on a common medium tank design—a modified version of the 25-ton Continental-powered M3 "General Lee" tank. By the British, it would be called the "General Grant", predecessor of the M4 "Sherman" tank. (The M3 Light Tank already in production was known as the "General Stuart" by the British and saw early action in North Africa.)

Dewar, head of the British Tank Mission, said his country needed a thousand tanks a month including M4 Medium Tanks, most of which would have to come from the United States. Knudsen turned to his friend and competitor, K. T. Keller, President of Chrysler, to head tank production and start construction of the huge Chrysler-operated Detroit Tank Arsenal to build the American tanks.

For the engines Knudsen turned to an old associate from the days when he was Vice President of Chevrolet. His choice—Jack Reese of Continental Motors, which would build most of the R-975 engines for both British and American tanks.

"Jack and Bill Knudsen were friends," observed Carl Bachle, "from their days together at Chevrolet, and they had confidence in each other. I suspect that if it hadn't been for Jack, the government might have gotten others into the act. I'm sure their friendship was an important factor in Continental getting the tank business."

Four days after signing a contract on September 9, 1940 to build engines at the rate of 200 a month by October 1941, Reese was asked to step up that delivery rate.

Arthur Purvis, head of the British Purchasing Commission, pointed out he needed 400 engines a month from the U.S. Reese agreed that Continental would undertake production of additional engines.

Letters approving the Continental orders were unique. Undersecretary of War Robert P. Patterson wrote to Knudsen and to Emil Schram, who succeeded Jesse H. Jones as head of the Reconstruction Finance Corp.:

> The creation of manufacturing capacity capable of producing twenty medium tank engines per day by Continental Motors Corporation of Detroit, Michigan is essential to the national defense of the United States.

The letter was said to be the first official recognition that it was important to the U.S. that Britain continue the war against the Axis. It also recognized the need to build up American war potential in advance of our own requirements.

By October 1, 1940, Continental had national defense orders totaling $26.7 million from the U.S. Government. Of this, $19.4 million was for tank engines; $7.3 million for radial aircraft engines for Army and Navy military training planes. All but $1 million of the orders were for work at Muskegon where employment had risen to 2500 workers.

Production of M3 medium tanks continued until August 1942, reaching a combined total of 5,236 British General Grant and U.S. General Lee models powered by Continental engines.

As an economy measure, Continental's directors in November 1938 had authorized the sale of the virtually unused Detroit plant, whose overhead expenses—taxes, depreciation, maintenance and insurance—were further hurting the company's deteriorating financial condition.

Detroit Production Capability 'Saved'

Of necessity, the sale would have to be approved by the RFC which held the mortgage on all Continental properties. After Reese took over as president it was decided to submit the proposed sale to stockholders for approval. Then, upon consolidation of operations at Muskegon, late in 1939, the Detroit plant was offered for sale at public auction.

James H. Ferry, Sr., went over to Detroit from his Glencoe, Illinois, home for a directors meeting. According to Ferry's wife, Mary, "They were going to meet someone from St. Louis, I believe, who was interested in buying the plant. Later it came out that they bid $574,000 for the plant. At my husband's insistence the bid was turned down as too low.

"Mr. Ferry came home very low spirited because they had not sold the Detroit plant. When he told me how he felt I said, 'Because you were offered such a ridiculously low price, you're not supposed to sell it. You should keep it; you may yet need it. Otherwise, it wouldn't have turned out this way.'

"He felt so relieved he said, 'I wish you'd tell Jack Reese about that.' So immediately we called up Jack, and I told him exactly how I felt.

"It wasn't too long after that, Continental Motors was called upon to produce tank engines for Great Britain and for our own government. If they'd sold the Detroit plant, they wouldn't have had the facilities or the chance to help the United States, and the war effort.

"Later on I went to Muskegon with Mr. Ferry for a directors' meeting. We were having dinner at the Occidental Hotel and Jack Reese said to me, 'You know, Mrs. Ferry, without your husband we wouldn't have any Continental Motors today!'"

Unfortunately, within months, Continental Motors did not have James H. Ferry, Sr. Following a serious fall while away on a fishing trip, he died on the operating table August 21, 1940. Jack Reese had lost his friend and sponsor. Of Ferry, he paid tribute in the 1940 Annual Report to Stockholders:

> His willingness to make heavy personal sacrifices during the dark moments of the corporation's history, and his unwavering faith in its future, make his loss keenly felt by all who worked with him.

First Continental products into combat overseas were W-670 tank engines manufactured at Muskegon for 12-ton M3 Light Tanks. Since 1938 the air-cooled radial power plant had been used in most American light tanks and in the many test models which were used in developing new combat equipment.

Germans, Too, Liked W-670 Engines

"American equipment was on the high seas," Carl Bachle recalls, "even as Franklin Roosevelt told the country we were not going to get into the war. Combat had spread to North Africa where Britain's remaining armored division had been sent to Egypt. The British needed help and had turned to America for more tanks. We, too, needed more armor."

JAMES H. FERRY, SR.
Serving Continental for nearly four decades, Ferry's initial confidence and investment got the company off to a good start. His willingness to make heavy personal sacrifices during the corporation's darkest moments assured its readiness to meet the production challenges of World War II

Bachle followed the service record of the W-670 engines because "I had been training these fellows on how to take care of the engines. In North Africa they were the most reliable engines on the battlefield. They were so reliable that when the Germans captured any tanks they made use of our engines in their own tanks. They even wrote a service manual in German for their maintenance people.

"The early tanks were light and too small and in time went out of production in favor of the later, larger M4 General Shermans powered by the R-975 engine."

As the war progressed, Continental-built R-975 tank engines of 420 hp rating replaced the earlier 250 hp W-670 for new medium tanks and tank destroyers as they went into production. The W-670 engine was then switched over to power LVT (Landing Vehicle, Tracked) amphibian tanks which later led the invasion forces on the beaches of the South Pacific.

By mid-1942, U.S. First Armored Division was training with Continental-powered M3 tanks in Northern Ireland

Richard P. Hunnicutt

General Motors

Lieut. Col. Jean E. Engler, Commanding Officer, supervised tests of R-975-powered tanks at Desert Test Proving Ground in California

Fortune was smiling on Continental Motors when directors rejected as too low the bid for its half million square foot Detroit factory. That decision nicely coincided with the British order and subsequent U.S. Government contracts for R-975 air-cooled engines to be used in Anglo-American M4 Sherman Medium Tanks.

Arsenal of Democracy

November 15, 1940 saw start of an $8 million top-to-bottom renovation and retooling of the Jefferson Avenue plant, which had been idle for the past year. All of the new machinery, equipment and facilities were to be provided by the Defense Plant Corp. and the completely modernized plant laid out for the most advanced mass production methods. Between 3000 and 5000 workers would be required.

Meanwhile Muskegon would be producing the 670 series aircraft engines for tanks and training planes and the A-65 engine for light military and commercial planes. In October alone Muskegon had produced 400 lightplane engines and 200 of the larger radials.

Lend-Lease legislation, primarily intended to aid Great Britain, had passed Congress in March, 1941. Production was being stepped up in America's Arsenal of Democracy. Continental received a new $40 million order for more than 9000 tank engines.

In record time, seven months, R-975 engines began coming from the Continental production line, most of them scheduled to go to the new Chrysler-operated Tank Arsenal in Detroit for installation in M3 Medium Tanks, and later in M4 Shermans which began coming off production lines in February 1942.

"The Army Ordnance Corps," Art Wild related, "moved bodily into Detroit and took over the Union-Guardian Building. They set up the Detroit Tank-Automotive Center, supervised contracts with engine builders and other suppliers and had other liaison facilities in the auto capital. It put them within reach of all their major suppliers and made the job easier for all of us."

One of the key Ordnance officers then was John K. Christmas, who helped get radial aircraft engines into tanks in the early thirties, and had recently been promoted to Brigadier General and Chief of Field Service Operations.

Another was 34-year-old Lieut. Col. Jean E. Engler, Commanding Officer of the Desert Test Proving Ground at El Centro, California. These extensive tests of R-975-powered tanks were conducted to secure the best air flow and maximum cooling in desert heat and operating conditions which "raised more dust than a Texas cattle stampede."

"Wright Aeronautical," Wild continued, "which had designed the R-975, had to concentrate on aircraft applications of that engine. At Continental we improved the basic engine and adapted it, as we had the W-670, for use in 30-ton M4 Sherman tanks since we had already solved the engine cooling problem."

Among the deadliest weapons powered by the R-975 engine was the huge, highly mobile M12 "Long Tom" self-propelled gun mounting a 155 mm. gun capable of knocking out or even sinking a heavy cruiser with a 95-pound projectile at a ten-mile range. Earlier the M3 Grant with 75 mm. gun had a remarkable success in combat in North Africa.

In line with an Armored Force recommendation of September 1941, the Ordnance Corps had contracted for Guiberson diesel engines for installation in as many medium tanks as possible. On the strength of that recommendation an entire new government-owned plant had been built at Garland, near Dallas, Texas.

But in February 1942, General Jacob L. Devers, Chief of the Armored Force, wrote to General Brehon Somervell, Commanding General, Services of Supply:

Gen. Jean E. Engler

Tank tests in California desert "raised more dust than a Texas cattle stampede"

90

In view of our past experience, and the present world situation as to the supply of diesel fuel, the Armored Force does not desire any type Guiberson radial diesel engines. Existing facilities should be utilized to increase the production of other standard types of tank engines.

Obviously, Continental's Detroit plant alone could not produce all the R-975 engines required. At Ordnance Corps request, Continental in September 1942 leased from the Defense Plant Corp. the Garland facility which had to be almost completely re-tooled for production of R-975 tank engines.

Several months were required before full production of engines and parts was achieved in this satellite plant which was placed under the direction of B. F. Tobin, Jr.

Glowing reports of Continental tank engines came from the British and from U.S. procurement and production officers who were well aware their reliability played a key role in General Erwin Rommel's defeat in North Africa and many subsequent engagements in Italy, France and Germany.

Wartime Tank Production

Colonel Joseph M. Colby, Chief of the Army Ordnance Development Section, who had conducted a survey of North African operations, called the American M3 and M4 tanks "the mainstay of British Eighth Army forces in the drive across Libya at the critical period when it was a case of stopping the Germans or risking loss of the war.

"In ten days of battle," said Col. Colby, "the percentage of U.S. tanks in a single brigade rose from 36 to 71. They carried the show from Tobruk to El Agheila [November-December 1942] through 32 consecutive days of fighting.

"The Continental engines received no pampering. They received gasoline and oil if the latter was available, and there were only 12 mechanical failures. Forty-eight mechanical casualties as a result of the fighting were restored to duty through service right in the field, since these engines can be pulled out and repaired under ordinary field conditions."

Outspoken Bachle held a somewhat different view, perhaps more realistic: "The M4 was a lousy tank but it was the only thing we had in quantity production and they made good use of it. The Army used to say they didn't care if it was inferior to the German tanks; all they wanted was more of them.

"Total wartime tank engine production was way beyond the capacity of Continental alone so the Army got everybody they possibly could into the act—Ford, Chrysler, General Motors. Everybody was producing tank engines."

While the R-975 did a commendable job, Lt. Col. Engler, by then an assistant to Col. Colby in Tank-Automotive Research and Development, recalled that "the radial aircraft type engine was not the ideal either from a design or maintenance standpoint. Broadly speaking, from an Ordnance point of view, the result was a confused effort and a jump off in many directions at once.

"Continental increased its engine production many-fold for the M4 and M4A1 model Shermans, the standard U.S. Army Medium Tank until 1943 when the Ford GAA 8-cylinder "V" engine, modified from an experimental V-12 aircraft engine, became available in the M4A3 model.

"Chrysler offered the approach of using a standard high-volume automobile engine and banking five 6-cylinder engines to get the horsepower needed. This became the M4A4 and was used primarily by the British. [Some 7500 Chrysler-powered Shermans were built].

"The Continental, Chrysler and Ford tank engines were all gasoline fueled. The National Petroleum Board had decreed that all U.S. ground equipment would use gasoline. This was based on their concern that fuel for aircraft would need the refinery capacity that might otherwise be utilized for diesel fuel. [There was also the problem of a duplicate supply system if both gasoline and diesel fuels were needed in combat zones].

"General Motors, however, paired two 6-cylinder two-stroke diesels as a power plant for the M4A2 which was used primarily by the Russians. They liked it because their other tanks were diesel powered."

Richard P. Hunnicutt

Red Seal Magazine

Col. Joseph M. Colby, a key figure in Ordnance Corps policy and engineering, provided analysis of tank combat in North Africa

British General Grant M3 tank with typical desert stowage during the North African campaign

91

First deliveries of Continental-built Ford-designed 500 hp liquid-cooled V-8 engines were for M4A3 versions of the Sherman tank

Red Seal Magazine

Sketch by Armada International shows installation of Continental R-975 air-cooled radial aircraft engine in Sherman tank as a wartime expedient

Courtesy ARMADA International

In late 1942, the M4 Sherman tanks, supporting and replacing M3s, began to arrive in North Africa in huge quantities. With the end of fighting there, the Continental-powered M4 and M4A1 Shermans became the standard tanks used in the Italian campaign. Thereafter Shermans appeared in actions elsewhere throughout Europe and on almost every major battlefield of WW II.

As the 500 hp Ford GAA engine for the M4A3 series of Sherman tanks began to be available, a second production source was needed and again Continental was asked by Army Ordnance to take on the added task.

About one-third of the Detroit plant, which was still in production of the R-975 radial engine and its spare parts, was tooled up in the Fall of 1944 to build the Ford liquid-cooled V-eight engine.

Production support came from the Garland (Dallas) plant which was responsible for connecting rods, pistons and cylinder sleeves; Muskegon provided crankshafts and camshafts. Additional production work, assembly and tests were done at three Detroit locations: the Jefferson, Bellevue and Boulevard plants.

Production of the GAA engine started in February 1945 with first deliveries coming in July, by which time the war in Europe was over.

The logistics problem of having so many different engines in production for many different tanks and combat vehicles was overwhelming. In time this led to a far simpler approach and a meaningful standardization program.

In support of its R-975 production program, Continental conducted engine operation and maintenance training programs for Army Ordnance personnel who would be going overseas. They were in turn followed overseas by Continental employees, usually test engineers, who became civilian technical advisers assigned to combat groups.

Overseas Tech Reps

As the war progressed, Continental opened a re-manufacturing facility at Detroit to rebuild engines which could then be shipped back to the front. In addition a large parts program was initiated to keep overseas service and maintenance depots supplied with replacement parts.

Starting in 1942, Continental service representatives began going overseas. John (Bud) Longnecker put in the longest uninterrupted period of service abroad, commuting back and forth across the Mediterranean between Africa and Italy. One crossing, interrupted by German U-boats which sank several ships in the convoy, required 17 days for the safe crossing.

Longnecker trained and supervised Army maintenance personnel on both sides of "Mussolini's lake." When the M18 "Hellcat" tank destroyers—Buick-built and Continental-powered—appeared in Italy in April 1944 he assisted maintenance units assigned to the support of armored troops on the Anzio beachhead. That done, he helped set up an engine repair line at Naples, then returned to North Africa at the request of the French.

CMC test engineer John L. Edrington was assigned to General Patton's Third Army in Germany. He and his Buick technical observer counterpart, E. E. Purcell, accompanied by the Army battalion commander and his driver, found themselves ahead of their own troops in pursuit of retreating Germans.

They decided to get a good night's sleep in a house in a deserted village only to wake up the next morning captives of the Germans.

"We were prisoners for five days," Edrington said, "and away from our unit seven days. As we had moved out of one village, our own troops were coming in the opposite side. It looked like we might be wiped out by the M18 'Hellcats' we had been working so hard to maintain. We walked perhaps 120 miles during the five days we were prisoners before we got back to our own units."

The experiences of Longnecker and Edrington were typical of the wartime assignments carried out by Continental tech reps. Others included Bill Hayes in North Africa, Al Ohlfest in Germany, Earl Bayard in England and India, and Lawrence Cass in Hawaii.

Employees who had left the company for military service abroad also reported back to the company. R. E. Bowman, a Navy Seabee master mechanic who had been a production foreman, wrote that "I landed on the Normandy beach on D-Day and came through safely.

"The 'rhino ferries', which we Seabees built and operated, transported many M4 Medium Tanks from ship to beachhead, and I saw and examined many Continental-built 975s in them.

"The performance of these tanks was marvelous. Never a fault or a misfire. The arrival of tank armament with such dependable engines was often referred to as the stuff that saved the day. I have also seen many replacement engines in their big black boxes labeled 'Continental' arrive safely over here. I know other service men appreciate the workmanship which I personally know is being given to the building and testing of these engines."

Allied as well as U.S. military officials were regular visitors to the Detroit plant to check production and to report on overseas combat operations.

One such visitor was Maj. Gen. F. F. Worthington of the Canadian Army, whose Continental escorts on a plant tour included Lewis Kalb, Art Wild, Bob Insley and Carl Bachle.

"Ever since the African campaign," General Worthington reported, "the American tanks powered with your engines have been favorites with our men. [The Canadian M3 version was the "Ram" cruiser tank.] They have done, and are still

Lieut. Gen. George S. Patton, famed commander of the Third Army, inspects R-975 tank engine (left) during armored sweep to the Rhine. At right, "Old Blood and Guts" poses in front of an M3 light tank.

John L. Edrington, CMC tech rep, looks over group of rugged M18 "Hellcat" tank destroyers. Edrington had a close call after capture by German soldiers

CMC worker Alex Saetta in crankcase department explains tank engine work to Canadian General F. F. Worthington under watchful eye of Lewis P. Kalb, Executive Vice-President in charge of Engineering and Manufacturing

ALL IN THE CMC FAMILY

CMC-Powered Service Unit Aids CMC-Powered Tank

Red Seal Magazine

Somewhere in Sicily, an R-975 engine is hoisted from its tank by a Continental-powered Ward-LaFrance field service unit

doing, a great job in Italy. Now they are in France too, stopping the best the enemy can throw against them. They are figuring very importantly in the allies' steady advance in Europe.

"One of our most urgent needs now is for replacements, both of finished equipment and of parts. A steady flow of repaired engines is essential to victory."

Jack Reese, at least vicariously, got a taste of combat operations when visiting Camp Hood in Texas in September 1944. Of special interest was the M18 Hellcat Tank Destroyer whose Detroit-built radial engine gave it a speed up to 55 miles an hour.

In the revived Red Seal Magazine (which had not been published since the late twenties), Reese wrote:

"Under conditions much like war we watched the Hellcat fire on disappearing targets—tank silhouettes bobbing up at various ranges—2500 yards, 5000 yards, 8500 yards. The crew of five, working as one man, sent ten of the big 76 mm. shells screaming at the targets in just 15 seconds.

"One Hellcat crew fired on the distant target first, and caught hell from the General. 'You can't do that,' he protested. 'In real combat you'd all be dead right now! Pick off the nearest ones first. Get 'em before they get you. Then take the others in their turn. First things first!'"

Reese also used the occasion to remind Continental employees that while the war was going well, it was far from over. "If fast-lengthening casualty lists mean anything, nothing could be further from actual fact. The increase in our own plant honor roll each month hardly squares with the theory that victory is in the bag."

Within a month, the first artillery shell fired into Germany left the muzzle of a self-propelled Continental-powered M12 'Long Tom' gun.

"It was a tense moment," said James Cassidy, NBC reporter, "as the crews of four Long Toms brought their sights into line. On the command to fire, the earth shook and the air was torn by the stupendous concussion of the big guns. The first shell, fired 20,000 yards into fortress Germany, was followed by 19 more, each weighing nearly 100 pounds." The date was September 10, 1944. The location, near the Belgian-German border.

[The Long Tom gun on one occasion fired special shells, filled with blood plasma,

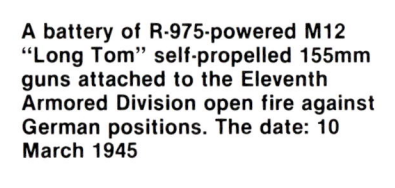

Richard P. Hunnicutt

A battery of R-975-powered M12 "Long Tom" self-propelled 155mm guns attached to the Eleventh Armored Division open fire against German positions. The date: 10 March 1945

94

morphine and sulfa drugs, to an American batallion fighting behind German lines in France.]

VE-Day—Victory in Europe—came eight months later, May 8, 1945. The General Sherman had been produced in greater numbers than any U.S. tank before or since; and from 1941 to 1945, Continental produced 54,104 of the R-975 tank engines.

In all, the United States built 88,410 tanks, most of them Shermans, between 1940 and 1945 vs. 24,800 by the British and 24,360 by the Germans.

As the war in the Pacific against Japan heated up, the seven-cylinder W-670 aircraft engines were put to a new use—this time to power LVT tracked landing vehicles.

Salt Water Solution

Variously nicknamed, "Water Buffaloes" and "Alligators", these amphibian tanks could cross swamps, reefs and lakes and knock over six-inch trees like matchsticks. They were carried aboard ship and launched overside with a full complement of armed men for an invasion force.

"We learned a lot," Carl Bachle says, "when we first installed an air-cooled aircraft engine in the cramped space of a tank. We learned more when we installed it in heavy duty seagoing craft where salt water was expected to be a serious problem.

"One of the oddities was that the salt water would condense on the cooling fins and block up the barrel with salt, but fortunately salt did not accumulate on the heads. When it became solid in the fins it didn't interfere with the cooling at all."

First-hand reports came in from Continental field service representatives. One on Okinawa wrote that "I've seen some of the Continental-powered amphibious tanks carry out wounded, and they sure do a good job. One driver I talked to told me his tank had over 500 hours and the motor was still in good shape. Keep up the good work. I hope to be back at my old job in Detroit as soon as Japan is defeated."

From a Navy commander on the scene came word that "The LVT was one of the Navy's best assets in the Iwo Jima invasion. Due to heavy surf, cluttered beaches and concentrated enemy fire, the amphibian tractors had to take over much of the work of the light personnel boats in getting the Marines ashore.

"Only tracked vehicles like the LVTs could make headway on the volcanic ash beaches in hauling weapons and equipment to support the landings.

"Many of the amphibian tractors were destroyed in action. They must be replaced with all possible speed for future assaults."

By war's end, Continental had produced over 15,000 model W-670 tank engines.

While the W-670 engines played their role in amphibious warfare, other operations in the South Pacific were supported by W-670-powered light tanks of the M3 series. Then, in late 1942 and '43, the larger R-975 radials began to see action as M4 and M4A1 Shermans joined in the island-hopping campaign across the Pacific.

Ordnance Corps

Continental W-670 seven-cylinder aircraft engines powered fleets of LVTs (Landing Vehicle, Tracked)

LVT "Water Buffaloes" land American troops on Gilbert Islands in South Pacific. LVTs had uncanny ability to surmount all barriers during landing operations

Red Seal Magazine

Continental-powered M4A1 Sherman tank goes ashore from an LST (Landing Ship, Tank) at Cape Gloucester, New Britain during campaign of late December 1943

Richard P. Hunnicutt

Boeing PT-17 primary military trainers powered by 220 hp Continental R-670 engines were used by U.S. and friendly foreign governments. Aircraft from top: Peru, Great Britain, China, U.S. Navy, U.S. Army Air Corps

Boeing Airplane Company, Wichita

Aircraft engines were not just for wartime use in land- and sea-based tanks, self-propelled artillery and amphibian craft. Continental also built the seven-cylinder 670 cubic inch displacement radial aircraft engine for military aircraft!

Aircraft Engines for Aircraft

With war on the horizon, the Army Air Corps in 1939 began contracting with civilian aviation schools for the initial training of military pilots. The R-670, 220 hp version of the radial air-cooled engine, was already being used to power the majority of popular-priced medium-size private planes, many of them biplane types similar to military trainers.

Boeing Airplane Co. produced the Continental-powered PT-17 biplane for the Army and a similar model for the Navy cadet training programs. The engines were also used extensively in Canada, Great Britain, China, Peru and other Latin American countries in their pilot training programs.

One civilian flying school training Army Air Corps cadets flew 350,000 flying hours in 2½ years operation without a single fatal accident, a rare tribute to the instructors, the airplanes and their dependable Continental engines.

For the war-support Civilian Pilot Training Program, Waco produced the Continental-powered UPF-7 biplane trainers. Gillis Flying Service in Montana reported that it ran the engines for 1,300 hours without a top overhaul. When a major overhaul was done the total cost for replacement parts was only $68.

When war-related pilot training programs began to taper off, Continental was able to switch production from the R-670 aircraft engine to the W-670 tank and amphibious vehicle engine which was urgently needed in the war effort against Japan in the South Pacific.

Long after the war, there were a lot of personal planes still flying which had been powered with R-670 engines—but by then there were few replacement parts. Fortunately there were W-670 tank engines available from war surplus stocks and many of these found their way back to the engine's original role as power plants, and parts, for use in commercial aircraft.

Most extensively used of Continental aircraft engines—in aircraft—was the four-cylinder horizontally-opposed A-65 model which powered the "Grasshopper" fleet of liaison planes in WW II.

Record-Setting Flights

Continental-powered light planes had attracted a great deal of attention in recent years in record-setting flights. November 29, 1938, Johnny Jones flew non-stop coast to coast; the following year Henry B. Chapman flew non-stop New York to New Orleans.

Bigger headlines were made in September-October 1939 at Rosamond Dry Lake, California, when Clyde Schliepper and

Experimental Aircraft Assn.

On golden anniversary of Lindbergh's New York-Paris flight, Experimental Aircraft Assn. found Continental R-670 war-time engine for its 1977 flying replica of Ryan "Spirit of St. Louis" monoplane

Wes Carroll remained in the air an entire month—726 hours— setting a new endurance record in their lightplane. That flight established reliability of the 'flat' A-50 engine beyond any question.

Continental engines also starred in high-performance as well as endurance tests. In the 1940 Firestone Trophy Races, Continental-powered planes took 1st, 2nd, 3rd and 4th. In 1941 they did even better, sweeping 1st to 6th places.

Early in 1940, Continental introduced a fuel injection system adaptable to its A series 65, 75 and 80 horsepower engines. This feature provided equal mechanical distribution of fuel to each cylinder.

Replacing the conventional carburetor, the new fuel injection system automatically overcame carburetor icing problems, a major step forward in reliability. In addition, the fuel injector reduced fire hazards, permitted faster warm-up, provided smoother operation and increased fuel economy.

To its previous customer list, Continental soon added Culver, Ercoupe, Interstate, Rearwin, Swallow and Welsh, but with wartime priorities set, production of engines for private aircraft came to a halt.

Early on there was skepticism in military circles as to what if any role light aircraft might have in a war situation. In the Spring of 1941, William T. Piper, Sr., whose company had already produced 7000 Cubs, began a campaign to sell the concept to the government. As a result, Piper supplied the Army with eight Cub planes which would participate in Army maneuvers to demonstrate their potential for artillery spotting and reconnaissance. His effort was supported by Aeronca and Taylorcraft which joined in the demonstration by also supplying planes and company civilian pilots.

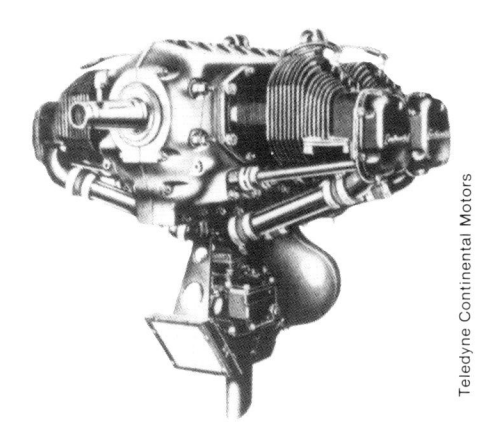

A-65, Continental's four-cylinder opposed air-cooled aircraft engine powered Army "Grasshopper" fleet

The planes of all three manufacturers were equipped with horizontally-opposed 65 hp Continental A-65 engines.

In Army war games in Louisiana in August 1941, the Grasshopper fleet was again demonstrating its capabilities, but there had been no contracts awarded nor any provision for paying the three companies for use of their planes.

One colonel evaluating the planes had himself learned to fly in a Cub in 1936 in the Philippines. Pending purchase contracts, he thought the Army might rent the planes, though this had never been done before. As chief of staff to Lt. Gen. Walter Krueger, Third Army commander, he knew his way through the chain of command and got the rental agreement signed. The colonel was Dwight D. Eisenhower.

Shortly before Pearl Harbor, the Army placed its first orders for Grasshopper light planes: eight planes each from Piper, Aeronca and Taylorcraft.

An L-4 Piper Cub liaison "Grasshopper" plane of U.S. Army takes off from a rice field on Luzon during Pacific War action in the Philippines in 1945.

97

Streets of Naples served as landing strip for L-4 flying command post of Gen. Mark W. Clark during Italian campaign

Gen. Joseph W. Stilwell, Commanding General U.S. Army, Pacific, returns to Okinawa base after observation flight in his L-4 Cub over enemy lines

At first the planes were given "observation" designations: 0-57 Taylorcraft, 0-58 Aeronca and 0-59 Piper. Later, with "liaison" designations following a Wright Field production order in February 1942 for 1500 Grasshoppers, they became L-2 Taylorcraft, L-3 Aeronca and L-4 Piper.

In the end, it was the olive drab L-4 Cub which is best remembered for the outstanding wartime combat role of the Grasshopper fleet of Continental-powered light planes.

Wartime Piper Cubs

They first saw service in North Africa, then in Sicily and Italy under leadership of Gen. Mark W. Clark who saw in the L-4 not only a superb aerial observation, artillery and bombing direction aircraft, and airborne command post, but also its unique capability as the general's own flying jeep.

Photographs were soon appearing in the press of Cubs not only in combat roles but with their general staff Army brass users—generals like Patton, Bradley and Eisenhower in Europe and MacArthur in the South Pacific.

After their introduction in 1942 in North Africa and Italy, the Grasshoppers next appeared in the Southwest Pacific in 1943; then in Western Europe after D-Day in June 1944.

Continental-powered lightplanes even flew the "Hump"—over the towering Himalayas—in the China-Burma-India war theatre.

No one was prouder of the combat performance of the L-4 Cubs than Corporal Emory S. Derr of Muskegon, whose father was superintendent of tooling in CMC's aircraft engine division. Young Derr served on Okinawa with a liaison squadron under General Joseph W. (Vinegar Joe) Stilwell, Commanding General of the U.S. Army in the Pacific.

In five weeks on Okinawa, Derr's squadron flew 1130 missions, evacuating 1215 wounded. Piloted entirely by enlisted men, the Continental-powered L-4 "eyes of the artillery" also directed fire control while exposed to everything from enemy small arms on the ground to fighters in the air.

"Can you imagine", young Derr wrote his father, "a flight of Navy dive bombers following a Cub, piloted by a staff sergeant, to a group of enemy landing craft attempting a flanking attack on the beach?"

"The Army had taken the Cubs over as they were built commercially, and used them with no charge whatsoever, except a paint job. While not built for the beatings which the pilots had to give them, they really performed fine. Using three and a fraction gallons of gas per hour, and practically no oil, the A-65 engines usually ran between 400 and 450 hours before requiring other than routine maintenance."

Continental engines in the 50 hp to 80 hp "A Series" also supplied power for Civilian Air Patrol planes patrolling coastal shores and similar areas. Other applications included commercially-operated planes in which Civilian Pilot Training Program (CPTP) pilots received their initial instruction.

The traditional cast-iron engines of automotive lineage also made their contribution to the war effort as Continental supplied "off the shelf" models to fill Army and car manufacturers' orders for engines used in light and heavy military trucks and jeep scout cars.

Powering the Invasion Fleet

For use in wartime marine applications, particularly in the South Pacific, Continental built thousands of "Commando" engines which powered invasion landing craft and heavy prime movers for hauling field artillery on the various battlefronts.

Early in the war Continental developed the 230 hp R-600 engine used in landing craft to put ashore tanks, jeeps, trucks and other military vehicles; and for use in ship-to-shore cargo lighters.

The R-600 also powered trucks, firefighting equipment and heavy battlefield prime movers like the M5 highspeed tractor built by International Harvester for moving artillery pieces. In combat the M5 could pull a 155 mm. howitzer weighing 7½ tons at speeds up to 35 mph over the roughest terrain.

The M-330 marine engine, which developed 70 hp had been in Continental's product line for five years and was used by the Navy in troop landing barges, patrol boats and other lighter craft.

Also seeing action on many war fronts were Continental electric generator sets, and portable lighting and "Tiny Tim" battery charging plants.

International Harvester's M5 military prime mover, equipped with R-600 engine, pulls Army's 155mm howitzer over rough terrain

Continental marine engines powered Higgins boats which landed invasion troops during island-hopping engagements in South Pacific

Scout cars, jeeps, trucks and other military vehicles are put ashore in specialized landing craft powered with various Continental converted engines

All photos Teledyne Continental Motors

R-600 Continental engine developing 230 hp was supplied in large volume to power military prime movers and landing craft

M-330 Continental marine engine developing 70 hp was used by U.S. Navy in patrol boats, landing barges and light craft

Continental Aviation and Engineering Corp. was formed to give greater attention to high horsepower aircraft engine development. Primary project was "Hyper" XI-1430 liquid-cooled engine for combat aircraft

Teledyne Continental Motors

As provided in its charter, Continental Aviation and Engineering (50.94% of whose shares were held by the parent company) confined its wartime activities to aircraft engines developing over 500 hp.

Getty Street Plant

Three projects were involved; (1) the "Hyper-cylinder" 1430 liquid-cooled engine development on which work had been underway since 1932; (2) production under license of a large radial aircraft engine for advanced training planes; and (3) production of the famed Rolls-Royce Merlin aircraft engine.

As part of the 1939 agreement with the Reconstruction Finance Corp., Continental had built a new aircraft engine test facility at the company's airport on Getty Street, Muskegon, not far from the main plant in that city.

Then, in July 1941, Jack Reese and federal officials announced that $5 million had been approved for expanded government-owned facilities at Muskegon and Detroit, but no further details were made public. The immediate purpose of the new facilities contract was assumed to be for production by Continental Aviation and Engineering (CAE) of the 12-cylinder, 1000 hp Model 1430 pursuit plane engines for the Army Air Corps.

At about the same time, Continental was asked to undertake production of the Pratt & Whitney 550 hp nine-cylinder R-1340 "Wasp" engine which would be required in large numbers to power North American Aviation's AT-6 and SNJ advanced trainers for the Army and Navy.

In April 1942, it was announced that a huge new plant would be erected in Muskegon on Getty Street for production of aircraft engines. The plant would be owned by the Defense Plant Corporation and operated by Continental Aviation and Engineering.

In late 1939 the Air Corps had restated its requirements for large liquid-cooled engines: (1) flat engines at 1800-2000 hp for submerged installation in bomber wings; (2) multibank engines of 1800-2400 hp for

Designed as a possible replacement for the P-38 "Lightning" fighter, Lockheed's XP-49 was powered by two Continental XI-1430 engines. Propellers rotated in opposite directions to counteract torque

Lockheed-California Company

100

First fighter designed by recently formed McDonnell Aircraft Company was XP-67, tested in 1944 with twin Continental XI-1430 liquid cooled engines capable of 1600 hp each

McDonnell Douglas—St. Louis

nacelle installation in bombers; and (3) inverted vee engines of 1500-1800 hp for pursuit planes.

For the first category, CAE made preliminary studies of an H-2860 engine; that is, a double 0-1430 arrangement of 24 cylinders. Continental's H-2860 design lost out to the Pratt & Whitney and Wright entries in that competition.

Hyper Engine for Pursuit Planes

In the inverted vee category, the Continental IV-1430 was the only entry. The company was given a new contract to make that engine a successful competitor to the Allison V-1720 which was already in production.

The Army felt that the IV-1430 could be brought in a reasonable time to a military rating of 1600 hp at 25,000 feet, with a turbo for use in an interceptor. To expedite the project Continental agreed to put in $250,000 of its own money without waiting for a written Army contract.

Several aircraft manufacturers were asked by the Army to design new pursuit planes around the IV-1430 engine and to assist the project further, the Air Corps helped finance the new Getty Street factory, nominally for the production of trainer plane engines, but actually tooled with equipment adequate for production of the IV-1430.

In May 1942 the engine, now redesignated XI-1430, passed preliminary tests at 1600 hp and a production contract for 100 engines was signed in November.

The XI-1430 was extensively flown during 1943 in the twin-engine Lockheed XP-49, a modified "Lightning" ordered in 1940. The 1600 hp Continental engines weighed 300 pounds less than the Allison 1475 hp engines used in the P-38L Lightning. Two XI-1430 engines were also tested in 1944 in the XP-67, first design of the McDonnell Aircraft Co. This twin-engine fighter had been ordered somewhat later than its Lockheed counterpart.

Allison and Continental were constantly jockeying for position in the Air Corps competition for pursuit plane engine business.

"When our 1430 model had been upped in rating to around 1400 hp," Carl Bachle recalled, "Allison was in production at about 1100 hp. When the military saw that we could get 1400 hp out of the same kind of displacement as Allison, they went to them and told them to up their horsepower rating as 'these fellows are doing.' And Allison did."

"They were always six months to a year behind us on rating, but they had a vast production capability. The 1430 was obviously the better engine, yet it was not tooled up for big production. So the Air Corps took a lesser engine and expanded the production on that rather than wait for the better engine. In wartime the military simply could not accept a six months lag in production."

When it became apparent that the planes and their Continental engines could not possibly be ready for use in the war, the 1430 model engine contract was cut to 50, then to 25 and finally to eight engines for experimental use. However, a total of 23 engines were actually delivered.

Teledyne Continental Motors

Under license, C.A.E. built Pratt & Whitney R-1340 "Wasp" engines at new Getty Street plant for use in North American AT-6 and SNJ advanced training planes

San Diego AeroSpace Museum

In writing about the wartime development of aircraft engines, consultant Sam D. Heron stated that "The chief cause of the slowness of the Continental development was not technical but administrative and economic. Needless delays were avoided by Rolls-Royce and all British manufacturers, since they could reach an understanding on informal terms with the government and then proceed with absolute assurance that they would be paid in full. The only way in which such delays could be avoided in the U.S. was by investing private funds [as Allison did] sufficient to bridge the gaps between government contracts."

During the Depression years when the project was started, Continental, of course, did not have the funds to bridge that gap and subsequently lost out to Allison.

After the war it was revealed that Continental's 1430 turbo-supercharged engine had, in August 1944, established a war emergency rating of 2100 hp (1½ horsepower per cubic inch of displacement) and that its weight was only 1640 pounds (just over ¾ lb. per horsepower). The low weight-to-horsepower ratio and small frontal area set performance standards never before attained.

By 1942, Continental's main Muskegon plant on Market Street, begun in 1906 but subsequently enlarged again and again, was getting worn out and its equipment had become obsolete, but the new government-owned Getty Street facility would be as modern and up-to-date as possible.

P&W R-1340 Engines

Construction began in June 1942 on a structure 450 feet wide and 950 feet long, to cost an estimated $7 million. All machinery, tools and equipment, as well as the building located on a 57-acre site, would be owned by the Defense Plant Corp.

Construction was primarily of wood, brick and concrete, with a minimum of critically short materials. Nature provided the only air conditioning—breezes from the neighboring forest from which the site was carved. CAE began moving into the new factory in November and commenced limited production of aircraft engine parts.

The first R-1340 advanced training plane engine, developed by Pratt & Whitney and built by CAE, was shipped in April 1943. Thereafter the production rate built up rapidly with volume deliveries starting in the Fall. The contract was completed in November 1944 with the shipment of 5100 engines.

In April 1940, the British Air Ministry approached North American Aviation with the intent of having them build Curtiss P-40 pursuit planes for the Royal Air Force. Instead, North American proposed a new fighter using the same Allison V-1710 engine as the P-40.

Rolls-Royce Merlins

The result was the famed P-51 "Mustang" which could outperform even the British Spitfire. Still better high-altitude performance was obtained with the Mustang when equipped with the British Rolls-Royce "Merlin" engine.

In the U.S., Packard began production of the Merlin V-1650 engine which was capable of delivering 1695 hp, but demand for the Merlin-powered Mustang was so great that Continental, through its CAE subsidiary, was asked to become a second source for the British-designed engine. By that time it was clear Continental's own IV-1430 engine would not go to production and plant space would be available.

The formal contract for 8500 Merlin engines was not signed until February 1944, although most details had been negotiated some months earlier after a letter contract had been worked out in August, 1943. Fifteen million dollars in additional facilities at the Getty Street Plant were required, as R-1340 Pratt & Whitney radial aircraft engines for advanced trainers were also being built by CAE in that factory. Total building and facilities cost at Getty Street soon totaled $55 million.

In a difficult on-again, off-again situation, CAE management had to coordinate production of the two engine projects. During 1944 there was a brief termination of the R-1340 contract, but a new contract calling for resumption of its production was signed shortly thereafter.

Some thought had previously been given to shifting R-1340 production to the recently leased Garland, Texas parts plant, previously occupied by the Guiberson Diesel Engine Co. in order to make room at

Muskegon lakefront view in 1940s showing power plant and individual buildings of Continental Motors in foreground

Muskegon County Museum

Built by Defense Plant Corp., operated by C.A.E., new Getty Street war production factory was 450 wide, 950 long and, with equipment, cost $55 million

Newest Production Facility

Getty Street for the Rolls-Royce job, but this did not come about according to Art Wild.

Meanwhile, CAE was going all-out to get the Rolls-Royce Merlin into volume production. Most of the Getty Street facilities expansion was in more machinery, tooling and other manufacturing equipment needed to assure "jeweled watch" precision in production of the Merlin—most intricate of aircraft engines.

Engineering and production planning were underway under direction of Albert B. Willi in Detroit, where close liaison was maintained with the Army Air Force, Packard and CAE's many subcontractors and suppliers.

The first Rolls-Royce model V-1650-7 was completed at Getty Street, Muskegon, in July 1944.

The plant had recently been re-tooled for resumed parallel production of the R-1340, which was just getting under way, when victory in Europe was achieved May 8, 1945. By that date, approximately one-third of the Merlin engines called for under the contract had been delivered. Contracts totaling over $50 million for both the Merlin and R-1340 engines were cancelled as of the end of May. Enough war materiel, the War Production Board indicated, was on hand to finish off the Japanese in the Pacific.

Equipped with British Rolls-Royce "Merlin" engine, North American's P-51 "Mustang" was Allies top WW II fighter. Continental's CAE became second source to Packard in producing engine in U.S.

Continental Old Timers

Veteran workers with over 25 years service, many employed since Continental came to Muskegon in 1906, gather around first Rolls-Royce Merlin engine built at Getty Street. Jack Reese at far right.

Final assembly of Rolls-Royce Merlin engines at Getty Street plant. Deliveries began in Summer 1944 but by May 1945 the war was over in Europe

The tremendous build-up in facilities and production capacity brought with it personnel problems unlike the company had faced in prior years.

Relations With Employees

Under pressure of war production requirements, Continental for the first time entered into union shop agreements with local unions representing workers at the Muskegon and Detroit plants. Under the contracts with the United Automobile Workers (C.I.O.), the company was required to deduct union dues from the paychecks of its employees.

Employment had doubled, and doubled again, as thousands of new defense workers both in the factories and offices were added to the payroll.

With the growing scarcity of men, an increasing proportion of new workers on the assembly lines were women. Training of new employees became an important task as those without technical skills were introduced to production tasks.

By 1942, most divisions of the Muskegon and Detroit plants were operating around the clock, seven days a week. For production efficiency, the plants and their employees were recognized by presentation of Army-Navy "E" Awards. The Treasury Department awarded the Detroit, Muskegon and Texas plants "Bullseye" flags for employee participation in the purchase of War Savings Bonds.

Everyone — management executives, labor leaders, run-of-the-mill employees, the military — pitched into the war effort wholeheartedly to speed engines from production lines to the war front.

Jack Reese praised the cooperation of Continental workers, pointing out that the production efficiency of its plants "bespeaks generally satisfactory working conditions and a full appreciation of the importance of our war production tasks."

From a pre-war low of 700 — all at Muskegon — company-wide employment rose to 6000 in 1941, to 14,000 in 1942, 21,000 in 1943 and soared to nearly 23,000 at the peak of production in 1944. Eleven thousand were employed at Muskegon, over 3000 of them at CAE's new Getty Street plant.

The military services drew off approximately 3750 employees who put on uniforms and went off to war. Women soon replaced men on the production line and made up one-quarter of the work force.

Continental factories, however, were not entirely free from labor disputes, but fared better than plants of many other companies operating in the same areas. Lest the public get the wrong impression, Jack Reese made it clear that "the vast majority of Continental employees have worked hard and conscientiously to speed production for war purposes. They have our sincere thanks for full cooperation in difficult times."

Cancellation or severe cut-back of war production orders in May and September 1945, after V-E and V-J Days, of necessity brought sharp reductions in employment and difficult personnel problems. By October, for example, employment at CAE's Getty Street plant was cut to 300 — one-tenth what it had been at the peak of wartime production.

Policies of the United Auto Workers required that national officers come from rank-and-file employees in industrial plants. UAW official Walter Reuther, fresh from a successful 113-day post-war strike against General Motors came to Jack Reese with a suggestion.

Reuther had a very promising young man with limited shop and union experience who looked like a natural for a future leadership role in the UAW. Would Jack hire him for at least one year, with the implied assurance that Continental could expect a minimum of union problems?

Thus, British-educated Leonard Woodcock became a Continental Motors employee and member of UAW Local 113 in the Muskegon plant. Within a short time, while on leave from Continental, Woodcock became a regional director of the UAW-CIO, then administrative assistant to Reuther when the latter became UAW president in 1946. Woodcock returned briefly to Continental Motors in 1947 and has been on leave ever since. The potential Reuther saw in Woodcock would later be even more fully realized.

With huge war production orders on its books, Continental in the early 40's again began to look attractive as an investment. To increase the working capital needed to handle the expanded volume of production, 350,000 shares of Continental stock were sold in 1940 bringing in $1.3 million in new funds. After the sale of this stock offering to the public, all of the company's authorized 3,000,000 shares were issued.

Young Ferry Gets Involved

The increased level of business also made it possible to reduce the loan from the Reconstruction Finance Corp. by $450,000, and in 1941 the company paid off the remaining $750,000 owed the RFC as well as the loan obtained from the Greater Muskegon Industrial Foundation to build the new test cells.

General business conditions throughout the country were improving as war production expanded, bringing increased demand for Continental's agricultural/industrial engines for the commercial market. New models were introduced including those for application in the oil fields of the Southwest, where Continental opened a regional office.

When James H. Ferry, Sr., passed away in August 1940, the board of directors was reduced to Jack Reese, B.F. Tobin, Jr., Lewis P. Kalb and Leslie L. Vivian, a partner in the brokerage firm of Fenner and Beane, who had joined the board the previous year.

As production expanded in 1941, Reese built up his team by adding Vice-Presidents to share the management load. Reese, Tobin and Kalb set policy; operations were carried out by the Vice-Presidents, principally Earl C. Ginn, the Company's cast iron automobile engine specialist, and Guy J. Harinton at Muskegon; and Art Wild and George E. Winters in Detroit.

James H. Ferry, Jr. was 23 years old when his father, a pioneer investor in Continental and long a key figure in management decisions, passed away in August 1940, making his son a beneficiary.

Young Jim Ferry, a graduate of Massachusetts Institute of Technology, was primarily interested in electronics and television, but corporate responsibilities were thrust on him at a relatively early age.

"After my father's funeral," Jim recalls, "Jack Reese came over to talk to my mother and me privately. He wanted to assure us of any support he could give.

"Father had been very supportive of Jack Reese and Ben Tobin, Jr., who were carrying the company load at that time. Before the RFC would loan money, a corporation had to put up collateral. It was not a good time to take risks, but Father put up his personal stock to help guarantee the loan the company so urgently needed. It took a lot of faith on his part at that critical time. Jack never forgot his support.

"I was just a youngster fresh out of M.I.T. and just starting a career. Jack put me on the payroll for enough to run the household so we didn't have to worry. Jack tried me out to see if I could be useful. He would send me out to check on design ideas which had come to us by mail to see whether or not they had merit. The company couldn't really afford to send a top engineer so I drew the assignment."

Young Ferry, however, wanted to strike out on his own so he went east seeking work at the Army's electronics center at Fort Monmouth, N.J. That didn't work out so Jim went to Boston to visit his contacts at M.I.T. only to be told, "I know you'd like what we're doing, but I can't tell you a thing about it. Do you want to sign up?"

"Sounds great. I sure do," was Jim's prompt response.

The next day was Pearl Harbor, December 7, 1941, and Jim Ferry found himself working at the famed Lawrence Radiation Laboratory, home of radar research.

"I stayed with the Radiation Laboratory until the war ended," he continued, "but a condition of my going to work there was that I could have a day or two off each month to go to Detroit and serve with Continental management."

On his first trip to Detroit, during the holiday season, Jim Ferry replaced his father on the Continental Motors Board of Directors, assuming a similar post with newly formed Continental Aviation and Engineering. A year later he was also named Treasurer of CAE.

During the war, Jim Ferry sat on the Continental finance committee with Jack Reese and Henry W. Vandeven, corporate Treasurer. "We had to go through all the government paperwork," Jim said. "I'll bet I signed fifty thousand papers!"

Red Seal Magazine

BEN F. TOBIN, JR.
Son of company's early chief executive, Ben Tobin, Jr., Executive Vice-President, was principal corporate aide to Jack Reese

JAMES W. KINNUCAN

Two of CAE's key engineering Vice-Presidents: Jimmie Kinnucan on aircraft engines; Ed Hulbert on tank engines

ED A. HULBERT

At Continental Aviation and Engineering, the developmental and production organization for "over-500 hp" aircraft engines, Art Wild was joined in overall management by Carl Bachle, the company engineering innovator, Bob Insley (who had returned to CAE after eight years absence), Al Willi (at Getty Street) and by Jimmie Kinnucan and Ed Hulbert.

Continental Motors added new industrial engines at both ends of the horsepower range—a small, four-cylinder industrial engine series and a new, large power output series.

After 11 lean years, Continental shareholders in 1941 received a 10 cents per share cash dividend, increased to 50 cents in 1942, 60 cents in 1943 and 1944, and 75 cents in 1945.

Production of some engine lines, notably those for use in farm tractors, trucks and buses, began to be curtailed as the war progressed, although the tremendous expansion of industry had more than tripled the demand for commercial engines. By 1943, however, there was some easing of governmental restrictions on production of commercial products.

Continental wisely began to set aside cash reserves for the time when the war would end and it would face the problem of post-war adjustments and reconversion of plants. But extensive financing of war production would still be required and so Continental arranged with banks for $30 million in standby "V Loan" credit for the duration of the war.

Continental Motors turned the corner financially soon after Jack Reese took over as president. Then as sales volume increased dramatically when war production contracts began to be filled, profits too rose sharply. And by early 1943, the company's backlog of unfilled orders reached a record $337.5 million.

Sales Hit Peak in '44

From 1940 net income of $663,814, profits increased to an average of $5.4 million annually for the next five years during which sales had grown steadily from $10.9 million in 1940 to a wartime peak of $258 million in 1944.

Financial figures in the company's Annual Reports to Stockholders had to be revised yearly to reflect wartime Contract Renegotiation, Excess Profit Taxes and rulings of the War Department Price Adjustment Board. (Excess profits taxes, alone, were from $13 million to $15 million annually.)

Adjusted for subsequent rulings, the tabulation following shows consolidated sales and net income for the five wartime years, ending October 31, for Continental and its subsidiaries.

Year	Sales	Net Income
1941	$ 31,564,631	$3,913,613
1942	126,401,565	6,214,815
1943	200,154,234	5,142,141
1944	258,067,814	6,056,000
1945	219,494,471	5,672,033

During the five years 1941-45, Continental Motors had after-tax profits of $27 million (3.2% of sales), and paid out dividends of $8.9 million. The net gain of $18.1 million more than erased the 1930-39 Depression years' loss of $14.3 million and got the company back on its feet financially before the inevitable post-war reduction in sales.

Until completion of the huge government-owned Getty Street plant in Muskegon, Continental Aviation and Engineering had been operating out of its Detroit engineering and factory facility. First appreciable production volume at CAE came from the R-1340 radial engine, being built under license from Pratt & Whitney for advanced training planes.

Sales of CAE for 1943 totaled $8.4 million compared with $2.2 million for the previous year but a net loss of $356,000 was sustained due in large part because production was moved to the Getty Street plant which was not fully tooled for volume production until eight months of the fiscal year had elapsed.

As with its parent company, CAE sales were at a wartime peak in 1944 when volume rose to $58.4 million on R-1340 production and the start of Rolls-Royce Merlin deliveries. Profit for the year was $628,078. In 1945, sales volume dropped soon after V-E Day, totaling $32.8 million on which net income of $44,553 was earned.

In 1945, CAE minority stockholder Armin Schlesinger of Milwaukee replaced broker David VanAlstyne, Jr. on that board of directors.

Prior to WW II, Continental Motors had been a supplier almost exclusively to commercial users of its products rather than to the military. Consequently Jack Reese and his team looked forward to the resumption of a peace-time economy and began to give thought to the company's post-war opportunities.

Continental Aviation and Engineering research and development work was centered at this Detroit location.

Post-War Planning

Although the company was just getting into full wartime production, Reese pointed out in his 1942 Annual Report that the company "would be favorably suited to participate substantially in the world reconstruction that inevitably must take place after the war.

"There should be a large accumulated demand for engines from industries served in the past—farm equipment, automotive, oil, transportation, marine, special purpose equipment and particularly aviation, which should become increasingly important."

In 1943, Reese got more specific about post-war plans and problems. "Our engines," he wrote, "will incorporate the high precision techniques perfected during the war. Cash reserves have been established to pay the costs of tooling and modernization of Continental plants which will start when reconversion becomes possible.

"A post-war feature of settlement of our accounts with the government will involve the separation of government-owned machine tools and inventories from those owned by the company, and perhaps the purchase of part of the government-owned facilities which can be used in peacetime operations."

Anticipating the demand for engines which had been accumulated since suspension or curtailment of production for several commercial uses early in 1942, Continental utilized the planning services of engineering and market research organizations not fully occupied with war work.

"We are planning new product lines," Reese pointed out, "to achieve greater diversification and a higher degree of stability."

An early step in that direction was establishment in 1943 of new headquarters in Dallas for the company's wholly-owned subsidiary, Con-Tex Petroleum Corp., formerly known as Continental Gas and Oil Co. The scope of its activities was broadened to more thoroughly serve the oil industry's engine requirements for drilling and pumping in Texas, Oklahoma and adjacent petroleum producing areas, and the exploration of its oil leases acquired in the Southwest.

By equipping its own oil fields with the most modern Continental-powered equipment to make them models of efficient operation, Con-Tex was also able to promote the growing acceptance of Red Seal engines among other oil operators.

Continental also maintained in Dallas a sales and service branch for its entire line of engines.

Although war production requirements had top priority on Continental's facilities and manpower, the company continued such commercial activity as conditions permitted.

Continental engines were being built to approximately 1100 specifications, a diversity practically double that of the pre-war years. The company featured scores of users for its Red Seal and Wisconsin engines (listed alphabetically) from Aircraft, Air compressors and Air conditioning to Water purifiers, Winches and Woodworking machinery.

To further fortify its position of leadership in the small and medium size aviation engine field, Continental introduced five new models ranging from 75 hp to 140 hp. These new "C" series horizontally-opposed four- and six-cylinder engines bridged the gap between the famous "A" series, widely used in Army liaison planes, and the R-670 radial 220 hp model used in Army and Navy primary training planes.

Long interested in the potential of diesel engines, Continental decided late in 1944 to begin manufacture of four- and six-cylinder models from 25 hp up as soon as government restrictions on manpower and materials could be lifted. They were expected to complement use of Continental gasoline engines in the industrial field and provide a high degree of interchangeability of parts and tooling.

To build up Continental's product line and increase its potential in small, air-cooled industrial engines, the company in 1943 purchased for $620,000 a 72% controlling interest in Wisconsin Motor Corp. of Milwaukee, Wisconsin.

Teledyne Continental Motors

First six-cylinder flat opposed aircraft engines were introduced in 1945 to fill post-war demands of civilian aircraft market

Teledyne Continental Motors

New diesel engines like this six-cylinder model complemented Continental's line of industrial, agricultural, marine and transportation gasoline engines

Wisconsin Motor Corp. Acquisition

Successor to a business organized in 1909, Wisconsin was exclusively a manufacturer of heavy duty internal combustion engines ranging from 2½ hp to 33 hp. Continental regarded the Wisconsin line of *air-cooled* power plants—for construction, agricultural, oil, railway maintenance and other industrial uses—as complementing rather than being competitive with its own line of *liquid-cooled* low-horsepower engines.

The new subsidiary's 1943 sales of $12.3 million, on which a $325,000 profit was earned, were the greatest in that company's history and Jack Reese felt that it would continue to do a large business in normal years, thereby amply justifying its acquisition.

At this time, Harold A. Todd, President of Wisconsin since 1937, was added to Continental Motors' board of directors. Director Leslie L. Vivian who had passed away earlier in the year, was replaced by Detroit attorney F. J. Kennedy, the company's general counsel.

The behind-the-scenes story of the acquisition of Wisconsin Motor may be apocryphal but with the passing of the years gained considerable coinage. Rumor had it that Wisconsin, due to financial difficulties, was deeply in debt to the First Wisconsin National Bank, which placed its employee, Harold A. Todd, into the position of President of the motor company to straighten things out.

Todd had worked hard and finally had the company in pretty good shape. Over drinks with Jack Reese in Chicago, Todd apparently disclosed, now that he had the firm pretty well 'slicked up,' the bank was going to let him buy controlling interest in Wisconsin.

"The next morning," one source reported, "Jack went to the bank's highest officers and bought the stock it held, giving Continental Motors control. Harold never forgave him for it. Those two guys used to sit at board meetings and just glare at each other."

HAROLD A. TODD
Reports are that Jack Reese got to the bank ahead of Wisconsin Motor's president.

In business since 1909, Wisconsin Motors had its Milwaukee plant at 53rd and Burnham Streets

WISCONSIN-POWERED PORTABLE CONVEYOR

Continental-powered Case tractor with Wisconsin (in circle) powered hay baler.

Most important of Continental's 1944 developments designed to strengthen its post-war industry position as the largest independent engine builder, was the $2.6 million acquisition on June 14 of the entire capital stock of the 39-year old Gray Marine Motor Co. of Detroit.

Gray Marine Motor Acquisition

The world's leading supplier of inboard gasoline and diesel marine engines, Gray's world-wide distribution system strengthened Continental's sales outlets abroad and, to a lesser extent, its North American distribution and service facilities.

In peacetime, Gray had been a major supplier of marine engines for commerical fishing and cargo boats, and for pleasure craft. During the war, the Navy and Army standardized on several Gray models which were suitable for military requirements and were produced on a mass production basis with no major changes. Primarily they were used for a vast armada of landing craft, bridge-erection boats and other small naval vessels.

Gray provided 60,000 wartime marine engines, totaling more than 12 million horsepower—about one-quarter of the total engine horsepower added by the U.S. Navy following Pearl Harbor.

For 17 years preceding its acquisition by Continental, Gray Marine held the exclusive world-wide conversion and sales rights for boat propulsion purposes on the complete line of Red Seal engines. In addition, it handled marine conversions of General Motors' Detroit Diesel engines.

For the 15 years before the war, Gray was the leading builder of inboard marine engines with a power range from five to 200 horsepower.

Jack Reese and his associates considered Gray Marine a most valuable corporate addition. Its peacetime market was particularly attractive.

Teledyne Continental Motors

Gray Marine Motor Co. plant on Detroit's Canton Avenue. Company also had a factory on motor city's Bellevue Avenue

Red Seal Magazine

Five Yards Building This Gray-Powered Craft

Seventeen-foot U.S. Navy line handling boat, used during WW II for towing seaplanes to anchorage, was powered by Graymarine model Four-22 engine with two-to-one reduction gear

"In getting back to normal peacetime business, the $64 question is going to be the matter of cost. On that we must stake our future." — Jack Reese

Despite reductions and cancellations of military contracts, Continental and its subsidiaries reported unfilled orders totaling $110 million at the close of the 1945 fiscal year—a month after Japan's surrender. Perhaps Continental could sustain its business momentum in peacetime.

That task would not be easy, Reese had warned 84 veterans of the Continental organization, each with 25 years or more service, at a September 1944 banquet in Muskegon. "The $64 question after this war," he said, "is the question of cost. If we reach a satisfactory cost level, our wartime plants won't be big enough to handle our post-war business."

Red Seal Magazine

Wisconsin Motor Mfg. Company
Milwaukee, Wisconsin

During 1908, Continental Motor Manufacturing Co., newly arrived in Muskegon, built just over 2000 engines, primarily for the growing number of automobile manufacturing companies. New firms building automobile engines were soon springing up all over.

Located across Lake Michigan from Muskegon was Milwaukee, Wisconsin, destined to be known as "the machine shop of the nation." There, two enterprising young men, Charles H. John and A. F. Milbrath, the latter a mechanical engineer, took the lead in forming Wisconsin Motor Manufacturing Co.

Formed March 1, 1909, the new firm, with John as President, started in a small shop in North Milwaukee determined to build engines, designed by Milbrath, for automobiles, trucks and marine applications. Eighteen months later the company moved to a new plant they had built in nearby West Allis.

The first Wisconsin product was a four-cylinder water-cooled "T"-head engine of 4¾" bore by 5½" stroke. The most famous user of this early Type "A" Wisconsin engine was the Stutz Automobile Company, which used it to power its famed Stutz Bearcat. Other autos using Wisconsin engines were those of the Case and Kissel companies.

Soon more water-cooled models were introduced until the product line included many sizes from 20 hp four-cylinder engines to larger four-stroke, six-cylinder units.

During World War I, the entire Wisconsin Motor facilities were devoted to production of a single engine, the Type "A" for the military trucks built by the Four Wheel Drive Co. of Clintonville, Wisconsin, for the Quartermaster Department of the U.S. Army.

At war's end, Wisconsin had only the one customer and of necessity had to build up an entire new line of engines and new customers.

Auto racing became a popular spectator sport and Wisconsin engines were used extensively by such drivers as Ralph de Palma and Sig Haugdahl. In 1922, the latter used a Wisconsin engine to become the first driver to reach three miles a minute—180 mph in an automobile.

While such specialized use promoted the company's product, it did little to offset the decline of the automobile engine market when the independent car makers fell by the wayside as the 'big three', which built their own engines, dominated the business.

When Prohibition went into effect in 1920 a new market opened up—marine engines. The powerful water-cooled Wisconsin "Whitecap" engines became the standard power source for the fast Coast Guard patrol boats that scoured the coastlines looking for rum-runners. When the rum-runners began buying Whitecaps for their own boats, the odds were evened.

Inventor, patent holder and engineer, Arthur F. Milbrath was co-founder of Wisconsin Motor

All photos Teledyne Wisconsin Motor

Wisconsin's first water-cooled engine, the Type "A" four-cylinder model, powered the sporty Stutz Bearcat

Type "V-A-U" engine developed 32.4 hp. Note the four priming petcocks

New markets had to be found and Wisconsin set about developing them by supplying engines for agricultural, industrial, construction, oil field and railroad equipment manufacturers. It was this diversification which allowed Wisconsin to weather the stormy weather resulting from changes in the auto industry.

With the stock market crash of October 1929 and the Depression which followed, Wisconsin found itself in financial difficulties. (As Continental had done some years earlier, Wisconsin Motor Company dropped the word "Manufacturing" from its corporate name).

By 1932 things were so bad the *Company* was reorganized as Wisconsin Motor *Corporation*, starting operations anew on March 9, 1933, twenty-four years after the original company was founded. Creditors owed less than $200 were paid in cash at the rate of 50 cents on the dollar; all others received stock which hopefully could be redeemed later at a face value of $10 per share, and holders of First Mortgage Bonds agreed to extend to 20 years the maturity date of the bonds.

In its first 20 years, Wisconsin had built only water-cooled engines. The early '30s brought a change when the company introduced several single-cylinder air-cooled engines. In 1935, a four-cylinder version of the air-cooled engines was introduced.

It proved to be one of the most remarkable successes in the history of engines. Demand for air-cooled engines rose so rapidly that by 1941 the air-cooled line had completely displaced water-cooled engines.

Despite this success, Wisconsin was still in financial difficulty. While operations of the new corporation in the early '30s were slow in starting, the air-cooled engines did breathe new air into the company. But not enough.

There were still financial problems. To try and protect its position, First Wisconsin National Bank of Milwaukee had to place one of its own executives,

In 1910 photo, this Bucyrus-Erie shovel, Wisconsin-powered, helps dig the Panama Canal which opened to ship traffic four years later

Harold A. Todd, in Wisconsin Motor as President of that company in May 1937.

Under Todd's leadership and with better controls, Wisconsin Motor made excellent progress in improving its financial position and liquidation of its long-term debt.

Taking full advantage of its leadership in heavy-duty air-cooled industrial engines, sales increased from $4.5 million in 1941 to $9.8 million the next year and $12.3 million in '43.

Soon after Continental Motors acquired the company in 1943 a substantial investment was made in new machinery and equipment and the plants enlarged for large scale production. Much of that production was for the war effort which had been the source of the increased sales of the past few years.

At the time of Continental's purchase of control of Wisconsin, its key executives, all of whom remained with the company, were Harold Todd, President; Phil A. Norton, Vice President, Sales, who joined the company in 1924; and Arthur A. Erlinger, recently hired as a manufacturing executive.

The first man to go three miles a minute, Sig Haugdahl had a 'big' Wisconsin engine under the hood when his 'Wisconsin Special' clocked 180 mph in 1921

111

GRAY MARINE MOTOR COMPANY

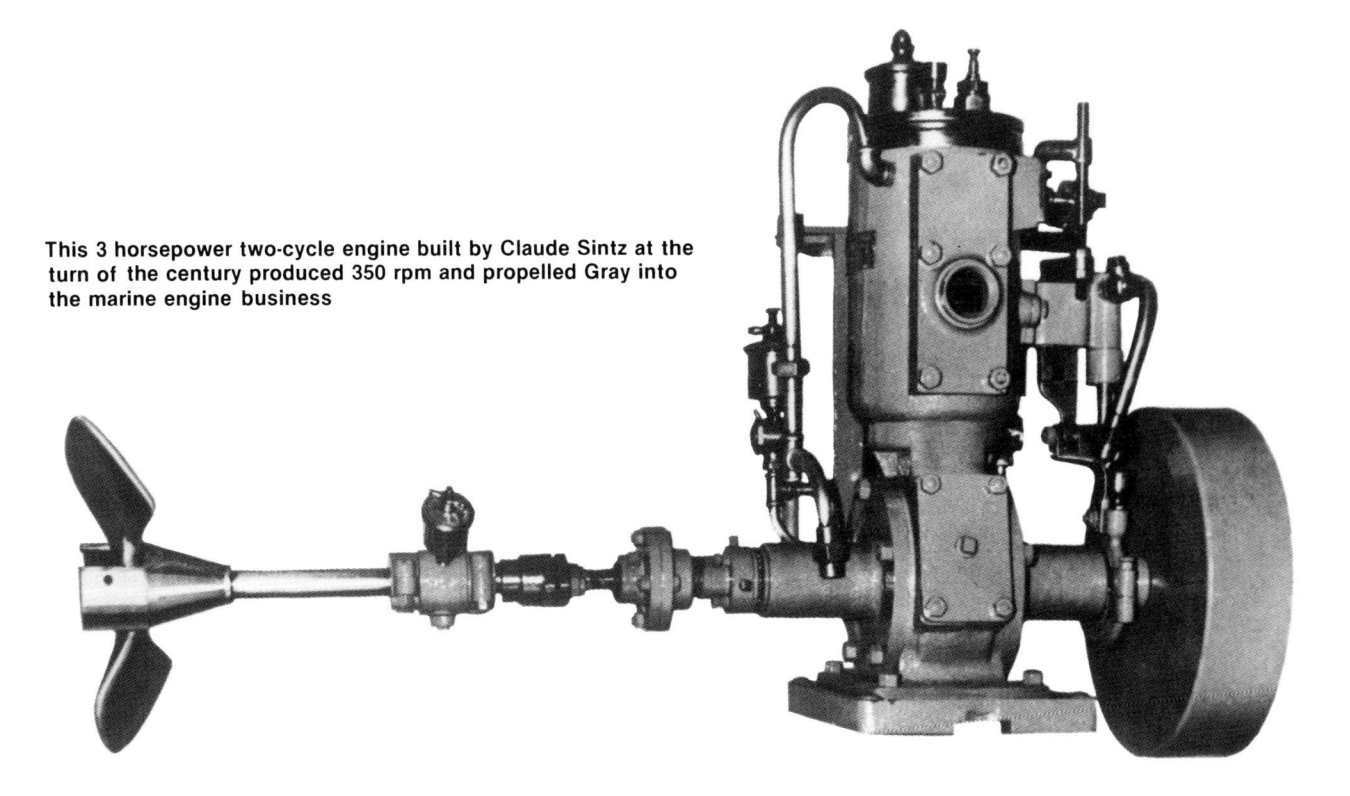

This 3 horsepower two-cycle engine built by Claude Sintz at the turn of the century produced 350 rpm and propelled Gray into the marine engine business

The year was 1906 and Continental Motor Manufacturing Co. had just moved from Chicago into its new plant in Muskegon, Michigan, to build engines for the makers of automobiles (formerly known as horseless carriages).

Some engines had also been built by Continental for marine use, but that was already a highly competitive market, particularly around the Great Lakes. Records of early boating magazines indicated that over a hundred makes of marine engines were being made and advertised at that time. Every town on the Lakes seemed to have a marine engine builder.

One early builder was Claude Sintz whose Sintz Gas Engine Co. had been making marine engines in Grand Rapids, Michigan, well before the turn of the century. His first engine was two-cycle, produced three horsepower, and had a rotative speed of about 350 rpm. One of Sintz' customers was the Michigan Yacht and Power Co., located in Detroit near the Belle Isle Bridge.

When Sintz was unable to supply engines fast enough, O.J. Mulford, head of the Detroit boat company, joined with his associates in 1895 to buy out the Sintz firm so as to assure an adequate supply of engines for their growing boat business.

Then, in 1906, John S. Gray joined O.J. Mulford in forming their own engine company, Gray Marine Motor Co. of Detroit. Mulford had been president of King Motor Car Co. and was also associated with Gray in Gray Motor Co. which built the Gray automobile and also supplied engines for Maxwell-Briscoe and Stoddard-Dayton cars.

Since the marine engine industry was older than the automotive, it was not surprising that some of the early auto engines were adaptations of marine engines. At Continental, the opposite had been the case.

In 1914 Gray Marine started using Continental engines, modifying them for marine use. By 1927 the two companies had agreed on a franchise arrangement giving Gray exclusive rights to Continental engines for marine applications.

After 17 years of that arrangement, Continental purchased all of Gray Marine's stock in 1944 for $2,616,910 during World War II. The stock was acquired from the estate of O.J. Mulford, co-founder of the company who passed away in 1943. However, in the industry, it had been anticipated that General Motors would buy Gray Marine and make it the marine division of that automotive giant.

Gray was a large peacetime supplier of marine engines for commercial fishing and freight boats and pleasure craft. Its distribution system covered the United States and some 41 countries abroad. During the war it was chiefly occupied with building engines for Navy landing craft.

Among wartime products were Detroit Diesel Quads (bank of four engines) modified and supplied by Gray for wartime use. Continental was able to continue government contracts for Gray Marine's modification of these General Motors engines, but lost rights for other conversions of their diesel power plants.

John W. Mulford, son of the founder and President of Gray Marine since the death of his father continued with the company as head of Continental's newest subsidiary.

Son of one of the founding fathers of Gray Marine, John W. Mulford continued as President after Continental bought the company

Gray Marine has won four stars for its "E" flag.

All Photos Teledyne Continental Motors

GRAYMARINE MODEL SIX-121 for heavy-duty service on inland waterways

GRAYMARINE LIGHT FOUR

113

POST-WAR TO KOREA (1946-1953)

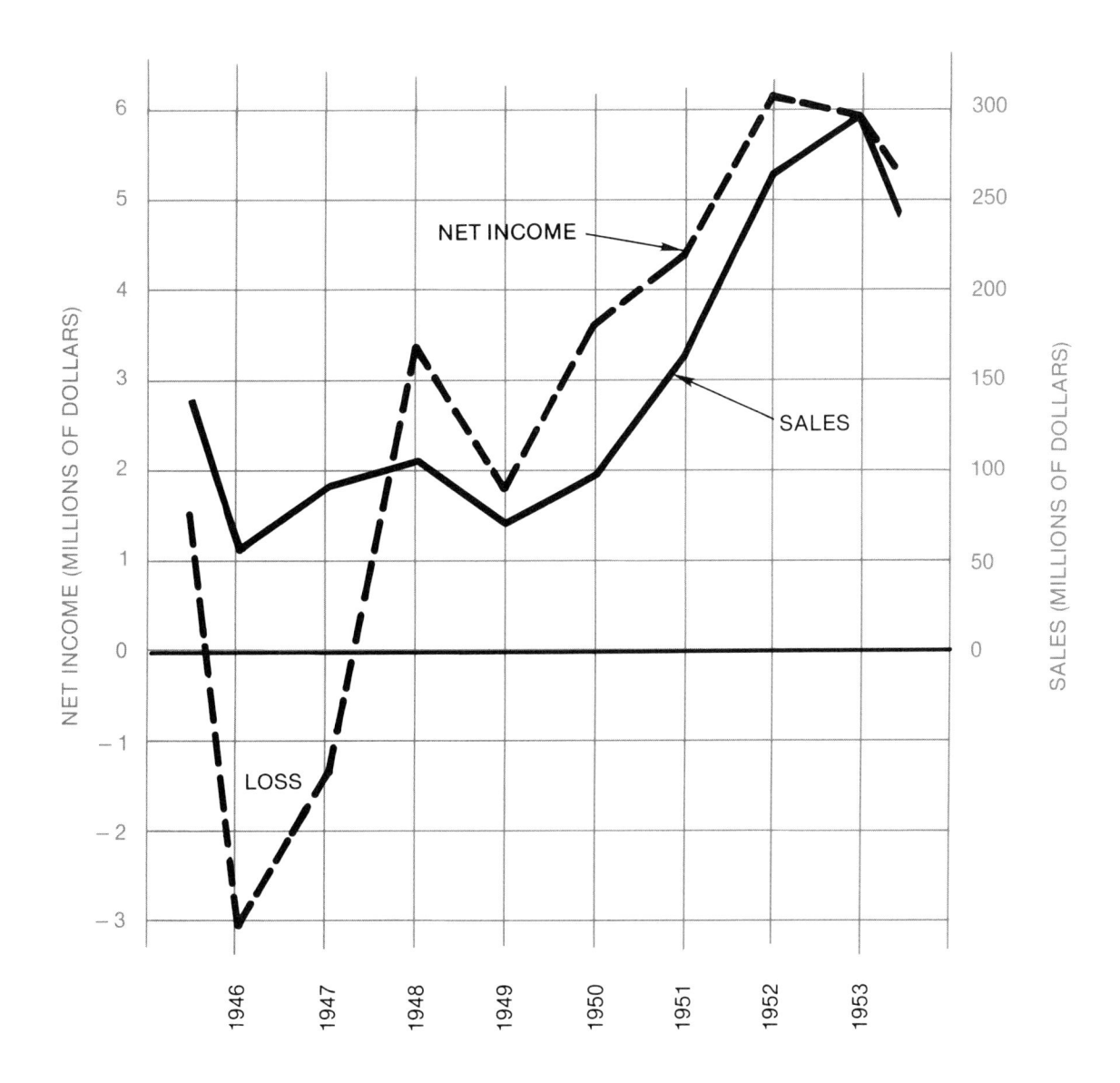

A new family of military engines developed for the Ordnance Corps opens the door to a long-range program for the company. So, too, does an agreement under which Continental Aviation and Engineering makes a strong entry into the jet engine business.

Pages 117 to 143

1946-1953

Post-War Reconversion Problems 117
Meeting Customer Needs 118
Agricultural Engines 119
Transportation 120
Aircraft 120
Industrial 121
Marine 121
CAE for R and D 121
Profitable Wisconsin 123
Con-Tex's Ferry Pilot 123
Kaiser-Frazer; Checker Cabs 123
New Ordnance Policy 124
The Stilwell Report 125
Family of Military Engines 126
Air-Cooled Tank Engines 128
Peacetime Economic Conditions 130
Gas Turbine Research at CAE 131
Speed and Endurance Flights 131
Putting Horsepower to Work 132
Tank Production for Korean War 134
Engines for Tracked Vehicles 135
A Diversity of Uses 136
Soaring Sales 137
Helicopter Engine Orders 137
Getting Into the Turbine Business 138
1952 — Golden Anniversary 141
Working for Jack Reese 142

Business as Usual

With return to a peace-time economy, Continental began to project its stature as the world's largest independent producer of engines. Five major commercial engine divisions were identified and extensively promoted: **Agricultural, Transportation, Aircraft, Industrial** and **Marine**.

Post-War Reconversion Problems

Although there was a large backlog of unfilled demand for commercial engines which could not be produced because of wartime restrictions, the reconversion to normal business operation was not without serious problems.

In his first post-war Report to Stockholders, Jack Reese pointed out that "A combination of adverse operating conditions—rising costs, price controls, material shortages and strikes in the plants of both customers and suppliers is resulting in unprofitable operations."

Reese also stressed the need for plant modernization, particularly at Muskegon. This would mean extensive changes in production layout, installation of new equipment and some plant additions. Facilities built in the 1920s were no longer adequate for the diversified output and production flexibility required for the changing post-war product lines.

Financial needs to accomplish the plan, and for working capital, were estimated at $12 million. Business conditions the first two post-war years, however, did not permit going ahead with the modernization program.

Despite the largest production schedules in peacetime, consolidated sales dropped from $220 million in 1945 to $60 million in 1946 then rose to $91.5 million in 1947.

Such a sharp reduction in sales volume brought an even sharper reduction in profit. Net income for 1945 was $5.7 million but net losses were posted in each of the next two years: $3 million in 1946; $1.3 million in 1947. (Before tax carry-back provisions of the federal income tax law, losses would have been $15.4 million in 1946 and $9.7 million in 1947.)

Dividends of 35 cents per share were paid in 1946. No dividend payment was made in 1947.

Under the wartime "V" Loan agreement with banks, Continental owed $24.2 million at the end of the 1944 fiscal year, but had paid the loans in full in March 1946.

Just before the close of the 1946 fiscal year, the company did arrange for additional financing, a $5 million loan from six banks and another $5 million from an insurance company. In addition, stockholders approved issuance of 350,000 shares of $50 par value preferred stock and an increase of authorized common stock from 3,000,000 shares outstanding to 5,000,000 shares. No additional shares, however, were sold at this time.

With new funds at hand, the company was able to begin its conversion program of plant modernization and replacement of equipment which had been operated almost continuously during the war years. Its full effect on more efficient operation, however, would not be realized for several years.

Although Continental was having financial problems during the post-war reconversion period, Jack Reese was attracting national attention as an up-and-coming business executive.

Under the headline, "Back to the Top," BUSINESS WEEK cited the company's up-and-down history: From producer, during the first quarter of the century, of engines for 90 percent of the cars on the road, to the brink of bankruptcy during the 30s.

With its $12 million modernization program, the magazine said, Continental was digging in to keep a large portion of the wartime gains that shot it to the top of the field.

"Jack Reese's accession to the presidency," BUSINESS WEEK wrote, "is the prime reason for Continental's success in the past seven years. He works 16 hours a day, wears out subordinates who try to keep pace with him and thrives on his intense schedules.

"His first moves were to strip Continental down to fighting weight and to make a strong bid for commercial business. As a result, Continental is no longer the third ranking competitor among diversified engine makers. It is the top builder with volume triple that of its nearest competitor. And in light aircraft, it has become a near-exclusive supplier."

Under the Reese management regime a new policy of giving priority to customer needs was adopted. Every effort was made to meet delivery dates; follow-up by service technicians was improved; quality control and parts availability were given increased attention. The number of distributor and dealer outlets, both domestic and foreign, was increased materially. Liaison with the sales and service outlets of equipment manufacturers using Continental engines was improved.

Meeting Customer Needs

As Reese explained, "While we were unable to produce as many engines as our customers would have liked, we nevertheless did produce more than ever before in peacetime—an accomplishment made possible only by going to every length to meet their delivery schedules.

"To keep shipments abreast of demand, we have been operating our plants six and seven days a week with excessive overtime labor costs which have resulted in unprofitable operations. This is the penalty we have been willing to pay to protect and enhance our competitive position."

In a characteristic, straight-from-the-shoulder talk to his engineers, Jack declared that "There are critical days ahead, but we must be prepared to go forward to the greatest business we have ever known.

"We have the plants and the facilities. We have the know-how. We have the product and the reputation. Now it is up to our team to meet the challenge."

His thoughts were echoed by other members of the 'Reese team'. Ben Tobin, Jr., Executive Vice-President, who had supervised CMC's activities in the Southwest since the opening of the Garland, Texas plant in 1943, declared that "We make the best damned engines in the oil fields. They have inherent qualities of stamina and ruggedness; they can run 24 hours a day, day in and day out, with little or no attention.

"Continental's on top and if we don't forget that we'll maintain our position. There is no reason why we shouldn't continue to lead the field."

The large government-owned Garland plant represented excess peace-time capacity, so CMC relinquished its lease on that property. Instead a new $250,000 assembly and service plant was built at Dallas.

Ben Tobin, who had long expressed an interest in having his own distributorship, moved out to Los Angeles in 1946, where his mother was living, and established Continental Sales & Service Company, heading up an intensified sales program on the West Coast.

George E. Winters, a long-time employee and production Vice-President since 1941, took over Tobin's corporate post as an Executive Vice-President, sharing that title with Lewis P. Kalb. Bert Brandana, former superintendent of the Garland plant, was selected to be branch manager at Dallas.

Additional branch offices were also established for the Pacific Coast, Pacific Northwest and Atlantic Coast areas under sales managers Don Parkin, L. E. Wheeler and Ed Rublein, respectively. And, to improve relations with dealers and distributors of Continental engines, C. Wheeler Johnson was named Vice-President in charge of general service and distributor sales.

GEORGE E. WINTERS
A native of Muskegon, Winters joined company in 1918, rising to Executive Vice-President 29 years later

C. WHEELER JOHNSON
Selected to improve distributor and customer relations, Johnson had been plant manager of an agricultural equipment company before joining CMC

POWER BY
Red Seal Engines
CONTINENTAL

CONTINENTAL... BUILDING THE HIGHWAYS OF PEACE

On the highways of peace, Continental Red Seal Engines are proving their stamina and versatility. In the crane that loads the trucks, in the trucks themselves, and in the spreaders that lay the pavement there's Red Seal Power. Every Continental Red Seal engine has the added stamina, the dependable power created by the Continental team of advanced engineering and precision manufacture.

Continental Motors Corporation
MUSKEGON MICHIGAN

The overseas market, especially Latin America, looked very promising to A.B. Bolthouse, export manager, after an extensive business trip south of the border. He was particularly optimistic about the outlook of CMC's new line of diesel engines because of heavy taxes in South America on gasoline fuel.

"With our biggest single competitor—Germany—out of the picture," Bolthouse explained, "we should hold our share and do $1 million in export business world-wide the first full year after the war."

Lewis Kalb, after a trip to England to investigate trade with the 'Sterling area,' was equally enthusiastic. "The British are anxious to buy Continental engines," he said, "because they know them and the reputation they earned in powering their tanks. Now they want to buy our industrial engines and they are interested in our light aircraft engines, too, because they have seen the "Flying Jeeps' and know what they can do."

To push the company's plans for reconversion to a peacetime economy, CMC launched a massive advertising program in 52 U.S. and foreign publications with a total circulation of 10 million copies. Highlighted was the story of how wartime research, engineering and production methods were being employed for the benefit of civilian customers in providing better, more responsive, more economical and more reliable Continental engines.

"No other manufacturer has ever offered customers so wide a choice of engines." Such was the 1947 claim of Continental and its Wisconsin and Gray Marine subsidiaries. Together they boasted a total of 106 models in production ranging from a new 1½ horsepower air-cooled unit to a 247 horsepower industrial engine. Models offered included air-cooled and liquid-cooled engines using gasoline, butane, natural gas, diesel oil and other fuels.

Wisconsin Motor Corp. offered 14 air-cooled heavy-duty engines from 2½ h.p. to 31 h.p. used primarily in agricultural and construction equipment. Gray Marine offered 22 marine versions of Continental engines plus six of its own models.

Continental was also achieving some needed degree of standardization and interchangeability. The 106 different engine models derived from 22 basic cylinder blocks by means of relatively simple variations in machining and by use of widely interchangeable parts.

Many of the major elements of Continental's new line of four- and six-cylinder Red Seal diesel engines were directly interchangeable with its carbureted gasoline engines of the same displacement. These diesels employed four-stroke cycle, overhead valves, and 'cushioned power' combustion chambers which caused delayed burning of the fuel and made possible low working pressures on the cylinder.

Good production runs were achieved for many years with CMC diesels employing the "Lanova" principle. While relatively poor in performance when judged against later developments, these diesels were 'adequate for their day' and a considerable improvement over the earlier limited success of "Oil-carbureted" engines which were started on gasoline, then switched to oil.

Diesels were offered in five basic models for industrial and agricultural applications; and in three models for trucks and buses.

The heavy-duty R-600 engine, developed early in the war, became the basic unit for many different gasoline and diesel power units sold commercially. All models based on the R-600 design were six-cylinder, overhead valve engines with a stroke of 5-3/8 inches offered in three bore sizes: 4-1/2, 4-3/4 and 4-7/8 inches.

In its major product lines Continental expanded the range of horsepower available to its customer companies, adding engines at both the lower and upper ranges of power output. With a broader product line, the number of customers increased and sales volume went up as the accumulated demand from wartime restrictions began to be met.

Agricultural Engines

Continental's Agricultural line of gasoline engines, confined to the 24 to 30 horsepower range in 1939 (before the Reese management 'team' took over), was expanded to a range of 12 to 65 horsepower, partly by acquisition of its 83.1% owner-

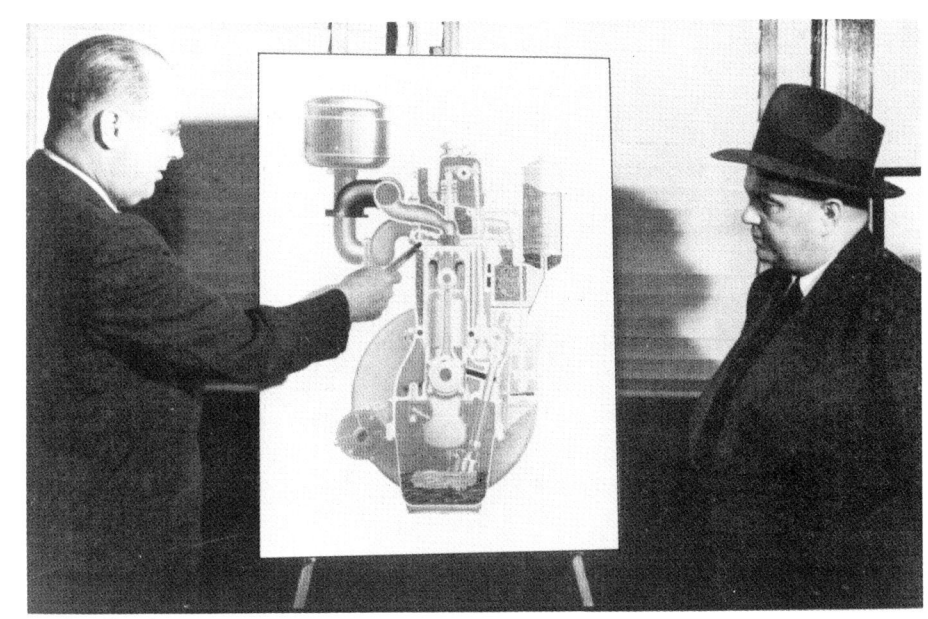

Red Seal Magazine

Earl Ginn, chief engineer of Continental's Industrial Engine Division, explains cut-away drawing of 'cushioned power' diesel to Jack Reese who, as usual, is wearing his hat

Wisconsin Air-Cooled Heavy-Duty Engines

from 2½ H.P. to 31 H.P.

ship of Wisconsin Motor Corp. In April 1946 the companion line of new diesel engines from 25 to 62 horsepower for farm use was added.

The number of agricultural customers was nearly doubled, and the 1946 sales volume of $5.6 million was three times greater than before the war. Agricultural sales rose to $11.6 million in 1947.

Typical agricultural uses were for tractors, combines, sprayers, hay balers, mowers, pumps and saw mills.

Transportation

Truck, bus and automobile manufacturers were the company's principal Transportation customers. Pre-war, Continental offered gasoline engines with ratings from 25 to 146 horsepower. After the war, range was extended upward to 250 horsepower in the wartime R-600 which could be used in heavy trucks, road machinery and other equipment requiring heavy-duty dependability. New diesel engines for transportation use ranged from 60 to 150 horsepower.

Sales of transportation engines at $7.4 million were four times greater in 1946 than for the 1939-41 yearly average, and forecast to be ten times greater in 1947. The actual sales figure that year was $20.7 million. Production of automotive parts and sub-assemblies for other manufacturers was an incidental phase of the business, but automobile engine sales as such were only 15% of the transportation division's volume.

As the 1946 fiscal year began, however, Jack Reese negotiated a contract with Joseph W. Frazer, President of Kaiser-Frazer, for Continental to build engines for the new, low-priced Kaiser and medium-priced Frazer cars to be built in the famous Willow Run bomber plant near Detroit.

To hold down production expense, Kaiser-Frazer wanted low-cost engines, so Continental offered six-cylinder models which had previously been in production for Graham-Paige, another Kaiser-Frazer company. It was perhaps the only post-war instance where a major automobile manufacturer went to an outside, independent company for its engines.

The 1947 Kaiser Sedan, powered by Continental's six-cylinder 100 horsepower engine

Six-cylinder "E" series opposed air-cooled aircraft engine was used in both Beech Bonanza and competitive Ryan Navion business planes

Aircraft

Largest percentage increase in sales, nearly 1000%, was for Aircraft engines as the light plane industry expanded rapidly after the war to sales of $100 million annually. Continental engines became standard on all production light-planes using power plants of less than 100 horsepower.

The company sold 34,358 aircraft engines in 1946 valued at $14.7 million. The following year sales dipped to $8 million as a depression hit the personal plane industry. This resulted in credit losses of over $400,000 due to financial difficulties of a few customers.

Nine horizontally-opposed air-cooled engines, with a large measure of interchangeability of parts, were offered in 1947. In production for light planes were the "A" series 65 horsepower model; 75, 85 and 90 horsepower four-cylinder "C" series engines; 115, 125 and 145 horsepower six-cylinder "C" models; and in the new six-cylinder "E" series, engines producing 165 and 185 horsepower.

One major user of the E-185 engine was Ryan Aeronautical Company for the Navion four-place personal/business plane. Originally designed and built by North American Aviation, the big, rugged, easy-to-fly plane attracted pioneer aircraft builder T. Claude Ryan whose company took over the project and began producing and selling the improved Ryan Navion—Continental-powered.

Another was the Navion's principal competitor, the Beech Bonanza powered by either the 165 or 185 h.p. flat six-cylinder Continental engine.

Two adaptations of the wartime R-975 nine-cylinder radial engine for 30-ton tanks were also available through CAE for use in medium-size planes. They were the 525 horsepower R-9A and the 600 horsepower geared GR-9A. In addition, some deliveries were still being made of the 220 h.p. seven-cylinder W-670 radial which had been used in both tanks and training planes during the war.

For rugged service many industrial firms selected the Continental-powered Ryan Navion business plane

Personally enthusiastic about flying and recognizing that for Continental the personal plane might replace the automobile as the company's best market for its transportation engines, Jack Reese became one of the personal plane industry's best salesmen.

When the 1947 market for small planes began to drop below estimates Reese decided Continental could best help by sponsoring a nationwide "Start Flying NOW" advertising program. Non-competitive, the ads were aimed at selling the idea of flying rather than promotion of a particular product. The company's major customers—Cessna, Piper, Beech and others—were indeed grateful for the engine-maker's leadership.

To make travel by personal plane more attractive and less costly, Reese introduced a new program, first of its kind, whereby used Continental aircraft engines could be exchanged for factory re-manufactured

Jack Reese, an enthusiastic aviation supporter, is flanked on his right by Michigan Governor G. Mennen Williams, and by Gen. Hoyt S. Vandenberg, Air Force Chief of Staff

engines on which was placed a new engine guarantee.

Few men did more than Jack Reese to advance the cause of aviation during its expanding years. Continental sponsored numerous programs involving the designing, building and flying of airplanes, and supported an even greater number of projects and organizations sponsored by others.

Over the years Reese served as an officer or member of nearly every organization interested in aviation—personal, business, agricultural, industrial and military. The Continental Motors Trophy Races for pilot-designed, pilot-built planes, the University of Detroit aircraft design scholarship competition and the Aero Club of Michigan were his particular interests.

Industrial

Increased sales of Industrial engines for such diverse applications as welders, drilling rigs and compressors reflected both the pent-up demand resulting from wartime curtailment of production and the wide range of products made by Continental's customers. Sales increased eight-fold compared with prewar levels, totaling $6.6 million in 1946, rising to $10.2 million in 1947.

New gasoline-fueled engine models were added on both the low and high power scale, so that a power range of eight to 124 horsepower was available to customers. The new diesel line offered industrial engines ranging from 25 to 115 horsepower.

Marine

Continental's peacetime Marine engine business was solidified and enlarged through acquisition in 1944 of Gray Marine Motor Co. as a wholly-owned subsidiary. The parent company had not built marine diesels before the war but with the introduction of CMC's new diesel line, Gray could also adapt these Continental engines as well as liquid-cooled gasoline types to inboard installations for marine use, greatly expanding the potential market.

Engines for marine use ranged from 10 to 190 horsepower. Sales for 1946 were $3.7 million, a peacetime record, climbing to $4.0 million the following year.

The majority-owned Continental Aviation and Engineering subsidiary had much the same post-war financial problems as did the parent company. Sales were off sharply in fiscal 1946, recovering somewhat the following year, but net losses were reported in both years.

CAE for R and D

Sales for CAE in 1946 were $2,232,878; in 1947 they rose to $4,981,228. But neither year was profitable; the two year loss was $566,000. In 1946, two-thirds of sales were

D. H. HOLLOWELL
Well-liked in the general aviation industry, Dee Hollowell was a great asset to Continental as the company's Vice-President in charge of aircraft engine sales

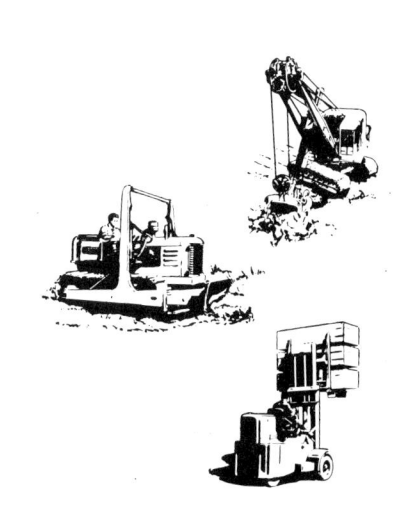

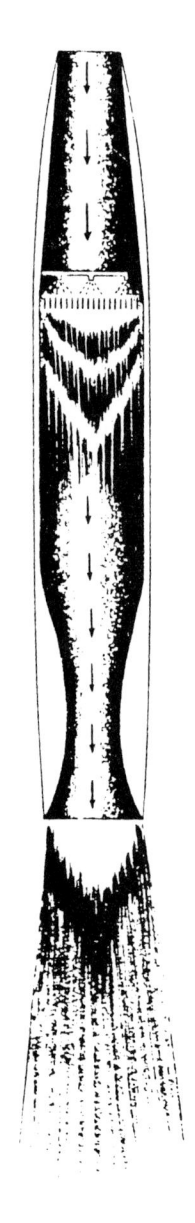

to the parent Continental Motors Corp.; the following year sales were 40 percent greater to other customers than to CMC.

With orders for military aircraft engines cancelled, CAE had to scratch for post-war business wherever it could be found. It would be six years before sales again reached the $10 million mark.

Following VJ Day, CAE began stressing its research and development work, with particular emphasis on ram and pulse jet engines of extremely high power; and on gas turbines, compound engines combining gas turbine and piston engine principles, and light-weight 200-300 hp piston engines for helicopters. All such development projects were either directly or indirectly sponsored by the government.

A production contract for $2.7 million had been obtained in 1945 from the Army Air Forces for 'intermittent' pulse jet engines adapted by CAE from the propulsion units which had powered German "buzz bombs."

Many commercial products were investigated and limited production contracts were obtained on such items as parts and sub-assemblies from automotive, farm equipment, household product and other industrial manufacturers.

Typical products manufactured were hydraulic brake cylinders, brake drums, refrigerator pistons and connecting rods, tractor components, field forage harvesters and lighting generators. In addition, CAE did commercial heat treating, plating and painting; and its machine shop made tools, jigs and fixtures for other companies.

A portion of the Getty Street military plant was leased by CAE for filling its commercial production contracts, while engineering, research and development projects were handled at the company's Detroit facility.

In line with national policy, the War Assets Administration put the $55 million, 850,000 square foot Getty Street plant up for sale or lease. In January 1947 there were two bidders. Midwest Motors of Grand Island, Nebraska offered $5.2 million cash but the complicated written offer was unacceptable and it appeared that the letter, on the stationery of a Chicago hotel, was from a 'paper' corporation.

CAE offered to lease one-quarter of the plant annually for five years, with an option later to buy the plant or negotiate further leases. The company also said it would employ every "able-bodied veteran in Muskegon." In Detroit, CAE did purchase from WAA the wartime engineering and research building it had been occupying there.

Lockheed chose Continental GR-9A engines for its twin-engine 14-place "Saturn" feeder airline transport. This commercial 525 h.p. engine was the CAE-

Largest helicopter of its day, the PV-3 'Flying Banana' was powered by a 'submerged' Continental R-975 radial aircraft engine

engineered geared aircraft version of the wartime R-975 nine-cylinder tank engine. The "Saturn", however, did not go into volume production.

Another customer for the GR-9A was Beech Aircraft, builder of executive planes for business travel.

Similarly, with its parent company as a customer, CAE began work to adapt both the W-670 and R-975 radial engines and one of the horizontally-opposed light-plane engines for use in helicopters.

In one important respect tanks and helicopters are similar in that neither can rely on forward speed for engine cooling. The heat transfer essential to power plant cooling must be aided by forced air movement with a stub fan as originally worked out by Continental on light tanks in the 30s.

Early Piasecki (P-V Engineering Forum) twin-rotor 'Flying Banana' helicopters, then largest in the world, were equipped with Continental R-975 engines in a 'submerged' installation in the aft end of the 48-foot-long fuselage.

"It turned out ultimately," Art Wild recalls, "that the helicopter was too heavy for the power, and we had a hell of a time'."

Another CAE post-war venture was development and manufacture of its "Skypower" controllable pitch propeller, primarily in configurations to match the horsepower range of Continental engines used in light planes. Designed to do for a plane what a gear shift does for a car, the new propeller was introduced in March 1946 after earlier development under direction of Peter Altman, consulting engineer. Claims for the propeller were that it would improve the plane's take-off and climb performance as well as obtain maximum cruising speed with minimum gasoline consumption. Pitch of the propeller blades was actuated hydraulically.

CAE's 'Skypower' controllable pitch propeller is tested with Continental C-85 aircraft engine

While sales and earnings of Continental Motors and CAE fell sharply from wartime levels in the first two post-war years, 1946 and 1947, those of majority-owned Wisconsin Motors Corp. increased sharply.

Profitable Wisconsin

From 1944 sales of $11,841,447, Wisconsin's business volume increased each year, reaching $21,659,696 in 1947. Similarly, profit rose from $486,535 in 1944 to $1,282,381 in 1947.

"Wisconsin's production capacity," Reese reported, "was increased 40% during 1946 by rearrangement and additions to manufacturing facilities. The company has also benefitted from the large demand for its present basic models, which has made it necessary to hold introduction of new models to a minimum.

"As a result of a court order liquidating Wisconsin Motor Company, predecessor of the present corporation, the stock holdings of CMC are increased from 72% to 83.1% of that firm's common stock."

Because the Garland wartime plant was no longer needed, CMC had given up its lease on that facility. And, because the product did not fit into the company's basic business, Continental disposed of its wholly-owned Con-Tex Petroleum Corp. late in 1947, taking a modest profit on the sale.

Con-Tex's Ferry Pilot

Con-Tex had been engaging in oil leasing, developing and producing activities in Texas and Oklahoma. Liaison with that subsidiary had been maintained by Jim Ferry, Jr.

"It just made sense for me to be able to nip back and forth by airplane," Jim said, "so I bought a small plane — Continental powered, of course — and learned to fly. I'd previously had some training at Boston while going to M.I.T. but my father didn't approve so I gave it up until after the war."

[Thirty-five years later, 1980, Ferry is still flying his own Continental-powered Cessna Skymaster business plane. His license includes instrument and multi-engine ratings.]

The automobile engine business, in which Continental had been a leader in the industry's early days, continued to elude the company. Although the Detroit plant had very little production business after the war, even the Kaiser-Frazer deal was not working out.

Kaiser-Frazer; Checker Cabs

"Kaiser was predicting great things", Art Wild relates, "and they insisted on a capacity we thought was way too high. It finally turned out that we reached an impasse.

JAMES H. FERRY, JR.
As his father before him, Jim Ferry was not only a stabilizing force in the changing fortunes of Continental Motors and its management but gave the corporation financial integrity by maintaining the family's long-time investments. Careers of father and son in the firm spanned the entire eight decades of the company.

"In March 1947 we leased that portion of the Detroit plant to Kaiser-Frazer on a combined rental and royalty basis under which they built the engines.

"The Detroit plant had been designated by the government as a stand-by war emergency production facility. Later I learned that Edgar Kaiser and his father went down to Dayton to the Air Force people and told them they had taken over the plant and would make the military engines called for in the war emergency plan. When I walked in on the Air Force two days later I almost got my head taken off'."

[A four-way controversy, which included the Defense Plant Corp., and War Assets Administration as well as the two companies, also erupted over Kaiser-Frazer's use of government-owned equipment in the plant.]

Kaiser-Frazer had complained that Continental was behind on deliveries. Auto industry sources guessed that CMC could make motors faster than K-F could use them and so could not make money on the

"This cab has gone 358,000 miles on its original Continental engine." — Tony Capocy of Chicago

comparatively small production K-F could absorb.

Even in the booming post-war auto market, Kaisers and Frazers were not selling well. Buyers, seeing a chance to get cars from the 'big three' after a wait of several months, were passing up an unproven product whose prices had increased nearly $400 since their introduction a year earlier. New cars with old names — Cadillac, Ford, Chevrolet, Buick and Chrysler — dominated the market.

That left Continental Motors with just one automobile customer, Checker Cab. However, sales of engines for buses and trucks continued in good volume.

Checker had long been one of Continental's most dependable customers. Cab drivers liked them because they could rely on the engine. Cabbie Tom Copocy said it all: "Continentals keep me moving and earning fares. They don't use oil top and bottom, so the plugs stay clean. This cab has 358,000 miles on the original engine."

As with Continental Motors, a major war production task of the "big three" auto makers had been building tank engines for the Army Ordnance Corps. Like Continental Motors, Ford, Chrysler and General Motors were anxious to resume their normal business—for them, building passenger cars and trucks. When they did so, they left a great business opportunity open for Continental.

New Ordnance Policy

The lessons being learned in WWII in the use of armor on the battlefield required that the U.S. military establishment continue to update its concepts and equipment.

In September 1943 the Army had published its Handbook of Combat Vehicle Engineering but that document clearly indicated the need for further studies of weapons and their related prime movers and transport vehicles in the light of wartime experience.

Late in 1944 and early 1945, a Board of Officers of the Army Ground Forces was convened to "Study the Equipment of the Post War Army." The Equipment Review Board report of June 1945 noted that:

Special engines that are developed for tanks have general application for all armored vehicles. These engines are so unlike engines for wheeled vehicles that *special development during peacetime* **will be required.**

For Continental, "special development during peacetime" — of engines for tracked military vehicles — was the golden opportunity. In fact, Continental was already working with Major General G. M. Barnes and the Ordnance Corps on new tank engine development, just as it had done a decade earlier in liaison with then Capt. John K. Christmas when adapting the radial air-cooled aircraft engine for use in tanks.

In 1942, the Industry-Ordnance Engine Advisory Committee had recommended the development of a 12-cylinder air-cooled gasoline engine for military use. To fill this need Continental offered its design of a 1790 cubic inch displacement, carbureted, spark-ignition engine planned to produce 810 horsepower at 2800 rpm. The contract to develop not just the "1790" but eventually a whole family of engines was awarded in 1943 to Continental Motors which assigned the research, detailed engineering and testing to its Continental Aviation and Engineering (CAE) subsidiary.

Subsequently, the Handbook of Combat Vehicle Engineering was updated. Its volume on Combat and Tracklaying Vehicles was revised in May 1945 under the general direction of now Brigadier General Christmas of the Office, Chief of Ordnance. This classified document for the first time made specific reference to the Continental V-12 Model 1790 development engine.

For the post war Army, the Equipment Review Board spelled out the need for three tank types: (1) An up to 25-ton **light tank** [T-41] for reconnaissance and security; (2) A not over 45-ton **medium tank** [T-42] — the principal weapon of armored divisions — for light assault action, exploitation, and pursuit; (3) a **heavy tank** [T-43] of about 75 tons for assault action and breakthrough.

The report also pointed out that "there will be continued requirement for amphibian tanks in sea-to-shore operations where Army ground troops will use them" and for amphibian kits "to float light and medium tanks ashore."

To power its tracklaying vehicles including tanks, self-propelled weapons and cargo carriers, the Army wanted a series of engines — 500, 1000 and 1500 horsepower — incorporating the maximum number of interchangeable parts.

Among some other specifications were requirements for operation on a wide range of fuels, minimum of 1000 hours of operation before major overhaul, adaptability to low silhouette hulls, ability to operate submerged in water and starting and operating in temperatures from minus 20° F to plus 140° F.

The Stilwell Report

The final report on equipment for the post war Army was issued October 8, 1945 by still another War Department Equipment Board, this one headed by famed General Joseph W. "Vinegar Joe" Stilwell whose name has since been used in describing the so-called "Stilwell Report."

Because of wartime security, virtually nothing was seen in the public press about new tanks and new tank engines. Only after the war, early in 1946, did CAE publish a picture and brief reference to "future tank engines" of 12-cylinder design in its Annual Report to Stockholders. (It was the first indication that CAE would broaden its scope beyond the "over-500 hp aircraft engine" field.)

A further development of long-range significance was the Ordnance Corps decision in June 1947 to have Continental begin design work on an air-cooled **diesel** engine.

During the 1942 Armored Force gasoline vs. diesel controversy, General Barnes and Colonel Christmas were the Ordnance Department representatives. General Barnes, vigorously dissenting from the no-diesel policy, wrote:

> "The Ordnance Department considers the diesel engine the proper ultimate engine for tanks and believes that every effort should be made to expedite the development of adequate diesel engines for all tanks."

The basic concept of the new Continental development contract was to obtain greater fuel economy, ligher weight, maximum power, minimum space occupancy and maximum reliability.

As retired Lt. Gen. Jean Engler later observed, "Once again Continental assumed the responsibility as principal developer and manufacturer of tank engines."

BRIG. GEN. JOHN K. CHRISTMAS

Origin of Species

Army Ordnance Corps officers inspect new tank engine developed by CAE in Fall, 1945. Left to right: Maj. Gen. Gladeon M. Barnes, Chief of Research and Development; Gen. J. L. Devers, Commanding General, Army Ground Forces; Col. Joseph M. Colby, Chief of Industrial Operations; and Carl F. Bachle, Vice-President, Research, CAE.

Red Seal Magazine

Simplicity of design of new family of Continental engines is shown by engine blocks for 8-, 6-, and 4-cylinder horizontally opposed engines differing only in length. (Opposed cylinders are on other side of blocks.)

Courtesy BUSINESS WEEK

Chart in back of Edward A. Hulbert (left) and Carl Bachle, CAE engineers, illustrates advantages of standardization.

Red Seal Magazine

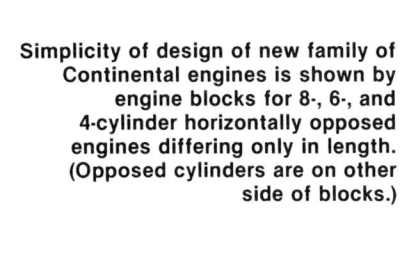

The concept for the development of a family of military engines stemmed from the 1943 Ordnance Corps research contracts with Continental.

Family of Military Engines

Col. Joseph M. Colby, Chief of Development and Engineering at the Detroit Arsenal, explained the Ordnance Corps' dilemma:

"Our World War II difficulties in obtaining an engine of approximately 500 horsepower for the medium tank was an excellent example of our military engine problem.

"We had to employ six improvised engines, build two new plants and retool four others. These engines came with 5,165 spare parts, six sets of tools, six sets of maintenance manuals and a constant flow of engineering changes. The effect was apparent because we as a nation did not have the vision to have an engine for military use developed, tested, and ready for the emergency."

Based on the design of a 1790 cubic inch displacement engine, Continental Motors and the Ordnance Corps set out to correct that situation. Next time around the U.S. would have a mobilization base consisting of production facilities and standard engines available to meet a national emergency.

The concept advanced was to expand the tank engine program to include other types of vehicles by developing six engines ranging from 125 to 810 hp using only two basic

Engines: Bore 4.62 × 4.00 stroke			
Model	c.i.d.*	Cyls	HP/rpm
AO	268	4	125 3000
AO	402	6	190 3000
AO	536	8	250 3000
Engines: Bore 5.75 × 5.75 stroke			
AO	895	6	375 2800
AV	1195	8	540 2800
AV	1790	12	810 2800
Supercharged			
AOS	895	6	500 2800
AVS	1195	8	665 2800
AVS	1790	12	1000 2800

*cubic inch displacement

cylinder sizes, and various numbers of cylinders: from four to 12. Cylinders for the three 125 to 250 horsepower horizontally-opposed engines were 4.62-inch bore by 4-inch stroke. The three 375 to 810 horsepower engines (one horizontally-opposed six plus 8- and 12-cylinder V-types) were 5.75 bore by 5.75 stroke.

By supercharging the large bore engines, a total of nine power plants could be produced, and top power rating could increase to 1000 horsepower.

Colonel Colby praised the new concept: "This is not an aircraft engine but rather a compact, lightweight, heavy duty engine designed for military use where mobility and reliability under conditions of heat, cold, dust, salt water, fungi, and other extremes are essential characteristics."

The entire program was under the overall direction of Art Wild, Executive Vice-President at Detroit, in collaboration with Col. Colby of Ordnance.

CAE's engineering and research effort was directed by the versatile, creative Carl Bachle assisted by Edward A. Hulbert, also a Vice-President.

The main features sought, according to Bachle, were "maximum interchangeability, lightest weight, minimum bulk, best utilization of space in the vehicle, use of standard Army gasoline and oil, waterproof for submersion, and suitability for extremes of arctic and tropical climates.

"Basic unit of the new engines is the individual cylinder, well suited for interchangeability because main wearing parts are all associated with the individual cylinder. In addition, individual cylinder construction is best for air-cooling. Also, many standard components such as fans, magnetos, oil filters, spark plugs, governors, etc., were considered appropriate for both sizes of engines.

"Air cooling, with cylinders finned like an aircraft engine, was selected as being preferable to liquid cooling. All things considered air-cooled engines are about one-third the weight of liquid-cooled, heavy duty vehicle engines, in part because approximately 40% of the weight of the former is aluminum. Air-cooling also does away with radiators, water pumps, hoses and coolants."

The fact that these engines operated in either vertical or horizontal position made it possible to install one in space little greater than its liquid-cooled counterpart required for radiator and fan alone.

Weight saving was very significant. So, too, was space. The new 810 hp air-cooled tank engine with cross-drive transmission was five inches shorter, yet produced 62 percent more power than its 500 hp WW II liquid-cooled counterpart with transmission and differential.

CARL F. BACHLE

Continental's engineering innovator, Carl F. Bachle, joined the company in 1927 after receiving his degree in Mechanical Engineering from the University of Michigan. For half a century Bachle sought out new concepts in engine design both in the United States and on the Continent, and supervised their successful development. Major accomplishments were in air-cooled engines for tanks and pioneering work in gas turbines. He continues to serve as a highly respected consultant to American industry and the government.

NOMENCLATURE

Engine families are identified by initial:

A = Air-cooled
O = Opposed
V = V-configuration
S = Supercharged

Later technical developments:

I = Fuel-injected
D = Diesel
L = Liquid-cooled

Basic configuration of the AV-1790 tank engine (Air-cooled, V-type of 12 cylinders and 1790 cubic inch displacement). This T40 tank was developed from the AV-1790-3-powered M26E2 medium Pershing tank, later standardized as the M46 Patton tank.

Compared with 5,165 kinds of spare parts for the six previous engines for medium tanks, the number of spare parts dropped to 954. The same mechanic, with a single set of tools, could service all models of the family of engines equally well.

Field tests with the AV-1790-3 (air-cooled, V-type of 1790 cubic inch displacement) engine in the M26E2 version of the Pershing tank were very encouraging. Ordnance had wanted a family of light-weight air-cooled engines ever since maneuvers in Alaska proved that liquid-cooled engines were impractical for such a climate. And, tests had shown that the air-cooled engine was preferable in desert areas where water for cooling was scarce.

As a result it was expected that the Army would equip most front-line vehicles from tanks to prime movers to trucks and weapon carriers with the new engines.

Things were moving along smartly with the Ordnance Corps' new engine program. To up-date U.S. technology, the government called on Carl Bachle in 1947 to serve as its technical consultant in making a power plant survey in Europe. As knowledgeable an engineer as could be found in his field, Bachle had been associated for 15 years with the application of air-cooled engines to tanks from the beginning of the U.S. pioneering effort in 1932.

After five years of development, Continental's new family of Ordnance Corps engines was unveiled in September 1948 with news splashes in major magazines including BUSINESS WEEK, TIME and LIFE.

Air-Cooled Tank Engines

Illustrations in the magazine articles visually showed the tremendous strides which had been made in design improvements. A LIFE photo showed a "new Continental 250 hp air-cooled [AO-536 eight-cylinder] engine weighing 777 pounds plus eight men balancing a standard liquid-cooled engine of the same horsepower which weighs 2400 pounds."

Another view showed the 12-cylinder version [AV-1790] against a background of four military vehicles which could be powered by the new engine: a heavy 70-ton tank, light 25-ton tank, 155-mm howitzer, and a 25-ton truck.

The contrast in engine space on two Army trucks was featured in BUSINESS WEEK photos. The air-cooled Continental, mounted vertically, showed the far larger cargo capacity of that truck's flat bed. Simplicity was featured in photo of 4-, 6-, and 8-cylinder engines with same bore for all, the only difference being in length of the blocks. As the magazine said, Jack Reese's new engines were built by sections.

Courtesy BUSINESS WEEK

On balance, Continental's new 250 horsepower engine weighing 777 pounds does work of 2400 pound water-cooled engine at right. Mounted vertically in military truck, background below, it gives Army far greater cargo capacity in truck.

First 1790 production engine for tanks was delivered in May, 1949. Jack Reese, right, congratulates Guy J. Harinton, left, and A.B. Willi, vice presidents at Getty Street operation.

Twelve-cylinder AV-1790 engine, foreground, can power wide range of military vehicles both wheeled and tracked, four of which are pictured here.

129

ALBERT B. WILLI

LEWIS P. KALB

THURA A. ENGSTROM

EARL C. GINN

All photos Red Seal Magazine

An $18.8 million production contract for 1000 tank engines, designated as Model AV-1790-5 was signed November 5, 1948. Final assembly of the pilot engine was completed May 23 and the first production engines were shipped in June 1949, eight months from the date of contract. These engines were initially used in the T40, later standardized as the M46 Patton Medium Tank, a major modification of the WW II Model M26 Pershing.

The November production contract provided authorization for an additional $9 million for tooling and facilities at the Getty Street plant to get standby production capacity up to 1200 engines per month. As the Air Force plant had been largely disassembled after the war it was necessary that it be renovated and reequipped. When reopened for tank engine production the Getty Street plant became an Army Ordnance facility.

On the same date that first deliveries of the 810 hp V-type 12-cylinder tank engine were started, Continental signed preliminary planning contracts for production of the AOS-895-3 supercharged six-cylinder 500 hp horizontally-opposed engine. The AO-895-4 unsupercharged version, rated at 375 hp, was also included in this program. "All out" capacity for producing the six-cylinder tank engines was set at 700 units per month.

Albert B. Willi, Executive Vice-President of CAE, was named a Vice-President of the parent company and placed in charge of tank engine production with Guy J. Harinton, another CMC Vice-President, as works manager at Getty Street.

In addition to the 5000 employed in the Market Street plant, 1200 more workers would be needed in Muskegon for tank engine production.

After two difficult post-war years, Continental got back on a firmer business foundation in 1948 with record peacetime sales of $108 million. Earnings rose to $3.4 million compared with a 1947 loss of $1.3 million.

Peacetime Economic Conditions

The upturn was largely the result of CMC's long-range program of product diversification and plant modernization which Jack Reese saw was carried out at an accelerated pace after the war. The price structure of the company's products was also changed to offset the increased costs of supplies and labor.

With increased mechanization on the farm, engines for implements and other agricultural uses accounted for 32% of total volume in 1948, increasing to 43% of the total the following year. Truck, automobile and bus engine sales were 21% in 1948, and industrial engine sales were 20% of the total.

Engines for aircraft and marine applications were both lower; in 1949 aircraft engine sales were only 4% of the total volume. Production was under way on important new military contracts for tank engines, but sales volume was not significant until the 1950 fiscal year.

Nationwide, the enormous production of both consumer and durable goods in 1947 and 1948 took the edge off the post-war sellers' market. Sales and earnings of many corporations declined and unemployment reached sizable proportions in many communities as the economy shifted to a buyers' market.

Continental Motors was caught in the same situation. Sales declined 32% in 1949 to $73.2 million and earnings for the year slipped 47% to $1.8 million. However, after two years of no cash return to stockholders, dividends were resumed in 1949.

The sizable loans from banks and an insurance company which CMC had arranged in 1947 were paid off in full at the end of the fiscal 1948 year. This was made possible by the sale through Van Alstyne, Noel & Co., of 300,000 additional shares of common stock at $7.50 per share in August 1947.

Consolidation of the financial statements of CMC and Wisconsin Motor, in which Continental owned an 83.1% interest, was effected in fiscal 1948. This resulted in an adjustment in consolidated financial statements back to 1943, the year CMC purchased its interest in Wisconsin Motor. [The adjusted figures are those used in this text.]

George E. Winters, CMC Executive Vice-President, who had joined the company in 1918, passed away December 7, 1948. At that time he was in charge of operations at Muskegon. Earl C. Ginn was selected to fill that executive vice-presidency.

Lewis P. Kalb, also an Executive Vice-President assumed a similar position with the Gray Marine subsidiary and was replaced in the CMC executive post by T.A. Engstrom, a 24-year veteran with the company.

Some indication of Continental's rather enviable position as an independent engine manufacturer, no longer overly dependent on either the auto industry or the military, was indicated in the accompanying chart. Peacetime production in 1948, expressed in horsepower, was nearly 80% of WW II peak military output.

Yet, in executive circles there was deep concern about the downturn in the general economy. A harried Jack Reese, recalling that Continental had a bank of $110 million in unfilled orders after VJ-Day, declared "This is a thing of the past.

"The employment outlook calls for plain talk. Much as I dislike saying it, there is little prospect — barring another war,

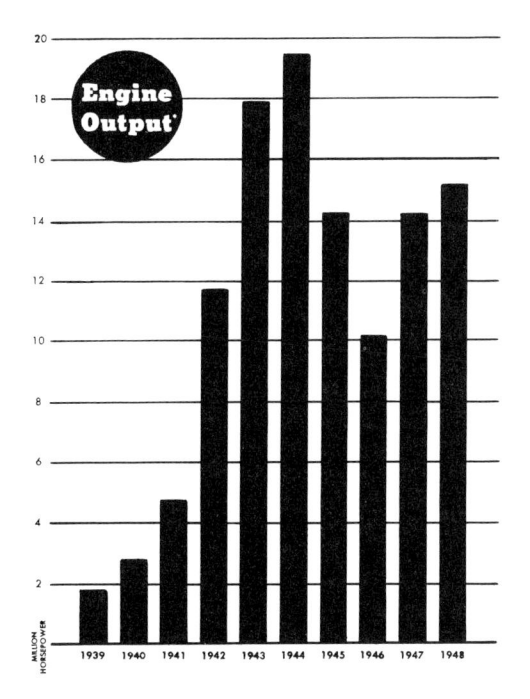

Engine Output

(Bar chart showing Million Horsepower from 1939 to 1948)

which none of us want — of any considerable number of our laid-off employees with low seniority getting their jobs back.

"Overtime pay is not in the cards any more. Competition for business is tougher than it has been for ten years and Continental cannot afford the luxury of inefficiency and high costs."

In line with its original objectives, the Continental Aviation and Engineering subsidiary again concentrated on research and development projects. Commercial manufacturing activities undertaken since the war at the Muskegon Getty Street plant proved unprofitable. As a result, CAE sales declined from the $5.0 million level of 1947 to $4.4 million in 1948 and $3.4 million in 1949, but operating losses were eliminated and a small profit was reported in 1949.

Gas Turbine Research at CAE

Research projects under way at Detroit for the Air Force included a 125 hp gas turbine engine and a starter for large jet engines, the latter deriving its power from the 125 hp turbine. A fuel metering device for the Air Force was also being developed.

For the Navy, CAE was developing two- and four-cylinder air-cooled diesel engines and a 50 hp gas turbine for portable fire pumps on naval vessels. Work also continued on a solid-fuel ram jet engine and on tank engine projects for the Ordnance Corps.

An initial pilot order was received from the Air Force for a small quantity of R975-34 helicopter engines to be delivered in 1950 and 1951. These were the nine-cylinder air-cooled engines adapted from the 525 hp radial aircraft engines Continental produced during the war for combat tanks.

Although the light plane industry was in a slump and sales of its engines sharply lower, Continental dominated what market was available.

Speed and Endurance Flights

New technical developments and many record-setting flights in Continental-powered planes kept the company's aircraft engines in the news. Trophies and purses which Continental sponsored for many lightplane events were eagerly competed for and the winning entries were well publicized.

At the Miami Air Maneuvers in January 1949, Steve Wittman hurled his 85 hp Continental C85-powered midget racer around a 24-mile course at 176.9 miles an hour breaking by 10.4 mph the previous record set by Wittman-trained Bill Brennand. A year later Wittman moved his own mark up to 185.4 mph.

On March 7-8, 1949, Capt. William P. Odom, flying a Beech Bonanza powered by a stock Continental 185 hp E185 engine, flew nonstop from Honolulu to Teterboro, N.J. The 5004 miles were covered in 36 hours and the engine used only $75 worth of gasoline. Two months earlier, flying the same plane, Odom had broken the Russian-held record for overwater flight in lightplanes with a non-stop flight from Honolulu to Oakland, California.

Hour-after-hour dependability of aircraft engines was frequently tested by endurance flights, which had become somewhat of a fad.

Shattering the 1939 mark Clyde Schlieper and Wes Carroll set in a Continental-powered Piper Cub, Dick Riedel and Bill Barris ten years later stayed aloft in their C145-powered Aeronca Sedan for 42 days (1008 hours of continuous engine operation). Total distance covered was over 75,000 miles—equal to three times around the world. When they landed at Fullerton, California, April 26, 1949, B.F. Tobin, Jr. head of Continental Sales and Service at Los Angeles was on hand to congratulate them.

The Fullerton fliers record was short lived. Less than six months later, also in a

Red Seal Magazine

Steve Wittman won trophy for 185 mph record speed behind 85 hp Continental engine

Red Seal Magazine

Coveted Continental trophy is awarded youthful speed pilot Bill Brennand by Jack Reese

In Continental-powered Beech Bonanza, Capt. William P. Odom flew record 5004 miles non-stop Hawaii to New Jersey

Beech Aircraft Corp.

Continental C145-powered Aeronca Sedan, Woody Jongeward and Bob Woodhouse of Yuma, Arizona, remained aloft for 1124 hours, bettering the old mark by nearly five days.

All engines in the record-setting flights were stock in every respect—identical with thousands of other Continental engines powering planes in everyday use.

The personal plane industry also had a prominent public figure enthusiastically selling aviation. Arthur Godfrey, popular CBS radio and TV personality, owned and flew a Continental-powered Navion and referred almost daily to the utility and pleasure of owning a plane.

The work-a-day jobs done by the wide range of Continental engines used in agricultural, industrial, transportation and marine installations became the theme of the company's expanded advertising and sales program. Satisfied customers telling their own stories of unique applications became CMC's best salesmen.

Putting Horsepower to Work

Wherever streets or highways were being built or repaired, it was a good bet that most compressors, pumps, graders, mixers and pavement-laying equipment were powered by Red Seal engines. Leading manufacturers of rollers, sprinkling machines, and fire-fighting equipment were Continental customers too.

A Red Seal Y-91 engine in an electrical generator plant made possible the complete electrification of the 8000-acre Minnesota ranch of the Chippewa Indian Tribe. Motion picture film for theaters throughout Pennsylvania was regularly delivered by a special truck powered by a Continental B-6371 engine.

A widow and grandmother, Mrs. Margaret Todhunter ran her 50,000-acre Diamond-L ranch near Deming, N.M., with the aid of the single-engine Cessna she regularly piloted for business and pleasure including trips into town to the beauty parlor and for shopping.

On a farm in Washington state, 71-year-old Charles Slusser was still operating the 1916 Continental-powered Federal truck which had served his needs for 32 years.

Much of the material moved into and out of warehouses throughout the country was carried to or from rail, ship or motor truck by Continental-powered fork-lift trucks. Work boats, fishing boats, pleasure boats were powered by Continental-Gray Marine engines.

One of the most dramatic changes in the country was in the mechanization of agriculture, brought about by increased use of tractors and especially by the development of self-propelled special-purpose harvesting equipment. For this broad market Continental developed many special, built-for-the-job engines.

Wherever power was needed, Continental could and did provide it. Thousands of stories were told of unique applications and tales were spun and re-spun of years-long service life and reliability. And are still being told.

Typical of the continued improvement in commercial power plants was Continental's T-6427 transportation engine. Designed to operate at higher engine rpm, this and companion Red Seal high-performance engines made possible faster over-the-road schedules for truck and bus operators. Higher gear ratios could be used, resulting in faster pickup, more power on hills, and higher road speeds.

Delivering 145 hp at 2600 rpm, the T-6427 was a six-cylinder overhead valve engine with sodium-cooled exhaust valves. Companion high-performance engines engineered expressly for transport uses were the overhead valve S-600 series and the L-head B-600 series.

Re-entering the consumer products field, Continental introduced a 1½ hp portable many-purpose power source under the registered trade-name "Multi-Tool." Engineered by Peter Altman, the new engine had a wide range of applications on the farm, in the shop, in the building and construction trades, on boats and in boat yards, on estates and around the home.

Available through hardware and implement stores as well as through Continental distributors and dealers, the Multi-Tool proved ideal for small cement mixers, pumps, feed grinders, conveyors, sprayers,

T-6427 heavy-duty transportation engines. Standard model above; horizontal model below

compressors, generators, and such tools as drill presses, lathes, sanders and saws.

In addition to Multi-Tool, Continental sought new markets by introducing ten small air-cooled single-cylinder, four-cycle L-head engines developing ¾ to 2 hp. They were designed to fill the growing need for power units for garden tractors, lawnmowers, compressors, electrical generators, and materials handlers.

In its 45th year the Gray Marine Motor Co. subsidiary offered 32 models (29 gasoline-powered and 3 diesels) in six lines including the Lugger, Phantom, Express and Fireball series, covering a power range from 16 hp to 180 hp.

As with its other products, Continental's Gray Marine engine users were that subsidiary's best salesmen. Edison Hedges of Atlantic City added to his world boat records with a new high speed mark of 57½ mph in his 17-foot runabout.

Gray Marine engines powered the lifeboats and tenders of the major transoceanic steamships of Cunard White Star, American Export Line and U.S. Lines.

To tote 400 bushels of oysters from the salt water ponds of Martha's Vineyard, the Vineyard Shellfish Corp. selected a four-cylinder Gray Express marine engine for its specially-designed 37-foot oyster boat.

The Army Corps of Engineers took delivery of three carloads of Express Six-244's for its specialized needs. W.A. Sheaffer, the pen king, had twin Super Six-427's installed in his 77-foot yacht.

When the Alaskan fishing industry was given permission to convert the salmon fishing fleet from sail to power for a 15-day season, a group of commercial fisheries standardized on the Gray Lugger Four-162, placing an order for 500 engines. Two years earlier the Venezuelan fishing fleet shifted from sail to power when 400 Gray marine engines went into service there.

Workman, right, demonstrates light weight and portability of many-purpose Multi-Tool engine which provides 1½ hp for wide range of uses in shop, on farm and in construction.

Edison Hedges

On shipping dock of Gray Marine's Detroit plant are three carloads of engines for U.S. Army Corps of Engineers

60-ton T43, largest U.S. Army tank, equipped with Continental's 810 hp twelve-cylinder AV-1790-7 gasoline engine, featured 120-mm gun

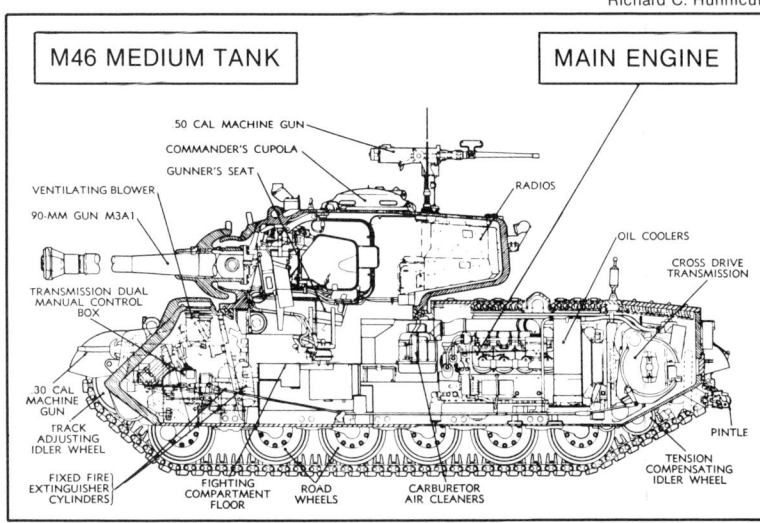

Installation of AV-1790-5 engine designed for specific use in M46 Patton tank is in sharp contrast to war-expedient use of radial aircraft engine (see sketch Page 92)

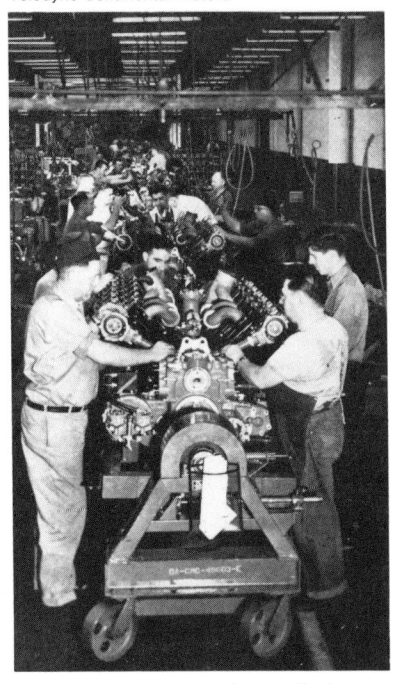

Final assembly of 12-cylinder 810 hp tank engines at Getty Street plant

The invasion of South Korea by North Korea on June 25, 1950 brought a prompt response from the United Nations and the authorization by President Harry S. Truman for U.S. military action in the area. It also set off a renewed emphasis on military equipment including the production of tanks and their engines.

Tank Production for Korean War

Once again Continental Motors was caught up in a situation where production of engines for military use was paramount. Once again Jean E. Engler, now a full Colonel, was deeply involved on the military side, later having responsibility for tank and automotive production for all three services.

When the Korean War started, Continental had delivered 625 Model AV-1790-5 engines for the M46, first of the series of Patton Medium Tanks, which began arriving in Korea in October, 1950. On August 1, the production rate of the 810 hp engines had been increased by the Army's Detroit Arsenal to 200 per month; on March 1, 1951, it was stepped up to 400 engines per month. Both increased quantities were based on a one shift 40-hour work week, although Continental had far greater round-the-clock capacity. By the end of May 1953, more than 20,000 engines in the 1790 series had been built.

For use in light tanks, Army Ordnance ordered Continental's AOS-895-3 (air-cooled, opposed, supercharged, 895 cid) engine into production just a month after the Korean War began. This six-cylinder lightweight gasoline fueled engine produced 500 hp; its unsupercharged twin, the AO-895-4, produced 375 hp and was included in the expanded production program for use in gun and cargo carriers. The first six engines were shipped eight months after contract.

21,250th twelve-cylinder engine in AV-1790 series was delivered late in 1953

Lesser production runs were scheduled for two other engines. The four-cylinder AO-268 model, which produced 125 hp, was used in an ammunition carrier. About 300 were built.

The 8-cylinder AV-1195, with 1790-type cylinders, produced 540 hp, but only about 50 engines of this model were built.

Employment at the Getty Street Ordnance Plant rose to 4000 in 1952, and to 5000 in 1953.

Demand for the Continental 1790 and 895 engines was so great that a second production source was considered necessary. As General Engler later explained, "Defense policy dictated that the production of key items of military hardware be dispersed to protect against a nuclear attack.

"The production of such items as tanks was planned in multiple geographic areas with their controlled subcontractors planned for the same area as the prime contractor. Under this program a tank engine plant was established under Chrysler at the old Michaud Ordnance Plant near New Orleans.

"Engineering control over the tank engines," Engler continued, "was exercised by Continental which assigned its Vice President, A.B. Willi, in September 1951 as liaison with Chrysler tank engine production. Starting deliveries in May 1952 this plant produced a relatively small percentage of total tank engine production before being placed on standby 14 months later after the Korean War."

Chrysler's initial contract for Continental-designed engines was reported to be $100 million and Art Wild observed that "We had to compete with them pricewise on tank engines for a while and that was a pretty hectic situation."

Another supplier also licensed to produce the 1790 engine was Lycoming.

In July 1952, the middle of the Korean War period, the Army unveiled its M48 Patton Medium Tank simultaneously at Chrysler, Ford and General Motors plants.

The Army had contracted for roughly $2 billion worth of the Patton tanks, with half of the contract value placed with Chrysler, which was also scheduled to take over production at the Detroit Tank Arsenal from the Ordnance Corps. The arsenal had been making the M47 tank which was outmoded by the M48 Patton.

A fifth source of Patton tank production was to be the American Locomotive Works.

All M48s were to be powered with Continental 12-cylinder 1790 gasoline engines, some of which would be produced at the Chrysler-run Michaud, Louisiana, ordnance plant.

Engines for Tracked Vehicles

In addition to the M46, M47 and M48 versions of the Patton Medium Tanks, 12-cylinder 1790 V-type engines were used in the following tracked vehicles built during the Korean War period: M43 Heavy Tank; 155 mm self-propelled M53 Gun; and 8-inch self-propelled M55 Howitzer. For its monster T51 Tank Retriever, the Army selected the AVS-1790-6 engine, the 1000 hp supercharged version of the engine powering M47 tanks. The same engine powered both the vehicle and its retrieval crane.

During the same period, the AO-895 and AOS-895 six-cylinder horizontally-opposed engines powered the T41 which went into production at Cadillac as the M41 Walker Bulldog Light Tank; also the 40 mm self-propelled M43 Gun, 105 mm self-propelled M52 Howitzer, components of the T10 Transporter, 155 mm self-propelled M44 Howitzer, M8E2 Cargo Tractor and M75 Personnel Carrier.

The Defense Department Equipment Board had earlier identified the continued need for development of amphibian tanks. For this task Continental produced a liquid-cooled version of the AV-1790 air-cooled engine for the Navy Bureau of Ships. Designated LV-1790-1 (liquid-cooled, V-type), this 12-cylinder engine powered the new LVT-5 (landing vehicle, tracked).

With the exception of the special liquid cooling components, all parts were common with the air-cooled engine and a high degree of parts interchangeability was secured. Shipment of LV-1790-1 engines began in November 1951.

All of the Korean War era Continental engines for tracked vehicles were built with carburetor fuel systems and embodied the latest engineering features then available for military applications. However, constant efforts to incorporate further technical improvements including fuel injection and the use of diesel fuel continued, but were not put into production until after the Korean War.

Teledyne Continental Motors

Assembly line for six-cylinder AO- and supercharged AOS-895 engines of 375 and 500 hp was established in 1951

Teledyne Continental Motors

AOS-895-4 air-cooled supercharged tank engine developed 500 hp

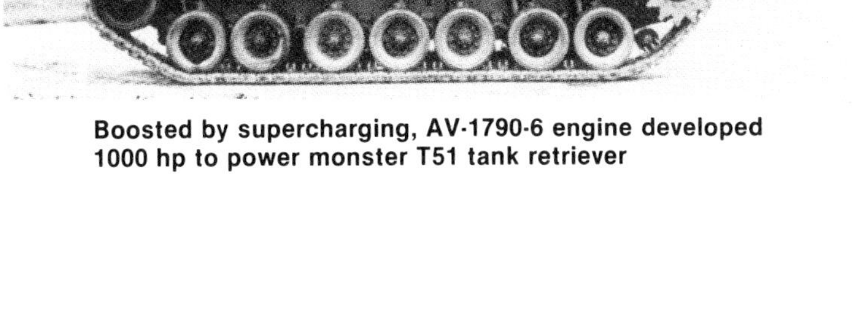

Boosted by supercharging, AV-1790-6 engine developed 1000 hp to power monster T51 tank retriever

This M8E2 tracked cargo carrier was powered by AOS-895 six-cylinder horizontally-opposed engine

Two thousand small AU-7B air-cooled engines were used in tent heaters in Korea

Cessna's popular Model 180

Army's L-19A 'Bird Dog'

Beech T-34 'Mentor' trainer

Continental aircraft and "Packette" air-cooled engines are assembled on same production line in recently completed plant addition, 1951

While America's attention was riveted on the war in Korea, every effort was made by Continental executives to carry on normal commercial business to the extent the national interest permitted.

A Diversity of Uses

Nearly every product line, however, had some military use. For example, the new line of small (up to 2 hp) air-cooled engines for such applications as garden tractors found use in Korea. There the biting cold presented a terrible personnel problem solved in part by using AU-7B engines to power heaters for tent shelters.

For this engine line, Continental introduced its own Contex ignition system which made it possible to check and adjust points without removing shroud or flywheel. This radically new system reduced ignition servicing time as much as 95 percent and prolonged the life of the spark plug and points.

In the aircraft field, Continental engines continued to set records in nearly all their power categories. In 1950, power output was increased to 225 hp in the E-225 model. At this time a new nomenclature system came into use where the numerical designation corresponded to piston cubic inch displacement (cid) rather than to horsepower. Thus the E-225 became known as the 0-470 (for opposed; 470 cid).

In production, the 0-470, with a new crankcase design, powered Cessna's popular Model 180 and their Model 310 twin-engine executive plane as well as the Air Force and Navy Beech T-34 "Mentor" training plane.

As with WW II "Grasshopper" liaison planes, their Korean War counterparts, Cessna L-19A Army Field Forces "Bird Dogs," were Continental-powered — by Model 0-470 engines.

The 0-470 series offered a high degree of flexibility including fan-cooled models for helicopters, supercharged versions and geared models.

For Air Force ground support installations, Continental won a design competition involving a series of five "Packette" engines adapted from certain standard Continental aircraft engines and their components. The "Packette" engines comprised one, two, four, six and eight cylinder models, ranging from 15 to 250 hp, specially engineered for all-weather operation.

The engines could be started at temperatures as low as 65 degrees below zero and operated in heat as high as 131 degrees Fahrenheit.

Special features included pre-warming of the engine by means of a self-contained system burning gasoline, and cooling by an axial-flow fan attached to the outside of the flywheel. Also available was a load-sensing governor which automatically increased engine speed as additional load was applied.

Produced side by side on the same Muskegon production line with standard commercial aircraft engines, the "Packettes" had an unusually high degree of availability and interchangeability of parts.

"Packettes" were used by the Air Force in fuel transfer units, compressors, starting units for large jet aircraft, mobile generator units and power plants, air conditioning units and other applications in support of military aircraft in the field. A former hours-long jet bomber refueling task, for example, could be performed in 15 minutes with a special unit equipped with a "Packette" engine powering a high-pressure pump.

From the same production lines, Continental supplied other standard commercial engines for use in a wide range of military equipment and essential civilian uses.

Through prime contractors building military vehicles for Army Ordnance, Continental built R-600 engines for 5-ton Army trucks and as replacements for prime movers. The same engine as well as the S-600 model went into Air Force crash trucks. And, as an example of Gray Marine participation, their 6-244 engine powered aluminum boats for the Navy.

Other engines for generator and lighting plants, road rollers, compressors, power shovels, lift trucks and a host of other uses were provided to customers manufacturing products for the Armed Services as well as for essential commercial markets.

Wisconsin engines, too, provided some of its smaller, air-cooled engines for such military equipment as air compressors, concrete mixers, auxiliary power in tanks, and for airplane refuelers.

Several new diesel engine models were also introduced as Jack Reese and his people continued to broaden the company product line for post-Korea peacetime markets.

Soaring Sales

By September 1951, Continental's sales were running at a monthly rate of $15 million; the backlog of unfilled military and commercial orders exceeded $300 million; employment at Muskegon, Detroit, Milwaukee and Dallas plants reached 12,350 compared with 4300 at 1949's low point.

During the year the company sold to Kaiser-Frazer Corp. the Jefferson Street portion — about two-thirds — of its Detroit facilities which had been under lease for the past four years and was no longer needed for CMC's operations. Continental kept the balance of the plant which then became known as "Kercheval Avenue." The entire plant had been used by Continental during WW II to produce R-975 radial engines for tanks. Part would now be used by Kaiser-Frazer to build Wright R-1300 engines for the Air Force. The auto company would also build some engines for its cars and Continental at Muskegon would also continue as a major supplier of Kaiser-Frazer engines.

As in WW II, the company arranged with a group of banks for a government guaranteed V-loan to finance its rapidly increasing military engine production programs, but at the end of 1951 only $21 million of the $30 million available was drawn down for use in the business.

After four pretty flat business years at the majority-owned Continental Aviation and Engineering subsidiary following WW II, a period of slow but steady growth was resumed.

Helicopter Engine Orders

At the expanded Detroit plant, a $7 million production contract for R-975 aircraft engines adapted for use in Navy helicopters got the new programs under way. The 9-cylinder engines, basically the same model produced for use in medium tanks during WW II, were for installation in Piasecki and Kaman helicopters for the Army, Navy, and for a new Air Force helicopter.

Along with stepped-up production of the 525-550 hp versions of the R-975 helicopter engine, CAE began a re-design program which resulted in a virtually new 600 hp unit designated R-975-38.

In addition, sizable orders were received from the Ordnance Department for replacement parts for an earlier model of the R-975 engine still powering many WW II medium tanks in service in NATO countries in Europe.

And, as a Korean War contingency, CAE negotiated a licensing agreement with Pratt & Whitney for military production of the same 600 hp R-1340 Wasp engine CAE had built in large quantities seven years earlier at Muskegon for advanced training planes for the Army and Navy.

Two other CAE military projects were significant. One was a fuel metering device for Air Force airplane engines of 150 to 800 hp. The other, a diesel engine research program similar to the air-cooled family of military gasoline engines CAE had developed in 1948 for its parent company and the Ordnance Corps.

Teledyne Continental Motors

Continental R-975 engines such as being assembled above powered tri-service Piasecki and Kaman helicopters including the H-25 "Army Mule." Navy version was Piasecki HUP.

Far overshadowing more conventional engines, however, was Continental Aviation's interest in the new field of gas turbine engines, first developed 1939-41 in England by Sir Frank Whittle, and in Germany by Hans von Ohain working with Dr. Ernst Heinkel.*

Getting Into the Turbine Business

Once again, the company went to the continental well.

Carl Bachle, more than any other company engineer, kept fully abreast of technical developments abroad since yearly trips to the Continent were part of his regular activity.

"At the time, 1951," Bachle related, "CAE had only one experimental turbine. Large turbines for jet transports and military planes were coming into their own, but small turbine development was lagging because in that era it was considered they would pay too serious a penalty on fuel consumption."

A need for small jet engines was developing in the U.S. but what was available was not entirely satisfactory.

One potential customer was Ryan Aeronautical Company which had won a 1949 Air Force contract to build the Q-2 "non-man carrying remotely controlled aerial target plane powered by a Frederic Flader turbo-jet engine."

The J55 Flander engine, built at North Tonowanda, New York, was still experimental and was expected to provide 700 lbs. static thrust. However, a competing engine, the Fairchild J44, was to become standard in early Ryan target planes for the Air Force (Q-2), for the Navy (KDA-1) and Army (XM-21).

"When I was in England," Bachle continued, "I dropped in to see my friend Air Commodore Francis Rodwell Banks, Director of engine research and development during World War II for the British Air Ministry.

" 'Rod,' I said, 'what is the best way for a small aircraft engine company to get into the turbine business?' "

" 'Carl,' he replied, 'why don't you try Turbomeca?' "

"So I did."

---

*Gas turbine describes a basic type of engine in which the power of expanding, burning fuel drives a shaft-mounted multi-bladed compressor supplying air to the burner and high velocity thrust-producing exhaust to propel the aircraft forward.

Modifications of this basic jet type include propellers driven by the turbine shaft (turboprop), and ducted fans and by-pass engines (turbofan) which ingest ambient air to augment the gases of combustion. There are many other jet engines variations.

Societe Turbomeca S.A. was located in Bordes, France and had developed a series of small and medium-size gas turbines in collaboration with the French Air Ministry.

Turbomeca was the brain-child of Josef Szydlowski, a young Polish engineer, whose interest in gas turbines started in 1927 because of a belief that the use of diesel power in airplanes would reduce the number of accidents experienced in gasoline-powered aircraft.

Szydlowski went to work on development of a two-cycle diesel type engine which involved use of a high-efficiency rotary compressor, not then available. The result was a compressor unit far superior to anything previously built.

In 1928, at the invitation of the French Air Force, he moved to France where he continued his work with the backing of the Air Ministry. By 1936 he had produced a compressor with variable air circulation with which many French engines were later equipped.

The Turbomeca company was organized in 1938 to produce turbo compressors, and later added gas turbines, but after four years had to cease production and development during the German occupation. At the close of the war full activities were resumed.

In Summer 1951, after months of negotiation and testing in the U.S. and France, CAE's parent company purchased from Societe Turbomeca the exclusive U.S. manufacturing rights to a family of eight small and medium-size gas turbines ranging from 200 to 1100 horsepower. Then, in October, Continental Motors sub-licensed CAE on a non-exclusive basis to produce the Turbomeca jet engines.

Bachle had successfully negotiated the arrangement with Turbomeca's Syzdlowski. "He was," said Bachle, "the most envied man I ever saw because he was the owner, the chief engineer, the head of sales, the director of manufacturing and the sole patent owner of Turbomeca. In 1980, at age 83, he is still around and still performing as usual.

"Turbomeca was so attractive to Continental because they had vastly reduced the previous serious penalty small turbines had to pay in fuel consumption to the point you could say it was almost break-even with the big turbines."

Among the Turbomeca designs were the Artouste shaft turbine (280 hp; 185 lbs. weight), Aspin ducted fan (500-800 lbs. thrust), Palouste compressed air generator, Palas jet turbine (330 lbs. thrust), and the Marbore turbo-jet engine (880 lbs. thrust).

In addition to fuel efficiency, other advantages of the Turbomeca family of jet engines were their long service life due to the absence of reciprocating parts, ability

---

"When I was in England I dropped in to see my friend Rod Banks"

The Jet Age

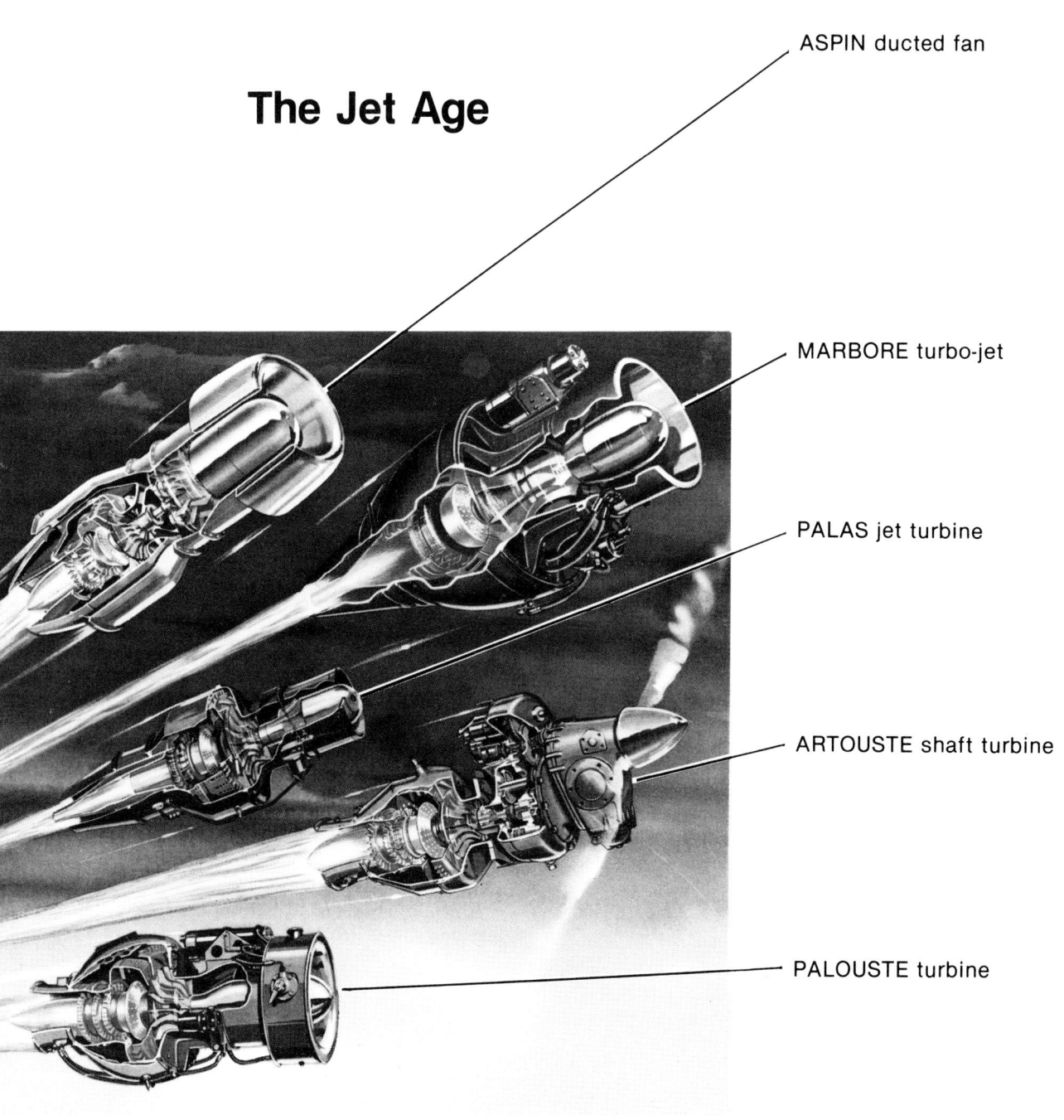

- ASPIN ducted fan
- MARBORE turbo-jet
- PALAS jet turbine
- ARTOUSTE shaft turbine
- PALOUSTE turbine

Teledyne CAE

to use a wide range of fuels, small size in relation to power, very favorable power-to-weight ratio, and interchangeability of parts among various models.

Arthur W. Wild was Executive Vice-President and general manager of CAE, and also the spark-plug of the company sales effort, particularly with the military services.

"The first production that we were able to develop and sell," Art explained, "was an air generator to the Air Force used to start large jet engines. Our MA-1 trailer-mounted unit contained the Model 140 compressed air generator based on the Turbomeca Palouste engine.

"About the same time, the Air Force had a competition for a side-by-side jet trainer to bridge the speed gap between piston-engine aircraft and jet fighters. Cessna won the competition with their T-37 twin-jet powered by two of our Marbore turbo-jet engines, which we then had to bring up to Air Force standards."

For the Flying Tigers cargo airline, CAE demonstrated how a Marbore jet engine could be slung beneath a conventional twin-piston-engine transport adding improved take-off performance, especially for fully-loaded planes. Other Continental-Turbomeca applications included use in helicopters and in Air Force Cessna L-19 reconnaissance planes.

Another prime prospect, of course, was

139

Under the knowing eye of G. Williams Rutherford, manager of Ryan Aeronautical's Torrance, California plant, production of Firebee target drones gets under way. Years later Rutherford was to play a major role in Continental's future.

Teledyne Ryan Aeronautical

Teledyne Ryan Aeronautical

First Continental J69 Marbore II jet engine for Firebee target drone is checked by Ryan's Forrest Warren

Ryan Aeronautical Company whose "Firebee" target drones were just coming into production for all three U.S. military services. Major Air Force contracts for the improved Q-2A model were being negotiated.

Carl Bachle picks up the story:

"Ryan had the Fairchild J44 engine already installed in its first production 'Firebee' targets. The J44 was touted as the best and cheapest available. It was sponsored and financed by the Navy, and everything was in favor of Fairchild continuing as the supplier.

"How were we going to get into that job?

"At that time Ryan was making exhaust manifolds in large volume for the Continental 1790 tank engines. On a routine trip to the Ryan plant, I went in to chat with Claude Ryan as I usually did. I hinted that we'd better get a little more serious attention on the Marbore engine for the Air Force Q-2A drones or something might happen to 'that good old exhaust manifold contract that is producing a pretty good profit for you.'

"Claude got the message; we got better attention after that!

"Because our Marbore engine was far more fuel-efficient we were able to give Ryan twice as much time on the target range as they could get with the Fairchild J44. That was a proper and convincing argument."

In June 1952, the first Continental Marbore II jet engine arrived at Ryan. Soon it had the official U.S. designation J69 and that engine and improved versions continued in production for Ryan Firebees, Cessna T-37s and other applications at increased thrust power for three decades.

Progress at CAE as measured by sales volume and profit had not been impressive since the 1944-45 days of war production, but the road back to better days began to change in 1951 as shown in this 12-year tabulation:

Year	Sales	Profit
		(Loss)
1942	$ 2,180,018	$ —
1943	8,431,331	(355,995)
1944	58,441,373	628,078
1945	32,751,293	44,553
1946	2,232,878	(356,979)
1947	4,981,228	(209,229)
1948	4,381,380	(42,829)
1949	3,404,482	21,806
1950	3,390,232	68,454
1951	6,083,200	122,566
1952	9,261,589	268,993
1953	14,523,719	325,101

Teledyne Continental Motors

Shipment of exhaust manifolds for assembly into Continental 1790 series tank engines received from Ryan Aeronautical factory in San Diego

140

Continental Motors, the parent company, reached the half-century mark in 1952 during the Korean War period which brought unprecedented sales volume, and profit levels comparable to those during WW II. To a large extent the increased activity was due to the strength of the company's advanced technology tank engine business.

1952 — Golden Anniversary

In 1950, sales volume was 31% above the prior year; in 1951 it was up 73% over 1950. Volume reached $264 million in 1952; then peaked at $298 million for fiscal year 1953.

Earnings showed similar increases, exceeding $6 million in both 1952 and 1953. (Normal and excess profits taxes paid to the government averaged $14.3 million each of these two years.)

But it would be 15 years, and under new management, before comparable sales and earnings would again be realized.

Dividends had been resumed in 1949 with cash payments of 20 cents per share. These were increased to 30 cents annually, then 45 cents, 60 cents and 80 cents per share during the four years 1950-1953.

After dividend payments, the net worth of the investment of the company's 31,000 stockholders increased by $3.4 million in 1953 to a new high of $42,254,564, or $12.80 per share on the 3,300,000 common shares then issued and outstanding. In the 14 years since he took over as president, Jack Reese had seen Continental's net worth increase nine fold from 1939's shareholder investment of $4.6 million.

In its line of commercial products, sales of engines for agricultural and industrial applications were at an all-time high. Transportation engines still provided about one-fifth of the commercial volume. Engines for aircraft and marine use, and sales of engine service parts all contributed to the company's continued business success.

Research and development work on diesel engines moved forward and, of course, the market for jet engines was being advanced by the Continental Aviation and Engineering subsidiary.

As more and more arid land was brought under cultivation throughout the country, the market for agricultural irrigation engines steadily expanded. To fill the need Continental introduced a specially-designed 136 hp LPG (liquid petroleum gas) power unit.

Wisconsin Motor Corp., 83.1% owned by Continental Motors, also reached a key milestone early in 1953 with delivery of the 2,000,000th engine built at its Milwaukee plant. Harold A. Todd, President, revealed that half of the all-time total had been produced in the most recent five-year period of the company's 44 year history.

For 12 years Wisconsin had concentrated on production of air-cooled engines. Demand was so high that three production shifts had been worked regularly since 1941. Five hundred manufacturers were using Wisconsin engines in their products, sold in 71 countries. The company employed 1850 workers at its Milwaukee facilities.

On its Golden Anniversary, Continental noted that more than 7,000,000 engines bearing its Red Seal trademark, and those of its Wisconsin and Gray Marine subsidiaries, had been shipped and placed in service throughout the world.

The year 1953 also marked the Silver Anniversary of the company's entry into the air-cooled engine business. During that quarter-century, sales of air-cooled engines and parts — primarily for tanks and aircraft — totaled over $1,100,000,000.

Completion of Wisconsin's 2,000,000th engine brings out company's (w) top brass as well as parent Continental (c) executives. From left: E. C. Wurtz (w), manufacturing official; A. F. Milbrath (w), Vice-President; James H. Ferry, Jr. (c-rear), Director; F. J. Kennedy (c-front), Director; H. W. Vandeven (c), Treasurer; Peter Zagorski (w), union president; Jack Reese (c), President; P. N. Hauser (w) Director-Secretary; Phil Norton (w), Vice-President; and Harold A. Todd (w), President.

Red Seal Magazine

141

John W. Mulford, President of Gray Marine subsidiary, recently elected President of the National Association of Engine and Boat Manufacturers, poses with Continental-Turbomeca Marbore jet engine at New York Boat Show.

In fourteen years, Jack Reese had given Continental the leadership needed to bring it from the depths of its near bankruptcy days to a strong and dominant position as the country's leading independent engine builder.

Working for Jack Reese

He had not done it alone. He had envisioned and inspired a close-knit team whose members had done a superb job under his 24-hours-a-day, seven-days-a-week drive and devotion. Jack was the ultimate workaholic and expected similar dedication from others.

"When you worked for Jack Reese," Art Wild pointed out, "you worked as many hours as necessary. I think during World War II I worked seven days a week for five years without a vacation.

"But Jack was one of the most generous men you'd ever run into. He'd give you the shirt off his back. He paid excellent salaries, but he didn't believe in vacations. He did not approve of retirement. He had no intention of retiring — he was then in his mid-50s — and he wasn't going to make it attractive for anyone else to retire.

"We had many fights about a retirement plan; it was a crime that we didn't have one."

A business executive who dealt with Reese over a period of years observed that Jack was oriented more to large sales volume and high production rates than he was to overall business administration and to the profitability of individual contracts.

"He was," our contact observed, "a master salesman who would rather have the business with little or no profit than not have the business at all."

Reese's pre-Continental experience as a purchasing agent in the automobile industry was a valuable asset.

"When it came to a purchasing question," Carl Bachle said, "Jack was an expert and he was constantly sharpening that side of the business. That was one of the reasons why the company was able to come back after the dark days of the thirties when multi-million dollar losses were sustained year after year.

"Reese was able to buy at minimum cost where others would accept the normal price. He was always making deals to buy things cheap.

"He was a complex character in some ways, but thoroughly understandable and normal in others. He had many virtues; one of them was to know when he was out of his depth. He would always step aside when it came to engineering questions; and often on manufacturing and financial decisions, too."

"Jack was a great guy to watch a man like me work," Bachle continued. "Years ago when we had a bad oil leak problem on the R-670 radial aircraft engine, I went up to Muskegon from Detroit to see if I could help.

"He followed me around for an entire Sunday. He was conscientiously trying to find out how I went about my work. He wasn't criticizing, he wasn't interfering, he wasn't helping, he wasn't hurting. He was just trying to learn. For this alone I admired him.

"Jack's formal education was limited, but he learned to use pretty sophisticated management techniques not the least of which was playing some of the 22 people who reported to him off against each other competitively."

Constantly on the go between his offices and homes in Detroit and Muskegon, with meetings scheduled Saturdays and Sundays as well as during the normal business week, Reese should have had more than enough to do. But he took on many civic and industry responsibilities as well, with particular emphasis on those that were aviation oriented. In addition he served a term as President of the Automobile Parts Manufacturers Assn.

Reese was a board member of all Continental companies and also of Lakey Foundry, a major supplier located adjacent to CMC's Muskegon factory. In Muskegon he was long a director of the Chamber of Commerce. For his civic interest and financial support of the project, the city's new neighborhood playground developed in 1951 was named "Reese Field."

BUSINESS WEEK magazine aptly described Jack Reese: "A fast mover even by standards of the automotive industry. His activity is motion with a purpose."

CLARENCE "JACK" REESE

From the depth of the Depression and the near-bankruptcy which followed, Jack Reese restored Continental Motors to a position of leadership as the largest independent engine manufacturer. A tireless worker himself, Jack demanded — and got — similar devotion from his management team during World War II and the war in Korea. During his quarter-century of leadership, Jack saw Continental's net worth increase 12-fold to $55 million

Portrait by James H. Ferry, Jr.   Richmond, VA 1957

ON THE HIGH PLATEAU
(1954-1961)

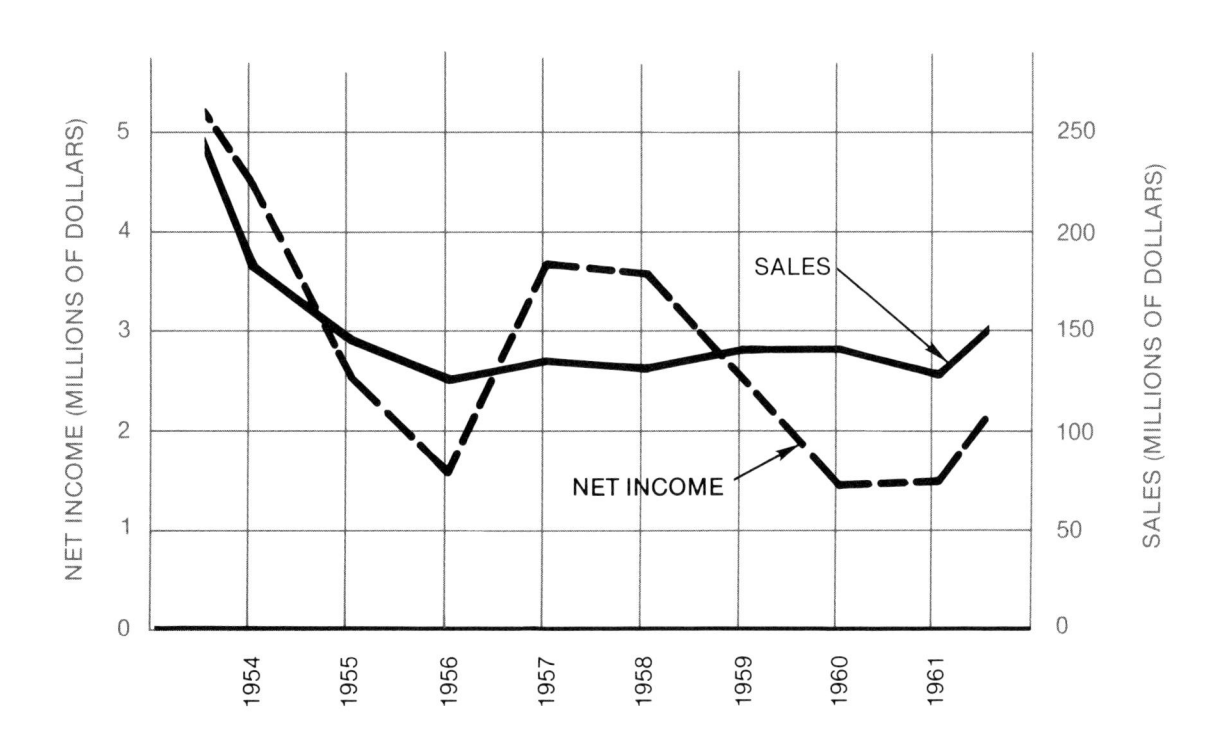

Business holds at a strong level but as senior management gets along in years there is too little room for new ideas and new people.

Pages 147 to 165

1954-1961

Production Volume Slips	147
Fuel-Injected Engines for Tanks	148
Air-cooled Aircraft Engines	150
"Cushioned Power" and Multi-Fuel	151
Military Standard Engines	151
End of the Tobin Era	152
Factory Branches and Subsidiaries	153
Jet Turbines from CAE	154
CAE's Toledo Plant	155
Lower Profits; New Ventures	157
Rolls-Royce and Fuji Licenses/Aircraft Engines	158
Multi-Fuel Engines for the Ordnance Corps	159
Technical Breakthroughs	163
Time Takes Its Toll	163
Six Decades of Progress	164

New Markets Opened

Continental Motors Corp. had done the greatest volume of business in its history in the twelve months ended October 31, 1953.

Three months before the end of that fiscal year, an armistice ending the Korean War has been signed and hostilities ceased. And, as in other armed conflicts, the end of war production brought new economic problems for the whole country.

Production Volume Slips

For Continental, it meant a 40 percent reduction in business volume the first peace-time year, from $298 million to $182 million in 1954, then a further 25 percent drop which saw company sales leveling off to an average of $135 million annually for the next seven years.

Similarly, earnings began to slip, declining from $4.5 million in 1954 to $1.6 million two years later, but climbing back to $3.5 million in 1957 and 1958. Dividends paid per share were 80 cents in 1954, then 70 cents, 25 cents, 35 cents, and 55 cents in the four succeeding years.

Initially, several bright spots in CMC's commercial product line helped stabilize business. "Man-made weather" — the use of Continental-powered equipment for irrigation on farms and ranches — became a new, expanding field for the company. However, sales were disappointing by 1957 because abnormally high rainfall that year held irrigation equipment sales to a much reduced level.

Secondly, CMC benefitted greatly from the highway construction program enacted by Congress in 1956. This called for 41,000 miles of new interstate highways to be built during the next 13 years at a cost exceeding $100 billion. At the Road Show highway equipment display in 1957 in Chicago, 43 percent of the construction items exhibited were Continental-powered. But delays in getting the highway program underway held back the volume of business CMC had anticipated.

Continental had long customized engines for the unique requirements of a wide range of manufacturers of specialized equipment. Rail equipment was an ideal built-for-the-job field.

Right-of-way maintenance had always been a problem for the railroads since the work required heavy labor and drudgery on the part of "section hands." In the mid-50s, however, a series of ingenious Continental-powered machines — tie replacers, ballast tampers, track brooms, spike drivers, track-bed undercutters and powered "handcars" — took over much of the heaviest work.

To separate research and development of new products from the work on production lines, CMC established a New Products Division in 1954. For this, the company purchased an existing 35,000 square foot eight-year-old facility in Detroit, ten miles west of the Kercheval plant, which became known as the Lyndon Avenue Plant.

The research facility was placed under the direction of Peter Altman, a CMC Vice-President since 1948. Highly regarded in the engineering profession, Altman for many years headed the aeronautical engineering department of the University of Detroit and served as consultant to many organizations.

In the mid-'50s, expanded markets for agricultural, construction and industrial engines included applications for irrigation, highway paving and railway maintenance

147

As expected, production of engines for military tanks, trucks and aircraft was sharply reduced, but Continental, having developed and built many of the new power plant concepts for Army tanks, was retained by the Ordnance Corps as sole post-Korean supplier of engines for tracked military vehicles.

Fuel-Injected Engines for Tanks

Favorable, too, was the fact that development work on improved power plants continued at the company's CAE subsidiary.

Sen. Lyndon B. Johnson (D-Texas), Chairman of the Preparedness Investigating Subcommittee, complained in February 1957 that while modern tanks were a high-priority defense item, no funds to buy them had been asked of Congress in the prior three years.

"Continuity of tank production is in jeopardy," said Johnson, the committee report adding that the Army had been scraping around for unspent funds to make tank purchases on a hit-or-miss basis instead of seeking new appropriations.

Continental engineers long felt there were great possibilities for engine improvement if military customers would accept **fuel injection** — gasoline sprayed directly into the cylinders — in place of carburetors which premix fuel and air before the vapor is fed into the cylinders. This research work had been going on at CMC under Ordnance Corps sponsorship since 1950.

Fuel injection had many advantages, the most promising being reduced fuel consumption which would not only increase vehicle range but also reduce operating costs and lessen the problem of fuel

Teledyne Continental Motors

AVSI-1790-6   12 cyl.   1000 hp

AVI-1790-8   12 cyl.   810 hp

AOSI-895-5   6 cyl.   500 hp

AOI-402-5   6 cyl.   205 hp

Teledyne Continental Motors

Above: M48A2 Medium Tank

Detroit Arsenal/Ordnance Corps

Below: M42A1 Self-propelled Twin Gun

transport on the battlefield.

Other advantages included easier starting and elimination of carburetor icing in sub-zero weather, and immediate engine response to the throttle without a warm-up period.

In spite of Senator Johnson's evaluation, Army Ordnance had proceeded with some tank engine contracts. The first Continental fuel-injected tank engine was the 12-cylinder AVSI-1790-6, a 1000 hp air-cooled, V-type supercharged version. Used in the M51 tank recovery vehicle, deliveries of these engines began in January 1954.

Other new fuel-injected engines were introduced in Summer 1956. Orders for unsupercharged AVI-1790-8 engines of 810 hp, used in the M48 A2 medium tank, came to $17 million. The six-cylinder AOSI-895-5 opposed engine delivered 500 hp and was installed in the M41A1 76 mm and M42A1 self-propelled twin 40 mm guns.

The fourth fuel-injected engine was introduced in October 1957. A six-cylinder unsupercharged opposed engine of smaller bore and stroke, the AOI-402 developed 205 hp and was used for the M56 self-propelled 90 mm gun. Over 650 of these engines were delivered.

In addition to its technical laboratories at the Getty Street plant, Continental's Military Division facilities included two cross-country vehicle test tracks and a fleet of tanks and tracked vehicles for final proof testing of all engine developments.

All four fuel-injected engines were developed as part of the 'family' concept of military engines started in 1943 under Ordnance Corps research contracts with Continental.

RESEARCH

PRODUCTION

TEST In addition to research and production at the Getty Street plant, this Muskegon facility also had its own test tracks on which the M47 and M48 tanks pictured are going through winterization trials

Aircraft Engine NOMENCLATURE

O = horizontally-Opposed cylinders
G = Geared crankshaft
I = fuel-Injected
TS = TurboSupercharged
F = Fan-cooled

Reduction Gears

Fuel Injection

Turbo-Supercharging

Air Force L-27 "light twin" transports powered by two Continental 470 series fuel-injected engines were military version of the popular Cessna 310 executive plane extensively used by business firms

Continental also continued to refine the performance of its line of flat, horizontally-opposed engines for the personal plane market and for light military aircraft.

Air-Cooled Aircraft Engines

In the four-year period 1957-60, Continental made its greatest advances in air-cooled aircraft engine technology.

Most aircraft engines were for years of the direct drive type with the propeller connected directly to the crankshaft, both components of course running at the same speed. However, such operation was not fully efficient for either the engine or for the propeller.

In 1957, Continental introduced its GO-300 model with a **reduction gear** system between the engine and propeller, allowing both to operate at their more efficient speeds — the engine at high rpm, the propeller at lower rpm. The GO-300 engine developed 175 hp at 3200 crankshaft rpm and 2400 prop rpm.

To overcome the disadvantages of conventional carburetor systems such as used in automobiles — principally the tendency of aircraft engines to form ice in the carburetor throat — the company introduced continuous flow **fuel injection**. This not only virtually eliminated the carburetor-icing problem but also achieved better general engine performance and economy through precise control of the fuel/air mixture. This system was first used in the 260 hp IO-470 engine whose carbureted version, the 0-470, had been introduced four years earlier.

The fuel-injected 470 engines first became standard equipment in single-engine Beech J35 Bonanzas and in the twin-engine Cessna Model 310 commercial planes and military L-27A Air Force liaison aircraft.

Also developed in 1958 was the conventional four-cylinder 0-200 engine which produced 100 hp. It was in continuous production for twenty years.

The third major step in improved performance came in 1960 with the introduction to general aviation of **turbo-supercharging**. It was first used in the IOS-470 engine developed from the basic six-cylinder fuel-injected model. Supercharging is accomplished by using the hot exhaust gases of a conventionally-aspirated engine to drive a gas turbine which in turn drives a compressor.

The compression of air introduced into the combustion chamber enables the engine to give sea-level performance at altitude, compensating for the rarified atmosphere during flight at high altitudes.

Earlier, in September 1955, a Cessna CH-1 helicopter, equipped with CMC's FSO-470 engine, had landed on Pikes Peak — altitude 14,109 feet — setting a new record for helicopters. Two years later, an Army Cessna YH-41 flown by Army Captain James E. Bowman and powered by a Continental FSO-526 engine rose to an altitude of 30,355 feet, exceeding by nearly 4,000 feet the previous helicopter altitude record, held by the French.

The FSO (fan-cooled, supercharged, opposed) series of engines were designed expressly for use in helicopters. Because of the submerged installation of the horizontally-opposed engine and minimum air flow at low speed, fan-cooling was necessary.

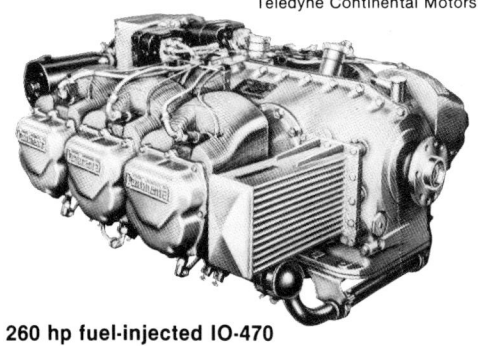

260 hp fuel-injected IO-470

Also offered was a Factory Engine Remanufacture plan which provided the user of utility planes a factory-remanufactured power plant carrying a new engine warranty and having zero hours on its log. This got the owners' planes back in the air in less time than required for periodic overhaul and at a modest, pre-determined cost.

The Aircraft Division, under a $10 million Air Force contract, continued production of "Packette" engines, the light, compact, all-climate packaged power plants developed by Continental from its aircraft engines for the Air Force standardization program. These mobile power plants had many applications in support of military aircraft in the field.

The policy of developing new Continental engines and components, and modifications to existing models, for industrial, agricultural and transportation use was seldom interrupted.

"Cushioned Power" and Multi-Fuel

New V-8s included a 240 hp overhead valve gasoline engine and a companion 182 hp "cushioned power" diesel. Both were shorter and narrower than conventional V-8s of comparable power output.

CMC began a strong merchandising effort for its line of Cushioned Power Diesels pointing out that they offered for the 1957 market "matching, interchangeable units — diesel and gasoline — at ten different power levels.

"Interchangeability of engines in the same mounting space, and interchangeability of many parts not only facilitates the matching of the power plant to its work, but simplified parts supply and maintenance problems."

The Continental distributor-dealer organization found the larger Cushioned Power Diesels a profitable source of replacement business in the heavy-duty truck and construction and agricultural equipment fields. And, interchangeability of engines in each "companion model" pair made it easy for equipment manufacturers to offer customers a power option — gasoline or diesel.

After World War II, Continental had adopted the "Lanova" principle of diesel engine design and produced a considerable volume of these engines. Other builders, however, abandoned the Lavona engine in favor of the "open chamber" design and drew off much of the available business. Only about 3% of Continental's business was diesel compared with 97% gasoline-fueled.

In the AU series of small heavy-duty industrial air-cooled engines, new 3 hp and 4 hp models were introduced. Extremely compact, they provided for operation on kerosene as well as gasoline.

And, of long-range importance, research went forward at the Continental Aviation and Engineering subsidiary on new principles in diesel combustion to make practical the use of multiple fuels in a single engine.

In 1957, Jack Reese forecast that tests then being run on "the new hypercycle, multi-fuel principle will have wide application, both military and commercial, in the years to come."

As engineer Carl Bachle pointed out, "For 20 years, the military had said they wanted multi-fuel capability. They told us it was the most important thing we could do for them."

CMC, CAE and Army Ordnance went to work on the problem, but it was some years before full-scale production was achieved.

In addition to large multi-fuel engines for its trucks, the Army was interested in standardizing its small engine requirements.

Military Standard Engines

Studies begun in 1948 showed that in World War II, the Armed Forces were using 340 different makes and models of small commercial gasoline engines. Of these, 78 were aircooled models spanning

Powered by Continental's fan-cooled FSO-526 engine, an Army Cessna YH-41 climbed to 30,355 feet

AU10 air-cooled 4 hp industrial engine

Cushioned Power Diesel enabled this tracked cargo transporter to wade and swim with heavy loads over muskeg in Northern Canada

an output range from one-half to 35 hp, and requiring more than 23,000 different parts for maintenance support.

Design evaluations conducted by Continental's Industrial Engine Division at Detroit and the U.S. Army Corps of Engineers resulted in a reduction to six standard models requiring only 800 parts. Research was done at the Lyndon Avenue plant; production at Kercheval Avenue.

Where the normal life of industrial type gasoline engines between major overhauls was from 100 to 500 hours, the military wanted a design that would deliver 1,500 hours. Such an engine, they said, should operate on any fuel from 70 octane to 100 — from the lowest octane general Ordnance fuel up to high test aviation gasoline — and tolerate detergent military lubricants, and the high lead content of military fuels.

In addition, the engines were required to run in any climate, at temperatures from minus 65° to a sizzling 125°, and at elevations up to 5,000 feet without carburetor adjustment.

More than 40 companies were invited to submit development proposals, and the contract had been awarded to Continental Motors on a bid basis, in February 1952.

Under direction of Peter Altman, CMC began producing the first three of the eventual six Military Standard engines in 1957. The concept was to use engines of two different bores and various numbers of cylinders to take care of most of the Army's requirements for small engines.

The one- and two-cylinder models provided the full power range from one-half to 20 horsepower. Their production was integrated with that of small CMC air-cooled industrial engines for use in lawnmowers, golf cars, scooters and similar applications.

The Military Standard engines were for such applications as engine-generator sets, engine-driven pumps, blowers, fans, and many other installations in the field where light weight, portability, dependability and minimum maintenance are paramount.

By 1960, production under the Military Standard small engine program, which had been underway since 1952, encompassed the entire line of six engines from one-half hp to 35 hp.

An analysis of interchangeable 'pieces' in the six engines showed that 94 percent of the parts in the 10 hp and 20 hp engines were common; 93 percent of parts in the 1½ and 3 hp engines were also interchangeable. This helped realize the Corps of Engineers' program to radically reduce the number of engines, and engine parts for military engine applications up to 35 hp.

A few of the air-cooled engines were sold commercially but the design life of 1500 hours between overhauls made them too expensive for most industrial uses.

PETER ALTMAN

39 percent of parts in 1½ hp engine, above, are interchangeable with 3 hp Military Standard Engine, below

Ford built Army's M151 MUTT using Continental-built, Ford-designed engine

Another military product whose engine production came Continental's way was the Army's M151 quarter-ton military utility tactical truck (MUTT). Ford Motor Co. held the prime contract for both the vehicle and its engine.

The Mutt power plant had been developed by Ford about 1955 and became a standard production engine. Ford, however, wanted the engine manufacturing capability for other uses and suggested to the Army they get someone else to build it.

The Army then chose Continental to produce the Ford-designed four-cylinder 71 hp engine, and a contract for over 7000 units was awarded CMC in Spring 1961.

At Los Angeles, Continental Sales & Service Co., headed by Ben Tobin, Jr., acted as Continental and Wisconsin Motor distributors on the Pacific Coast.

End of the Tobin Era

For twelve years, 1944-1955, there had been no change in CMC's seven-man Board of Directors: Jack Reese; production expert Lewis Kalb; lawyer Fred J. Kennedy — all Detroiters; investor Jim Ferry of the Chicago area; Ben Tobin, Jr. now of Los Angeles; Wisconsin Motor's Harold A. Todd; and investment banker David A. VanAlstyne, Jr. of New York.

Then, in January 1956, Ben Tobin, Jr., on the Board since 1919, resigned to be replaced by Henry W. Vandeven of Muskegon, Treasurer since 1969, who had joined Continental back in 1917.

In 1956, Lewis P. Kalb left the Board, and the following year Robert C. Trundle, a principal in the Cleveland industrial consulting firm which Reese had retained in the early 40's, became a director. Kalb passed away in 1957 at the age of 69. He had been with Continental 36 years.

Keeping alive a family tradition, Ben F. Tobin III joined CMC after the Korean War in the Los Angeles distributorship. Not only were his father and grandfather senior executives; his great-uncle Arthur W. Tobin was a co-founder of the company.

After three years as a sales representative covering Arizona and Southeastern

California, young Tobin was appointed assistant sales manager of Continental Sales & Service Co. As his father went into retirement because of poor health, the son moved up to Vice-President and sales manager, positions he held when his father passed away in August 1959 at age 68.

Tobin III reportedly had many run-ins with Continental dealers in his sales area and eventually became such a problem to CMC management that the distributorship was terminated. Claiming unfair treatment, he filed suit against the company.

At this late date (1981) it is difficult to sift fact from fancy, but the Auditors' Note to financial statements in the 1961 Annual Report to Stockholders is interesting:

The Corporation and Wisconsin Motor Corporation have been named defendants in a suit brought by Continental Sales & Service Company, a former distributor, claiming treble damages and other amounts aggregating a maximum of approximately $5,600,000 arising from the termination of distributorship agreements.

The Auditors further noted that management's opinion was that there was no merit to the plaintiff's claim. Notes to the 1962 Annual Report listed the claim as having been reduced to $2,150,000.

Since the contingent liability item did not appear in subsequent Annual Reports, the matter is believed to have been settled out of court.

To serve the expanding Canadian market, Continental Motors of Canada, Ltd., was granted its Ontario provincial charter at the start of the 1955 fiscal year and a new plant at St. Thomas, only a hundred miles northeast of Detroit, was opened in 1957 for fabrication, assembly and warehousing operations.

Factory Branches and Subsidiaries

Factory branches at Dallas, Texas, (built 1946), and Atlanta, Georgia (1952), were expanded to serve the fast-developing South where sales increases were anticipated especially in engines for the irrigation and highway construction fields.

However, effects of a nationwide steel strike in 1956 on the company's manufacturing customers contributed to lower-than-expected sales volume and profits.

For 105 days, from May 2 to August 15, CMC's Wisconsin Motor Corp. was closed by a strike of employees, but the subsidiary made a rapid recovery as all important original equipment customers remained loyal to their principal engine supplier.

The Gray Marine subsidiary, leading manufacturer of inboard marine engines, broadened and improved its lines of both gasoline and diesel engines during its 50th anniversary year. One example was its revolutionary new "Quick-Align" mount, available in 1956, which greatly reduced the time required to align engines either at time of original installation or at periodic maintenance checks.

Gray, whose 31 gasoline and five diesel engines were said to be powering more models than those of other manufacturers exhibiting at annual boat shows throughout the country, came up with other sales-expanding ideas. One was introduction in Spring 1959 of its fourth V-8 model, the Fireball 188 hp engine. At that time John W. Mulford, President of CMC's marine subsidiary, reported that April was the greatest month in the company's history.

Then, in 1960, as the market for pleasure and work boats continued to build, the company introduced a unique inboard-outboard engine known as the "Stern Drive" which was favorably received by the expanding pleasure boating market.

Mulford had suffered a heart attack in 1959 and relinquished the presidency to P.C. Chamberlain, sales manager. However, Mulford continued as chairman of the Gray Marine board of directors.

Teledyne Continental Motors

New plant of Canadian Motors of Canada, Ltd., at St. Thomas, Ontario

Red Seal Magazine

Gray's 225 hp version of Fireball V-8 marine engine

Red Seal Magazine

Gray Diesel-Powered Seiners for Alaskan Service

The Continental Aviation and Engineering gas turbine program, begun in 1951 with the parent company's license agreement with Turbomeca of France, made rapid progress and by 1954 displaced R-975 radial aircraft engines as CAE's largest source of revenue.

Jet Turbines for CAE

Initially, French-made engines were imported so that potential American users could experiment with the new power plants until CAE could get squared away to produce turbines on this side of the Atlantic.

Not only was it necessary to "Americanize" each French model, but each had to be engineered specifically to its application. For example, in the change-over of the French Palouste air generator to the Continental Model 140, six hundred specifications had to be altered. Then sources had to be established for materials, parts and sub-components, and assembly facilities provided.

The Model 140 air compressor became the heart of the MA-1 portable generator unit built by CAE for the Air Force for starting combat aircraft including the North American F-100, McDonnell F-101 and Convair F-102 jet fighters; and the four-jet Boeing B-52 bomber.

The 880-pound-thrust J69 jet — Americanized version of the French Marbore engine — and later up-rated engines became standard for Ryan's Firebee target drones and for Cessna T-37 twin-jet trainers, both of which were in volume production for many years.

These two programs were the mainstay of CAE's business which saw sales expand from $11.3 million in 1954 to $43 million annually in 1958-59. In the latter two years, net profits reached $1.3 million annually.

By 1961, sales were down to $23 million because of reduced Air Force T-37 jet trainer requirements; smaller orders for MA-1A air generators; reduced Air Force target drone requirements, and a slow start-up of Navy target drone production.

A third turbine showing great promise in the mid-50s was the Artouste turbo-prop (or shaft turbine) which Continental offered in two versions. The Model 210, developing 280 hp, powered Cessna's L-19C military liaison plane. It was also used in the Bell H-13 helicopter.

The 425 hp Model 220 powered the Sikorsky XH-39 helicopter which established world helicopter records for altitude (24,500 feet) and speed (156 mph).

One of the real engineering challenges CAE faced with the J69 engine was to increase its power output to meet the requirements of customers who were building jet aircraft for the military services.

Carl Bachle, CAE's top engineer explained:

"As we received the prototype turbine from Turbomeca, it had a thrust rating of 880 pounds. That was the J69-T-3 engine we called 'Marbore II' which went into the Ryan XQ-2 target drone in 1952.

"In the course of negotiations with Cessna, it turned out they needed 920 pounds of thrust to meet Air Force performance guarantees. We said, 'Why, sure, we can give you 920 pounds just as well as we can 880.'

"Then we spent millions of dollars and two years of heart-breaking development getting to 920 pounds thrust.

"However, it was no great problem in conversion between inches and metric measure because we had been through that before with the British Rolls-Royce Merlin engine during WW II. We minimized the

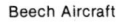

CAE's Model 140 air compressor provided power for MA-1 portable generator used to start combat aircraft engines

Model 210 shaft turbine powered military liaison planes and helicopters

J69-T-9 engine powered high performance Model 73 jet version of Beech's popular T-34 Mentor trainer

problem for ourselves and our customers because we didn't convert everything. Only what we had to: for example, studs — so we could use nuts which were common in this system. The starter was completely American. The fuel control was metric, but we had no problem."

After up-rating the J69 to 920 pounds thrust in the T-9 version for the T-37A Cessna, the same principle was applied to the T-19 model, giving Ryan 1000 pounds thrust for its Q-2A production drones. Then, in 1958, the J69-T-29 model was introduced at 1700 pounds thrust for the improved Ryan Q-2C Firebee. The 60 percent gain in thrust was achieved with only a six percent increase in weight.

Similarly, the 1960 "B" version of the Cessna T-37 trainer was powered with J69-T-25 engines rated at 1025 pounds thrust as compared with 920 pounds in the original twin-trainer.

Other aircraft using various models of the J69 included the Temco TT-1 Navy primary trainer (T-2 model engine) and the tandem-seat Beech Model 73 jet-powered (T-9 engine) version of its propeller-driven T-34 "Mentor" standard primary military trainer, the latter powered by Continental's 0-470 piston engine.

And, based on the successful T-37, Cessna in 1959 introduced its Model 407 four-place military utility aircraft powered by T-29 engine models de-rated to 1400 pounds thrust for use in manned aircraft.

In 1954, CAE completed and occupied its new research and engineering facility at Detroit, but because of expanding production schedules for its cart-mounted air generators and jet engines, it was necessary to look elsewhere for additional capacity. Originally, it was expected that a jet engine plant might be built in Muskegon, but soon thereafter, at Air Force suggestion, negotiations were opened for CAE's use of a Government-owned production plant at Toledo, Ohio.

Air Force Plant 27 at Toledo appeared to be ideal for CAE's needs. The 300,000 square foot production facility had been built during WW II for the Lycoming Division of Avco, just as the Getty Street plant in Muskegon had been built for Continental Motors' use.

CAE's Toledo Plant

However, from 1943 to 1949, it had been occupied by Packard Motor Co. and used for production of aircraft engines. The next occupant was Frederic Flader, Inc., which conducted research and development work there for a short period on jet engines. One such research project was the jet engine originally scheduled for Ryan Firebee target drones, but "beaten out" in the market place by CAE's J69 Marbore engine.

For five years, 1950-1955, A.O. Smith Corp., auto parts manufacturer, used the Toledo plant facility for production of landing gears for Air Force B-47 and B-52 bombers.

The plant had been idle for a year when CAE took over use of the Government-owned facility in Spring 1955. On September 16, the first production model, a J69 turbojet, came off the line. CAE's

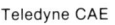

Ryan Aeronautical's tri-service Firebee targets provided realistic training for Army, Navy and Air Force pilots and anti-aircraft gun crews. At left are early versions of pilotless jets. At right, the Q-2C drone.

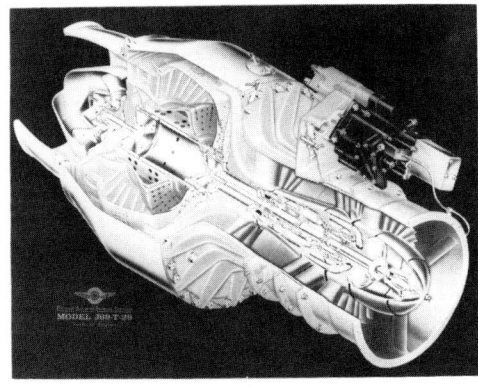

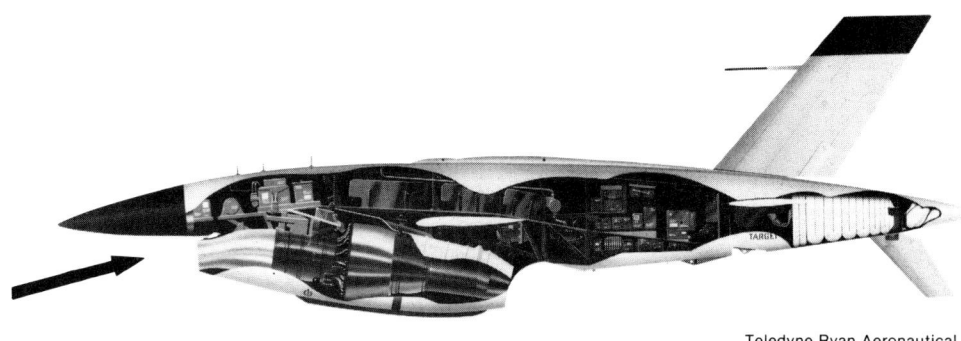

CAE's model J69-T-29 jet engine, up-rated to 1700 lbs. thrust, gave Ryan's Q-2C Firebee greatly increased performance

Raymond P. Powers, right, took over management of new Toledo plant and got CAE jets into production. In center is Jack Reese and at left is H. M. (Mel) Parker of Detroit headquarters, Director and Treasurer of CAE.

backlog of orders rose to $60 million and the Air Force pumped $2 million into plant facilities including test cells and additional machine tools and equipment.

But all was not well. Costs to produce J69 engines had exceeded the contract amount, and CAE filed a claim with the Government for $2.2 million in contract price relief. [The claim was denied; CAE accepted the decision in 1957 without appeal.] Manufacturing schedules were in disarray, too. A. C. Dickson, plant manager, was on the hot seat.

"When we got the Toledo plant," Art Wild, CAE Executive Vice-President recalled, "we were all set to go, but were having considerable production problems. I found I was spending as much time down there as I was in Detroit and Washington."

"Then we got Ray Powers and he turned the whole thing around."

The man responsible for getting Raymond P. Powers was Robert Trundle, Cleveland industrial management consultant and a new member of the Continental Motors Board of Directors.

From a contact at the National Bank of Detroit who handled financing for CMC and for Packard, Bob Trundle learned that production expert Powers was 'at liberty'.

Ray Powers had a fine track record as a manufacturing specialist. He had spent 20 years with General Motors and was a graduate of the General Motors Institute. For three years, he was general manufacturing manager of the Lincoln-Mercury division of Ford Motor Co.

Jack Reese had known Ray Powers for years, and when he learned from Bob Trundle of Powers' availability, struck a deal for him to join the Continental Motors organization.

Just prior to joining CAE in 1957 as Vice-President and Assistant General Manager at Toledo, Powers had been Vice-President, Operations of Studebaker-Packard.

The J69 program in particular was in trouble. As Powers said, "We were not delivering engines for the Cessna T-37 on schedule and Cessna was not helping the situation any by referring to the stored planes awaiting engines as 'gliders'."

But by "putting the right people in the right place," as Powers described it, things soon turned around.

"We put Ray in charge of production," Wild said, "and he soon got us on schedule, and our reputation with the Air Force went sky-high. He was also able to get the Air Force to make available a great deal of Government-owned equipment which we badly needed for efficient production."

Separation of research and development at Detroit, and manufacturing at Toledo, greatly improved operational efficiency. Company-wide CAE employment in 1958 reached two thousand, with 900 workers at Detroit and 1,100 at Toledo. Facilities at Toledo were further improved in 1957 with acquisition of a well-equipped component test laboratory.

CAE was greatly interested in the potential market for its turbine engines in both military and commercial helicopters and turbo-prop aircraft. Development work was begun in 1959 on the Model 217 shaft turbine for these applications.

In 1961, ten years after signing an agreement with Societe Turbomeca, CAE reached a new agreement, concluded through Continental Motors, with the French turbine manufacturer. This covered sales and manufacturing rights to additional engine models to be offered commercial aircraft customers.

Air Force Plant 27 at Toledo, Ohio became Continental Aviation and Engineering's main production facility

Heavy demand for J69 jets to power Cessna's twin-engine T-37 military trainers kept CAE production lines busy for two decades

San Diego AeroSpace Museum

Despite a multitude of problems, including a nationwide business recession, Continental Motors in the late 1950s and early '60s operated at a fairly high plateau of peacetime sales volume. However, profit as a percentage of sales was only about two cents on the dollar and dividends per share had to be reduced from 60 cents in 1959 and '60 to 40 cents in 1961.

Lower Profits; New Ventures

As CMC entered the sixties, Jack Reese reported that "rising labor costs, shrinking profit margins, and increasing competition have become the major current problems.

"The challenge looms larger each year, but this is nothing new to Continental. Our present diversification had its origin in just such a challenge, when motor car builders began manufacturing their own engines many years ago."

Looking ahead, Reese was optimistic because "we have built our business on the principle that we will never leave a customer 'high-and-dry' by discontinuing an operation around which he has built his operation. That is the reason for the multiplicity of specifications to which our engines are manufactured, and why our customers stay with us year after year."

CMC sales people explored every potential commercial market for business, seeking to expand the list of customers in the agricultural, industrial, transportation, marine and aircraft engine fields.

The Wisconsin and Gray Marine subsidiaries promoted new markets in their specialized areas as did Continental Aviation and Engineering. The factory branches at Dallas, Atlanta, and in St. Thomas, Ontario, broadened the potential for business as did export marketing agreements with distributors and dealers abroad. The possibility of a Latin American branch in Sao Paulo, Brazil, was also studied.

Engines for oil field equipment used in production, distribution and refining were typical of the specialized markets exploited. The breadth of the Continental line of engines — air-cooled and liquid-cooled; able to operate on gasoline, diesel or liquified petroleum gas (LPG) fuels — was a big plus in the oil equipment field as elsewhere.

And the automotive market, though far from what it once had been, was not neglected. Engines for leading manufacturers of highway trucks and tractors, fire engines, buses and delivery vans continued to be built, and special mention was made of "Continental engines for the taxicabs of the Checker Manufacturing Co. of Kalamazoo, and for its new line of cars and station wagons now in production."

On the theory that his company's heavy-duty taxicabs would be suitable for personal ownership as well, Morris Markin, President, introduced Checker's Marathon and Superba line of four-door, eight-passenger compact but roomy limousines and station wagons, all powered by Continental Red Seal engines — either 80 hp or 122 hp.

Because annual model changes were not considered necessary with cars good for 200,000 miles of lifetime usage, they were thought to be more economical and were offered at "half the cost of comparable cars." Long range, it did not work out that way.

Of equal importance with trucks and

Red Seal Magazine

Checker Cab chose Continental Red Seal engines for their Superba limousines when expanding its market beyond traditional cab business

157

New 1959 facility purchased was Novi Equipment Co., manufacturer of speed governors

buses was the military automotive market involving production of R600 truck engines for the U.S. and its allies.

New enterprises here and abroad were brought into the Continental orbit.

The Wisconsin Motor subsidiary loaned half a million dollars to Ronaldson Bros. & Tippett, Ltd. of Ballarat, State of Victoria, Australia, in 1958 to improve that company's facilities as a manufacturer of Wisconsin engines. The loan was convertible to stock in that company. An engine builder since 1906, the Australian firm had been producing Wisconsin engines under license since 1954.

At home, Wisconsin heavy-duty air-cooled engines remained the dominant power plant for agricultural and industrial use in the 3-½ hp to 30 hp range.

The Novi, Michigan plant and machinery of the Governor Division of the Novi Equipment Co. were purchased in August 1959, giving Continental a modern, well-equipped facility supplying governors for most of its industrial and agricultural engines requiring governed speed regulation.

The new Novi Division also supplied governors for engines manufactured by other companies as well as providing sheet metal and aluminum stampings to other Continental plants at lower cost than outside sources.

Governing devices produced included a hydraulic governor for fuel-injected engines; a load-sensing governor for DC generators; fixed-speed governors; variable speed controls for road building, lift truck and agricultural equipment; belt-driven governors; and crankshaft and other governors 'buried' in the engine.

Novi load-sensing governor assembly regulates direct current generator sets in accordance with load requirements

In the aircraft engine field, Continental also worked out new agreements with foreign producers. Fuji Motors of Japan, licensees of Continental under an agreement signed in 1954, began production in 1960 of Continental E-185 aircraft piston engines sold to aircraft users in its territory.

Rolls-Royce and Fuji Licenses Aircraft Engines

More significantly, Continental entered into a cross-licensing agreement in October 1960 with Rolls-Royce Limited of Derby, England, covering the full range of Continental aircraft piston engines — four- and six-cylinder air-cooled types from 65 hp to 400 hp.

Cooperation between Rolls-Royce and Continental dated back to World War II production by CMC of the Rolls-Royce Merlin engine for U.S. pursuit aircraft. "We knew 'em from top to bottom," was one Continental executive's evaluation of the relationship.

The new arrangement was worked out by Jack Reese and Dee Hollowell with John Herriot of Rolls. Part of the rationale for the license was that the English motor company found it too expensive to design its own engines for the private/utility plane market, but production by Rolls was primarily confined to the Continental 0-200 and 0-300 models.

The license gave Rolls-Royce exclusive rights for the sale of engines and parts in Europe, and for Rolls-Royce-built Continental engines in Australia and New Zealand. The agreement opened to Continental new markets previously restricted through international trade barriers; and also permitted Continental to build and market selected Rolls-Royce engines in the U.S.

For the military engine market, Beech Aircraft was an important intermediary. Continental's E225 piston engine (later models were known as O-470) powered the Beechcraft T-34 Mentor series of all-metal low-wing primary trainers not only for the U.S. Army and Navy but also for friendly foreign governments.

Beech also licensed Fuji Heavy Industries to build its airplanes for the Japanese National Safety Forces. A similar arrangement for Canadian production of the T-34 added the Continental-powered trainer to the inventory of the Royal Canadian Air Force.

The personal/business use of utility aircraft continued to expand throughout the world, and Continental engines were in a near-dominant position. No more convincing proof of their dependability could be offered than the many records Continental engines established.

Two 1958 records stood out. Both bet-

Capt. Boling and his Beech Bonanza

Refueling Heth-Burkhart Cessna

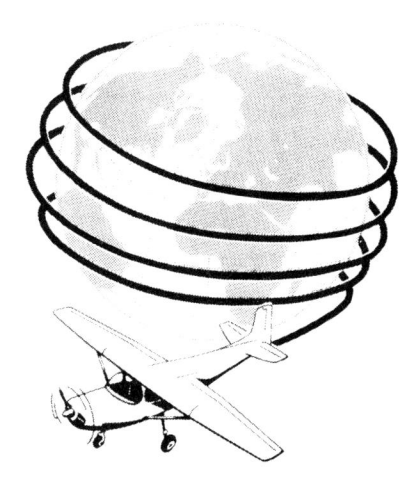

tered records set earlier by planes with Continental power.

Veteran airline pilot Capt. M. L. Boling flew 7,000 miles non-stop in his single-engine Beech Bonanza from Manila, Philippine Islands, to Pendleton, Oregon, practically all over water. He bettered, by some 3,500 miles, the record established nine years earlier by Capt. Bill Odom, also in a Continental-powered Beech Bonanza.

Boling's plane was powered by an IO-470C engine with Continental's exclusive continuous-flow fuel induction system. The flight lasted almost two full days.

In more than *seven weeks of continuous flight*, Jim Heth and Bill Burkhart flew their Cessna 172 for 1,200 hours during which its Continental 0-300-A engine never missed a beat in a flight equivalent to four times around the globe without stop.

The Heth-Burkhart Cessna was serviced by a speeding truck from which gasoline, oil, food and drink were hoisted into the plane by one of the pilots.

The previous record, set in 1949, with a Continental C-145-powered Aeronca, was 1,124 hours of continuous flight.

The Heth-Burkhart record was short lived. Within a few weeks, Robert Timm and John Cook, in the same type Continental-powered Cessna, added 15 days to the record, bringing continuous flying time to 1548 hours, or over nine weeks.

Peter Gluckman of San Francisco was more than a match for Capt. Boling when it came to long-distance over-water flights. Starting with a 1953 round-trip crossing of the Atlantic in a Continental-powered Luscombe, Gluckman's ocean-hopping appeared to have culminated with a round-trip San Francisco-Hawaii flight in 1957 in an E225-powered B35 Bonanza.

Two years later he topped even that record with a 29-day round-the-world flight in a Meyers 200 all-metal monoplane powered by Continental's new fuel injection IO-470-D engine. In circumnavigating the world — 28,000 miles in 198 hours flying time — Gluckman set a new world's record for single-engine aircraft.

Professor Paul H. Schweitzer's newsletter always received a careful reading by Continental's engineering virtuoso Carl Bachle. A professor at Pennsylvania State College, Schweitzer was a celebrated researcher on diesel engines who traveled frequently to Europe as technical observer and tourist.

Multi-Fuel Engines for the Ordnance Corps

Bachle was constantly searching for an answer to Army Ordnance's long-standing requirement for a multi-fuel engine able to "burn any fuel that will run through a pipe."

That's why an item in Professor Schweitzer's newsletter caught Bachle's attention in the early '50s. It described a demonstration of the MAN "whisper engine" truck which had been made to the professor while in Germany.

MAN — the acronym for Maschinenfabrik Augsburg-Nurnberg — was, Bachle said, "the famous German engine company where Rudolf Diesel built his first commercial engine in 1897. Since then it remained in the forefront of diesel development.

"The MAN whisper engine was the product of Dr. S. J. Meurer who was both a scientist and a practical engine man with an instinct for combustion. Over the years I learned a great deal from him.

"MAN engines had the reputation of having the loudest combustion noise, so I was interested to find out how they had transformed it to the quietest."

Once again technical developments on the Continent beckoned the perennial traveler, Carl Bachle.

"After two quick trips to MAN," he recalls, "I had satisfied myself that the 'whisper engine' was multi-fuel; that it would run well on any fuel — as well as being quiet in operation.

"Vastly exceeding my authority, I made a deal for Continental to take out a license at a small royalty figure with zero dollars entrance fee, all contingent on MAN supplying an engine behaving in a certain way during tests in Detroit.

159

Continental's LDS-427 Hypercycle multi-fuel compression-ignition engine in which fuel is sprayed directly onto the wall of the spherical combustion chamber (shown in cutaway photo)

In Arctic tests, Army trucks with new multi-fuel engine ford ponds and streams and plow through hub-deep mud on a 'good' Alaskan gravel road

"This precipitate action was to prevent our competitors from getting wind of what I was up to.

("My free-wheeling action at MAN probably was a factor in the company later assigning a lawyer, Al Massnick, to accompany me on many of my 80 trips to Europe. Fortunately, he was a delightful fellow traveler.")

"The MAN engine proved just as advertised and we immediately started to convert the six-cylinder 427 cubic inch displacement Continental gasoline engine to the 427 'Hypercycle' diesel engine."

Continental Motors used "Hypercycle" to describe the combustion principle developed by MAN's Dr. Meurer which was to spray fuel directly onto the combustion chamber wall instead of into the air of the combustion space in normal diesels.

Through the use of a special intake port, a swirl is induced in the induction air, and this swirl, scrubbing the fuel from the combustion chamber wall, results in a smooth and uniform rate of burning.

The controlled combustion prevents knocking even when low-octane fuels are used. Noise, smoke, and engine shock are reduced sharply.

"When Dr. Meurer first described the principle in a 1956 technical paper," Bachle continued, "there was a great upheaval in the diesel engineering fraternity. It was considered heresy to squirt fuel onto combustion chamber surfaces since great effort had always been expended to do the opposite. But today the principle is thoroughly understood and accepted as not in defiance of conventional diesel combustion theory."

On the basis of early tests by Continental Aviation and Engineering, the company went to the Army with the news that they, at last, had a multi-fuel engine for Ordnance Corps use. The Army was not convinced.

"It's too good to be true," was the reply. "We don't believe it, so prove it."

"Prove it, we did," said Bachle. "We put on a demonstration in a truck where we had six or seven different bottles which you could see. We could switch them on and off, and the fuel-injected engine would burn on any of those fuels — kerosene, turbine fuel, any octane of ordinary gasoline, diesel, even alcohol or drained crankcase oil.

"The Army finally conceded reluctantly that maybe the engine was multi-fuel, and that's how the enterprise grew."

First public indication that Continental was on to something good came in the 1955 Annual Report to Stockholders which revealed, without details, that the company had arranged to carry on exploitation and production in the U.S. of a radically new principle of diesel combustion. The following year, mention was being made of the Hypercycle engine.

Testing of the engine continued and early in 1958, Continental received a $2.9 million Ordnance Corps order for a pre-production quantity. The contract called for field testing the Army's 2½-ton truck, powered by the LDS-427 engine (Liquid-cooled, Diesel, Supercharged), in the Arctic and on the Arizona desert.

The order was especially significant because the announcement was made to coincide with public disclosure by Maj. Gen. Nelson M. Lynde, Jr., chief of the Ordnance Tank-Automotive Command in Detroit, of the Army's new policy to switch combat vehicle production from gasoline to diesel engines.

Having successfully passed all performance demands in 400,000 miles of testing under extreme conditions of climate and terrain, the LDS-427 multi-fuel Hypercycle engine for the standard Army 2½-ton truck went into full production in 1961 with the award of $14 million in contracts.

Supervising tests of LDS-427 multi-fuel engine are production head Thura Engstrom and, at right, Jack Reese, President

Although Continental was operating in a peacetime economy, Jack Reese frequently pointed out that "the military continues to be our largest single customer." Even as research and development work was being done on advanced engine concepts, production of established models was being stepped up. But then came a new development in the military engine picture.

The Military Services go to Diesels

During World War II, the National Petroleum Board had decreed that all U.S. military ground equipment use gasoline. This policy did not change until after the Korean War.

In February 1958, the Army announced a giant program to change nearly all combat vehicles, including tanks and trucks, from conventional gasoline spark-ignition engines to diesel-type compression ignition engines within five years.

In cooperation with Army Ordnance, CMC and CAE for many years had been working to adapt Continental's "family" of carbureted military engines to diesel and to gasoline fuel injection. A diesel version of the 1790 cubic inch displacement 12-cylinder engine was first proposed about 1948 and by 1950 Ordnance let CAE start work on a single cylinder. Too, four fuel-injection engines had been introduced in the 1954-57 time period. (See page 148.)

While the change from carburetor to fuel-injection systems reduced fuel consumption as much as one-third, the diesel compression-ignition engine appeared to offer still greater advantages.

Continental had been building air-cooled tank engines for a quarter-century and planned to continue the air-cooling practice when going to diesel. But experts in the diesel field said it couldn't be done.

Carl Bachle explained some of the problems:

"When we first started in on conversion of the spark-ignition 1790 engine to compression-ignition for diesel fuel, I was told by Art Rosen, chief engineer of Caterpillar Tractor and the 'pope' of the diesel engine in those days, that it was impossible because diesel depends on not losing heat.

"In a liquid-cooled diesel, you'd have a glow plug to give the heated air of compression that last push so that the fuel squirted in will burn and start combustion. When the piston comes up on compression it heats the air, but if the engine is air-cooled, Rose contended, you lose that heat and the air-cooled engine can't overcome that problem."

But Continental did solve the dilemma. "In noble style," said Bachle, explaining further. "You can produce the temperature in which the fuel will burn either by compressing the air or by heating the air first, and then compressing it, which gets it to the final temperature needed. By heating the air outside the cylinder, we solved the problem."

Among other specifications, the Army required tank engines to operate under water with the use of a snorkel for air intake and engine exhaust. One demonstration required submerging the engine in ice water for 15 minutes, then starting the engine while it's still 15 feet down at the bottom.

It was this test, in particular, that the experts said could not be met by an air-cooled diesel.

"We had to prove all these things," Bachle said. "In order to do it we built a half-million dollar cold room, and made a terrific investment between 1955 and 1959 to finally win the contract award."

Development work by CAE on the air-cooled diesel engine for tanks and tracked vehicles was directed to providing not only greater fuel economy but also minimum space, maximum reliability and, because of extensive use of aluminum, light weight with maximum power.

Result of the five-year program was the 12-cylinder 750 hp model AVDS-1790-2 engine (Air-cooled, V-type, Diesel, Supercharged). Fuel consumption was 40 percent less than its same displacement gasoline fuel-injection counterpart (AVI-1790-8) and 53 percent less than the companion carburetor fuel system engine (AV-1790-7C). This helped the Army attain the cruising range requirement it had established for tanks.

At Last! Diesels for Tanks

Teledyne Continental Motors

Continental AVDS-1790-2A Diesel Engine

Assistant Secretary of Army Frank H. Higgins, second from right, and Brig. Gen. Jean E. Engler, Army Ordnance director of procurement, left, inspect Continental's new AVDS-1790 tank engine. With them (between visitors), are Carl F. Bachle, CAE research head, and (far right) Continental President Jack Reese.

The significance of the new engine was stressed by Assistant Secretary of the Army Frank H. Higgins during a June 1958 visit to the Getty Street plant at Muskegon.

"The importance of the new Continental diesel," Higgins said, "cannot be overestimated. It is of great significance in the area of Army logistics planning as we change from conventional to diesel-type compression ignition engines."

New funds appropriated by Congress for Army tank procurement brought a revival in military vehicle production.

A limited quantity of AVDS-1790 diesel tank engines was ordered in April 1959 under an initial $5.6 million in contracts to CMC. Deliveries began in December; then full production of this model was scheduled in late 1961 under a $34 million contract for use in the M60, the Main Battle Tank for U.S. and Allied Forces. It was the first new tank ordered into production since the M48 Patton built during the Korean War.

At the same time, the new production orders also covered Continental's 850 hp fuel-injection engines (AVI-1790 series) for M88 Tank Recovery Vehicles.

Smaller versions of the AVDS family, ranging from 375 to 550 hp and including an eight-cylinder model of the 1100 cubic inch displacement engine, were also being developed. Late in 1960, the first were tested in motor gun carriers.

Continental's new orders had resulted from plans by the Defense Department to purchase 720 M60 Medium Tanks to be produced by Chrysler at the Detroit Arsenal, and 212 of the M88 Tank Recovery Vehicles to be built in Pennsylvania.

M88 Tank Recovery Vehicle, above, powered by fuel-injected AVI-1790 gasoline engine. Below, M60 Main Battle Tanks, powered by new air-cooled AVDS-1790 diesel engines.

Over a half a century, what had been Continental's greatest technical accomplishments? For an answer we went to Carl Bachle:

"In the broadest terms it was the proof that air-cooled engines could have long life in tanks. Also outstanding was the fact it was possible to have an air-cooled diesel engine in tanks."

Technical Breakthroughs

Tank historian Richard P. Hunnicutt was inclined to agree:

"Only the United States has been committed to the air-cooled engine despite its obvious advantages. In Europe, aircraft engines were installed in tanks (as Continental did as early as 1932), but overseas they were liquid-cooled as in the Rolls-Royce Meteor used for many years in Britain.

"American liquid-cooled engines lost out to Continental's 1790 air-cooled series which were designed specifically for the tracked vehicle job.

"Russia has modified and used almost the same liquid-cooled diesel since World War II. They don't seem inclined to drop a reliable engine and gamble on anything new.

"The people who developed the later European engines had extensive liquid-cooling experience and were probably more comfortable with familiar solutions to their problem. It certainly involved less risk than striking out in a new area as Continental did."

There are those who contend that the U.S. uses air-cooled tank engines (and the rest of the world liquid-cooled) because of Carl Bachle's 'selling.' His response: "Perhaps. But one man or one company could not keep a thing like that sold all these years unless the concept was right.

"In the military sense, getting rid of the liquid for cooling is tremendously important. We first learned this in North Africa during World War II with the Continental W-670 air-cooled 'aircraft' engine in light tanks.

"In the desert there you couldn't *find* water. And in the Arctic you can't *use* water.

"The Germans wrote a W-670 instruction manual for our engines retrieved from captured tanks. It made an excellent case for air-cooled vs. liquid-cooled.

"Time has proven that air-cooled demands expertise in handling the cooling area whereas with liquid-cooled you could always cover up lack of expertise by a bigger radiator or something of that sort."

Senior management at Continental Motors — Jack Reese, Henry Vandeven, Earl Ginn, Albert Willi, T. A. Engstrom, Wheeler Johnson, Art Wild, Dee Hollowell, to name a few — had served long and well, but time and hard work had taken their toll. And, unfortunately, behind the first line of the "Reese team," aggressive new managers had not been fully developed.

Time Takes Its Toll

The top workaholic was, of course, Jack Reese whose seven-days-a-week devotion to business had gone on without interruption since he took the helm as president in 1939.

Now, twenty years later and with 27 years of service to Continental, he was nearly sixty. Commuting regularly by company plane between Detroit and Muskegon with scheduled business meetings every Saturday and Sunday as well as during the normal work week, it was little wonder that members of his team with whom he was most intimate began to notice subtle changes in Jack's performance. Was he on the verge of a breakdown?

"I knew it about 1958," observed Carl Bachle. "I went to my cohorts who had little noticed his troubles yet and said something ought to be done. Because it smacked of being disloyal, none of them were willing to do anything to correct the situation.

"One of the things that Jack instilled very effectively was the idea of loyalty. It was probably his chief contribution in those days. Loyalty to the team. Never mind titles; never mind salary; never mind anything except be loyal to the team.

"Loyalty was such a strong influence that when it became obvious to my friends that Jack was in trouble, they wouldn't act. To me, it was obvious that he should not be president any longer.

"Take an incident during the time we had an intensive campaign on to sell the multi-fuel engine to the Army and win a production contract. First they wanted to look us over.

"Army Assistant Secretary Frank Higgins said he'd like to come to Detroit and meet Continental's president. I said 'fine, but I'd like you to visit Muskegon and see the plant where we propose to build the multi-fuel engines.'

" 'That's even better,' Higgins replied, 'I've got to be in Muskegon anyway for ground-breaking ceremonies of the new Army Reserve Armory there.'

"So, this was all arranged.

"The Assistant Secretary's Army plane flies into Muskegon, and Jack Reese is well alerted that he's supposed to be our principal actor. We are all standing at the airport

"One of the things that Jack instilled very effectively was the idea of loyalty"

> "It was the ability to adapt to changing conditions which brought us through that crucial time"

at attention. I naturally thought that Jack would come forward and shake hands and otherwise make our visitor welcome. But he wouldn't.

"Jack just stood there. So out of the pack, since I knew Higgins, I walked forward, shook hands and performed like the president of a company should.

"This looked very odd to Higgins. Then I said to Jack, 'You should ride with the Secretary when we go to the plant and otherwise be his companion.' But Jack declined, and asked me to do it. So I did, but I was embarrassed for the company because, for the team's sake, we were looking bad."

The incident was, of course, not serious in itself, but as a harbinger of problems ahead, it was a matter of growing concern to those associates of Jack Reese who were discerning enough to realize the long-term implications.

As the year 1961 drew to a close, Jack Reese recapped sixty years of company progress in a special RED SEAL magazine feature directed to his associates. It was a succinct review of six decades of great accomplishment.

Six Decades of Progress

As the accompanying sketch suggests, products of the Continental family now encircle the globe. It should be noted that the picture shows only the broad general groups of Continental-powered end-products — transportation, agricultural, industrial-construction, military, aircraft, and marine. Specific applications running into the hundreds were omitted for lack of room. And of all those shown, and those omitted, the automobile is the only one that was in existence at all, when Continental Motors was founded, 60 years ago.

On the farm and on the highway, "horsepower" then meant just that. Oat-burning horsepower was king. The only farm tractor was the horse. He pulled plow, harrow, grain drill, cultivator, mower, reaper and rake. He powered hayfork and stoneboat. Off the farm the horse drew the fire engine, as well as most of the scrapers and other road machinery then in use. He hauled sand and gravel, in slat-bottomed wagons which men dumped by hand, turning the slats on edge one by one to let the load trickle through.

When the job was too heavy for the horse, it was not gasoline, but steam or electricity, that got the call. Threshing machines and road rollers derived their locomotion from steam; steam donkey engines powered derricks, mixers and cranes, and steam had the marine field entirely to itself.

Electric interurbans, all but extinct today, scampered about the landscape where superhighways now carry air-conditioned buses.

In their bicycle shop in Dayton, the Wright brothers were experimenting with a flying machine. It hadn't gotten off the ground yet. Lots of people didn't think it would.

As for the military tank in our picture, it didn't exist even as a dream. For hadn't the world entered on an era of permanent peace?

The 1920s brought a jolting readjustment which many firms failed to survive. Tightening competition in the automobile industry forced company after company to become more nearly self-sufficient — to build its own engines or quit. Continental customers fell away.

But Continental didn't take adversity lying down. And it was the ability to adapt to changing conditions which brought us through that crucial time. This can be said in all modesty, since the product diversification that has progressed so far in recent years originated with the management of that day. Continental brought all its resources of technical skill and production know-how to bear on the two-part problem of finding new jobs for Continental power, and engineering that power precisely to each job.

Gradually, one by one, new applications unfolded. Aircraft destined to change the world's whole way of life; highway trucks; farm tractors and various agricultural implements; rollers, pavers, mixers, ditchers; generator sets, compressors and pumps; power for oil field production, distribution and processing; air conditioning; specialized construction machinery of all sorts. The list goes on and on. It is still growing, too. It will, I believe, be limited by only one thing: our ability to keep step with a fast-moving world.

And "world" is the right word, too. For not only our market, but our competition as well, is now global in scope. The ability to keep pace is no longer the simple thing it once was—no longer merely a matter of producing engines of new types and sizes. More than ever before in our 60-year history, it means keeping guard over engineering design, quality, service—and price.

Clarence Reese

President

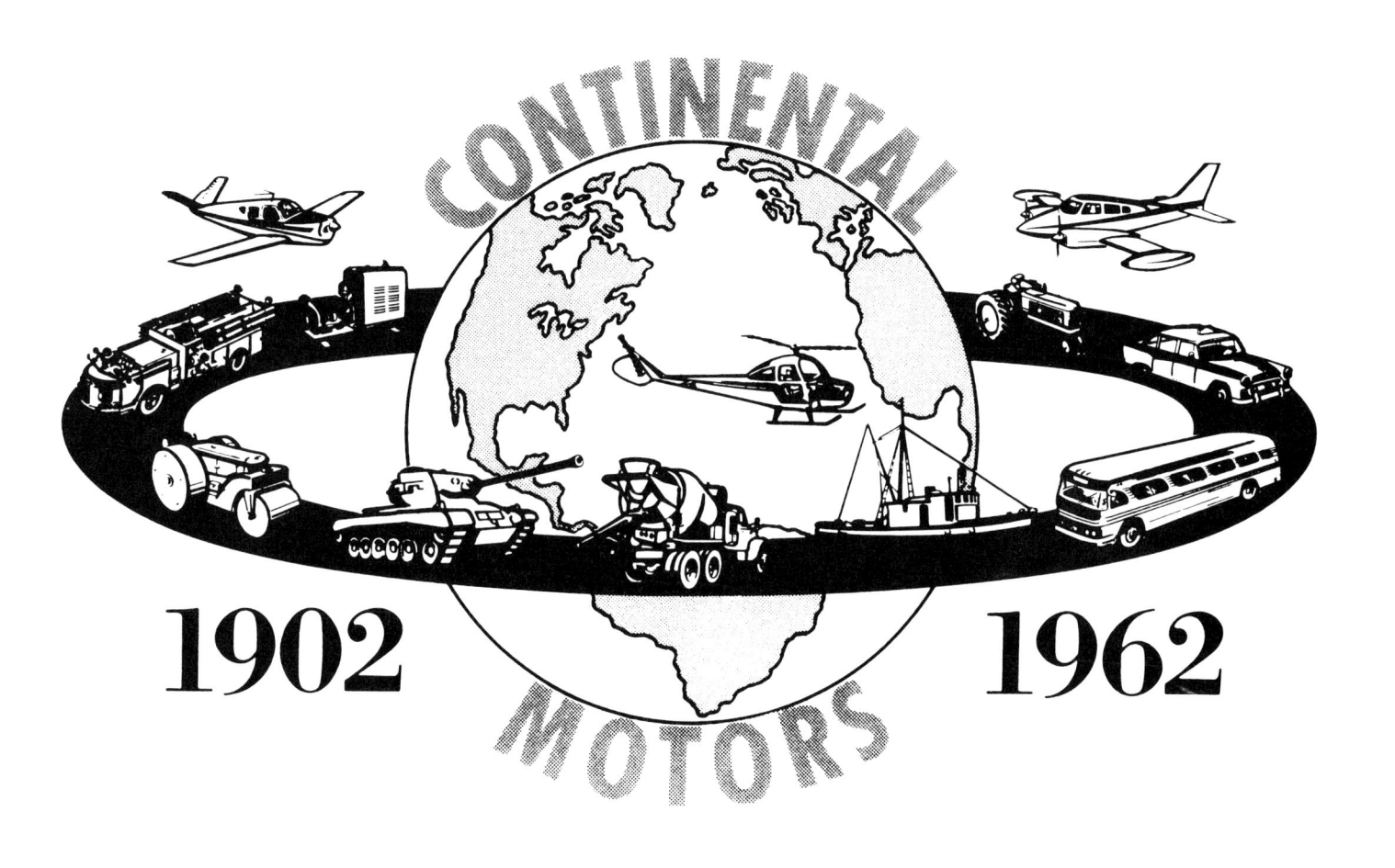

CONTINENTAL MOTORS

1902 — **1962**

THE RYAN AND TELEDYNE ERAS (1962-1975)

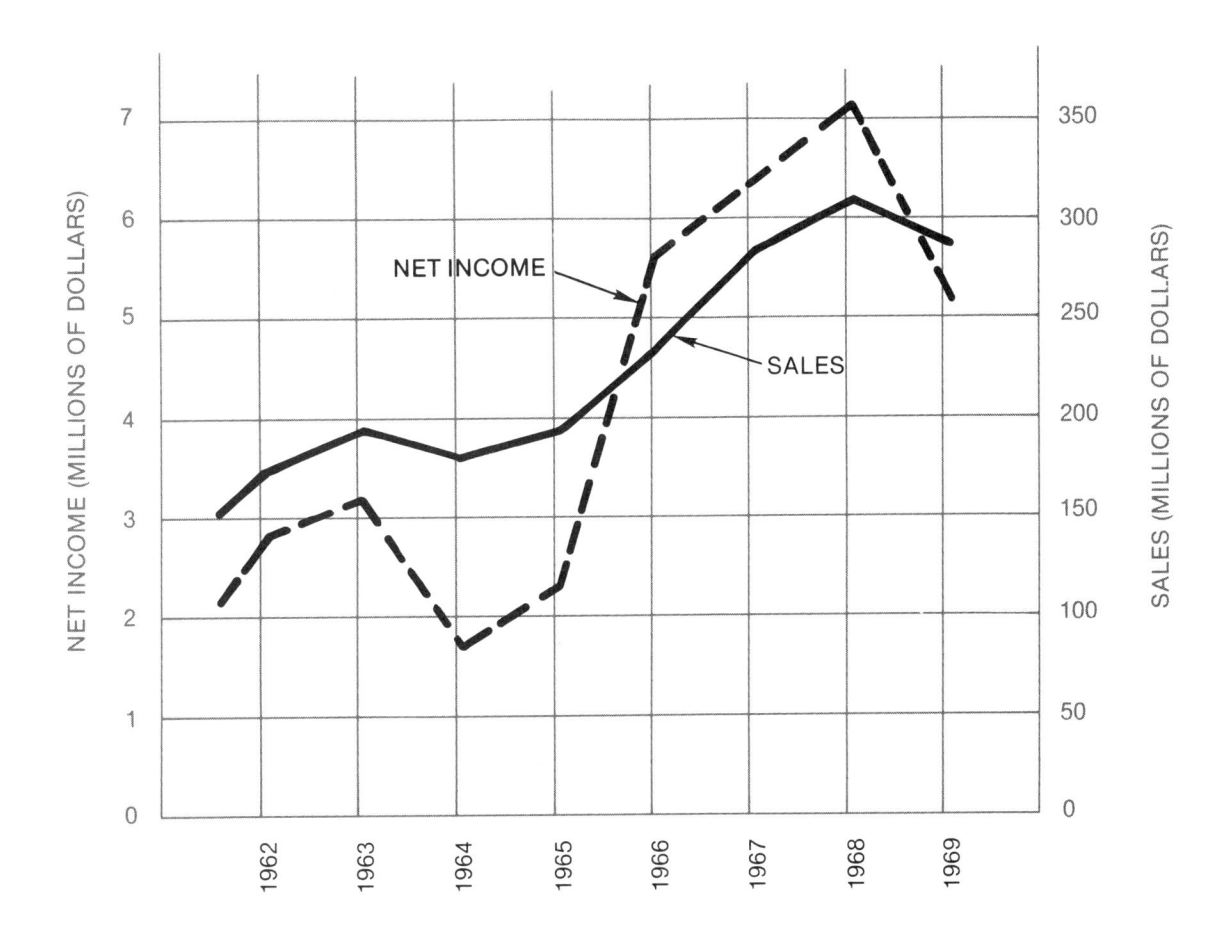

Aggressive, profit-oriented Ryan Aeronautical Company of San Diego makes a stock investment in old-line Continental Motors and in four years gains control of the company. Then Teledyne, Inc. buys out the Ryan-Continental group of companies.

Pages 169 to 204

1962-1975

Ryan's Investment	169
The Chicago Meeting	170
Business Better in 1962-63	171
Ryan's Advance Men	172
Major Management Changes	173
A Comprehensive Review	174
Ryan Gets Majority Control	175
Reese's Man-Killing Pace	175
New Trends in 1964-65	176
Product Profitability	178
Creative Executives Needed	178
Senior Managers Stayed On — and On	179
The Employment Contracts	179
Central Management Concept	180
Continental's Superior Engineering	181
VCR — Variable Compression Ratio	181
Tank Engines	182
Military Truck Engines	183
Military Standard Engines	185
Aircraft Engines	185
Industrial/Automotive, Marine Engines	186
CAE Gas Turbines	188
New Plant Facilities	190
Civic Responsibility	191
Stock Ownership Changes	193
Rutherford Named President	193
New Sales and Earning Records	194
Teledyne Buys Ryan	195
Ryan People Retained	195
Wisconsin and CAE Become Divisions	196
Continental Folded Into Teledyne	198
Independent Units	198
General Products Division	199
Aircraft Products Division	200
New Generation Tiara Engines	201
Planes in the News	202
Industrial Products Division	203
Teledyne CAE	203
Teledyne Wisconsin Motor	203

What Future Role for Ryan?

Early in 1962, Ryan Aeronautical Company of San Diego, California, issued its 1961 Annual Report to Stockholders. For the first time the firm disclosed that it had made "an investment of $3,285,079 in a marketable security." No further explanation was given.

Ryan's Investment

A year later the word came out from both companies that Ryan had been steadily buying shares of Continental Motors Corporation on the open market. At the October 31, 1962 fiscal year end Ryan reported that it owned 21.1% of Continental's 3,300,000 shares.

An 'Addendum' stapled to Continental's 1962 Annual Report showed that Ryan had increased its ownership to 23.9% as of January 31, 1963, the record date for the annual meeting of Continental stockholders.

What was the story behind the pioneer aeronautical firm's investment in an engine manufacturing company?

Ryan had been founded in 1922 by an enterprising young Army reserve pilot, T. Claude Ryan, whose original company, Ryan Airlines, Inc., went on to build Charles A. Lindbergh's famed "Spirit of St. Louis" monoplane.

The Ryan company continued to prosper and began attracting knowledgeable investors, among them George Knox, a partner in the Los Angeles investment firm of Harker & Co., and Knox's fellow Harvard Graduate School of Business classmate, Robert C. Jackson.

Harker & Co. customers began to purchase stock in the promising Ryan Aeronautical Company in 1947 and in 1956 joined Knox and Jackson in forming the Emtor, Inc., investor group. Eventually, Knox and his associates, through Emtor, controlled 26% of Ryan, while founder T. Claude Ryan held 10% of the outstanding shares.

Knox was a great student of financial reports—as astute a security analyst as one was apt to find. If anyone could see financial opportunity in a set of cold figures it was George Knox. In Continental Motors he saw a potentially rewarding investment for himself and his associates acting through their stock interest in Ryan Aeronautical Company.

When Ryan made its first purchases of Continental shares, the engine company was doing $135 million in annual sales, and earning a net profit of from $1.5 to $3.5 million per year. But both sales and earnings had declined more than 50% from levels of a decade earlier and the profit on sales seldom exceeded 2%. The company and its management was aging. However, despite reduced business volume and profits, net assets had increased about 25% in ten years to $50 million.

Although Continental's book value was $15 per share, its stock was selling on the New York Stock Exchange for $10 per share, at which figure Ryan was only too happy to make its "investment in a marketable security." An added attraction to Ryan was the fact that Continental Motors held a 51% interest in Continental Aviation and Engineering Corp., providing participation in the growing jet engine market.

Before proceeding any farther, however, the Los Angeles investor group dispatched a financial analyst from another brokerage firm to inspect the Continental property. When he returned he advised that Ryan was making a terrible investment and that the Continental stock they had already purchased should be sold immediately. His advice was overruled.

Through the company's stock transfer agent, Continental's Treasurer, Henry W. Vandeven early on became aware of Ryan's purchases of the engine company's shares. In turn when this came to the attention of Jack Reese and particularly of Art Wild, Executive Vice-President of CAE, there was concern as to Ryan's long-range intentions. Would Ryan continue its purchases to the point where they demanded a role in management?

James E. Murray

**Financial Planner
GEORGE KNOX**

Brilliant behind-the-scenes financial expert (shown at '29 class reunion in Boston), Knox masterminded Ryan's acquisition of Continental Motors

Top management of Ryan Aeronautical Company strongly supported the firm's investment in Continental Motors. Key executives were pioneer aircraft manufacturer and company founder T. Claude Ryan, left, Chairman; and money-wise Robert C. Jackson, President.

Richard Stauss

The Chicago Meeting

When pressed for his reaction, Reese was a bit more relaxed than Wild. "That's all right, Art. Don't forget, Ryan's a good customer of ours." Reese also told the Wall Street Journal, "We couldn't have better stockholders than Claude Ryan and his company, who have been customers for years."

For their part, George Knox and Claude Ryan well understood the feelings of Continental management. After all, Ryan himself had experienced the same situation when Knox and his associates bought into the Ryan company. What emerged then was a friendly relationship between founder Ryan and his management team and investor Knox and his financial friends.

In any case, the facts about Continental would soon become public, because Securities and Exchange Commission regulations required a publicly held company to disclose its ownership in another corporation whenever that ownership represented more than 10% of that firm's outstanding shares. (In its 1961 Annual Report, Ryan had only disclosed—without further comment—"an investment of $3,285,079 in a marketable security.")

Under the circumstances, Knox and Ryan decided they should contact Jack Reese and lay all the cards on the table before their 10% ownership of Continental had to be made public. From joint service on the Aircraft War Production Council, Ryan and Reese were well acquainted. Ryan phoned Reese and suggested a meeting. Reese proposed they fly to Chicago and meet with him and his company's attorney at the Blackstone Hotel.

As was his custom, Knox had little to say at the Chicago meeting with Continental's Jack Reese, major stockholder Jim Ferry, an attorney from Fred J. Kennedy's law firm, and Treasurer Henry Vandeven.

"Jack," Claude began, "as you know, any company whose officers hold only a small percentage of the outstanding shares is very vulnerable to a take-over by what could be unfriendly financial groups. Our approach is a friendly one. George Knox is very experienced in investment matters and has been of great help to us.

"We think we can be of similar assistance to you, to your associates at Continental and to your shareholders. We have many talented young men coming along in our management structure; they are available and can help your company do a better job. And, we have the capital to make a major investment in Continental since we believe this is the best use Ryan can make of the cash we have available.

"Your management is well seasoned, but getting along in years. We intend to continue buying Continental shares and we want close, friendly relations during a transition period which may take several years."

In recounting that meeting many years later, Ryan recalled that "Jack Reese seemed relieved that our intentions were entirely friendly." Jim Ferry's comment was that the meeting "was absolutely the most open discussion there ever was. What could be more straightforward than buying stock for cash on the open security market?"

While there was some apprehension in CMC executive offices about Ryan's future role in the firm's affairs, (and wild speculation about 'Mr. Knox, a mysterious financial genius'), it was business as usual between the engine company and its customers. In fact, business was showing an

170

upturn from the $135 million average annual sales level of the past seven years.

Business Better in 1962-63

Jack Reese attributed 1962's increase of 34% in sales volume to "increased deliveries of military equipment to the Armed Forces and to increased civilian aircraft engine orders from commercial customers." Business volume increased another 11% in 1963 to $191 million, the highest in ten years. Net income rose from $1.4 million in 1961 to $2.7 million in '62; then to $3.2 million in '63. Cash dividends held steady at 40 cents per share annually.

Production moved ahead on tank engines with $25 million in additional orders for 750 hp diesel engines for M48 and M60 Army medium tanks, and 850 hp fuel-injection engines for M88 tank recovery vehicles.

Work continued with Army Ordnance on further development, testing and initial production of the LDS-427 Hypercycle compression-ignition engine for Army 2½-ton M35 trucks. The multi-fuel engines operated equally well on gasoline, diesel fuel, jet fuel or any combination of the three.

Six models of the ½ hp to 35 hp Military Standard Engines which Continental had developed for the Army Corps of Engineers continued to be built under contracts totaling $10 million.

Due largely to the growing interest in private and business flying, now supported heavily by government-sponsored expansion of airports for smaller aircraft, Continental aircraft engine business was growing rapidly.

Indicative of the trend in the private plane market was Cessna Aircraft's delivery in Spring 1963 of the Cessna Skyhawk which marked the 50,000th aircraft built by that pioneer company. Like the great majority of Cessna's planes—as well as all of the Cessnas built in recent years—No. 50,000 was powered by a Continental air-cooled engine.

Through its cross-licensing agreement with Rolls-Royce of England, CMC was gaining an important share of the European engine market for private and executive aircraft. And in the Far East, engines were being distributed through the Japanese licensee, Fuji Motors of Tokyo.

The export market for industrial engines was also tapped by a licensing agreement with the long-established Belgian industrial firm LaMeuse.

Continental's subsidiary companies and divisions made significant progress in developing new product lines and engine models, broadening markets and increasing distributor service.

Adding to its reputation as the largest producer of inboard marine engines, Gray Marine Motor Co. introduced a number of new models and also became North American distributor for Rolls-Royce marine engines.

Essentially a designer and assembler of marine modifications of other companies' engines, Gray built up its marine power units from basic engine blocks supplied by Continental (Market Street-Muskegon), the Buick Division of General Motors and American Motors.

Major pleasure boat builders like Chris-Craft and Owens Yacht produced their own engines, increasing Gray's problem to continue to operate efficiently. In fact, in the 13 years 1950-63 average profit was an unimpressive $35,000 annually.

Unlike the automobile market, most builders of pleasure boats would install any engine of the individual customer's choice, provided it would fit the boat.

Wisconsin Motor Corp. of Milwaukee maintained its position as the world's largest builder of heavy-duty air-cooled engines. Ranging in power from 6 hp to 60 hp, Wisconsin engines were used primarily in the agricultural, industrial and construction fields—powering everything from heavy equipment such as road paving and

Red Seal Magazine

Against snow-draped Mt. Rainier, a Fairliner Jethawk with 170 hp Gray Marine engine speeds over waters of Puget Sound

Cessna Aircraft Company

A prime customer for Continental aircraft engines, Cessna delivered its 50,000th plane — a Skyhawk — in 1963

"... fewer and fewer units of more and more items."

highway maintenance machinery, and large farm equipment, to small lawn and garden tractors.

CMC's sales and service organization was strengthened by opening of a new branch at Salt Lake City to better serve the West and Pacific Northwest. Branches at Atlanta and Dallas, and Continental Motors of Canada (at St. Thomas, Ontario), stocked over 300 different engine models, and up to 15,000 different engine parts, to adequately service all lines of CMC automotive-industrial, aircraft and marine engine types.

In addition to supplying parts, service assistance and training for distributors, dealers and customers in their areas, the branch plants were given the facilities to customize and remanufacture engines.

The recently acquired Novi Governor Division expanded its established engine speed and control product line to include water pumps.

At important 51%-owned Continental Aviation and Engineering, the subsidiary reported somewhat reduced sales but higher profits. Research continued on CAE's model 217 free turbine engine from which were developed T65 and T72 turbo-shaft engines for helicopters. And for the parent company, CAE development work went forward on the LD-465 and supercharged LDS-465 multi-fuel engines for military trucks.

Not content with the preliminary analysis of Continental Motors they had received from Will Richeson of Dean Witter & Co. some months earlier, the Ryan investors in April 1963 dispatched one of their own executives—Winthrop C. Henderson—to Muskegon and Detroit to take a more exhaustive look at the company in which they were investing.

Ryan's Advance Men

Henderson had joined Ryan in 1960 and most recently had been an administrator monitoring the business side of the company's extensive aerospace engineering activities.

He had come to Ryan after six years as Financial Vice-President of General Paint Corp., a firm in which Knox, Harker & Co. and their clients had made an important investment. Henderson understood what they needed to know about Continental's operation.

For four months advance-man Henderson researched the key elements of CMC's past record, current business and future prospects. His findings were reported back to Bob Jackson in San Diego.

"Major changes have taken place in the internal-combustion engine market in the past ten years," Henderson wrote. "The automobile industry has expanded heavily its use of V-8 engines, and the pleasure boat industry has followed this trend.

Teledyne Continental Motors

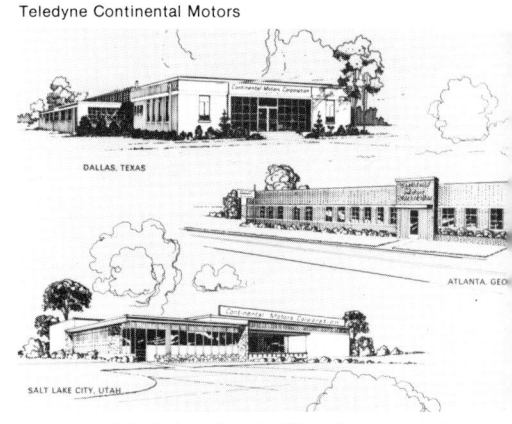

Salt Lake City facility, bottom, joins customer service branches at Dallas and Atlanta

"Diesel engines have gained a large share of the market for highway trucks, and have increasingly been used in foreign countries. Small, lightweight, low-horsepower air-cooled engines have been produced by the millions to power an increasing variety of 'handyman' tools. Turbine engines have been developed for a variety of applications, and are becoming increasingly favored.

"But Continental has not experienced any substantial growth during the past ten years, although a bulge in Army orders for tank and military truck engines caused a substantial increase in sales volume in 1962-63. Continental has developed only one new V-8 engine and has no 'open chamber' diesel. As a result in the past 15 months the company shipped only 2800 diesel engines, 40% of which went to the Gray Marine subsidiary and the company's own branch plants.

"Meanwhile, sales of Cummins Engine Co., a major competitor particularly for diesel engine business both domestic and export, have grown four-fold since 1950. Briggs & Stratton, a principal builder of small air-cooled engines, has likewise increased its sales volume 400% in the past decade.

"At the Market Street plant, 70% of the sales are automotive engines, sold to commercial customers at only about 2% gross profit. This division has a highly complex product line of 120 models of liquid-cooled engines manufactured to 5000 or more specifications plus over 25,000 service parts for current engines and those built in past years. The company rarely discontinues anything.

"Most of the 4400 pieces of machinery are over 14 years old, and some equipment has been in service for half a century.

"Continental tries to operate the plant on a policy of providing any customer with any quantity of any engine in the shortest possible time at the lowest possible price. Production orders tend to be for small lots so the factory in effect is a job shop rather than a production line operation. Regardless of financial results, Reese simply cannot turn down an order.

"As this keeps up, the product line becomes fewer and fewer units of more and more items. Eventually it could consist of no units of everything!"

Continental also faced another serious competitive threat, this one in the military market. Most research and development of engines for military use is done under government contract and therefore designs are available to any qualified manufacturer when new contracts are put out for bid. Cummins, Hercules Motor Company and Lycoming, as well as the 'big three' automakers, cut into Continental's share of the military engine market.

"Reese appears to recognize," Henderson also reported, "that the ratios of profits to sales and invested capital are low, but he seems to feel that this is an unfortunate characteristic of the engine business and that nothing much can be done about it.

"He also seems to foster the impression of genteel poverty. General offices are at Market Street and give a very poor impression. Even the parking lot is unpaved; instead it is surfaced with oiled sand which is tracked into the buildings. Jack feels the appearance of poverty impresses customers who feel they are dealing with an economical vendor.

"In very few respects does the company show signs of progress or change.

"None of the officers or directors are substantial stockholders, except Jim Ferry, who inherited his stock. None—Reese and Vandeven included—has apparently considered Continental's stock to be a bargain at the low prices it has reached in recent years.

"Reese, assisted by Vandeven, makes all major and most minor decisions for Continental and for Gray Marine. Wild, with Reese's general supervision, runs CAE. Harold Todd runs Wisconsin with practically no interference from anyone."

For his part, Jackson made no secret of the fact that "Ryan is buying Continental stock on occasion when we think it is a good buy. And, if the opportunity is good, we will continue to buy. I might add, that the Continental shares we now have were purchased at some $5 million below their book value."

Representing the Emtor holding company investors, Robert C. Jackson became a Director of Ryan Aeronautical Company in 1957, Executive Vice-President two years later, and was elected President in 1961 at about the time Ryan began its purchase of Continental Motors shares.

Major Management Changes

Money-wise Bob Jackson had been a Certified Public Accountant, World War II Army Lieutenant Colonel, wartime finance officer in Europe and Washington and was a business executive of rare capability.

In December 1963, by which time Ryan's continued purchases brought its ownership to 33% of Continental shares, Jackson became a member of CMC's seven-man Board of Directors, replacing David Van Alstyne.

The next month, Henderson, who had just been employed by Continental as special assistant to Jack Reese, was elected Treasurer of Continental, replacing Henry W. Vandeven. Then, in March 1964, Henderson also replaced Vandeven on the Board of Directors. It was the beginning of the take-over of CMC management by Ryan people.

Vandeven, age 70, had been with Continental since World War I, advancing steadily through the company ranks for 45 years. Named Treasurer in 1939, he was elected to the Board of Directors in 1956. By the time Ryan got into the picture, Vandeven was Jack Reese's second in command, serving also as officer and director of all of CMC's subsidiary companies.

"Vandeven was well along in years and knew all the reasons why a new idea wouldn't work," recalls Henderson. "He didn't actually retire. We bought out his employment contract (more about that later) but he did step aside from management responsibility. In a month or two we moved him to an office in the Hackley Bank Building in Muskegon. Our people felt that Vandeven was too old-fashioned in his approach to financial and accounting matters, and the company simply needed to have him out of the way.

"Reese made every attempt to keep his management team intact, resisting retirement of his people. Vandeven was a good example; so too was Dee Hollowell, Continental's well-liked aircraft engine sales Vice-President. But Dee was 68, suffering from arthritis and the after-effects of a stroke. Willi, 68, was in reasonably good health. Guy Harinton, 68, another Vice-President, was in possession of a plastic tube as a major artery to his brain. Mrs. Beda Clowar, Assistant Secretary and Reese's personal secretary, was probably in her mid-seventies.

"All of his senior people, no matter how hard they are trying, are slowing the company down, not only by their actions or failure to act, but by the restriction of opportunities which should otherwise be available to younger people in the organization."

J. Lynn Richardson, Assistant Controller of Ryan, was sent to Detroit in March 1964 to check on CAE financial matters and

Richard Stauss

**Advance Man
WINTHROP C. HENDERSON**

Red Seal Magazine

Veteran No. 2 man at Continental for many years was Treasurer Henry W. Vandeven

CMC's government contracts. B. Kenneth Goodman, Ryan's Corporate Secretary and General Counsel, began looking into similar business areas at CMC as did Walter J. Herbert, Ryan's labor relations and pension plan expert.

Other executives from San Diego moved into the CMC management structure, some for short periods, others to remain permanently. To revitalize the dying CMC organization, Ryan continued to pump in new blood and new ideas. Howard Dunlap went east to survey CMC's commercial marketing; Frank Light to take control of accounting functions.

Hard-hitting, no-nonsense Ryan plant operations Vice-President L. M. (Larry) Limbach went east in April to survey manufacturing activities and was appalled at their run-down, decaying condition, especially the outdated equipment in the ancient Market Street plant in Muskegon adjoining which was the equally outdated Lakey Foundry in which Continental had a 27% stock interest. It was the first of Limbach's many regular trips to CMC plants.

In October, Limbach was named Vice-President, Plant Operations, of CMC. He in turn moved Ray Powers up a notch to Vice-President, Military Plants because of his ability to thread his way through the government facilities maze. At the same time, Richardson was elected Vice-President and Controller and Henderson was named Secretary-Treasurer. By then Ryan owned 43% of Continental's shares.

The make-up of the Continental Board of Directors was changing, too, involving two long-time associates of Bob Jackson's. Businessman Lloyd M. Smith of Los Angeles, Chairman of the Board of Emtor, replaced Robert C. Trundle, the Cleveland industrial management consultant. Attorney Arthur J. Hair, a Ryan director and Emtor shareholder, also of Los Angeles, replaced CMC's attorney, Fred J. Kennedy, who had been a board member since 1943.

The most significant management change involved one of Ryan's most promising young executives, George Williams Rutherford, Vice-President, Marketing and Programs. A Phi Beta Kappa out of Stanford University, with degrees in Economics and Law, Bill Rutherford had been a World War II navigator on trans-Pacific transport planes.

Joining Ryan as a tax attorney in 1951 he moved up to Vice-President and head of the Electronics Division in 1959; then took charge of both electronics and aerospace activities including the highly classified unmanned reconnaissance planes (powered with CAE jet engines) later used in the Vietnam War.

Production Head L. M. LIMBACH

A high regard for Rutherford's management potential had been developing at the top executive and investor level in the Ryan organization. Increasingly, Bob Jackson and George Knox were discussing with Bill the acquisition of Continental stock. "Not really consulting me," Rutherford recalls. "It was just conversation.

A Comprehensive Review

"But in June 1964, Bob and George said they thought I should go back there full time. So, I said I'd be glad to give it a whirl."

Rutherford well remembers his introduction to Muskegon and Continental.

"I got there a couple of days after the Fourth of July. I'll never forget that day as long as I live. I'd had dinner with Win Henderson, then went to the Occidental Hotel where Continental people had traditionally stayed.

"The next morning when I turned on the shower the water came out absolutely rust red. No matter how long I let it run it never changed color. It was bad enough to have to shower in rust-red water, but when it came to shaving and brushing my teeth I had had it!

"So I packed up my bags and moved out of the "Accidental Hotel" as I went over to Continental that morning. Incidentally, my name for their favorite hotel never endeared me to anyone in Muskegon.

"At the plant I was received cautiously. That's the best way I can put it. Jack Reese had arranged a meeting with the principal executives based in Muskegon. Every one of them was at least twenty years older than I. After a brief movie which Jack screened for my benefit, each of the executives was asked to describe his role in company management.

"They were terribly nervous and not used to conducting briefings for interested visitors, least of all someone they felt was intruding into Continental affairs.

"That afternoon we went into the Market Street plant. I had never been in anything like it; it was absolutely in a shambles. There was a lot of production, but the plant was old. It was dark; it was dirty. The machinery was old. The workmen were old.

"I walked along one production line where there was some scaffolding. Two fellows up above were fixing a broken steam line. One of the guys said in a loud voice, 'If that son-of-a-bitch comes under here, I'm letting him have a wrench on his head.'

"All this was for my benefit, I'm sure, although I believe the guy on the scaffolding just thought I was part of Continental management. I looked up and said, 'You s.o.b., if you drop anything off that scaffolding while I'm around here, I'm coming up there after you, so you better be prepared.'

"That story went around the plant pretty good. As a matter of fact, after that I got a little better consideration around the factory than I did in the offices."

By the end of the day Bill Rutherford had gone into every nook and cranny of every department in that sprawling facility, had met all of the management people and had heard all their stories.

"I walked away from the plant that evening," Bill recalls, "with the worst headache I've ever had in my life. I got in the car alone and drove along Lake Michigan as far north as I could go. There was an inlet, and no bridge, so I had to turn around and went back to Muskegon, checking in at the Holiday Inn. As I crawled into bed that night I wondered if every day at Continental would be like that! But there I was in Muskegon, completely detached from Ryan and permanently assigned to Continental!"

Rutherford came to Continental to take a thorough look at every phase of the company—products, pricing, contracts, finance, engineering, manufacturing, organizational structure, labor relations. And thorough he was. More Ryan people came aboard: besides Frank Light in Accounting and Howard Dunlap in sales, there was Mike Kissinger in manufacturing and quality assurance.

James W. Wells, head of Ryan's Washington office, was named a Vice-President of CAE in March 1965. (Early on, two of the author's assistants, Don Bennett and Phil Whitacre, were dispatched to handle public relations and special projects for Rutherford.)

To get some control over the deplorable Market Street operation, Rutherford and Limbach selected a seasoned Ryan factory superintendent, Harold Rouse, as works manager of that run-down, out-of-date facility and its myriad collection of engine models in production.

An earlier observation by Henderson about Market Street: "General Offices are old, crowded. Reese and Vandeven are only ones who have office rugs, and Vandeven's looks as if it was second-hand when installed."

In January 1965, Jack Reese discussed the changes in management philosophy in his Annual Report to Stockholders:

> "A comprehensive review of product lines and production facilities was undertaken early last year . . . so as to channel the company's resources into production of those goods and services offering the highest profit potential . . . and to streamline all efforts so as to reduce costs and achieve more efficient production methods."

The presence of Rutherford and other Ryan-trained people had been felt.

Reese's "President's Letter" went on to explain that the plants previously occupied by Gray Marine and Novi had been closed and were subsequently sold. Gray Marine operations at Detroit were transferred to Market Street in Muskegon. The Novi governor and controls work was moved into the Kercheval Avenue plant in Detroit.

Ryan Gets Majority Control

Two months after stockholders received Reese's assessment of the 'comprehensive review,' Bob Jackson was named Chairman of the Board and CMC's Chief Policy Officer, and Bill Rutherford was elected Executive Vice-President. Ailing Jack Reese, President and Chief Operating Officer, was carefully sandwiched between Jackson and Rutherford. B. Kenneth Goodman of Ryan was named General Counsel of CMC and in May elected Corporate Secretary of that company.

By October 1965, with just over 50% of Continental stock in its hands, Ryan held full control of the long-established engine maker.

How was Jack Reese, the heart and soul of Continental and a compulsive workaholic, taking all the changes within the company which had been his life work?

Reese's Man-Killing Pace

Early on, Bob Jackson had been tipped off by Art Wild that Jack's behavior had become a little strange. Jackson in turn discussed the situation with Henderson and made it clear that one of Win's prime responsibilities was to make the situation as comfortable as possible for Reese and his devoted wife, Pat.

"My impression," Win says, "was that Jack was suffering from arteriosclerosis—hardening of the arteries—and that his memory, in particular, had been impaired.

"I became aware of this on my first plane trip with Jack from Muskegon to Detroit. Eight times during the trip—I counted them—he asked me if this was my first visit to Detroit. He was vague about that, and he had trouble knowing what day of the week it was. He would ask his driver, 'Johnny, what day is today?'

"Jack had the habit of wearing his hat all the time from when he got up in the morning until he went to bed at night. It had nothing to do with his poor health and mental condition. As I recall, he told me that when he was a young man it had been the custom of manufacturing executives in industry to wear their hats in the office. He became a manufacturing executive; therefore, he wore a hat.

"Jack's associates, of course, couldn't

Richard Stauss

**Legal Eagle
B. KENNETH GOODMAN**

After an early breakfast, Jack Reese was always at the office Sunday morning — as usual.

help but be aware of his deteriorating condition. Their feelings varied with the individual and his attitude toward Reese. Some were fully aware that Jack was not the man he had been. Others, perhaps, not so much so.

"His schedule certainly was a man-killer.

"At 6:15 every Monday he would appear for breakfast at the restaurant across the street from Muskegon's Occidental Hotel where Jack and Pat lived most of the time. The office was only a couple of blocks away and he'd arrive at seven and be occupied with meetings there and trips into the plant until noon when he'd be driven to the restaurant for lunch. At one o'clock it was back to the office until six o'clock, then he would return to the same restaurant for dinner alone.

"Jack didn't drink then so he avoided the fancier side of the restaurant, where cocktails were served, in favor of the plainer area where a regular table was reserved for him every night. After dinner he'd return to the office at seven o'clock and generally stay until at least 9:30 p.m. Then it was home to the Occidental Hotel and bed.

"This was Jack's daily routine Monday through Friday morning when he would leave his office at eleven to be driven to the Muskegon Airport for his regular flight to Detroit. By one o'clock he'd pick up the car he kept at Detroit City Airport and drive to his office in the Ford Building in downtown Detroit. After four hours there he'd keep his weekly appointment for a working dinner and evening with Mel Parker, Assistant Treasurer, who was pretty much general manager of Continental Motors operations (but not those of CAE) in Detroit.

"By eleven o'clock Reese was on his way to his permanent residence in Grosse Point where he spent the night. Saturday morning found him bright and early in his Detroit office, where he met until noon with Art Wild. After lunch prepared by a maid in his Grosse Point home, Jack drove to the airport and picked up his plane to Muskegon. By four o'clock he was in his Muskegon office for several hours before leaving for dinner at his regular restaurant.

"It was just another business day for Jack since he returned after dinner for his usual Saturday evening meeting with Wheeler Johnson, his Vice-President in charge of branch plants and customer service.

"Sunday morning started no different than any other business day. Breakfast as usual; to the office at seven as usual. But Sunday did bring change. This was the day for the weekly morning plant tour of Muskegon facilities with Thor Engstrom, Executive Vice-President in charge of the Market Street plant, and various manufacturing assistants.

"If the weather was at all decent, Jack would be driven up to the company's retreat at Bitely for Sunday dinner with his wife. On their return to Muskegon, he would drop Pat off at the hotel before going to the office at five o'clock for the rest of the evening.

"That was Jack's weekly schedule, seldom changed except perhaps to accommodate meetings of the Board of Directors.

"Jack never took an extended vacation. You couldn't get him to go any place—except maybe shooting ducks or hunting deer—for a day or two. Although they had a fine home in Detroit, Jack and Pat spent most of what time they had together in a very small apartment on the top floor of the beat-up Occidental Hotel!"

Ryan management policies continued to replace what had become stagnant, business-as-usual practice at Continental.

New Trends in 1964-65

The company began to purchase additional shares in its subsidiary companies just as Ryan kept purchasing Continental shares. CMC's percentage of ownership in CAE, which had been 50.9% since that company had been formed 24 years earlier, was increased to 61% at the end of the 1964 fiscal year and to 75.7% at the 1965 calendar year end. Similarly, the percentage of ownership in Wisconsin Motor was increased from 83.2% to 87.9% in October 1964 by that company purchasing and retiring 24,915 shares of its own common stock. Such purchases, CMC said, would likely continue.

In 1964, Continental and subsidiaries earned $1.7 million on a sales volume of $179 million, a profit of barely 1% on sales. The year 1965 was somewhat better: profit $2.3 million on sales of $184 million. The less-than-spectacular performance in earnings was due in large part to changes in accounting practice resulting from the 'comprehensive review' which Ryan had initiated.

On the plus side was a change in the funding requirements for pension plans for all employees. This was one of the areas which Wally Herbert, Ryan's labor relations and pensions expert, had been dispatched to investigate.

Originally, Continental and its subsidiaries had been required to make contributions to trust funds at fixed rates for each hour worked by employees. As a result of negotiations with the UAW, the plans were amended to require contributions only in the amounts necessary to maintain them on an actuarily sound basis.

United Auto Workers vice president Leonard Woodcock, on extended leave since 1947 from his last employment at

Continental, and in charge of bargaining with General Motors and the aerospace industry, contended that the change in funding resulted in an unjustified financial windfall for the company since it reduced the next year's contribution by Continental.

Because the pension plan applicable to top executives provided only the same payment of $51 annually for each year of qualifying service as for all other salaried employees, Ryan tried to find some way to meet normal industry retirement standards which related pension amounts to salaries paid. This was not then possible because the cost to adequately fund past service of senior executives at higher benefit levels was prohibitive.

However, under Ryan management Continental later funded an improved salaried pension plan which with each year of new service after 1969 also picked up a past year of benefits retroactive to 1964 when Ryan came into a management role.

Herbert and Woodcock, who maintained his seniority with Continental, were already friendly adversaries having previously been on opposite sides of the negotiating table at Ryan Aeronautical Company where the UAW had labor contracts in which Woodcock had represented the national union in bargaining at the San Diego plant.

By comparison with west coast labor practices, Herbert found a far more hostile environment when he went to Muskegon, Detroit, Toledo and Milwaukee to look into union relations there. What he found was militant unionism in which labor leaders, not the company, dominated the work environment. And Market Street at Muskegon was the bellwether plant.

"Continental employees," Herbert related, "were so steeped in unionism that they believed the union did everything for them, and that certainly included their thinking. They felt the union was responsible for giving them everything: the money, and every benefit they ever got.

"The company, in effect, received no credit so it was very easy whenever the new Ryan management took a firm stand for the union to point out that 'this isn't the way it used to be' under the Reese regime. To them, Ryan was trying to upset their whole way of life. More than anything, Ryan people tried to get the attitude in company-union relations changed.

"The union was the focal point of life for most Continental employees. The turnout at union meetings was unbelievably large to those of us who had seen more passive participation by workers on the west coast. For labor contract ratification meetings the UAW had to rent the Walker Arena in Muskegon which could accommodate 5,000 people!

"One difficult area for us was the plan the union had negotiated which set standards on how much a worker could produce on his shift. Employees would work very hard to get their day's production quota, then sit around at their work stations and read the rest of the day."

At Wisconsin Motor, one effect of the incentive plan which imposed individual production ceilings was to place a lid on what a worker could earn.

In 1965 Herbert headed the Ryan negotiating team which reached new three-year contracts covering production and maintenance employees at CMC, CAE, Gray Marine and Wisconsin Motor. Included in the settlement were increased pension plan benefits for all employees.

"After Leonard Woodcock became an officer of the UAW national leadership" Herbert said, "he continued to negotiate the 'big table' issue for all Continental companies with Jack Reese. These included four items: pension plans, supplemental unemployment benefits (SUB), preferential hiring and the transfer agreement.

"Other issues were negotiated by local union officials with Ted Hughes, personnel director at Muskegon, and with his counterparts at other plant locations, all of whom reported on labor matters to William G. Raven, a CMC and CAE Vice-President based in Detroit.

"Our personal relations with Woodcock helped get us by some otherwise very difficult days. Leonard was very competent, very cooperative, very smart. We each understood the necessity of reaching reasonable compromise for the mutual benefit of the company and the employees the union represented.

"Of course Leonard moved on up in the UAW hierarchy to the presidency of the union on Walter Reuther's death and to national prominence. He was the first labor leader to endorse Jimmy Carter for President in 1976. Then, having retired from union office, he was available for national service. In 1977, President Carter appointed Leonard Woodcock the first United States Ambassador to the People's Republic of China."

The comprehensive review—not only of labor relations but also of products and plants—brought further changes. Volume manufacturing operations in Detroit (at the Kercheval Avenue plant) were shut down and moved to Muskegon.

Production rights to Novi governors and controls were sold, as were manufacturing rights to 2½-to-5 hp air-cooled, heavy-duty, four-cycle industrial engines—both of which were being produced in the Kercheval plant. These particular low volume operations—less than a million dollars a year—were discontinued because of their unprofitable nature and incompatibility with larger volume product lines.

Teledyne Ryan Aeronautical

**Labor Expert
WALTER J. HERBERT**

Manufacture of Novi products for Continental engines was moved to the Market Street plant in Muskegon.

A new branch plant was established at Chicago for the more efficient computer-controlled handling of engine and spare parts sales and service requirements, and engine overhaul and rebuilding. The company also leased a facility in Walterboro, South Carolina, for some light assembly and packaging operations.

Manufacturing and office facilities in the Market Street plant were extensively refurbished and modernized. Production lines were rearranged and new factory, electronic computing and office equipment purchased and installed.

"Continental," Rutherford always said, "was weakest in the financial area and for this deficiency Henry Vandeven was largely responsible.

Product Profitability

"Henderson and Richardson had done a good job of shaking down financial reports, so we had the skeleton of some workable financial documents. Continental had respectable balance sheet accounting but the cost accounting was non-existent. Price estimating was a shambles and most inventory, production and material control records were totally archaic. We had to construct and install all new systems from scratch, and train the people to use and operate them.

"They never analyzed product by product for profitability. Basically they estimated their jobs and then costed them to match the estimate so they showed a profit. Trouble was they had terrific variances which they just wrote off against everything. With that system you really couldn't get to the bottom of true cost of products.

"CMC's policy was that they could satisfy any customer's requirement for any kind of an engine, because they had such a multiplicity of them. They had become custom, short-run manufacturers but because many of their people—Jack included—had come out of the car business, they had the mistaken idea that the total volume of business would cure everything.

"They just couldn't let an order get away from them. It was unheard of to say, 'Well, $800 is our price for this engine and that's the least we're going to sell it for and if you don't want to buy it for that, good-by.' So on some theory or other they'd take the order anyway for the customer's $700 offer. All you had to do was look at the profits of Continental over a long period of time and you could see this."

One report, never fully confirmed, was that one of Continental's competitors, unwilling to take business at a loss, repeatedly referred bargain-hunting customers to Reese knowing full well that he would take the business—at a loss. Henderson agreed with that generalization. "Jack might very possibly take the business, overlooking the fact that he was going to lose money on it."

Checker Cab was an excellent example.

"As soon as I got checking into that account," Rutherford observed, "I found it always showed a very heavy loss. Jack said he considered their business just like advertising.

"'When you get into a Checker Cab', he explained, 'you always ask the driver how he likes his cab. His answer invariably is that it's a good car. Then the rider asks what kind of engine it has, and the driver explains that it's a Red Seal Continental. That's word-of-mouth advertising about the reliability of our engines that you couldn't buy any other way!'.

"So, we all killed ourselves laughing, raised the price of the engine to cover production costs...and lost the account! Everyone at Checker was mad at us. All the cab fleet operators and drivers were mad at us. Everybody was mad at us. But we stopped the losses, or 'advertising' expense —depending on how you look at it.

"For years after that I never got into a Checker Cab without asking the driver, 'what kind of car is this?' and he says, 'Checker.' "What kind of engine?

"'Continental Red Seal. It's the greatest engine that ever existed!'

"Even today if you ask a Checker Cab driver if he has a Continental engine—and he doesn't—he will take an hour to tell you he wished it did!

Creative Executives Needed

"If Jack Reese had had a very creative financial executive either above him—like a George Knox—or below him—like Ryan's Vice-President and Controller, Josh Wooldridge; or Lynn Richardson—CMC would have been a howling success.

The ubiquitous Checker Cab for years was one of the best 'advertisements' for Continental engines.

"Ryan would never have been able to buy Continental because they had everything else. They had ability, they had product, they had good people, they had access to money, they had a fine reputation. But they just let the company run down. And Vandeven, whose thought processes were old, was the oldest of the old-timers—and boy, that was old!

"Vandeven's old-fashioned attitude was 'Well, we'll get along with what we've got, because we can't afford any of these high falutin' new ideas.' That sent a chill over everything.

"By contrast Jack literally worked himself to death for the company. He was a finished marketing executive, a good leader and a really charismatic kind of guy who was backed by wonderful engineering.

"As Ryan people got into the picture it should be remembered how kind Jack was to all of us. He was a real gentleman. I believe he realized he was in a lot of physical trouble, and I know Pat did.

"During the entire time I worked in the same set of offices as Jack he made it very easy for us to come in there and assume management of the company. He never gave us a tough day.

"We never asked him for any advice because we wanted to do things our way. We knew he wouldn't agree, and we didn't want to embarrass him by involving him in the decision process. During what could have been a very difficult period for him, he was an absolute gentleman.

"With a limited blood supply to his brain, Jack was having big memory lapses. His long-time associates told me he had an absolutely fabulous memory. He could remember anything—part numbers, dollars, customers, all the customers' children's names, everything you could think of—but his brain just gave out on him."

The early days in Detroit and Muskegon were not all roses for the newly arrived Ryan executives. "We made our shares of mistakes," Rutherford readily admits. "We didn't know much about the engine business. We just knew something about business in general.

Senior Managers Stayed On—And On

"It was in many ways a hard interface between Continental people and Ryan people. But what made the interface bearable was that over a long period of time Jack had prevented his senior executives from retiring. By any standard he held people way over retirement age. That meant there hadn't been any role for younger management. By the time we came aboard, we had to fill that void with Ryan people.

"Jack positively did not want any change. He insisted that his long-time associates stay in place to be there with him. With the problems he was beginning to have physically, their continued presence made him feel secure. That's the main thing he wanted—stability and security.

"I asked Jack one day, 'Who would be the logical person to run Continental Motors in the event something happened to you?' His answer was he really didn't have anyone, but supposed the closest person would be Art Wild. Except, he added, that Art Wild (just turned sixty) was way too young!"

As assistant to the president, Win Henderson was especially close to Reese because part of his assignment was to help Jack with his personal problems including adjusting to Ryan management's take-over.

The Employment Contracts

"Jack had something like 25 people—most of them in Muskegon—reporting directly to him," Henderson says. "He just didn't develop any subordinate levels of future management. After 25 years as president he was a one-man show—the boss of everything. But he did let Harold Todd run Wisconsin Motor essentially on his own. Art Wild, too, was pretty much in charge of his operation at CAE. Anyway, I don't think Jack was too interested in the turbine engine as such.

"Some of the problems stemmed from the fact that the senior officials had five-year employment contracts, which each year were extended so that these old-timers always had five years job security 'in the bank,' so to speak. As far as Jack was concerned he was just going to keep everybody going until they died."

The fact that these people were getting along in years, with their continued employment assured, made them less open to new ideas and more modern business management methods. That didn't leave much chance of 'upward mobility' for new, younger people in the organization.

It was perhaps natural that employment contracts for such executives as Vandeven, Wild, Johnson, Hollowell—and Reese—were renewed every year. The practice dated, in fact, from 1939 when the Reconstruction Finance Corp., in extending loans previously made to Continental Motors, approved Reese's plan to give five-year employment contracts to the executive heads of sales, engineering, manufacturing and treasury. The contracts were, he said, "designed to provide stability of management."

"Henderson had the job of getting those employment contracts settled," Rutherford explained. "I never got involved in them; never even looked at them."

Henderson recalls that in the case of Henry Vandeven, as with others, Ryan

"... it should be remembered how kind Jack Reese was to all of us."

ARTHUR W. WILD
Executive Vice-President and General Manager of Continental Aviation and Engineering Corp., and a Vice-President of the parent company, Art Wild was Continental's well-known and highly-regarded government contact and marketing expert. Wild had 42 years service with the company when he was moved up to President of CAE in 1966 and to the Continental board of directors in 1967.

management agreed that the contracts should be honored, though details were on occasion renegotiated. "I made a deal," Win explained, "with Vandeven to cut his down from five years at $70,000 a year to ten years at $25,000. He came out very well tax-wise, as did the company. So, Vandeven didn't actually go off the payroll until he was 80 years old.

"In any case, starting in 1964, the contracts were not renewed, but allowed to run themselves out."

Many of the senior executives at Continental, Wisconsin and CAE had been anxious to retire for some time so when Ryan entered the picture as a major factor it provided an easy out for them. They didn't want to cope with new management and made it clear that they weren't about to do so.

Central Management Concept

Albert Willi, Executive Vice-President at Muskegon, was a good example, as cited by Bill Rutherford. "He and I had one meeting and that was the end of that. He retired the next day, but I certainly didn't want him to go that quickly. Like others he was tired and just wanted out.

"There were a few more progressive executives like Art Wild and Carl Bachle with a lot of loyalty to Continental who wanted to stay and hold the company together. They felt an obligation to get the new crowd of managers in place and essentially teach them the engine business."

They were held in high regard. Jim Ferry recalls that "riding in a car with Bob Jackson he remarked that Art Wild was the best-liked guy in the engine business in Washington or anywhere else, which was a proper appraisal of Art."

"Both Art and Carl" Rutherford said, "were well-known at Ryan as a result of business dealings, principally involving CAE's J69 jet engine which powered Ryan Firebee target drones. Then there were people like Ray Powers who never agreed with Continental management anyway. He was just glad to see someone else come along, and he helped us a lot.

"Essentially CMC lacked a strong, upcoming middle-management group. The people who should have been there to take over realized before we ever got there that it would be a long time before they got a chance, so they went elsewhere.

"We didn't know much about marketing engines but we did bring in people like Jim Murray we knew could help us with government marketing to work with Art Wild who had done so well in that arena for so long. From San Diego we had brought in Howard Dunlap who spent most of his time on commercial marketing, trying to get that part of the operation better organized.

"We totally redid the financial units with people from Ryan and a lot from the outside. Lynn Richardson, principally, led that campaign.

"We wanted to impose Ryan's concept of central management on Continental with one key man in each area. Continental had central management and *it* was Jack Reese in *every* area. For operations we settled on Larry Limbach; for finance it was Rich (ardson). In marketing we were happy to have Art Wild supported by Jim Murray. And for engineering, Carl Bachle, although some of the plant units never recognized him as the **chief** engineer.

"These men were central to our management technique. They could dabble and supervise and hire and fire down into the operating units in each of their own specialties. That was a real trauma for Continental. The established people didn't like it; they resisted it at every turn. But it had been successful for us at Ryan and we introduced that kind of organization at Muskegon, Detroit, Milwaukee and Toledo. We were least successful at Wisconsin, partially successful elsewhere, but mostly we had to put our own people into the principal jobs.

"Then we had Bob Jackson and George Knox as our link out of the group of management people into the owners of the companies.

"I picked Detroit as the location for our central management unit out of which to oversee the total operation. Art Wild and Carl Bachle were already headquartered there, and they were the people who best knew the engine business and were willing to take the time to teach it to us.

"On this we spent from 1964 to 1969, imposing our form of management over Continental. In the long run the results were very gratifying."

Through it all, Rutherford retained his position as Vice-President and Assistant to the President of Ryan, commuting regularly between his Detroit office and apartment to San Diego where he maintained his family and his permanent residence.

Jim Ferry, whose family had the largest and longest-lasting financial interest in Continental, and whose father had put Jack Reese into the top management spot in 1939, saw the situation in proper perspective.

"While there was resentment when the Ryan people came in," he explained, "there was also considerable relief that something was going to happen to resolve the company's ossified condition and the problems related to Jack's health.

"In such a situation, everyone is scared about his job, but you have to look past that to what is happening in total and try to cushion the people the best you can. There is no question about it; people were hurt. But I don't see how you could do it any smoother, any easier, and hurt fewer people, while really benefiting nearly everyone.

"Continental had become well diversified, but there was usually some product area that was losing money and pulling everything else down with it. Ryan came in, analyzed the problems product by product and moved things around to where the total operation was much more profitable."

It seemed that everything at Continental had to be restructured. But there was one exception, as explained by Bill Rutherford.

Continental's Superior Engineering

"They had terrific engineering; really super engineering under Bachle's leadership. So we didn't bring in any new engineering people.

"Turbines, diesels, gasoline engines, air-cooled, liquid-cooled. You name it, they had it. It was an asset so outstanding that Continental didn't even realize how good it was.

"I believe they had the strongest total all-out engineering capability for engine design in the United States and probably one of the three or four best in the world.

"They could design in prototype and launch any kind of an engine you could imagine from a large turbine to a 2-horsepower gasoline air-cooled engine, and everything in between. They absolutely had no limitations that I could see. In addition to Bachle's group in Detroit, they had outstanding engineering units in each of the plants, so we had no requirement whatever to bring in engineers."

Art Wild, who had to market CAE's and CMC's engineering capability agreed on the quality of their people. "In addition to Carl," he said, "you have to mention Ed Hulbert from the design end on tank engines. Bob Insley was very effective in getting Continental going in the aircraft engine field. Jimmy Kinnucan did more in liaison work between ourselves and Wright Field and other government agencies than anything else."

The famed air-cooled tank engines were a prime example of how a basic concept could be broadened through new technology to provide far greater utilization over an extended time span.

The original 12-cylinder V-type 1790 cubic inch displacement engine and its 6-cylinder horizontally-opposed 895 cid counterpart started out in the mid-40s as *carbureted, spark-ignition* gasoline engines. (Four and eight-cylinder versions were also developed).

In the mid-50s, Continental offered *fuel injection* for its tank engines—gasoline sprayed directly into the cylinders. Typical was the Model AVI-1790 (Air-cooled, V-type, fuel Injected) engine, and the AVSI version, a *supercharged* gasoline engine with fuel injection.

When the Army decided in 1958 to change from conventional gasoline spark-ignition engines to *diesel compression-ignition* engines for ordnance equipment, Continental responded with the supercharged AVDS-1790 engine.

That, however, was not the ultimate configuration.

Carl Bachle was not just a fine engineer; he was a visionary who not only had ideas of his own but made it a point to keep in touch with new engineering ideas worldwide. A tireless traveler in pursuit of new technology, Bachle made frequent trips to visit colleagues on the Continent and in Great Britain.

VCR — Variable Compression Ratio

One of Carl's best American contacts was diesel expert Art Rosen, chief engineer of Caterpillar Tractor, who also had good sources abroad. One of those contacts was BICERI, the British Internal Combustion Engine Research Institute, a non-profit cooperative which had been formed by 15 English companies for the betterment of engine design.

> "Their engineering was so outstanding that Continental didn't even realize how good it was."

Double the Power With VCR

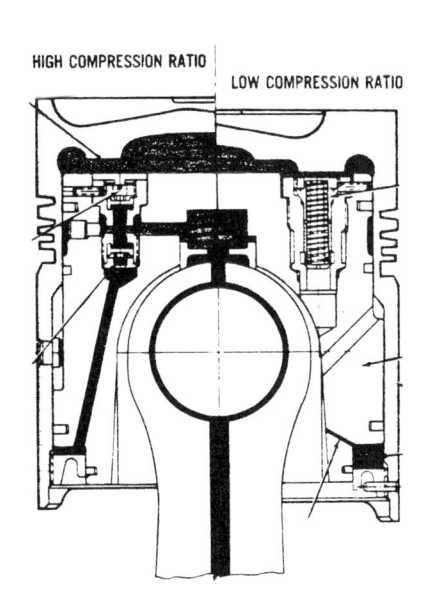

"For years," Bachle related, "the dream of all diesel engineers was to develop a variable compression engine to provide high compression for starting and lower compression under load. Bill Mansfield, the head of BICERI, was the patent holder for a variable compression ratio (VCR) piston. When Art Rosen stumbled on this development, BICERI invited him in before they published their first technical report.

"I got into the VCR experiments in 1957 and rushed right over to BICERI to have a look. We were then working on the new 550 hp AVDS (air-cooled, vee, diesel, supercharged) tank engine of 1100 cubic inch displacement (cid). Looking for a way to obtain more power, we were developing a Unisteel cylinder; then Continental obtained the license in the early 1960s to use the VCR patents and began our own program to further up-rate the engine. You put the two together — VCR and Unisteel — and you have the capacity for real high power output.

"On the 1100 cid engine at 550 hp we had some cylinder heads blow off, and this is always a threat in any engine. They blew because the compression ratio and the pressures being generated were too high. We felt we could cure the problem with VCR."

The unique VCR principle incorporates a hydraulically-operated piston-within-a-piston assembly to control firing in the engine's variable volume combustion chambers. This is accomplished automatically while the engine is running, adjusting compression ratio according to load demands. No change in engine displacement is involved.

Such an engine could deliver unheard-of power per cubic inch displacement and would weigh about half as much as engines of comparable output.

With VCR, the engine's horsepower potential was doubled (to 1100 hp) over that obtained with the same bore, stroke, rpm and structure as the basic engine with fixed compression ratio. With Unisteel cylinders would come even greater power output. While the potential was there, results of the first practical application of this new principle did not come easily. Most of the insiders at BICERI were skeptical, but CAE made it practical.

"We broke our hearts during development of the VCR piston," Bachle continued. "We had to do it over and over because we were crowding the potential to the very limits. We had a 1964 contract with the Army which had as a goal output between 1300 hp and 1500 hp, and that was a killer.

"Eventually that version ended up as a 1475 hp engine of 1360 cid after 10,000 hours of background operation and 3000

Richard Stauss

The VCR piston-within-a-piston gave engineers the variable compression ration they had long sought.

miles in the M48 tank. VCR has been very useful for extremely high power output military demands, but not quite worth it for commercial applications."

In 1964, the agreement between Continental and BICERI was extended to 1973.

The results of CAE's and Continental's superior engineering during the 60s showed up in many products other than VCR for the military and for commercial customers.

Tank Engines

By the mid-sixties, CMC had built over 150,000 engines for tanks in the 30 years since installation of its first air-cooled spark-ignition engines in T2 tanks.

New contracts for 750 hp AVDS-1790-2 compression-ignition (diesel) engines for the Army's M60 tanks scheduled production through 1966. Another order provided modification kits to convert gasoline-powered M48 series tracked vehicles to tanks with AVDS-1790-2A supercharged diesel engines. Other kits updated 1600 earlier model AVDS engines to the latest configuration, and an overhaul and retrofit program re-equipped M88 tank recovery vehicle with AVSI supercharged fuel-injected gasoline engines.

Besides their tank application, the AVDS-1790 engines are widely used as power for other tactical armored units such as amphibious vehicles, weapons carriers, landing, crawling and swimming vehicles, and for such ancillary equipment as bridge launchers, recovery vehicles, and engineer units for bulldozing, mine-clearing and other specialized equipment.

In Vietnam, the AOSI-895 horizontally-opposed 6-cylinder engines for tracked vehicles as well as the 1790 V-12 series tank engines were in service; and their maintenance as power plants for M48 tanks, M88 recovery vehicles, armored personnel carriers, and self-propelled howitzers was provided by military personnel.

In 1964, CAE was awarded a $10.7 million contract for the design and manufacture of prototypes of the advanced 12-cylinder AVCR-1100 engine, using variable compression ratio pistons, for the new Main Battle Tank (MBT-70) being developed for use in the 1970s as a cooperative project for the U.S. Government and the Federal Republic of Germany (West Germany). The contract, scheduled to cover two years work, was awarded by General Motors, prime contractor and administered by the Army Tank Automotive Center.

The first AVCR-1100 engine was delivered on schedule in March 1966 and the following February, in tests at Muskegon, developed a record 1498 gross horsepower. In 1968, the AVCR-powered MBT-70 was first shown publicly.

For Continental, the foreign market for tank engines became very attractive since NATO and allied nations were scheduled to retrofit many of their American M47 and M48 tanks with newer equipment, mainly Continental's AVDS diesels. Largest potential existed with the military services of Italy, West Germany, Greece, and Turkey, plus South Korea and some Middle-East countries.

M60 series 55-ton Main Battle Tanks were powered by 750 hp CMC supercharged 12-cylinder diesel engines.

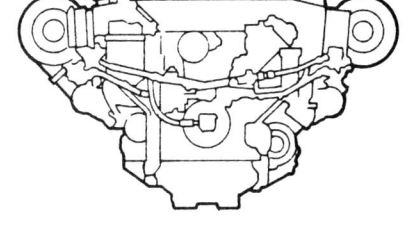

Military Truck Engines

The need for even higher power output for military trucks led to further refinements of Continental's 'Hypercycle' multi-fuel engine of the late 1950s. Structurally, that engine had evolved from one used in industrial equipment and commercial trucks — the TD-427. It provided the "skeleton" — crankcase, block, crankshaft and gear train for the military engines.

For increased power, supercharging was first used in the LDS-427 model; then further power upgrading came with increases in displacement for LD-465 series engines. Fortunately, dimensions of the block had permitted enlargement of the bore, with gains in piston displacement but without the necessity for other major modifications.

The growth version 210 hp LDS-465 "run-on-anything" supercharged engine won plaudits in 1964 when demonstrated in the Army's MX656 cargo truck built by Ford. Carrying a 10,000 pound payload while towing additional 13,000 pounds, the eight-wheel 5-ton cargo truck completed 40,000 miles of durability testing over every type of rugged terrain during an eight month demonstration period.

Its LDS-465 multi-fuel engine made it possible for MX656 cargo truck to climb 27-inch-high step.

MBT-70 'new' Main Battle Tank, joint project of U.S. Army and Federal Republic of Germany, had 1475 hp Continental AVCR-1100 engine with Variable Compression Ratio.

"... a 465 series Multi-Fuel engine can be used in either a 2½-ton or 5-ton truck."

The multi-fuel, supercharged engine went into prototype production for 5-ton trucks in 1965. Follow-on contracts for $36.3 million were obtained later in 1965 for 16,000 of the six-cylinder engines, and this figure was increased to 21,000 in 1966.

The multi-year contracts called for increased deliveries over a three-year period. Liquid-cooled, the truck engines operate on a variety of fuels, including kerosene, gasoline, diesel and jet fuels, with the capability of switching from one to another while running. They feature compression-ignition and hence are not subject to electrical ignition failures.

The naturally-aspirated unsupercharged 140 hp version, LD-465 (also of 478 cubic inch displacement) was already in production for the Army 2½-ton truck series under similar three year contracts funded for $57 million.

So vital was the LD-465 series of truck engines to the country's commitments in Vietnam that "Red Ball Express" fast delivery of replacement engines was undertaken. From nearby Grand Rapids Airport, and from Detroit headquarters of the Ordnance Corps, military C-141 cargo planes flew hundreds of engines in Summer 1967 to the Far East via Travis Air Force Base in California.

The urgency of combat conditions in Vietnam was further exacerbated by the large turnover of military personnel, introduction of diesel powered trucks, which provided 85% of the cargo carriers, and the use of inexperienced drivers and mechanics. The Army needed technical support which Continental supplied by a selected dozen of fifty top engine mechanics who volunteered for overseas duty.

In Continental test facility, new LD-465 is checked out in Army's M35 2½-ton truck

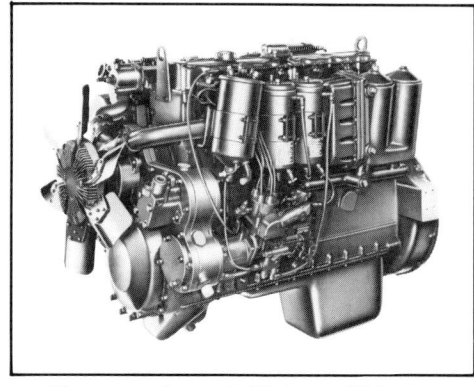

The supercharged 210 hp multi-fuel LDS-465 'run-on-anything' engine had 30-year production span.

Basing at such locations as Cam Ranh Bay, Long Binh, Pleiku and Da Nang, the Continental Military Field Service tech reps shared heat, humidity, insects, infiltration and the threat of enemy mortar fire with GI units to which they were assigned.

Other Continental tech reps provided similar assistance to Army units in Europe also using the LD-465 and LDS-465 engines.

Citing the commonality of parts, Lt. Gen. William W. Quinn, Commanding, Seventh Army in Germany, noted that "It is no longer necessary to stock spare engines separately for the 5-ton and 2½-ton trucks. By using or not using the supercharger, a 465 series engine can be used in either truck."

In retrospect, engineer Carl Bachle had these observations on multi-fuel truck engines: "The British military at Cobham scolded me about our work since they felt that now they had to have their own multi-fuel engines. With an opposed piston engine principle, made by Rolls-Royce, they had a disastrous experience. While it was good on multi-fuel it was very expensive to produce. I was also scolded by Jo Szydlowski at Turbomeca who held that the piston engine was finished and I'd do better to concentrate on gas turbines.

"The 465 engine is phenomenal in military engine experience because the production span from 1958 will probably be 30 years. Ten years is more normal. About a hundred thousand engines will have been built in that time for military trucks.

"Each year the contract would come up for bid — the Army held the design rights — and Hercules won it nearly always after Continental's first four or five years.

"The Army had somewhat ambivalent feelings about multi-fuel engines. The Continental-designed 465 was the first and only such engine they had.

"For years they said they wanted multi-fuel but because no one had come up with such an engine, they said it couldn't be done. Later they said, 'It's nice to have it but we don't really need it because if it costs any more we'll eliminate it.'

"In Vietnam, although the military was losing some interest in multi-fuel, there were first-class examples of its merit; why it was important. When the 2½-ton trucks ran out of diesel fuel on the battlefield, they were able to use their second choice fuel — turbine fuel for helicopters, or gasoline."

Multi-fuel went over big with GIs manning the trucks. Instead of having to wait at a long line to fill up with some specific fuel, they could ease up to any pump at the fueling depot, fill up and be on their way.

Another major award by the Army in the mid-60s was a $12 million three-year contract for 28,000 L141 engines for M151 quarter-ton Military Utility Tactical Trucks (Mutt). Over 13,000 units had already been delivered under the original 1960 contract with Ford Motor Company, builder of the vehicle. The new order, for installation in trucks to be built by both Ford and American Motors was the first in which the Army Mobility Command contracted directly with the engine manufacturer for Mutt power plants.

Military Standard Engines

During 1965, Continental also manufactured 40,000 engines for the Military Standard Engine Program. This program had started in 1952 under direction of the Army Corps of Engineers, resulting in CMC's development of an entirely new family of industrial-type, air-cooled engines which substantially reduced to six the number of ½ hp to 20 hp engine models required by the Army.

Aircraft Engines

As they had for many years, Continental engines powered the majority of business and personal aircraft produced in the U.S., with Cessna and Beech, the largest plane builders, as principal customers. Abroad, the demand for Continental aircraft engines was being supplied in large part by Rolls-Royce under the fifth year of a licensing agreement.

To meet the demand for ever-increasing performance, Continental engineers in the early sixties came up with further refinements to their popular line of aircraft engines.

Higher power in four-cylinder engines was achieved with the large bore, fuel injected IO-346 which produced 165 hp. The IO-360 six-cylinder engine was developed in 1962 for the Cessna Skymaster series. This 210 hp engine proved to be one of Continental's most popular power plants.

By upgrading the basic 0-470 engine through larger bore and higher crankshaft speed, the IO-520 model delivering 285 hp was introduced, while a new version of the fuel-injected 470, with propeller reduction gearing in the crankcase, developed 310 hp at 3200 crankshaft rpm.

Production of Military Standard Engines was moved to Wisconsin Motor subsidiary where similar small commercial engines were built.

On Continental's own test track at Muskegon, Army's LDS-465-powered M36 truck gets a workout.

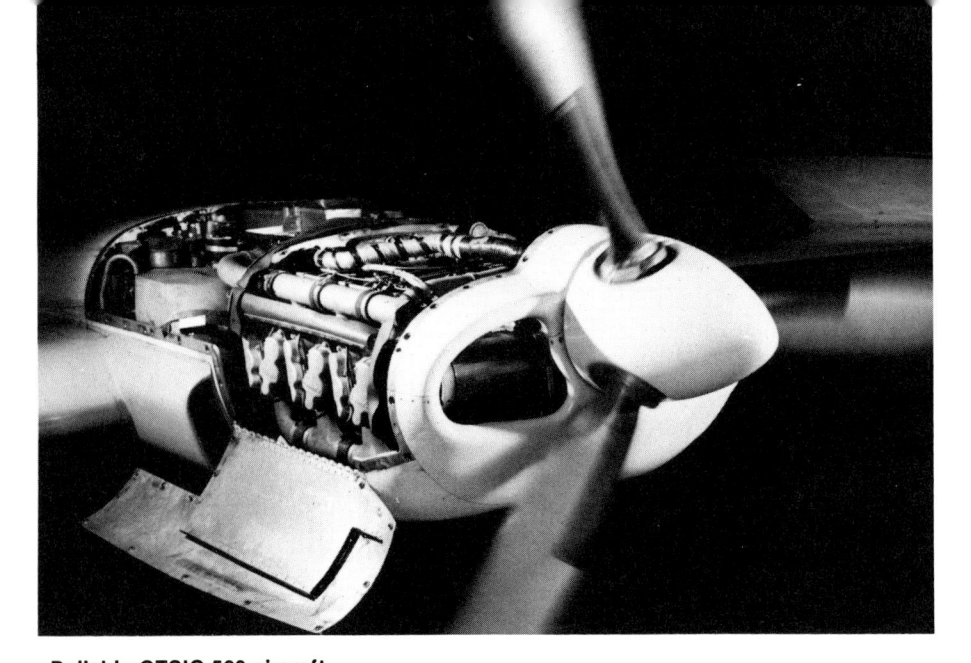

Reliable GTSIO-520 aircraft engine was the product of years of development and test

Widely-used Cessna model 172 became Air Force T-41A primary trainer in off-the-shelf purchase by military

Teledyne Continental Motors

Eleven-year-old Continental-powered Cessna 180 was flown solo around the world by aviatrix Mrs. Jerrie Mock

Cessna Aircraft

Largest in the Continental engine line was the GTSIO-520 (geared, turbo-charged, fuel-injected, opposed, 520 cubic inch displacement) at 340 hp. Later refinements brought the power rating up to 375 hp and eventually to 435 hp @ 3400 rpm.

During this period, when aircraft engine sales were running at a 5000 annual rate, the activity was headed by well-liked Dee Hollowell, Vice-President. His principal assistant was Rodney M. (Bob) Tinney, based at Wichita, Kansas, home of Beech and Cessna, to give those important accounts the attention they deserved.

An important consideration which Jack Reese frequently mentioned was his concern that Ryan's increasing role in management might 'rock the boat' with Cessna. Ryan had previously been a major builder of personal/business planes competing with its Ryan Navion against Beech and Cessna in this market. However, Ryan showed no interest in reentering a field which it had dropped at the start of the Korean war.

In Viet Nam and other world trouble spots, Continental-powered business aircraft adapted to military missions and pilot training programs were in wide use. Through the Military Assistance Program, 14 free-world countries were being supplied light cargo and similar Continental-powered aircraft.

In a departure from recent practice, the Air Force training command decided that cadet pilots should receive their first 30 hours of training in single-piston-engine primary trainers. As the result of competition among three manufacturers, the Air Force selected the T-41A "off-the-shelf" military version of the Cessna 172.

Both the military and commercial models of the popular Cessna are powered by Continental O-300-D and IO-360 engines which have been standard equipment in 10,000 Cessna 172 aircraft.

From the T-41A, Air Force cadets will graduate to the Cessna T-37 400 mph twin-jet trainers which are powered by two CAE J69 gas turbines.

Increasingly, women pilots were proving their capabilities in the air. For the fifth time, the transcontinental "Powder Puff Derby" was won by Mrs. Frances Bera flying a Continental-powered Beech Bonanza. Mrs. Marion Hart, a 70-year-old grandmother and engineering graduate of M.I.T. for the second time flew her Bonanza across the Atlantic to Ireland.

Then, early in 1964, Mrs. Jerrie Mock, in her eleven-year-old Continental-powered Cessna 180, became the first woman to fly solo around the world. It was the latest, dramatic proof that the single-engine light airplane had arrived as a useful transport capable even of globe-circling flights with a woman at the controls.

Industrial/Automotive Marine Engines

Liquid-cooled industrial and automotive engines off Muskegon's Market Street plant assembly lines found their way to a multitude of uses throughout the country, serving all types of Original Equipment Manufacturers (OEM) whose end products filled requirements of industry, construction, transportation and farm equipment for reliable power.

For material handling equipment such as fork lifts and industrial tractor-tugs used in warehousing, on docks, at air terminals, factories and in the holds of cargo ships, Continental supplied the engine requirements of 90% of the manufacturers of such equipment.

The 6 to 65 hp heavy-duty, air-cooled engine market serving agricultural, garden, construction, industrial and recreational needs continued to be filled from its Milwaukee plants by CMC's Wisconsin Motor subsidiary, world's largest builder of such engines.

For marine applications, requirements continued to be met by the wide selection of models available from the Gray Marine Division. Largest volume production was the V-8 model line of engines ranging from 185 to 280 hp, which were used either singly or in pairs. Introduced in 1965 was a new 150 hp six-cylinder model with stern drive suitable for inboard-outboard installations.

Massey-Ferguson Continental-powered row-crop tractors are in wide use

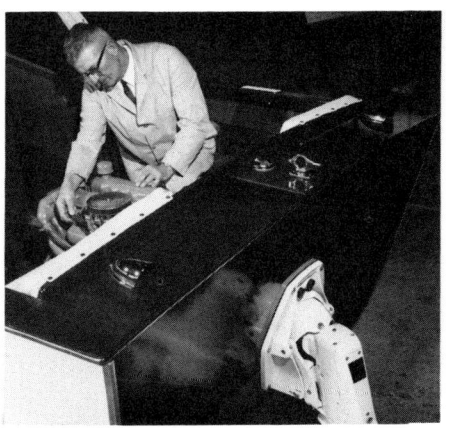

Gray Marine offered '232' engine for inboard/outboard installation

CMC has long been a major supplier of industrial lift truck engines

Typical of wide variety of construction industry equipment is this earth borer

Makers of paving equipment for interstate highway system relied on Continental power

CMC-powered seaplane is lifted from water by Continental-powered Hyster lift truck

Wisconsin four-cylinder air-cooled heavy-duty engine powers New Holland haying machine

For U.S. Air Force, FWD Corp. built four-wheel-drive Continental-powered fire trucks

F-245 industrial engine powers 15-ton road roller manufactured by Acme Iron Works

Photos Teledyne Continental Motors/Richard Stauss

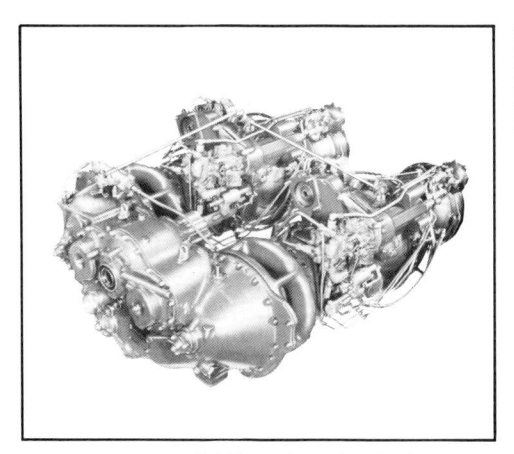

CAE's twin-turboshaft T67 engine powered Bell UH-1D helicopter

In addition to its research and development work for Continental Motors and the Ordnance Corps on VCR and other internal combustion engines for tanks and military trucks, CAE was busy expanding the market and product line for its own gas turbine engines beyond the production contracts already held for the J69 jet engines.

CAE Gas Turbines

Special attention was directed to development of new versions of the basic Model 217 turboshaft engine; that is, a turbojet engine with a free turbine which produces rotary motion to drive propellers or helicopter blades.

In 1962, the military had contracted for development of the 250 hp T65 turboshaft engine as the powerplant for the Army's LOH light observation helicopter competition. A parallel project, company-sponsored, was the larger 500-700 hp T72 model. From this was developed a twin-turboshaft configuration (military model T67). The twin configuration was envisioned as suitable for both fixed wing aircraft and helicopters in commercial as well as military applications.

Combining two engines into a common gear box, providing 1400 hp, would give the helicopter or aircraft twin-engine reliability. Overrunning clutches permit either single or twin operation or automatic single-engine operation should one engine fail. By alternating engines during single engine operation, flight time between overhauls can be increased substantially.

Although the smaller T65 model had met all design and demonstration requirements, military support of the project was terminated in 1964. However, development work continued on the T72 single engine version of the twin-turbo-shaft model T67. The latter was test flown in 1965 in a Bell Helicopter/U.S. Army UH-1D Iroquois.

Company-sponsored projects like the T72 were undertaken because such programs held promise of production contracts on which larger sales volume and favorable earnings might be expected. However, many proved costly.

In the two fiscal years 1963-64, CAE reported a net loss of $1.1 million, largely due to the fact that development expenses were $1.4 million in 1963 and $750,000 in 1964.

During the four years 1962-65, CAE sales averaged $21.4 million annually.

Another important research contract with the Air Force, won as the result of a design competition, called for development of a light-weight demonstration turbojet lift engine. For use in vertical takeoff and landing (VTOL) aircraft, the lift engine was designed to supply vertical thrust to supplement thrust of the jet engines used by aircraft in normal operation. Providing high thrust-to-weight ratios, the lift engine gives otherwise conventional aircraft the flexibility of VTOL operation.

Yet another application of gas turbine technology involved a study to adapt the J69 engine to use as a helicopter rotor-tip turbo-jet for use in Army "flying crane" rotary wing aircraft.

A commercial application was also investigated and demonstrated in which a 460 hp natural gas-burning turbine (Model 231-9) provided the total energy system — light, heat, power and air conditioning — for office buildings.

For the Army's Engine Research and Development Laboratories, CAE began work under a three-year contract on a family of gas turbine engines of 60, 90 and 120 hp which could be used as prime power for generators and other military applications.

The growth of research and development contracts necessitated expansion of CAE's engineering organization and the installation of new laboratory and test equipment at its Detroit facility. Modernization of facilities and installation of additional test cells and precision equipment at the Toledo production plant, in cooperation with the Air Force, were also required to meet higher delivery schedules of J69 engines.

Richard Stauss

Lift engine for VTOL aircraft is tested in vertical test cell

The primary source of CAE's production business was the extension of previous contracts for J69 series gas turbine engines and their spare parts.

Production of these engines for Cessna T-37 twin-jet trainers continued at a steady pace. In the first six years of operation of the T-37 primary jet trainers, Air Force Training Command pilots flew the equivalent of 1272 round trips to the Moon without a fatal accident due to operational failure of the CAE J69 jet engines.

Orders for similar J69 engines for Ryan's tri-service jet targets, and classified unmanned reconnaissance planes, were significantly higher. The latter application involved development of advanced, higher thrust J69 model engines.

For the Navy's new Firebee II supersonic training target, CAE supplied the J69-T-6 engine with afterburner, giving the drone a speed of Mach 1.5 at 75,000 feet.

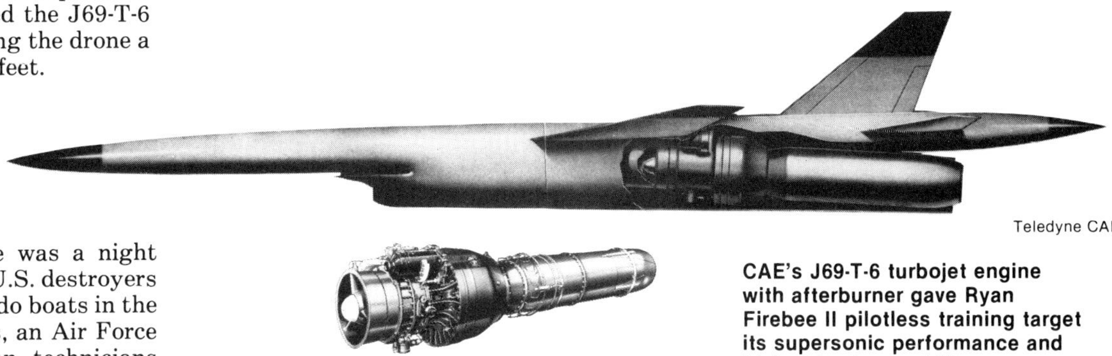

CAE's J69-T-6 turbojet engine with afterburner gave Ryan Firebee II pilotless training target its supersonic performance and high altitude capability

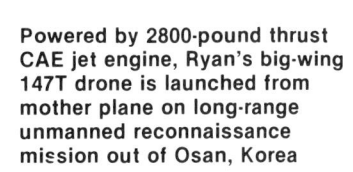

On August 4, 1964 there was a night naval engagement between U.S. destroyers and North Vietnamese torpedo boats in the Gulf of Tonkin. Within days, an Air Force group supported by civilian technicians was dispatched to begin operating Ryan unmanned jet 'spy planes' over Southeast Asia.

First into service were Model 147B "Lightning Bug" planes, larger-wing versions of the Firebee training target drones. These first camera-equipped 'birds' were powered with 1700-pound-thrust J69-T-29 engines.

When higher altitude performance was needed over mission areas, CAE developed the T-41 version of the J69 engine to provide 1920 pounds of thrust for Ryan 147G and 147H pilotless reconnaissance planes.

The ultimate challenge in high altitude performance came when the Air Force ordered the 147T reconnaissance vehicle. For this mission, CAE added extra axial flow and turbine stages to the basic J69 engine. The new J100 model increased thrust to 2800 pounds, 45% more than available for the engine in the 147H bird. This enabled the T-bird to operate at 60,000 feet, with a fuel-out altitude of 75,000 feet at which time the plane was recovered by parachute.

Continental's CAE engines powered all of the pilotless Ryan reconnaissance aircraft in the 3435 operational missions flown in Southeast Asia during the 1964-1975 period.

Research and development work on new engines — except piston engines for aircraft — continued to be concentrated at

Powered by 2800-pound thrust CAE jet engine, Ryan's big-wing 147T drone is launched from mother plane on long-range unmanned reconnaissance mission out of Osan, Korea

Dave Gossett

Continental Aviation and Engineering facilities, but there were a few disappointments.

The Army awarded CAE a $3 million contract in 1966 for development of a new six-cylinder 700 hp version of Continental's 12-cylinder Main Battle Tank engine for use in military vehicles in the 1970s.

Designated AVCR-700, it incorporated the variable compression ratio (VCR) piston concept, and was expected to be used in self-propelled guns and mechanized infantry vehicles then under study by the Army. However, because of cutbacks in Defense Department R&D budgets, work on this VCR engine was terminated by the Government in 1968.

CAE had two excellent turbo-shaft engines which had been developed for military helicopter and commercial aircraft applications but was unable to obtain production contracts. The company offered its uprated 1400 horsepower T67 twin-shaft turbine in a competition for Navy twin-turbine-powered helicopters, but was not successful. CAE also had available the T65, a 310 hp single turboshaft engine for the Army's light observation helicopter program.

Led by manufacturing-oriented Larry Limbach and facilities-wise Ray Powers, Continental management continued to improve the companies' physical assets.

New Plant Facilities

In November 1964, the Defense Department announced the planned phase-out of its Brookley Air Force Base in Mobile, Alabama. It was the kind of information that was grist for Ray Powers' mill.

Civic officials in Mobile had begun a campaign to find industrial activity to replace the outgoing military program. The necessary facilities were there, and would otherwise be unused. In a three-way agreement in June 1966 the Department of Defense leased many of the Air Base facilities to the City of Mobile which in turn subleased 180,000 square feet to Continental Motors.

Initial operations by CMC included rebuilding CAE turbine engines, remanufacture of Continental commercial aircraft piston engines and overhaul of military tank engines. Engine overhaul had been a primary government activity at Brookley which had much to offer in the way of suitable facilities and a pool of technically qualified personnel.

Selected by Limbach as works manager was Ryan production veteran Ray Ortiz, who two years later was named Vice-President, Mobile operations.

By 1969, the company had exercised options for additional space and was using 925,000 square feet of space and part or all of 21 buildings at Brookley. The remanufacture of all piston engines — all models of Army, Navy, Air Force and commercial aircraft engines, three models of Army truck engines, and four models of Army tank engines — was being accomplished at Mobile.

"Zero Time" was the marketing name for remanufacture of engines for general aviation in aircraft ranging from single-seat agricultural models through a wide variety of aircraft for personal transportation, air taxi, commuter airlines, cargo, business and corporate travel, patrol and similar activities.

Under the program, owners of Continental-powered aircraft could exchange their original engines for a like model off-the-shelf, factory-remanufactured, FAA-certified, Zero Time powerplant — with new log book — that had been rebuilt to new engine standards.

Over the next few years, getting out from under militant union conditions and the outdated facilities of the Market Street plant, CMC's piston engine aircraft manufacturing activity was moved to the modern Mobile plant.

Since the physical move would mean loss of 250 jobs in Muskegon, company and union officials agreed to make the transition over a period long enough for the elimination of jobs to be accomplished through normal attrition in the labor force.

During a three-year period other important changes in plant facilities were made.

Construction began in 1966 on a small new aluminum casting facility at Panama City, Florida.

The Wisconsin Motor subsidiary added two plant sites totalling 340,000 square feet. The second of these, located on the northeast side of Milwaukee and known as Plant 4, was leased from Pabst Brewing to house production of Military Standard Engines, which Continental had transferred to its Wisconsin subsidiary upon obtaining new three-year manufacturing contracts for the 1½ to 20 hp engines.

During the year Wisconsin announced that production of its single-cylinder

Mobile Manager RAY (BUTCH) ORTIZ

Large portion of Brookley Air Force Base, Mobile, Alabama, has become headquarters for production of Continental aircraft engines

engines had begun in Sao Paulo, Brazil, under a licensing agreement. A program was also under way to expand production facilities of its Australian licensee, Ronaldson Bros. & Tippett, Ltd.

World-wide distribution of Wisconsin engines continued to be expanded and a 1968 agreement with Hirth Motorren KG of West Germany gave Wisconsin rights (except in certain European countries) to eleven Hirth heavy-duty, lightweight two-cycle single and multi-cylinder engines of from 11½ to 52 hp.

The year 1968 was a banner one for Wisconsin with 2400 employees at work delivering engines at an unprecedented rate. Sales for the year reached an all-time high, exceeding $60 million due in large part to increased shipments of 1½, 3 and 6 horsepower Military Standard Engines.

A total of 60,759 military engines were delivered compared with 15,627 in 1967. And, in 1968, production also got under way on the 10 hp and 20 hp military engines.

To improve parts service and delivery to its customers, including its extensive network of distributors and dealers, the company established near Chicago's O'Hare Airport a centralized Product Support Center which also took over direction of all branch plant operations. Selected to head the support center was Fred Rathert, a veteran Ryanite, who was advanced to a CMC vice-presidency in 1968.

The Continental Motors of Canada subsidiary closed its plant at St. Thomas, Ontario in 1968 and the lease on the Salt Lake City branch was permitted to expire. The centralized support center at Chicago picked up the work as it later did for the Atlanta and Dallas branches whose land and buildings were sold.

Used to community involvement, the invading San Diegans had not been hesitant about plunging into participation in civic affairs in Muskegon and other plant cities.

Civic Responsibility

As the advance man for Ryan — and successor to Henry Vandeven as keeper of the Continental purse strings — Win Henderson was invited to serve on the boards of three Muskegon banks. Those offers were declined by Henderson only because of the heavy requirement to devote adequate time to familiarizing himself with Continental's problems and to avoid any conflict of interest.

Soon, however, Henderson accepted the presidency of the Muskegon Area Development Council, a broader-gaged group than the parochial downtown-merchant type of Chamber of Commerce it succeeded.

One point which Henderson stressed was that downtown Muskegon could never be redeveloped properly until the city got rid of the unsightly, dirty Lakey Foundry and the deteriorating Occidental Hotel. That would come to pass some years later under leadership provided by Ryan executives who arrived later on the scene.

As to the Lakey Foundry, Henderson tried to get the local Campbell, Wyant and Cannon foundry, owned by Textron, to take it over and close the old facility. Henderson also tried to 'give' Continental's 27% stock interest in Lakey to Caterpillar Tractor in the hope that they would move the business to their Peoria, Illinois, plant. Lakey eventually went bankrupt, solving the problem.

Rehabilitation and modernization of the decaying Market Street plant and offices served as a catalyst for later mall-type redevelopment of downtown Muskegon under the direction of civic groups on which the transplanted Ryan executives from San Diego served.

Ryan had always been a strong financial supporter of community projects in San Diego and Bob Jackson saw to it that through Henderson's participation Continental began to contribute more than in the past to similar projects in Muskegon.

Ray Phillips, then Director, Personnel and Industrial Relations, took on the top fund-raising task in Muskegon for the United Negro College Fund Drive and joined Henderson in leadership of the Junior Achievement program in local high schools.

And, in his first try for political office, Richard Stauss, a Ryanite and marketing support supervisor, was elected an Alderman of the City of North Muskegon.

Many other examples of civic involvement were to follow in succeeding years.

There had been, of course, conflicts as well as cooperation, especially within the Continental family, as related by Phillips:

"When Ryan people first arrived, Continental management, workers in the factory and people in the Muskegon community were not too receptive to us. For Muskegon it was the first acquisition of a major local industrial complex by an outside firm, and the people didn't really understand it.

"Muskegon was an old, established community with old families, a lot of old money, a lot of successful businessmen. And many poor people. We had come from San Diego, a growing, youthful city, though its roots went back to the days of Spanish California.

"Ryan management was young, ambitious and talented, with a lot of savvy. It was aggressive and sometimes abrasive. We were told to turn the company around, and we did.

WISCONSIN
HEAVY DUTY ENGINES

Ryan Aeronautical Library

Product Supporter
FRED RATHERT

> "... what we brought was a management style and energy, plus the ability to make decisions."

"It was not easy to tell people who had been with Continental all their working careers that they were wrong, and we were right. But their management was old, unimaginative and ultra-conservative. They were very successful when the company was young, but failed to develop people behind them. In some areas there were four levels of supervision, all in their sixties. They had no young management people. Ryan had legions of such people, all with a lot of enthusiasm to get on with the job. Anyone who moves in and changes the order of things is an irritant. No wonder there were conflicts."

All was not hostility between the Ryan and Continental camps. Lynn Richardson, like Bill Rutherford, headquartered in the Detroit offices which were presided over by Dolores Lyngaas who served as Jack Reese's personal secretary while he was in the motor city. She was also an Assistant Secretary of the corporation. In 1975, Dolores Lyngaas became Mrs. Lynn Richardson.

Harold Rouse, an old Ryan factory hand who had arrived in Muskegon even a year before Phillips, found the atmosphere in the Market Street plant, where he took charge of production of industrial and aircraft engines, "one of some hostility, especially from the union's point of view."

Eventually Rouse became director of all plant operations not only at Market Street and Getty Street in Muskegon but also at other plant cities.

"In addition to modernizing Market Street, we found it necessary to move some work out of there. The warehousing of spare parts for industrial and aircraft engines was moved to a central location in Chicago. The overhaul of aircraft and tank engines was moved from Market Street and Getty Street to the new facility in Mobile, Alabama. Later, of course, all aircraft engine manufacture was moved to Mobile.

"Following that we started a plant in Walterboro, South Carolina, for manufacture of industrial engine governors and some sub-assembly work.

Ryan graphics designers introduced modern new symbol for Continental companies and products as seen in this view of refurbished Market Street facilities at Muskegon

Neosho, Missouri plant formerly used for rocket engine production was leased by CAE for precision machine capability applicable to its gas turbine business

"To further break up some of the problems we had at Market Street we increased the number of components, like water pumps, which were built for us by various suppliers under sub-contract.

"Getting back to our invasion of Muskegon, the Continental establishment saw that we were young and thought, 'Who are you to come in here and tell us how to make engines.'

"But what we brought was not engine know-how but a management style and energy, plus the ability to make decisions. We gave other people responsibility and authority they had previously not been able to exercise themselves, and held them to it. Even their vice-presidents had little authority when we came aboard. There was a top and there was a bottom in the Continental organization, but there was no one in the middle."

Ever alert to the need to upgrade Continental's facilities, Ray Powers took leadership in the decision by CAE to lease yet another government plant being phased out by the Department of Defense. This was the 375,000 square foot plant in Neosho, Missouri, formerly occupied by the Rocketdyne Division of North American Rockwell for production of rocket engines for NASA and Air Force programs. Its manufacturing equipment ideally matched CAE's requirements for turbine engine work.

Through his military facilities connections, Powers had also been instrumental in 1968 in Continental closing agreement with the U.S. government to purchase the government-owned Getty Street tank engine plant in Muskegon which it had been operating for 25 years. The purchase price was $10 million, payable over a ten-year period. The 890,000 square foot plant and 57-acre site was a major acquisition but title was not formally taken until two years later. After that the company was free to produce commercial as well as military products although a major stipulation was that capacity to produce tank engines be maintained for at least ten years.

During that year Continental sold the assets of the Gray Marine engine division to newly-formed Graymarine Corporation, with headquarters in Coldwater, Michigan. Continental had earlier discontinued sales of its marine engine models in order to concentrate on larger volume product lines.

Changes in the stock ownership structure of the various Ryan-Continental units continued during the 1966-68 period. Ryan's percentage of Continental Motors ownership, which reached a controlling 50.14% at the end of Ryan's 1965 fiscal year, was increased steadily until reaching 62.2% in September 1968.

Stock Ownership Changes

In turn, Continental continued to buy stock of its subsidiary, increasing its share of ownership in CAE from 75.9% in 1965 to 82.9% in 1966 at which time the American Stock Exchange suspended trading because the amount of stock then in public hands was less than the required 100,000 shares. (At the 1968 fiscal year end, CMC owned 85.9% of CAE's shares.)

At Wisconsin Motor, that firm purchased and retired additional of its own shares which resulted in Continental Motors' control going from 88% in 1966 to 92.5% in 1968. Wisconsin's ownership in its Australian affiliate was also increased — from 24.3% to a controlling position of 51.1%. At that time, November 1966, Robert C. Jackson went on the Ronaldson Bros. & Tippett board.

Many of the officers and directors brought into the various Continental units from the Ryan organization were spread across CMC, CAE and Wisconsin in so many capacities and titles over a period of years that to enumerate all would be pointless. However, because of the key roles some filled over an extended time, mention of them is appropriate.

Rutherford Named President

In September 1966, G.W. Rutherford was named President and Chief Operating Officer of Continental Motors and went on the boards of the CAE and Wisconsin subsidiaries. Bob Jackson, Chairman and Chief Executive Officer of CMC also took over as Chairman of Wisconsin, whose former Chairman, Harold A. Todd, passed away in June 1967.

A late 1966 addition to the CMC management team, as Vice-President and assistant to Rutherford, was James L. Murray, former Vice-President of Douglas Aircraft and President of Rockwell-Standard's aircraft divisions. An Air Force officer with both test pilot and program management experience, Murray was project officer on development of the B-52 bomber and while in industry was general manager of the Douglas division building the C-5A military transport.

Due to failing health, Jack Reese resigned from the CAE and Wisconsin boards, but remained in the largely honorary post of Vice Chairman of the parent company which he had served so long and devotedly.

Art Wild, Continental Vice-President, Engineering and Marketing, also moved up to President of CAE succeeding Reese and joined the CMC board of directors a year later. Ray Powers moved into Wild's former job of CAE's Executive Vice-President. When Reese resigned from the CAE board he was replaced by Carl Bachle, Vice-President, Research and Engineering. Ira W. Nichol, a 12-year veteran engineer with CAE was named Vice-President of that subsidiary in 1966 and two years later became Vice-President, Military Marketing of CMC.

Lynn Richardson, one of Ryan's 1964 advance men, took on ever increasing responsibility, first as a board member, then as Vice-President, Finance of CMC. Frank Light, Controller in 1967, won a CMC vice-presidency the next year. Larry Limbach joined the CMC board in 1967;

ARCHITECTS OF CHANGE — 1966
Major management roles at Continental were filled by key executives from Ryan Aeronautical Company. Left to right, with their Continental positions: Robert C. Jackson, Chairman of the CMC Board; B. Kenneth Goodman Secretary and General Counsel; Winthrop C. Henderson, Treasurer; J. Lynn Richardson, Vice-President and Controller; L. M. Limbach, Vice-President, Plant Operations; G. Williams Rutherford, President.

Teledyne Wisconsin Motor

PHIL A. NORTON
Norton succeeded Harold A. Todd as President of Wisconsin Motor

one of his key men, Harold Rouse became Vice-President, Muskegon Operations, in 1968.

Ray Powers, who philosophically was oriented to Ryan management methods, took on added duties as Executive Vice-President of CAE. At Wisconsin, Phil Norton took over as President in February 1967 a few months before Todd's death. At CMC, Howard F. Dunlap was named Vice-President, Commercial Marketing.

In May 1968, Jim Wells, Ryan and Continental's Washington representative, passed away. He was succeeded in that role, and as a Vice-President of CAE, by Raymond A. Ballweg, Jr., well-known in aerospace and government circles. Ballweg had been military assistant to several Air Force Assistant Secretaries concerned with research and development.

This, then, was the cast of principal characters who in four and one half years managed to turn around the declining fortunes of Continental Motors.

New orders — not without a lot of hard selling, pencil sharpening and negotiation — continued to flow in to Continental plants, replacing the steady stream of completed engines shipped to customers.

New Sales and Earnings Records

Largest volume items were piston engines for military vehicles — tanks and trucks — and for business and personal aircraft; and jet turbine engines for remotely piloted aircraft and military training planes.

From Getty Street, Muskegon, came the 750 hp AVDS-1790 series tank engines, principally for M60 battle tanks. In October 1968, the 10,000th AVDS-1790-2A engine was delivered to the Army.

Muskegon's Market Street plant also produced thousands of LD- and LDS-465 multifuel engines for 2½ and 5-ton Army trucks. (Huge numbers of industrial, automotive and material handling engines in the 33 to 95 hp range were also being built at Market Street, as were 260-330 hp engines for large highway trucks, including the military 465's companion commercial L-478 series engines for use in transportation and agricultural equipment.) And more than 40,000 engines for quarter-ton Army Mutt trucks were built.

The new Mobile plant, and Market Street, produced horizontally-opposed, air-cooled aircraft engines, up to 435 hp geared turbocharged models, for general aviation and light military aircraft.

At Milwaukee, Wisconsin Motor's major commercial engine customers were agricultural, construction, industrial and outdoor power equipment manufacturers, with farm machinery the heaviest user. Wisconsin's compact, lightweight designs were especially attractive to producers of self-propelled agricultural equipment.

CAE's Toledo plant built thousands of J69 jet engines for Ryan drone training targets and, more importantly, for use in Ryan's still secret unmanned reconnaissance planes flying intelligence missions in Southeast Asia. J69 engines in large volume were also supplied for Cessna jet trainers.

In all, nearly half a million engines bearing the Red Seal tradition were being built annually by the Continental Motors companies.

From CAE's 1962-65 average production volume of $21.4 million annually, and net yearly losses averaging $100,000, this subsidiary made remarkable progress in the following three years:

	CAE Sales	CAE Earnings
1966	$29,113,603	$427,110
1967	40,201,279	581,970
1968	50,360,915	794,210

After ten years, 1955-1964, on a sales and profits plateau, total CMC business results made sharp gains:

	CMC Sales	CMC Earnings
1965	$184,003,189	$2,298,299
1966	232,442,113	5,544,590
1967	279,051,594	6,406,905
1968	308,503,701	7,134,306

Rutherford, in his 1968 Annual Report to Stockholders:

"The results for the 1968 fiscal year marked the first time . . . sales and earnings have reached such levels. This . . . is the result of many factors, primarily realignment and modernization of facilities to achieve more efficient production, concentration on the manufacture of those product lines offering the best profit potential, and an extensive program of cost reduction.

"The beneficial aspects of these efforts have been reflected by the constantly improving financial results achieved since they were initiated several years ago."

The significance of those "constantly improving financial results" was not lost on others. Continental Motors and its parent company, Ryan Aeronautical Company, were ripe for plucking. Just as Ryan had taken over Continental, it in turn became the object of take-over bids by other, larger holding companies. After all, its founder-Chairman, T. Claude Ryan, was 72 and had already spent half a century in aviation. It was, perhaps, a good time for other, younger management to take over. The lesson of Continental's mature but unimaginative senior leaders was well learned.

194

By late 1968, the combined Ryan-Continental group's financial, production and technical success, with a business volume which had grown to $430 million that year, made the parent Ryan Aeronautical Company a prime target for acquisition.

Teledyne Buys Ryan

For more than a year nearly a dozen expansion-minded conglomerates had been sending out feelers, usually through investment banking houses, to determine whether or not Ryan's key stockholders would be willing to sell their holdings — at an attractive figure — and influence other owners to do likewise.

Meanwhile, based in part on take-over rumors circulating in investment circles, Ryan shares on the New York Stock Exchange were trading at around $40 per share compared with about half that price a year earlier.

Some behind the scenes negotiations had taken place before November 6, 1968, the date when Teledyne, Inc., a broadly-based multi-company advanced technology firm headquartered at Los Angeles, offered to purchase at $50 per share up to 100% of Ryan's 2,570,898 outstanding shares.

In mid-September 1968, the writer's office issued a press release announcing that "discussions are in progress with more than one responsible financial group concerning possible cash tender offers . . . at prices higher than present market values."

During this period, Bob Jackson had been on a business trip to Australia visiting Ronaldson Bros. & Tippett, Wisconsin Motor's affiliate. On Jackson's return, Claude Ryan went on vacation to southern England but he and Jackson arranged to keep in touch by telephone on the various negotiations under way.

Ryan wondered what Jackson's reaction may have been when asked by his secretary to return a call to Ryan's overnight lodge in England — "the Lobster Pot in Mousehole." *It hardly had the ring of a Big Business gathering place.*

Ryan and Teledyne had the services of the same investment banking firm — Dean Witter & Co. of Los Angeles. At the company's request, Guy Witter, a senior partner, had served on the Ryan board of directors for two years during the 1960s.

As competing investment firms vied for position, Dean Witter was instrumental in bringing Ryan and Teledyne together. Claude Ryan recalls a preliminary meeting in his office.

"George Knox had been meeting separately with Teledyne's founder, Dr. Henry E. Singleton, in Los Angeles. Both came to San Diego to meet with Bob Jackson and me so we would be better informed of the status of their discussions.

"We hit it off well with Dr. Singleton and he seemed satisfied with the background information on our company that Teledyne had already acquired through contacts with George and Dean Witter. The price of $50 per share was satisfactory to both parties and we agreed to go ahead with the deal. The four of us then had lunch together; and that was about it."

Teledyne, Inc. was the 1960 creation of Dr. Henry Singleton, a brilliant M.I.T. engineer with industry experience at Hughes Aircraft, North American Aviation and Litton Industries. The first product line developed was semiconductors and other electronic components. By acquisition of other companies, Teledyne then expanded into metals and other industries. With purchase of Vasco Metals (formerly Vanadium Steel Co.) in 1966 came Dr. George A. Roberts, now Teledyne's President, a Singleton friend and classmate at Annapolis.

In response to Teledyne's $128 million purchase offer, T. Claude Ryan, founder-Chairman; Robert C. Jackson, President; and other Directors tendered their Ryan holdings and urged other stockholders to do likewise. By the end of November nearly all Ryan shares had been tendered or purchased. Thus, on January 2, 1969, Ryan became a subsidiary of Teledyne, Inc. Teledyne's purchase, of course, included Ryan's 62.2% ownership of Continental.

Then began a step-by-step process to fold the rest of Continental shares and 100% of its subsidiaries' shares into Teledyne, Inc. The integration was a two-pronged approach, one involving the legal corporate structures, the other the operating organizations.

Bill Rutherford, having been the point man on Ryan's take-over of Continental, wanted to make the transition to Teledyne's control of Ryan and Continental as smooth as possible. Dr. Singleton was an old friend so Rutherford called to congratulate Teledyne's founder on the purchase and reassure him of his desire to cooperate.

Ryan People Retained

"I assumed Henry had someone in mind to take over management of Continental," Rutherford said, "so I told him I would do everything possible to help the new guy, and that there would be absolutely no hard feeling on my part. His response was 'We don't have anyone to send back; you just stay right there. You'll hear from George Roberts.'"

During the first month of Teledyne ownership, Dr. Roberts, President, became a member of Continental's board of directors, and Ryan-Continental's Bob Jackson joined Roberts, Dr. Singleton and three others on the six-man Teledyne board.

DR. HENRY E. SINGLETON
Chairman of the Board
Teledyne, Inc.

DR. GEORGE A. ROBERTS
President
Teledyne, Inc.

(Jackson served in that post until his death in February 1979.)

Because Teledyne did not staff Continental with its people, but retained Ryan's, there was not the kind of psychological shock to the organization there had been six years earlier when Ryan took over. However, Clarence J. (Jack) Reese gave up his last official connection with the company he had served so long and well.

When Jack left the board, his fellow directors recognized his contribution, noting that "He assumed the presidency of Continental Motors in 1939 when the fortunes of the corporation were at an all-time low, and through his wise counsel and direction guided it to a position of world-wide recognition and leadership in its field." It was a proper but inadequate tribute to a great industrialist.

Reese spent the next year with Pat in Florida, but no relaxation in his strenuous schedule could repair the increasing loss of his faculties.

"Jack was wintering in Sarasota," recalls his long-time friend Jim Ferry. "One morning he was out walking... up and down, up and down the road. He wasn't at all sure where he was. It was time to do something. We flew him back to Michigan where he and Pat had a little cottage on a lake north of Muskegon. It was just right for him to enjoy retirement, but he wasn't that kind of a guy. He had tremendous vitality and if he had a weakness it was that he didn't delegate responsibility enough.

"Eventually he had to be placed in an institution in Traverse City. The hardest thing in my life was going to visit him because he'd be with you for a little while and then his voice got so soft you could hardly hear him."

That voice was finally stilled January 23, 1972. He had joined Continental 45 years earlier when 26 years old.

Another long-time associate, Art Wild, also shared his memory of Jack. "It was really amazing that when he died his memory had already failed, because when he was working, he had a memory like an elephant. I learned pretty quickly that when he told you to do something you better do it because he wasn't going to forget it.

"To have this memory loss was pathetic. Except for a series of mild strokes, he was perfectly healthy. It was fortunate, I guess, that Ryan solved the problem for us by moving in and taking over."

Josh Wooldridge, Ryan's Vice-President, Finance, was named to the Continental board replacing Reese who had retired, and Lynn Richardson was appointed Executive Vice-President of CMC and Jim Murray named Executive Vice-President of CAE.

To give Teledyne management some idea of the physical plants and product lines they had purchased, Rutherford and Roberts organized a scouting expedition led by Continental's young Jean Engler (son of the General of the same name); Teledyne's Berkley Baker, assistant to Dr. Singleton; and the writer, as Ryan's public relations officer. In the matter of a few days, the group of Teledyne financial and administrative executives had visited Muskegon, Detroit, Milwaukee, Toledo, Mobile and Neosho.

A few weeks later George Roberts called and asked Rutherford if they could take the same tour of Continental facilities, giving him an opportunity not only to size up plants and products but also the management organization and Rutherford's own performance. Roberts conclusion: "Things seem to be going okay, Bill, but you could probably be doing something else besides this." That came to pass very soon.

To simplify the corporate structure, Continental Wisconsin Corp. was formed and to this new entity Continental Motors transferred the shares owned in its two majority-owned subsidiaries, Continental Aviation & Engineering Corp. and Wisconsin Motor Corp. Then on March 20, 1969, after stockholders had approved the plan, the new Continental Wisconsin unit was merged into the parent Continental Motors Corp.

Wisconsin and CAE Become Divisions

An interesting story, perhaps apocryphal, concerns the 14% of CAE stock that Continental had not yet purchased. It later was learned that a Beverly Hills stockbroker, who knew that George Knox was behind Ryan's increasing ownership of Continental Motors, began buying CAE shares for his own and his clients' accounts, thus gaining a bit of leverage of his own in the subsequent take-over.

CMC's board of directors was expanded to eleven members, taking in Phil Norton, President of Wisconsin, and Jim Murray, who had just been named President of CAE.

No longer separate corporations and subsidiaries of CMC, Wisconsin and CAE became Divisions of the parent company. Instead of the three corporations, only one now remained — Continental Motors Corp., with three semi-autonomous operating divisions of its own.

Heading the Continental Motors Division (piston engines) was Lynn Richardson. Jim Murray served as President of the Continental Aviation and Engineering Division (turbine engines) with Frank Light as Executive Vice-President. The Wisconsin Motor Division (industrial air-cooled engines) had Phil Norton as President with Arthur A. Erlinger as Executive Vice-President. All division heads reported to Bill Rutherford, President of CMC.

"Ryan solved the problem for us by moving in and taking over."

G. WILLIAMS RUTHERFORD

World War II navigator, Stanford-trained in law and economics, tax attorney, division manager for aerospace and electronics, Bill Rutherford was the up-through-the-ranks executive selected in 1964 by Ryan Aeronautical Company to spearhead its management and subsequent take-over of Continental Motors Corp. Named Continental's sixth President in 1966, Rutherford became a key group executive for the newest owner when Ryan in turn was acquired by Teledyne, Inc., of which he has been Vice-President since 1969.

In June, Rutherford was named a Vice-President of parent Teledyne, Inc., and, as a follow-up of Roberts' evaluation of 'something else,' came the announcement that Teledyne had established a Ryan-Continental Group based at San Diego with Rutherford as Group Executive and Jackson as Group Chairman. Seven additional Teledyne companies, mostly in California, were also placed under Rutherford's management in what became the Pacific Group.

Rutherford, when Roberts asked him to oversee Ryan and other companies, as well as Continental, and headquarter at San Diego: "I never had moved away from San Diego so that wasn't any big thing!"

W.E. (Gene) Lewis, who had come to Continental in 1966 after service in the aircraft industry and as a financial analyst for the Air Force, was named Vice-President, Finance, and Treasurer in September 1969. William. A. Wiseman, a key engineer in Continental's aircraft engine department since 1945, was appointed Vice-President, Aeronautical Engineering.

With considerable regret, Rutherford accepted the resignation of Art Wild, one of the company's most highly respected managers and, with 45 years employment, its senior executive in terms of continuous service.

Having 'done their thing,' Ryan's early advance men, Win Henderson and Larry Limbach, resigned their Continental posts as did Ray Ballweg.

Next logical step in the simplification of the corporate structure would be for Teledyne to buy up all available Continental shares so as to merge that company into Teledyne, Inc. Through Teledyne's ownership of Ryan, they already had 62.2% of Continental's 3.3 million shares.

Continental Folded Into Teledyne

With CMC's shares selling at $18 on the New York Stock Exchange, Teledyne, Inc., in June 1969 offered to exchange one $30 principal amount 7% subordinated debenture, due 1999, for each share of its publicly outstanding common stock. Paying $2.10 per year, the debentures provided an attractive annual yield of better than 12% to those then tendering their shares.

With Teledyne by then controlling more than 80% of its shares, Continental Motors announced in December 1969 that stockholders had approved merger of the company into Teledyne, Inc. The former Continental Motors Division was then redesignated *Teledyne Continental Motors* with Lynn Richardson as President. The other divisions took on new names: *Teledyne CAE* headed by Jim Murray and *Teledyne Wisconsin Motor* with Art Erlinger as President, replacing Phil Norton who retired, and Fred Rathert as Executive Vice-President.

Ryan and Continental had been run very successfully under a central management concept with key men in each area — finance, engineering, marketing, manufacturing, etc. — spreading their talents over all units in the group. By contrast, Teledyne was made up of over a hundred separate companies, each quite autonomous and self-sufficient.

Independent Units

George Roberts often discussed Teledyne's management concept with Rutherford but never imposed it on the Ryan-Continental Group. However, in its first year of ownership by Teledyne, Continental had at least been separated into its three product divisions: piston engines, turbine engines, and industrial air-cooled engines.

Smaller units, Roberts contended, give management better control and make the local manager fully responsible for the success of his own operation. At the time, Rutherford's first reaction was, "Oh, boy! I never heard anything like this; it's the last thing I have on my mind. We'd been exactly the opposite as far as Ryan and Continental were concerned."

Later, Rutherford allowed that "I listened and, after quite a period of time in Teledyne management, I finally went to George Roberts and told him it was time to get busy and break Continental into individual units."

J. LYNN RICHARDSON

"Rich" was in the vanguard of Ryan executives who moved into the Continental Motors management structure in 1964. Soon after joining Continental he was named Vice-President and Controller of CMC and also served as an officer of CAE and Wisconsin Motor. In 1969 he became Executive Vice-President of the Continental Motors Division. Three years later he was named President of Teledyne Continental Motors and Midwest group executive for Teledyne, Inc., filling the latter post until his death in 1981.

Teledyne CAE under Jim Murray and Teledyne Wisconsin under Art Erlinger were already separate units. It was Teledyne Continental Motors which needed further surgery. The scalpel was applied to the 'Siamese triplets' in February 1972.

Teledyne Continental Motors was split into three units with Lynn Richardson, President, as Group Executive.

The *TCM General Products Division*, headquartered in the Getty Street plant, was headed by Harold Rouse, Vice President, who was advanced to President of that Division in October 1974. At the same time, Ira W. Nichol, Edward F. Blackburne and Alfred E. Kugler were named Vice-Presidents.

This Division was given product responsibility not only for power plants for tanks and other military tracked vehicles, but also for engines for military trucks. The latter work was transferred from Market Street which had already built 91,000 multi-fuel military truck engines.

Because the government owned design rights, Market Street several months earlier had lost a $10 million Army quarter-ton truck engine contract as they were underbid by a competitor. Getty Street also lost continuation of the contract for the Main Battle Tank AVCR-1000 engine when Congress failed to approve additional funding.

The *TCM Industrial Products Division* took over the Market Street operation in Muskegon, producing industrial engines. Nominally, Richardson served as General Manager with Ramon J. Phillips, a former Ryan industrial relations executive and later in the same position at Continental, as his right-hand man. Phillips became President in October 1974.

The *TCM Aircraft Products Division* at Mobile, Alabama, was placed under Vice Presidents W. E. (Gene) Lewis, former financial executive, and Ray Ortiz, originally from Ryan.

Looking back on the Ryan to Teledyne transition, Rutherford noted that "We've taken about 110 people out of Ryan to put into other Teledyne companies in management positions. It's a real tribute to Ryan that we had enough management to take so many out."

Teledyne's decentralized management of smaller, independent units where each company, reporting through a group executive, is responsible for its own fate had a great deal of merit. Each president, in effect, has his own company. As long as he's accomplishing what has been set out and approved as a basic plan for the year, no one from the Teledyne corporate office in Los Angeles is going to bother him very much. It's only when things don't work out the way they have been forecast under a constantly updated 'sales and profit plan,' and annually-approved capital expenditures budget, that higher management needs to take over. Thus Teledyne has been able to manage more than a hundred companies with a minimum headquarters staff.

Because Teledyne's annual and quarterly reports to stockholders are compiled on a consolidated basis for the entire operation, sales and profits of the individual 'companies' in the corporation are not a matter of public record.

The last Ryan financial statement, issued as a press release to the investment community, was made for the 1968 fiscal year, and by Continental for the 1969 fiscal year. The last printed, illustrated Annual Reports to Stockholders were issued by Ryan for 1967 and by Continental for 1968.

There has been a tendency among laymen like the writer to derisively refer to practitioners of the accounting profession as "bean counters." At Ryan, the financially-oriented executives were upgraded by we unsophisticates to the role of "money mechanics." They were superb at their task. Now, Teledyne has gone a league further with their successful financial policies. With the engineering background of their two top management executives they are truly "fiscal engineers."

At the General Products Division (Getty Street), new technologies continued to be explored. After nearly a decade of development, Continental's Unisteel cylinder won acceptance with a December 1972 contract for $4.5 million for units to be installed in AVDS-1790 diesel engines for M60 Main Battle Tanks.

General Products Division

The new cylinder, incorporating the use of a forged steel dome with aluminum cooling fins attached through a shrink-fit process, provided improved durability and increased maximum engine performance from 750 hp to 900 hp.

Conflicting national interests led to cancellation in 1970 of the joint United States-West Germany project to develop the MBT-70 tank. In this country, using technology from the MBT-70 effort, work continued on the XM803 version of the Main Battle Tank with Continental offering its AVCR-1100-3B variable compression ratio diesel engine.

General Products teamed with General Motors in a new competition for development and production of the Army's new low-silhouette XM-1 tank. Continental supplied the up-rated AVCR-1360-2 supercharged engine of 1500 hp mated to an Allison automatic transmission with four forward and two reverse ranges. With this package, double the power of older tanks, the XM-1 could accelerate rapidly to 52 mph versus the M60 tank's 30 mph.

Although the GM/Continental entry was considered by experts to have superior performance and lower cost, the contract award went to Chrysler whose entry was powered by an unproven turbine engine.

There was some consolation, however, in new government contracts for $44 million for continued production of AVDS-1790 engines as retrofits in older tanks and for installation in new Army vehicles.

Earlier in 1972 General Products completed tests on two models of its LED-500 (low emission diesel) engine, winning approval not only of the Environmental Protection Agency (EPA) but also meeting the more rigid California state exhaust emission standards. For gasoline engines, Continental had attacked the problem by obtaining low carbon monoxide emission in advance of, rather than after, combustion. This required carburetors calibrated to meter fuel and air more precisely, thus gaining greater combustion efficiency. However, the Arab Oil Embargo soon brought a shift in emphasis for emission control to fuel economy.

In a departure from past practice, General Products in Spring 1972 submitted bids for production and assembly of complete military vehicles — the Army Scout and Army 2½- and 5-ton trucks — but was not successful in either effort.

Popular Beech Bonanza V-tailed personal business plane was introduced in 1946. Twenty-five years later, nearly 10,000 Bonanzas had been delivered to their devoted owners. All Bonanzas were powered by Continental horizontally-opposed, air-cooled engines

Beech Aircraft

Army contracts for continuing production of Continental-developed LD-465 and LDS-465 military truck engines, and the smaller Ford-developed L-141 engine, previously built by Continental, were being won by lower bidders, principally Hercules (White Motor).

Because Continental had developed the original LD-465 engines, the company was asked to respond once again to a change in Army fuel policies. Since the military no longer required multi-fuel capability, CMC developed modifications to convert the engines to straight diesel operation.

In export business, the Republic of China (Taiwan) contracted for sets of engine parts for assembly of LD-465 and L-141 engines.

A new product, the Maintenance Indicator Panel (MIP) was developed to visually provide military vehicle operators with vital engine information which, if neglected, could result in engine failure or unnecessary maintenance cost.

In a new program to improve tank engine performance through redesign of major engine components, time between engine failure under simulated combat conditions was increased from 51 hours to 131 hours. Time between overhaul was improved from 3180 miles to 3682 miles, and the availability for tanks employing the 12-cylinder supercharged diesel engines was increased from 77% to 95%.

For use with its diesel engines, General Products developed a "variable flow area" system which permits new superchargers to operate at high efficiencies throughout a broad range of engine speeds and loads.

Under an $8 million government Energy Research and Development Administration contract, development of a new automotive diesel engine using variable compression ratio (VCR) pistons was undertaken in 1975. Objectives of the four-year program were to develop a system which would greatly improve fuel economy over that of spark ignition engines.

In the commercial diesel engine field, 300 heavy-duty air-cooled versions of the 750 hp 12-cylinder AVDS-1790-2D engine were purchased to power extremely large earth-moving equipment in South Africa.

Despite the ever-increasing importance of jet and turboprop engines for large transport aircraft, the majority of modern aircraft have single or multiple gasoline engines in the 100 to 500 hp range. The piston engine has maintained its place in the market, and has evolved into a highly refined and reliable power source for most aircraft.

Aircraft Products Division

Continental aircraft engines employ a flat, horizontally-opposed configuration of four, six or eight air-cooled cylinders. A major advancement in design was the use of **fuel injection** for better performance and economy, achieved through more precise control of the fuel/air mixture. Fuel-injection also has virtually eliminated the problem of carburetor icing.

To compensate for the rarified atmosphere at high altitudes, **turbo-supercharging** was developed with hot exhaust gases driving a gas turbine and compressor pumping pressurized air to the engine.

A **reduction gear** system between engine and propeller makes it possible for the engine to operate efficiently at relatively high speed while the propeller turns at the lower speed where it is most efficient.

An outstanding example of the longevity of good aircraft design is the distinctive V-tailed Beech Bonanza personal/business plane. It made its debut in 1946, powered by a Continental E185 engine. By its 25th anniversary, 9,478 Bonanzas, all Continental-powered, had been delivered. Latest versions were powered with 285 hp IO-520 fuel-injected engines.

At the Aircraft Products Division, work continued on further development of a Hydra-Torque engine, research on which had been started in 1965 under William A. Wiseman, chief of aircraft engineering at Muskegon.

New Generation Tiara Engines

Concerned that Continental's position in the four-cylinder aircraft engine market could be jeopardized because others might produce a similar engine for less, Wiseman set out to design a completely new family of engines. Crossing of the one-pound-per-horsepower barrier was a primary goal of the development program.

Wiseman's proposal for the four-cylinder 100 hp market was to make the engine inexpensive; by making it high-speed it was possible to get more power for the same cost in material and parts. Displacement could be reduced, so weight and over-all cost would come down.

More compact than other engines, the all-new Hydra-Torque engine would permit the plane builder to use a shorter, more streamlined nacelle, leaving more cabin room. Lighter engine weight would also mean greater aircraft payload.

The Hydra-Torque name came from a totally new, hydraulically actuated torsional vibration control (VTC) system which greatly reduced vibration. With VTC the propeller driveshaft is driven either solidly or flexibly by a quill shaft providing a "soft drive" system.

In addition, the camshaft gear was used to get a 2-to-1 reduction in the ratio of engine/propeller speed. With the propeller turning at half the engine speed, this eliminated the need for separate reduction gears. Thus the engine could run at the high rpm where it is most efficient while the propeller operates in the range of its greatest efficiency and at reduced noise levels.

Many other innovative design and production details were also included. A series of nine transfer machines were designed and built for the Mobile factory to machine Tiara crankcases while similar equipment automatically performed machining operations on each cylinder head.

Christened "Tiara," the new engines included six- and eight-cylinder supercharged versions with a great commonality of parts. Spanning a horsepower range from 160 to 500, they were introduced to the general aviation industry in 1970 but never fully realized the potential of wide usage which the modern automated production line at Mobile was forecasting.

Before being turned over to aircraft manufacturers for service-testing, Tiara engines had already logged hundreds of development flight test hours in Continental's own engineering fleet of Cessna, Beech and Piper aircraft.

Flight demonstrations in Tiara-powered aircraft flying in competition against identical models powered by existing engines were impressive. "The difference," said one observer, "was obvious. The Tiara-powered planes were off the runway quicker and climb-out was increased sharply. With the prop running at 2000 rpm, the 285 hp Tiara could take off with a greater weight than the same plane when powered by a competitor's 300 hp engine running at 2800 rpm."

"The Tiara," explained veteran Continental engine publicist Don Fairchilds, "was

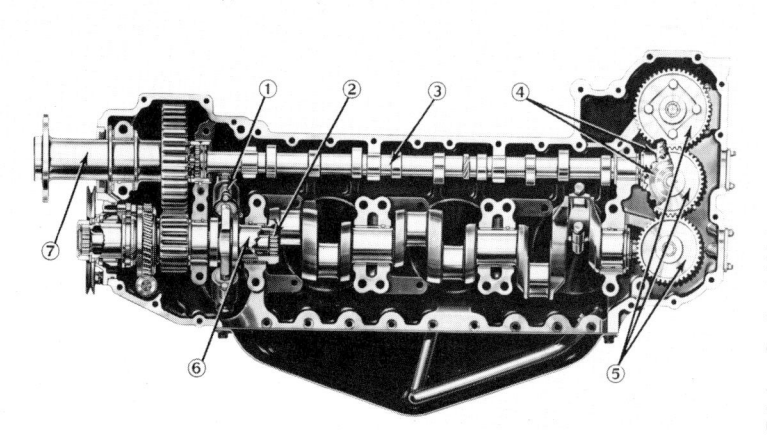

Piper Aircraft

After extensive testing in Continental's own fleet of planes, new Tiara engine was flown in hard-working Piper Pawnee Brave agricultural plane under severe operating conditions

Tiara Hydra-Torque engine legend: (1) Vibratory Torque Control (VTC) unit; (2) Quillshaft; (3) Camshaft; (4) Hypoid Gears; (5) Accessory Drive Train; (6) Prop Driver Shaft; (7) Propeller Shaft

Teledyne Continental Motors

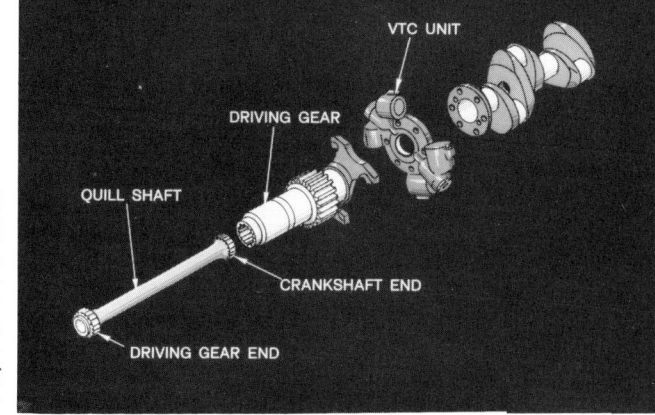

one of the finest and most tested new piston engines to come along. Unfortunately for its appeal to the general aviation market, it was introduced in the wrong type of airplane — the hard-working Piper Pawnee Brave ag-plane."

Leslie Waters, who — after an interim chief engineer — succeeded Wiseman as Vice-President, Engineering, was more specific:

"Although advanced in concept and incorporating many novel design features, the engine did not initially show enough advantage to be convincingly superior to the well-proven engines already in use. One disappointing feature was fuel consumption because high speed produces high friction, resulting in less than desired fuel efficiency.

"Moreover the first commercial application of the engine was in the extremely arduous duty of agricultural crop spraying which was not conducive to a good demonstration of reliability. Agricultural aircraft work in conditions of high load, abrasive dust and high temperature which impose the severest possible conditions on an aircraft engine.

"Very much on the plus side was the first new device for dealing with torsional crankshaft vibration I'd seen in my 32 years in engine design work. The Hydra-Torque VTC system was an excellent mechanism."

Had the engine gone through the normal refinements in detail, as extended operating experience was gained, there is no doubt the market would have responded positively. It is one of the paradoxes of new products that when they are no longer available their merit seems more appreciated.

As the largest producer of engines for general aviation use, Teledyne Continental Motors was always happy to help publicize the record-setting performance of planes using its air-cooled piston engines.

Planes in the News

Powered by two 435 hp fuel-injected GTSIO-520F engines, a pressurized Rockwell Commander flown by James L. Badgett and Hal Fishman attained a record 35,450 feet altitude, topping by 2642 feet the previous business aircraft mark held by West Germany.

A different kind of recognition came from Lufthansa German Airlines and Southern California's PSA commuter airline. Under a unique agreement, PSA trained future Lufthansa pilots. The training aircraft? Continental-powered Beechcraft — nine G33 Bonanzas and six B55 Barons.

In a similar airline pilot training program, Beech Bonanza and Baron aircraft were used in Civil Aviation College of Japan under a government-sponsored program.

Making news in the executive/air taxi field was delivery of ten Continental-powered twin-engine Cessna Model 402 Businessliners to Taxi Aereo Marilia (TAM) of Sao Paulo, Brazil. The sale was not unique but typical of the expanding foreign market for American aircraft.

To its fleet of Cessna aircraft, the Bolivian Air Force added eight Skywagon 185s and two Turbo Centurions — all Continental-powered. "The Turbo Centurions," said Major Luis Rivero, "will be based at 13,340 foot La Paz, due to their ability to operate efficiently from the highest commercial airport in the world."

Top management of the Aircraft Products Division changed hands in June 1974 when Donald G. Bigler was named President, replacing Gene Lewis, Vice-President, as chief executive. Bigler had been President of Teledyne Neosho, formerly a unit of CAE. He had joined the CAE jet engine company after extensive industry experience including manufacturing and engineering responsibilities related to aerospace engines for Aerojet-General.

Because of the high capital investment and seven year time lag required to develop and market entirely new built-for-the-job industrial engines, TCM's Industrial Products Division entered into marketing agreements with two major European engine makers, Renault Moteurs of France and Rheinstahl-Hanomag of West Germany.

When an engine is no longer available, its merit is more appreciated.

Cessna Aircraft

First three of ten new Cessna Model 402 Businessliners which TAM airline will operate throughout Brazil

Continental-powered fleet of Bonanza and Baron Beechcraft were operated by San Diego-based PSA in training transport pilots for Lufthansa German Airline

Power Reporter

Industrial Products Division

Under these agreements, the company added 12 new 4-cylinder gasoline engines in the 10 to 86 hp range, marketed in the U.S. and Canada under the "R" series designation. Three "H" series Hanomag diesels of 59, 81 and 124 hp were also offered.

Industrial Products continued the product revaluation begun by Ryan and discontinued unprofitable engine models, including five in the '400' series and four models in the '600' series. Retained for continued manufacture and sales were the F, Y and Z engines in the '400' series and the F-600 model.

A "Marathon" engine project based on F series industrial models was undertaken looking toward development of power plants capable of 10,000 hours of maintenance-free operation. Technical innovations included a vapor-cooling system to maintain constant engine temperature, a completely encased air cleaner, and a revolutionary ignition system.

Developed in connection with Clark Equipment Company, builders of Continental-equipped lift trucks, the Marathon project did not result in production engines as agreement was not reached with Clark over a debated three-year exclusive use contract.

In 1968, the Market Street industrial engine complex was manufacturing 13 different series of engines. By 1972 they were down to five and by 1974 to just three engine series. Ray Phillips' group had eliminated unprofitable accounts and products, dropping all which accounted for less than a thousand units annually, but had retained a small but profitable product mix.

Although never confirmed, one report circulating at Market Street was that consideration was being given to disposing of the Industrial Products Division. Dr. Singleton, Teledyne Chairman, is said to have responded, "We don't buy companies to sell them. We buy them to run them."

Ford Motor Company attempted to take over the gasoline engine business for forklift trucks and Hercules Motor Company made a run at the engine market for welding equipment. But Continental did not lose a single customer during this highly competitive era.

Under U.S. Air Force sponsorship, Teledyne CAE in 1970 initiated development of an advanced gas generator, the basic core of all gas turbine engines, to which other components are added to make a complete turbojet, turbofan or turboshaft engine.

Teledyne CAE

A three-year U.S. Navy development contract culminated with pilot production and qualification of a CAE low-cost, expendable turbojet engine. It was used to power "Harpoon," the Navy's answer to anti-ship missiles such as the Russian "Styx" with which Egyptian patrol boats sunk the Israeli destroyer Elath in October 1967.

Twelve inches in diameter and only 30 inches long, the 600-pound thrust Harpoon engine weighs less than a hundred pounds.

A longer-life version of the basic Harpoon engine was supplied for the Army's Variable Speed Training Target (VSTT). Because of its similarity to the expendable Harpoon engine, minimum modification and developmental testing was required.

CAE was selected as one of two competitors for a small turbofan engine for the Air Force Subsonic Cruise Armed Decoy (SCAD). This same engine was entered in the competition for competitive fly-off between two entrants in the Navy's Sea Launched Cruise Missile (SLCM) program. While the prime contractor with which CAE was teamed did not win the competition, CAE became the second source for the engine (Williams) which powered the winning entry.

A major milestone in the 62-year history of Wisconsin Motor of Milwaukee was reached in 1971, less than two years after it became a part of the Teledyne organization. The event was delivery of the 5,000,000th heavy-duty Wisconsin engine; in this case an 18 horsepower two-cylinder air-cooled model.

Teledyne Wisconsin Motor

Wisconsin's first air-cooled industrial engine — a single-cylinder model — was built in 1931. Forty years later the product line comprised 22 basic models of one-, two-

Power Reporter

F-series industrial engine powers six-row corn detassler designed by HOE Corporation. Continental gasoline engine provides power for both propulsion and the cutters

Teledyne Wisconsin Motor

ARTHUR A. ERLINGER

Manufacturing executive Erlinger replaced Phil Norton as Teledyne Wisconsin Motor President in 1969

Five millionth Wisconsin Motor was delivered in August 1971, 62 years after company founding and only 18 years after two millionth engine was built

and four-cylinder long-life engines ranging from 4.6 hp to 65.9 hp. Before 1931, only water-cooled engines were offered.

In addition to its manufacturing plant in Milwaukee and three in the suburb of West Allis, the company in 1971 operated production facilities in Australia, Argentina, Brazil, Colombia, Mexico and Turkey plus sales and service in 92 foreign countries.

Supplementing its line of Hirth engines from West Germany, including a low-silhouette 60 hp twin-engine for recreational vehicles, Wisconsin also entered into a 1971 agreement with Fuji Heavy Industries of Japan for manufacture to Wisconsin specifications of lower-horsepower "Robin" engines.

The arrangement with Fuji was entered into only after extensive design and performance testing of the compact, long-life Robin engines by Wisconsin engineers. First of the four-cycle air-cooled engines to be distributed by Wisconsin were single-cylinder 4.6 hp and 6.5 hp models.

Further strengthening its competitive position, arrangements were made with Motorenfabrik Hatz KG, also of West Germany, for rights to four-cycle air-cooled diesel engines ranging from 3 hp to 82 hp.

Besides long-established industrial and agricultural uses of Wisconsin engines, Art Erlinger pointed out that "recent import arrangements provide us with the industry's most complete line of engines for powering snowmobiles, all-terrain vehicles and hover craft.

"The most significant benefit of these engines is the availability of 'de-noised' single-cylinder diesels to comply with the trend to noise abatement."

This, then, is the record of the first seven and a half decades of Continental Motors and its affiliated companies

THE FIVE COMPANIES...

...in the '80s

Precisely eighty years ago — 1902 — Ross W. Judson built the first Continental engine.

Now the ninth decade opens with five companies carrying on the Continental Motors tradition.

Pages 206 to 230

Continental has been successful for 80 years because of the steady evolution of sound technical ideas; not because of some single revolutionary development. As Carl Bachle has pointed out, "New developments in engines have usually been but a rediscovery of old ideas in need of perfection.

"Alternatives to basic principles are awfully hard to find and inventions merely for the sake of being different have never been productive." [Cadillac's innovative 1981 model V-8-6-4 engine, for example, that downgrades 8-cylinder power to four cylinders to save fuel.]

The fundamental principles of internal combustion engines still apply. Pistons still go up and down within the cylinder. The connecting rod is still the link which gives rotary motion to the crankshaft, spinning up the engine's driving force to turn wheels or propeller.

Through the evolutionary years, refinements in fuel injection, gearing and supercharging have enhanced basic design precepts to give us the modern gasoline and diesel engines.

The gas turbine has also gone through similar evolution since the early 1930's work of Sir Frank Whittle in England, Hans von Ohain in Germany, and Josef Szydlowski on compressor design in France.

Management techniques, too, have been refined and modernized. At Continental Motors, a mature but tired management was succeeded by younger, more aggressive talent from Ryan Aeronautical Company. A few years later that pioneer aircraft firm and its Continental subisidary became part of multi-company Teledyne, Inc.

Ryan, and then Teledyne, brought to Continental Motors not so much by way of advanced technology; rather they supplied a great deal of know-how and experience in modern, forward-looking management systems and financial concepts.

Current challenges to industry center around national economic conditions brought on primarily by a half-century of living beyond our means, requiring deficit financing in which government spending has consistently exceeded income.

These challenges must be faced by today's managers in each of the five Continental Motors units, and also in the broader national and international economic spheres.

It's been an interesting eight decades. Many more interesting years lie ahead for Continental and its people.

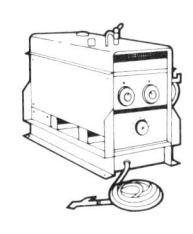

TCM Industrial Products Division

In many ways, Americans have priced themselves out of some markets for industrial products. The inroads that have been made by Asian and European products — automobiles and electronics, for example — is universally recognized.

One way to meet the problem of keeping American products competitive was advanced by Ramon J. Phillips, President of Teledyne Continental Motors Industrial Products Division.

"When it comes to designing entirely new engines," Phillips explained, "it is often more cost-efficient to contract for such services than to maintain a large, permanent, in-house engineering organization.

"Today our engineers are primarily applications engineers. That is, they take the various engines we manufacture or distribute and tailor them to the specific application desired by the original equipment manufacturers with whom we do business.

"The firm that we selected to do new design work was Ricardo Engineering of England with whom Continental already had a consulting agreement. Sir Harry Ricardo's firm was established in 1927 and has a long, successful record in internal combustion engine technology.

"Ricardo consults for many American companies and designs, develops, builds prototype engines, tests and evaluates them for customers all over the world.

"In this case, we wanted to be able to offer new overhead-valve engines to replace the L-head family Continental had been building for so many years. And in so doing we wanted to go to metric engines as this would make it possible for Teledyne to tap world-wide markets not otherwise open to us."

RAMON J. PHILLIPS

Ray Phillips was among the first Ryan executives to migrate east to assist in the modernization of Continental Motors. His first assignment as Personnel and Industrial Relations Director at Muskegon paralleled his career experience at Ryan. Soon Phillips' responsibilities with Continental and Teledyne were broadened into general business management. He became Vice-President of the Industrial Products Division in 1972 and was named its President in 1974.

Photos TCM/IPD except as noted

Richard Stauss

Modern-day Muskegon, Michigan, with new shopping mall in left foreground, TCM's refurbished Industrial Products Division at right in old Market Street plant location. Gone from the scene are Occidental Hotel, Lakey Foundry and other old structures, replaced by new office building, mall and parkway.

One of Continental's widely-used industrial engines was the model Z-145, available in both gasoline and diesel configurations. Thousands of the gasoline version were built for use in Massey-Ferguson farm tractors.

Phillips continued, "We had Ricardo evaluate this engine to see if we could bring it up from 145 cubic inch displacement to 164 cid. Then we gave Ricardo a contract to design modern, metric, overhead valve engines using the latest technology."

Designating the new models as "Litrengines," the first to be introduced — in 1980 — was the TM2.7 four-cylinder 2.7 litre displacement (164 cu. in.) metric gasoline/LPG in-line engine developing 70 horsepower. Available a year later was its diesel counterpart, the TMD2.7, which develops 66 horsepower. All Litrengines are water-cooled.

When the entire Litrengine line is complete it will consist of eight engines in two-, three-, four-, and six-cylinder gasoline/LPG and diesel configurations. The six-cylinder 4.0 litre engines range up to the 95 horsepower supercharged model.

Over 80 percent of the parts between the gasoline/LPG and diesel engines are common, making them the only interchangeable gasoline-diesel engines in the world. They are extremely fuel-efficient, operate at a very low noise level, and are the first all-metric engines built in the U.S. for industrial applications.

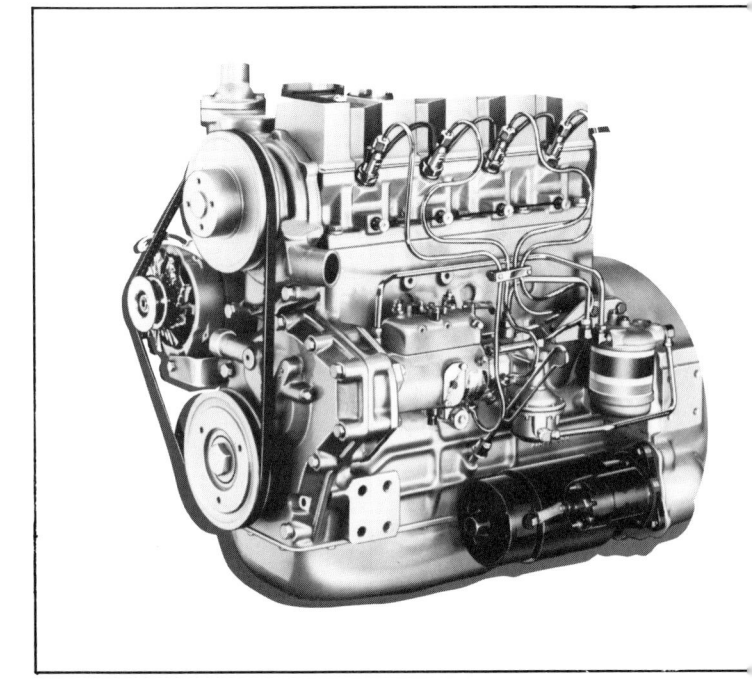

Photo Art Studio

Eight new all-metric gasoline and diesel engines are being introduced by Industrial Products Division. This is the 66 hp four-cylinder TMD2.7 diesel Litrengine

While the Litrengines were in development, Industrial Products introduced a new two-cylinder 56 cid gasoline engine based on its own widely used Y112 four-cylinder model. Developing 17-25 horsepower, the new "Tomcat" TC56 engine was designed for the commercial turfgrass market — mowing equipment for golf courses and for park maintenance.

There are, of course, many other industrial applications for Tomcat engines — welders, generators, construction equipment — where quiet, dependable power is needed in a small, rugged package.

The inherently quiet liquid-cooled design makes it easier to meet stringent restrictions on noise pollution, and allows the engine to operate in high ambient temperatures without overheating.

Industrial Products continues the volume manufacture of a number of its long-established L-head water-cooled gasoline and diesel engines, ranging from 15 to 85 horsepower.

Used in portable engine-driven welders, material handling trucks, front-end loaders, agricultural equipment and in construction and off-highway machinery, these engines include the popular four-cylinder Y112 (37 hp) and F163 (58.5 hp) models. Also, the six-cylinder F227 (78.5 hp) and F245 (80.5 hp) engines.

Hyster Lift Truck powered by Continental six-cylinder F-245 gasoline engine tackles a tall assignment

New Litrengine Model TMD2.7 diesel provides power for Allis-Chalmers fork lift truck

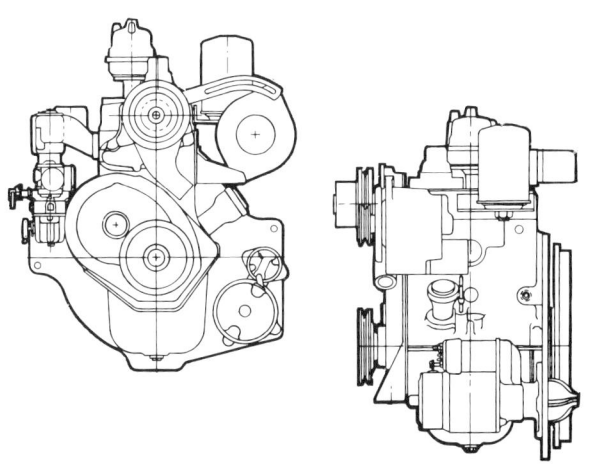

Industrial Products' new Tomcat engine, line-drawing above, is power source for Excel's Hustler Mower

Above: Development testing of TMD Litrengine on dynamometer stand. Left: Blocks, pistons and connecting rods for F-227 engines on powered assembly line

Toro mowing equipment for golf course and park grass maintenance is powered by Renault engine imported for Continental customers

In addition to the Litrengine, another solution to the problem of overseas competition is for American companies to contract with foreign manufacturers to build products designed to meet the needs of the domestic customers they usually serve.

The Industrial Products Division did just that in the early '70s when arranging for distribution in the U.S. and Canada of industrial engines built by Renault Moteurs of Billancourt, France. This added importantly to Teledyne Continental Motors' line of gasoline power plants tailored precisely to customer needs.

(As noted in the opening chapter, Ross W. Judson, founder of Continental Motors was greatly influenced, when he started in 1902, by the advanced design of the French Renault engines.)

Four Renault-built engines are presently offered in the 27 to 49 horsepower range. All are four-stroke, in-line, high-performance overhead valve gasoline engines.

It was the early 1920s when salesman Louis J. Kanitz directed Continental's attention to the potential market for industrial and agricultural engines to somewhat replace the declining sales of Continental automotive engines as the 'big three' automakers began producing their own motors.

For the past six decades Continental engineers have been working to take the drudgery out of manual labor while constantly up-grading the efficiency of industrial engines which work under heavy load in adverse conditions of dust, temperature and vibration.

Unlike automotive engines which operate at high RPM, those in industrial usage require high torque at low engine speeds. Their long stroke pistons extract more energy from fuel and provide improved exhaust emission. To operate efficiently under heavy service requirements, industrial engines are designed and built more sturdily than ordinary engines.

Design innovations which have greatly improved efficiency include twin-ignition systems with spark plugs that do not fire simultaneously, accurate solid-state electronic timing set at the factory for the life of the engine, new fuel induction systems, and a low-emission system which does not require add-on pollution control devices such as catalytic converters.

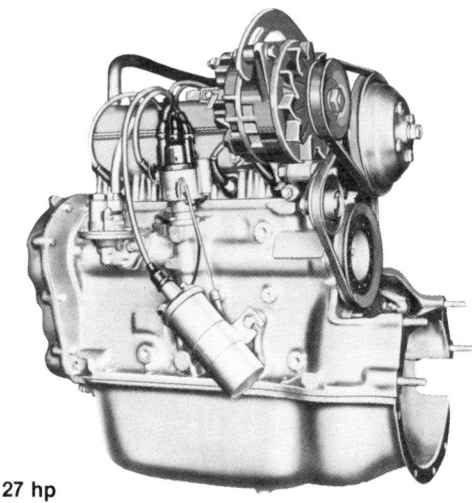

R839-46 four-cylinder 27 hp industrial engine built in France for Continental

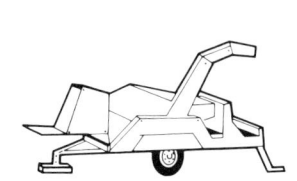

TCM Aircraft Products Division

Three years after Charles A. Lindbergh electrified the world with his New York to Paris flight—and gave the fledgling aviation industry its greatest impetus — Continental Motors introduced its first horizontally-opposed aircraft engine. (Earlier, Continental's seven-cylinder radial aircraft engine had been in production.)

In the 52 years since development of the 38 hp four-cylinder model A-40 air-cooled engine, the flat horizontally-opposed piston configuration pioneered by Continental has proven ideal for the general aviation market.

Today, in an energy-conscious world, the operational advantages and fuel efficiency offered by general aviation aircraft are becoming better understood.

Little more than one percent of the 14,000 airports in the United States handle 97 percent of all airline traffic. For the person who must travel often between low-traffic cities, a single- or twin-engine business aircraft is the answer to his needs. Available to him are 13,600 airports not served by scheduled airlines.

The typical single-engine business plane offered by Beech or Cessna provides 72 seat-miles of travel per gallon of fuel consumed. By contrast a four-jet Boeing 747 averages 40 seat-miles per gallon. Even light twins use fuel more efficiently than the latest Douglas DC-10.

Companies in Fortune Magazine's listing of leading corporations are large users of scheduled airline service; yet over half operate their own business aircraft, many of them in the up-to-ten-passenger category.

Teledyne Continental engines for such aircraft come in both naturally aspirated and turbocharged models — some with direct propeller drive and others with geared drive.

1927

1983

Although research and development continues on new concepts, the Aircraft Products Division's principal output is of seven basic six-cylinder models of 360, 470 and 520 cubic inch displacement, the fundamental configurations of which have been in production for some years.

"Further development of these air-cooled, opposed engines," says Donald G. Bigler, President, "has — in recent years — been evolutionary, not revolutionary. The past decade has been a period of consolidation and improvement of product rather than new design.

"The technical gains of the '70s in terms of turbocharging, fuel-injection, improved carburetion and gearing for these engines are still valid. Power output has been increased and there has been a dramatic improvement in durability, but these have been improvements to an already proven line of aircraft engines."

In this age of gas turbines, the piston engine has retained its place in the 100 to 500 horsepower range for general aviation aircraft. Continental's primary line of engines currently in production ranges from the fuel-injected model IO-360 (210 hp) to the carbureted O-470 (240 hp) and the top-of-the-line geared, turbocharged, fuel-injected GTSIO-520, which develops 435 hp.

Photos TCM/APD except as noted

Lightweight six-cylinder air-cooled horizontally-opposed TSIO-520 is Teledyne Continental's newest engine for general aviation market

Cessna Aircraft

Cessna's six-place twin-engine Crusader has Continental's new Lightweight TSIO-520 turbocharged power plants

Newest model is the Lightweight TSIO-520 fuel-efficient engine. It is the result of a major redesign program aimed at reducing overall weight of this turbocharged, fuel injected engine by ten percent while maintaining its structural integrity.

Where possible, lighter weight materials are used as in the case of substitution of magnesium for aluminum in certain areas. Additionally, many components have been redesigned to reduce weight. Examples: A new camshaft lighter yet 15% stiffer than its predecessor; and redesign of cylinder head fins for weight reduction and optimum cooling.

The Lightweight 520 engines give Cessna's new six-place Crusader executive plane the highest time-between-overhaul (TBO) of any turbocharged twin-engine aircraft. It also has the best fuel efficiency of any competitive twin, yet delivers a cruising speed of 207 mph and a range of over 950 statute miles.

For improved directional control, the three-bladed propellers of the Crusader are counter-rotating, both turning inboard. The Crusader's 250 hp engines are backed by Teledyne Continental's 'Gold Medallion' warranty which provides six months (or 240 hours) comprehensive coverage, plus pro-rated coverage all the way to TBO.

Redesigned (left) and original (right) components of new Lightweight 520 Series engine. New design resulted in 10% weight reduction

212

DONALD G. BIGLER

Continental's services to customers and its "Gold Medallion" warranty policy get the personal attention of Don Bigler, President, who came to the Aircraft Products Division from Teledyne CAE

Charles Beck

The National Aeronautics and Space Administration (NASA) has sponsored a number of design studies for future engine concepts suitable for use in general aviation in the next decade. Based on such studies the agency would develop new technology which would be made available to the aerospace industry.

NASA's interest and that of the military services, as well as the General Aviation Manufacturers Association (GAMA), is to encourage continued research which will lead to more efficient aircraft.

Among studies being done are those in fuel management, improvements in engine and propeller efficiency, reduction in aerodynamic drag, composite materials and structures, high altitude flight in pressurized cabins with advanced turbochargers, jet and diesel fuels, and turbine technology applicable to lighter aircraft.

In several of these areas, Continental has done research and development work for the military services and NASA, as well as cooperative programs with aircraft manufacturers and other engine companies.

Continental was selected for and completed a NASA-funded technology study contract for advanced spark-ignition engines. For the U.S. Army the company developed and demonstrated a mini two-cylinder 20 hp engine suitable for low-cost RPVs (remotely piloted vehicles).

A high-performance, four-cylinder, low fuel consumption aircraft engine has been developed jointly with Rolls-Royce of England for the 150 to 220 horsepower range. The '368' series engine was installed in a Cessna 172 and test flown for evaluation purposes by both Continental and the aircraft manufacturer. Due to recent economic conditions, the engine has not yet been placed in production.

Engineers routinely monitor design improvements of engine components

Skilled mechanics, in teams of two, work at one of five assembly lines

213

While Cessna and Beech are the largest users of Continental engines — as they have been for four decades — deliveries continue to be made to other manufacturers for their latest lines of general aviation business and personal planes. Among the latest: Piper's Turbo Arrow single- and Seneca twin-engine models, and the Mooney Turbo.

A major service provided owners of Continental-powered aircraft is the company's exclusive Gold Medallion engine rebuild program. Factory rebuilt engines, available through the Continental distributor organization, are given 'Zero Time' log books, carry the same warranty as original engines and cost about one-third less than new engines.

One further advantage of rebuilt engines is that the owner need not wait while his old engine is being overhauled. Rather, he merely turns it in on a rebuilt engine which has been upgraded to the latest specifications and given a new serial number.

Continental also produces a considerable quantity of service parts and rebuilt assemblies such as fuel injection systems. In fact, Continental's own fuel injection system has proven to be an excellent selling feature since competitors must buy similar equipment from outside suppliers.

Manufacturing and engineering work is centered in headquarters facilities located at a former Air Force base leased from the City of Mobile, Alabama. (See photo Page 190).

These six aircraft are all powered by 520 series engines

Beechcraft Baron 58TC

Beechcraft Bonanza V35B

Piper Turbo Arrow

1983 Piper Seneca III

Cessna Golden Eagle

Cessna Pressurized Centurion

TCM General Products Division

Soon after Ryan-trained Harold Rouse took over as President of the General Products Division in 1972, he looked for new opportunities for the company to expand into equipment lines associated with the end-product military vehicles powered by Continental engines.

"It was also obvious to me," Rouse explained, "that there was a market for engine modernization packages for upgrading older, battle-tested armor to standards comparable with the performance of new, more modern battle tanks. Such modernization could be the most cost-effective method of quickly increasing the combat effectiveness of ground forces.

"Too, we began looking at ways to offer 'mated' power packages of engine and transmission; then expanded into suspension systems, gun stabilization and laser fire control systems for tanks, and to complete military vehicles.

"There was also, we felt, a real need on the part of friendly foreign governments to modernize their armor at minimum cost through engine retrofit programs.

"The power range of our 1790 series engines has since been increased from 750 hp to 950 hp as part of this program. With variable compression ratio (VCR) pistons, the same cubic inch displacement engine was then brought up to 1200 hp. And, a new 1360 cubic inch displacement VCR engine was developed to produce 1500 hp."

The success of General Products under Rouse's leadership is evident by the rapid growth of this Division which, by 1975, became the largest manufacturing company in Teledyne. This number one position in sales volume has been maintained since that time.

Photos TCM/GPD except as noted

HAROLD W. ROUSE
President of the General Products Division, Rouse was a Ryan factory superintendent before taking on major assignments at Continental Motors virtually as a group vice-president for manufacturing operations at all plant cities. In civic affairs he played a key role in redevelopment of downtown Muskegon, Michigan

Super M60 offered by Continental as a cost-effective way to modernize U.S. Army's main battle tanks

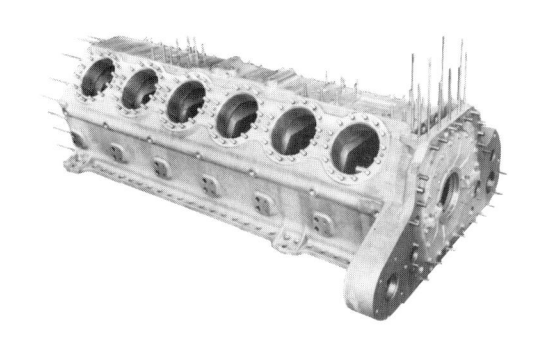

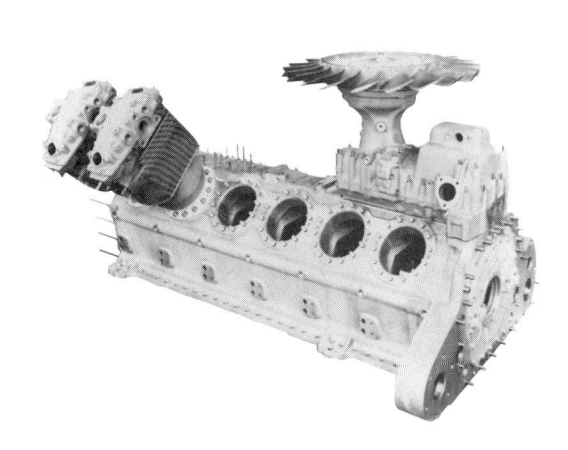

Continental engineering has long featured a continuing product improvement program to upgrade performance and reliability. One result has been the RISE engine developed as part of the U.S. Army 'Reliability Improvement of Selected Equipment' program. Many operational tanks have been converted to the RISE engine configuration.

Over 32,000 AVDS-1790 series engines have been produced, principally for the M60 tank and for converting M47, M48 and Centurion tanks from gasoline to diesel power. Including earlier, gasoline-powered engines, the 1790 power plants have set a record for continuous production 1947 to 1983 — over 35 years.

The -2AC and -2CC versions are special models configured for use in British Centurion tanks, widely used in the Middle East, when replacing the original power plants with Continental air-cooled diesels.

Several other variations of the basic AVDS-1790 series engines are available, including the -5A model up-rated to 900 hp, and the -7A model rated at 950 hp. The -8A version, now in development, will be rated at 1050 hp.

Typical of the 'mated' power packages offered is the combined Continental engine/Allison transmission unit which was specified in the General Motors proposal for the low silhouette XM-1 tank. The XM-1 competition between General Motors/Continental and Chrysler/Lycoming was expected to provide a new Main Battle Tank as successor to the Continental AVDS-equipped M60 tank.

A similar engine/transmission power package is the high-performance 1200 hp AVCR-1790-1A variable compression ratio diesel mated to the Renk hydromechanical transmission. Like others, this AVCR model for tanks up to 62 tons is air-cooled, turbosupercharged and fuel injected.

This new series of diesel tank engines feature modular construction which permits use of weight-saving aluminum components. The engines' 90-degree upright Vee-design facilitates engine cooling, and easy access for routine maintenance. Cylinders are arranged in two banks of six individually mounted Unisteel cylinder assemblies.

In the early '70s it was apparent to observers of military strategy that the day of gasoline engines — especially those liquid-cooled — in combat tanks was waning. By modernizing battle-tested tracked vehicles with new air-cooled diesel power plants, their service life could be extended at minimum cost.

So that Continental could offer a more complete modernization package, Harold Rouse led the company program to acquire rights to a hydropneumatic suspension system (HSS) from the National Water Lift Company of Kalamazoo, Michigan. "We also bought a tank gun and turret stabilization system from them," explained Rouse.

"Additionally we took over the prime contract with the U.S. Government for the High Mobility/Agility Vehicle (HIMAG) laboratory-type tank.

"In 1973, the U.S. Government permitted us to disband the capability to build the old-line gasoline tank engines which took up a lot of space and equipment in the Getty Street plant so we could concentrate on the diesel retrofit programs.

"The initial modernization effort was centered in the Middle East. We re-fitted hundreds of British Centurion Mark Series battle tanks — as well as U.S.-built M47s and M48s — with diesel engines and with new transmission suspension, fire control, and weapon stabilization systems. It was a huge undertaking.

"To expedite the modernization program, we bought our own Centurion tank and had it shipped to our Getty Street plant in Muskegon so as to integrate the design features and modifications."

Modernization kits have also been provided for the affordable upgrading of U.S. M60, M47 and M48 tanks. French AMX-30 battle tanks were also upgraded in performance while at the same time provided with more satisfactory cooling for desert operations.

Perhaps unique among industrial executives, Rouse concentrates much of his effort in direct personal contact with government officials abroad, traveling extensively all over the world. As a result the tank modernization program has been adopted by the military services of Pakistan, Jordan, Greece, South Korea, Israel, Switzerland, Norway, Sweden, Taiwan, Turkey, and Spain to mention some of the friendly foreign customers involved.

For production models of the Israeli 'Merkava' tank, which performed so well in the Lebanese conflict against Russian T-72 tanks operated by the Syrian Army, Teledyne Continental developed the 900 hp AVDS-5A engine.

The Middle East has been a particularly sensitive area in which to do business but, as Rouse says, "I won't tell any customer about what's going on in another country." Thus, he has retained friendships on both ideological sides throughout that strife-ridden area.

So far Rouse has had no personal difficulty in his travels, except for customs formalities, although he was in Thailand when the government was overthrown and in South Korea the night President Park was assassinated.

Continental's own Centurion tank arrives at Muskegon for modernization and testing on company's test track adjacent to Getty Street plant, below

HIMAG test vehicle equipped with hydropneumatic suspension 'barrels' over rough terrain without slowing down

217

Richard Stanier

Many British Centurion tanks in the Middle East have been re-equipped with Continental diesel engines in modernization program

The hydropneumatic suspension system is a vast improvement over the conventional torsion bar system. Its 'soft-ride' feature greatly increases crew comfort, vehicle mobility and firing accuracy.

HSS-equipped tanks can now operate over rough terrain without having to reduce speed. Tracked vehicles are able to operate at twice the speed they could attain with only torsional bar suspension. The system was extensively tested on the MBT-70, HIMAG and M60 tanks before being produced for wider usage.

The new, faster-acting weapon/turret stabilization system provides HSS-equipped tanks with the ability to fire on the move while going cross-country, with a 90% hit probability at 1000 meters.

Another important technical development under U.S. Army contract has been in turbosupercharging. A new variable-area turbocharger developed by General Products for high output diesel engines provides increased torque at low speeds, reduced exhaust emissions, lower fuel consumption and maximum efficiency at any point during the range of engine speeds.

'Kneeling' feature of hydropneumatic suspension system is demonstrated on MBT-70 tank during test program

A simple engine induction air dust detector system has also been developed to warn of any air cleaner filter failure or of dust leaks into the induction system. It is expected to prevent many expensive engine overhauls.

To provide tanks and other tracked or wheeled vehicles with improved protection against enemy weapons, Teledyne Continental Motors offers new applique armor packages using high-hardness steel plates coupled with ceramic modules.

One design incorporating many of Continental's newest techniques for tracked vehicles is the Republic of Korea Indigenous Tank (ROKIT). The design, for which a full-scale mock-up was built and air-lifted to Korea, incorporates features which would permit easy local production by that government.

Continental's laboratory test tank during slide-slope testing at Army's Aberdeen Proving Grounds

Looking to development of tomorrow's fighting vehicles, the U.S. Army has contracted with the General Products Division for the sophisticated High Mobility/Agility Vehicle (HIMAG), a 44-ton full-tracked laboratory test bed capable of speeds to 65 mph.

The original Army contract for HIMAG was awarded to National Water Lift (NWL) in 1976 and included development of new gun turret stabilization and chassis suspension systems. Continental was subcontractor for the AVCR-1360 variable compression ratio 1500 hp air-cooled diesel engine mated to an Allison transmission.

Having worked with NWL during the design phase to assure proper engine integration and cooling, Continental was familiar with the entire project, which was novated to the Teledyne unit after General Products Division acquired NWL's gun stabilization and suspension systems.

HIMAG features the latest equipments (all previously mentioned) plus a lightweight, rigid hull; variable height suspension; and automatic target tracking. Lightweight and extremely compact, the engine features 12 replaceable cylinder assemblies set in a 120-degree Vee for reduction of overall engine silhouette.

Test data generated by the HIMAG vehicle was transmitted by telemetry to an instrumentation van for analysis. Program testing has been completed and the final report submitted.

Although General Motors/Continental had lost the XM-1 Abrams main battle tank contract to the Chrysler/Avco-Lycoming team, the General Products Division continued to push the conviction that its air-cooled diesel engine better suited the Army's needs for the tank to replace the proven M60.

The Chrysler version faced many challenges because it was powered with a gas turbine engine, something new for tracked vehicles which must face the rigors of difficult environment on the battlefield. The principal problems were that it was a new design and that ingestion of dust created serious operational conditions for a turbine engine.

Originally it was understood the Army had recommended the General Motors version with Continental's newest AVCR diesel engine, the 1500 hp 1360 cid model. But when the recommendation went to the Defense Department it was reversed and, after a delay of some months, the award made to Chrysler.

It was reported the Army testified that the turbine engine was ready for production with no further development cost. However, right after the decision was made in favor of Chrysler, additional development money for the turbine engine was authorized.

In addition to reliability and durability problems with the new turbine, initial tests indicated, because of high fuel consumption, that combat range of the tank was less than required and that costs were nearly double what had been expected.

To protect against a worst-scenario situation, the Army, at Congressional insistence, has contracted with Continental for a back-up diesel engine program for the XM-1, covering the installation of new AVCR-1360 air-cooled engines in two M-1 tanks for planned extensive testing in 1983.

Proven in HIMAG, new variable compression ratio AVCR-1360 diesel engine delivers 1500 hp and is ready for tests in newest M-1 tank

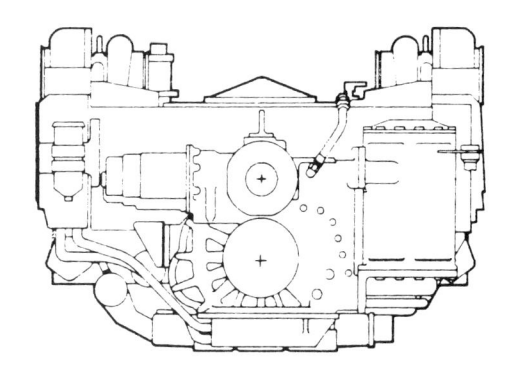

Powered by AVCR-1360 engine, High Mobility/Agility Vehicle (HIMAG) 'makes the grade' in Army slope tests

Up-graded version of main battle tank, Continental's Super M60 incorporates new 1200 hp variable compression ratio diesel engine, hydropneumatic suspension, weapon/turret stabilization and other advanced features

While waiting for the dust to settle over the XM-1 controversy, Rouse and his people got busy on a project to modernize the M60 series main battle tanks, all of which had been powered with Continental diesel engines. The result was the Super M60.

This up-graded version of the basic M60 achieves its high performance by substitution of the 1200 hp AVCR 1790 engine with Renk transmission for the standard 750 hp AVDS model of similar displacement mated to an Allison transmission.

Apart from the pistons and related parts, most components of the two engines are interchangeable. Also, the power pack can be easily removed from tank hulls and replaced by the new self-contained Continental/Renk package with minimum modification.

The 60 percent increase in available power plus installation of hydropneumatic suspension, a new, lower silhouette commander's cupola and greatly increased armor protection brings the Super M60 up to latest standards, extending their service life at a fraction of the cost of procuring new tanks.

The Super M60's automotive performance (maximum speed 45 mph vs. 30 mph for the standard M60) is similar to that of the XM-1 and Leopard 2 tanks and is made possible both by increased power and improved suspension. For this reason the Super M60 can accept the increased weight of better armor protection without adverse effect on its performance.

The add-on armor and side skirts provide added protection and a new ballistic shape. Cross-country over rough terrain the Super M60 can average 24 mph while the standard M60 can average only 9 mph.

AVCR-1790 diesel engine for Super M60 tank provides 1200 hp vs. 750 hp in standard tank version

Engineering drawing of Super M60 tank shows details of modernization program including armor applique

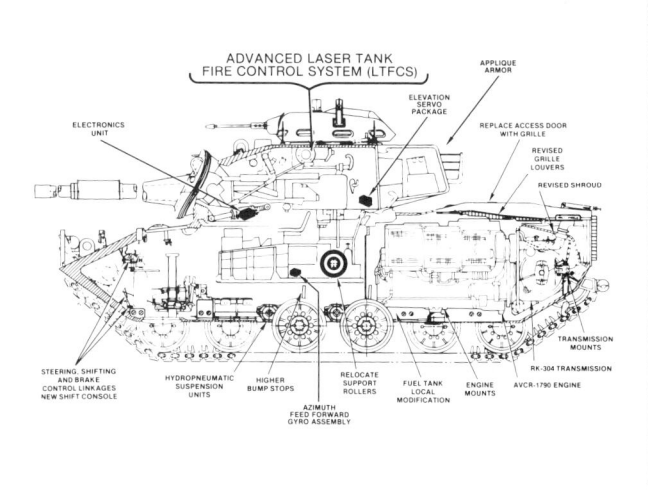

Since 1977, the General Products Division has been developing a complete multi-purpose military vehicle to meet the Army's latest needs in the ¼-ton to 1½-ton range.

For the Combat Support Vehicle competition, Teledyne Continental Motors responded with its rear-engine "Cheetah," two versions of which were built and tested.

In 1979 the Cheetah vehicle was superseded by a front-engine design for the Army High Mobility Multipurpose Wheeled Vehicle (HMMWV) which will replace the M151 Jeep, the Gama Goat and related equipment. This new version, dubbed, "Humvee," has been through three generations of further development and extensive service testing in the U.S. and abroad.

During 1982, TCM General Products delivered eleven HMMWV prototype vehicles to the Army for tests which were successfully concluded in October. In November the company submitted its proposal for delivery of 55,000 vehicles over a five year period.

Because first production vehicles must be delivered eight months after award of contract to the competition winner, the company has a new plant under construction at Seneca, South Carolina, for "Humvee" production. Located on an 80-acre site, the new facility will have 240,000 sq. ft. of manufacturing area and 34,000 sq. ft. office space.

From the very beginning Teledyne Continental engineers designed its low, lean, tiger-tough vehicle to meet all operational requirements and multi-mission capability.

As the General Products Division does not build diesel engines in the lower horsepower range, it selected as the fuel-efficient power plant for its HMMWV entry International Harvester's 170 hp 420

Head-on view of Continental's low-silhouette entry in Army multipurpose vehicle competition

cubic inch displacement V-8 diesel engine mated to a General Motors turbo-hydromatic transmission.

The 4 x 4 tactical vehicle has a low silhouette, high ground clearance, and four-wheel independent suspension. It is three feet shorter and over a ton lighter than the Gama Goat. Cargo bed height is six inches lower than in conventional designs. It is easily maintained in the field and has excellent durability and survivability on the modern battlefield. Highway speeds can exceed 70 mph.

HMMWV is easily air-transportable to forward positions. Its multi-purpose design and available kits assure versatility as cargo carrier, squad car, ambulance, communications van and weapons carrier. It has the same chassis and body components for all mission roles.

This is "Humvee," the High Mobility Multipurpose Wheeled Vehicle (HMMWV) developed by the General Products Division to meet Army needs in the ¼-ton to 1½-ton range

Richard Stauss

Teledyne Continental's new factory now under construction at Seneca, South Carolina, for "Humvee" production

Versatility of basic "Humvee" vehicle is illustrated by weapons carrier, above, and ambulance, below. Same chassis is used for all kits

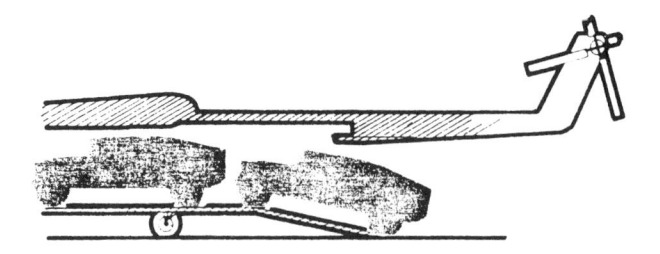

Air-transportable HMMWV can be air-lifted by helicopter, left, or two vehicles can be carried inside as sketched above. C-5A Galaxy transport can carry 15 vehicles in its cargo hold

Several new research and development projects, both company-sponsored and contract-funded, are on the drawing boards, including those for various government agencies.

Looking to future requirements of general aviation, NASA has funded a number of studies, one of which is for design of a diesel aircraft engine, which is attractive because of its lower operating and life cycle costs.

Continental has received a new three-year contract covering further development and testing of diesel aircraft engine components. This is part of the study which has been under way for four years. Current thinking centers around a two-cycle low-compression configuration. Lower operating pressures, with air preheated by a turbine compressor, eliminate the need for the heavy structures associated with diesel power.

General Products also has a fully-developed eight-cylinder water-cooled diesel which can be rated from 650 to 850 horsepower. It is suitable for many commercial and military applications.

A new Army contract is for a configuration and design study of an advanced diesel propulsion system for the 1990-1995 time frame. This would be the basis for engines to be used in the next generation of tanks to be produced at the turn of the new century.

General Products also has two Advanced Vehicle Concept Design contracts with the U.S. Army, one for the Mobile Protected Gun (MPG) system and the second for the Future Close Combat Vehicle System (FCCVS). The FCCVS concept will be the next generation of tanks for the 2000-2010 time period.

Concept design and prototype work is beginning on the Medium Multi-purpose Wheeled Vehicle (MMWV), which will be a new 2½-ton truck for the U.S. Army for the late 1980s.

The next generation Hydropneumatic Suspension System for main battle tanks of all weights is under development, which incorporates an in-arm system which reduces the overall width and weight of the unit, and will be substantially less expensive.

Turbine Engines

Teledyne CAE

JAMES L. MURRAY
President

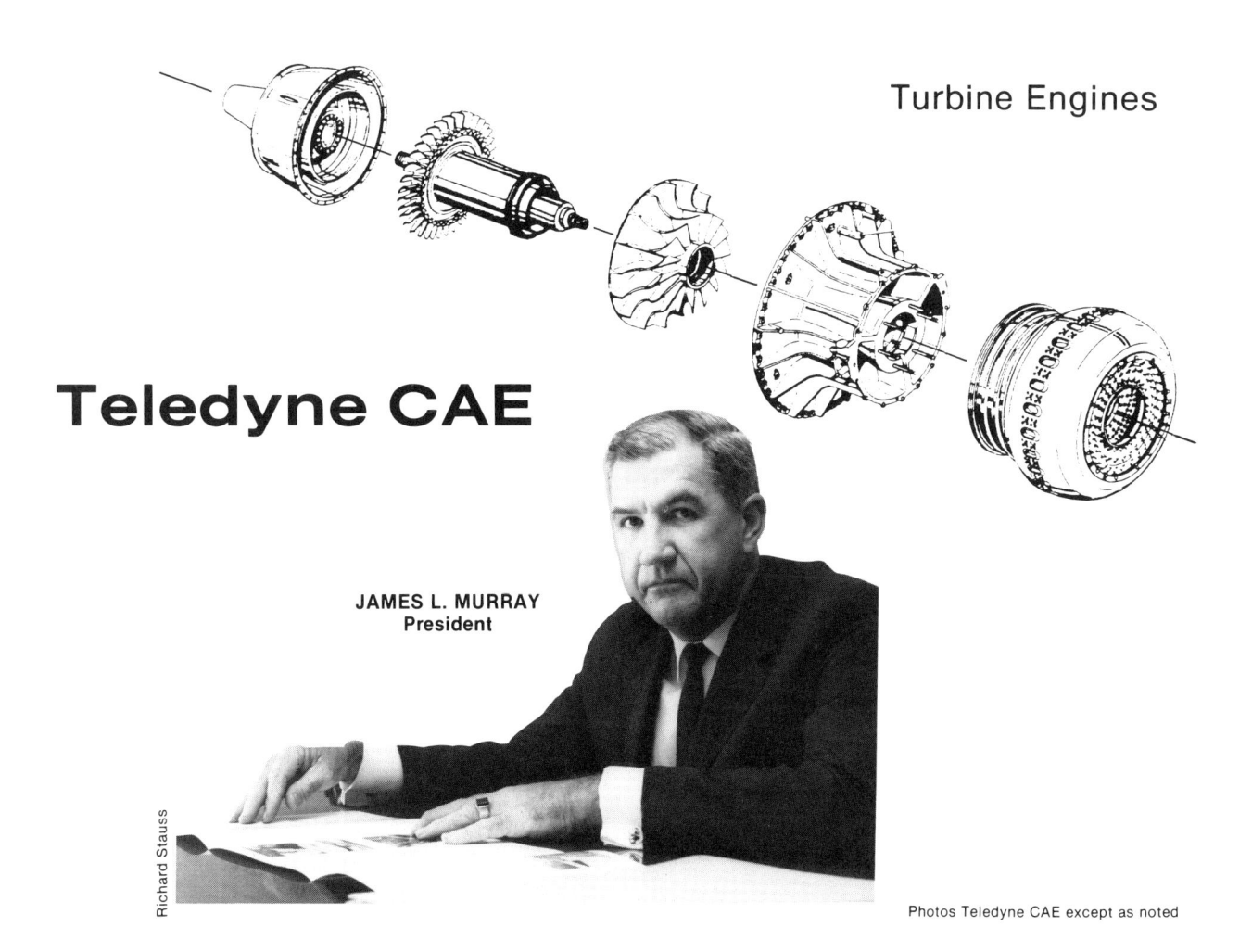

Photos Teledyne CAE except as noted

In the early '50s, Continental set as one of its jet age objectives a major role in the expanding gas turbine business. At that time, the large jet engine field had been pre-empted by such industrial giants as Pratt & Whitney and General Electric.

Additionally, as engineer Carl Bachle explained, "small turbine development was lagging because in that era it was considered they would pay too serious a penalty on fuel consumption."

Despite these apparent obstacles, Continental Aviation and Engineering staked out and achieved its own special place in small turbine engine development and production. More than three decades of experience have made it possible for the company to solve the unique design and manufacturing problems associated with small turbines.

Today, Teledyne CAE turbines are a primary source of power for target drones, RPVs, stand-off and cruise missiles and trainer aircraft.

The company is headed by James L. Murray, President, former Air Force officer and aviation industry executive, who joined the Continental organization in 1966 soon after it became a subsidiary of Ryan Aeronautical Company. When Ryan was in turn acquired in 1969 by Teledyne, Inc., Murray was named President of the Continental Aviation and Engineering Division which was renamed Teledyne CAE later that year.

CAE's headquarters, engineering labs and manufacturing plant occupy 375,000 square feet in a government-owned facility, located on 79 acres in Toledo, Ohio.

In the not too distant past, enemy warships were sunk primarily by guns, torpedos and more recently by air-launched bombs. However, modern tactics now require "smart" weapons with stand-off, over-the-horizon capability as complementary to the longer-established anti-ship systems.

Under Navy sponsorship such a weapon, capable of defending over 8,000 square miles of ocean against hostile ships, was developed by McDonnell Douglas Astronautics. The resulting "Harpoon" stand-off missile is 12½ feet long, has aerodynamic surfaces, and is powered in sustained low-level sub-sonic flight by a Teledyne CAE J402-CA-400 turbojet engine.

Just 12 inches in diameter, the expendable one-shot turbojet engine weighs only 100 pounds yet develops a maximum thrust of 660 pounds.

The small diameter of the engine — scaled down from the J69 series — was a primary requirement so the Harpoon can be launched from a torpedo tube as well as by surface ship launchers, and from aircraft pylons. Another consideration was minimum cost with maximum reliability since the engine would be used only once on a mission of perhaps no more than 15 minutes duration.

When Harpoon is launched from ships or submarines, initial power is supplied by a booster rocket after which the CAE turbojet sustains flight in a low-level trajectory to the target. Air launches, of course, do not require the initial booster equipment.

Another major requirement for the Harpoon and its turbojet engine was that the missile must be capable of

223

being stored 'on-the-shelf' for up to five years fully-fueled and ready to go on a moment's notice, the same as required of artillery shells.

Teledyne CAE was awarded the engine development contract in 1971 and began production in 1976. By the end of 1982, more than 2600 engines had been delivered.

The Navy's ship and submarine launched Harpoon is designated RGM-84A; the air-launched vehicle, AGM-84A. In addition to operation by U.S. Navy ship, aircraft and submarine units, Harpoon missiles are reported to be deployed with 13 Allied nations.

Recent anti-ship exercises with the Atlantic Fleet were very successful. Of six versatile Harpoon missiles launched — from two aircraft, two surface ships and a submarine — all scored direct hits on the target. Nearly 200 test missions have been operated with more than 95% reliability.

Designed to 'get its hooks' into enemy ships, the Navy's Harpoon missile is launched from submarine (lower right) and sustained in aerodynamic flight (upper left) by Teledyne CAE's volume-produced 660-lb. thrust turbojet engine

General Dynamics

Medium Range Air-to-Surface Missile (MRASM) under development for Air Force and Navy is powered by derivative of CAE engine used in Harpoon anti-ship missile

The success of the Harpoon engine design has resulted in a number of variants suitable for other programs which require a low-cost turbojet in the 600 to 1,200 pound thrust range. A prototype, which retains the 12-inch engine diameter, has been tested in a Teledyne CAE-sponsored project. This up-rated model provides about the same thrust as CAE engines (installed in trainer aircraft) which are twice the diameter and weigh three times as much.

The CA-401 derivative of the J402 series engine is designed to power the Medium Range Air-to-Surface Missile (MRASM) which is now in the development stage under Air Force and Navy sponsorhip.

A tactical weapon with conventional warhead, MRASM is needed for use against fixed ground targets. Because it will be air-launched, the engine must have high altitude start capability.

A recent $8.7 million contract awarded Teledyne CAE is for a 26-month program calling for full scale engineering development, testing and qualification of its MRASM engine. The missile is a derivative of the Tomahawk cruise missile built by General Dynamics.

Most widely used variant of the Harpoon engine is the CA-700 version of the J402 series of turbojets. Teledyne CAE entered this longer-life engine in the 1972 competition for the turbojet to power the Army's new Variable Speed Training Target (VSTT).

The engine competition was won by CAE and the MQM-107 vehicle production contract was awarded to Beech Aircraft. Since production began in 1975, CAE had delivered more than 450 engines for the Beech "Streaker" training target.

The VSTT Streaker is a cost-effective system which can realistically simulate an enemy threat, making it possible to test a wide variety of missile and gun systems fired against the target.

The swept-wing, 16-foot-long MQM-107 target drone is ground launched. Its 640 pound thrust variable speed CAE turbojet engine is pod-mounted below the fuselage.

In addition to its use by the U.S. Army for personnel training and weapons evaluation tasks, the Beech VSTT is used for similar missions by friendly foreign governments.

A growth version of the CA-700 engine will produce 730 pounds thrust, making it suitable for additional uses including higher performance targets and larger missiles. It has been successfully tested in the VSTT target vehicle.

Army's MQM-107 Variable Speed Training Target (VSTT) is sustained in flight after launching by rocket by CAE turbojet engine seen beneath fuselage

Beech Aircraft

225

Techniques demonstrated operationally by Ryan remotely-piloted reconnaissance drones, and more recently by Harpoon short-range tactical missiles [both systems CAE-powered], are now being further refined in long-range cruise missiles.

The U.S. is building three versions of strategic cruise missiles which fly at high subsonic speed and at very low altitude where they are virtually undetectable by enemy radar until too late to be intercepted. Like Harpoon, they can be either air, surface or submarine launched.

Teledyne CAE was selected in 1978 as the licensee to co-produce the Williams International F107 turbofan engine which powers the Air Force ALCM (air launched cruise missile built by Boeing), and the Navy's sea-launched SLCM and Air Force ground launched GLCM (both built by General Dynamics).

Comparable in size, weight and thrust to CAE's Harpoon turbojet, the F107 turbofan engine is a foot wide and a yard long.

An important factor that led to the selection of Teledyne CAE as co-producer was its long experience in developing and manufacturing jet engines of similar size. Such second-source procurement is essential to the Department of Defense leader/follower approach for key high-volume production programs.

Teledyne CAE has a $77.7 million contract covering 16 months of cruise missile production engine deliveries, the first of which were made in October, 1982, two months ahead of schedule.

Long-range cruise missiles, advanced versions of earlier remotely-piloted vehicles (RPVs), are powered by Williams F107 turbofan engines, lower left, for which Teledyne CAE has been selected as co-producer. Above, the Boeing air-launched cruise missile for the Air Force. Below, the General Dynamics sea-launched Tomahawk for the Navy

Continental Aviation and Engineering (CAE) was formed in 1940 as the engine research and development arm of the parent Continental Motors Corporation.

While Teledyne CAE and its predecessor organizations have produced thousands of turbine engines, research and development of advanced concepts continues to be given major emphasis by management.

Two current programs, both structured to demonstrate advanced technologies required for propulsion systems for cruise missiles, advanced trainers and fighter aircraft in the next decade, are of particular significance.

The Advanced Turbine Engine Gas Generator (ATEGG) program is an on-going project of the Air Force Propulsion Laboratory in which CAE has been a major participant for 14 years. New contracts totaling $9.4 million extend the work for another two years.

The Air Force and Navy together sponsor the Joint Technology Demonstrator Engine (JTDE) program which CAE has conducted for the past seven years. Generally, the hardware technology demonstrated is applicable, within acceptable scaling limits on size, to engines in the range of 1,500 to 7,500 pounds thrust.

One derivative of the ATEGG/JTDE was the 1,500 pound thrust Model 444 Turbofan, proposed as the power plant for Cessna's entry in the Next Generation Trainer (NGT) competition.

While the Cessna twin-engine primary trainer entry did not win the competition, CAE's engine has demonstrated that it can deliver twice as many training hours on the same amount of fuel as the current J69 model.

Yet another development is CAE's patented "Excentric" three-spool (compressor and turbine) turbofan engine. This new concept, requiring exotic materials technology, should ultimately provide a pressure ratio of 30-to-1, compared with a range of approximately 15-to-1 for existing cruise missile engines.

Complex casting for CAE turbojet engine used in Navy's Harpoon missile. Same casting is used in engines for VSTT and MRASM vehicles

4000 hp compressor test facility enables prototype compressors to be evaluated under simulated engine operation

Instrumented test cells at Teledyne CAE permit full-scale engine operation from sea level to high altitude conditions ABOVE

BELOW **Teledyne CAE headquarters, laboratories and production facilities are in government-owned facility in Toledo, Ohio**

Teledyne Wisconsin Motor

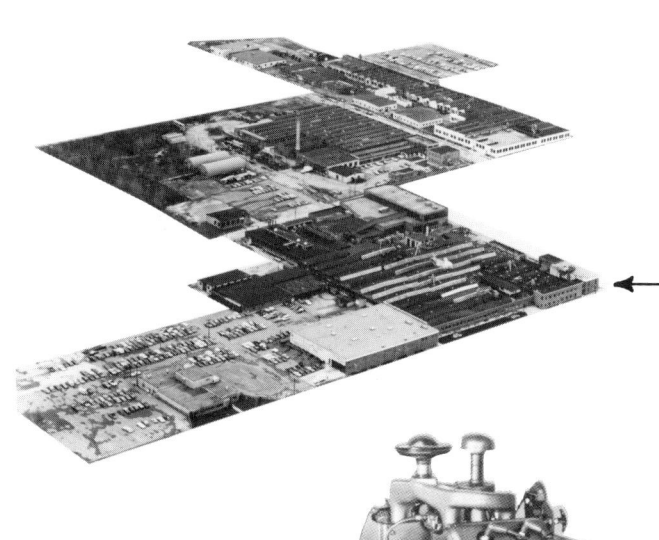

Administrative headquarters of Teledyne Wisconsin Motor and its three-plant factory at West Allis (Milwaukee), Wisconsin

Genack Studio

30 horsepower VH4D L-head Wisconsin engine (right) gives Midmark Power's trencher (below) outstanding performance

Photos Teledyne Wisconsin Motor except as noted

Teledyne Wisconsin Motor has been building internal combustion engines for industry, construction and agriculture for seven decades. Since the early 1930s it has been the largest producer in its field, with the most complete line of air-cooled heavy-duty engines.

Today Teledyne Wisconsin offers three product lines covering a power range of from 3 to 65 horsepower. Two series of engines—gasoline and diesel models—are built abroad for Wisconsin.

In its long-established line of Wisconsin-designed, Wisconsin-built engines, the Milwaukee firm produces 16 cast iron, gasoline engines of one- and two-cylinder configuration, plus the 65.9 horsepower four-cylinder V-465D valve-in-head engine.

In demanding *construction* industry applications, Wisconsin engines are used to power trenchers, front-end loaders, concrete saws, tampers, and mortar and cement mixers. In the *industrial* field, they are used in material handling equipment, welders, generators, air compressors, sweepers and railroad maintenance. The *agricultural* market employs these engines in balers, sprayers, and specialty farm and gardening machinery. Other applications include golf course and park maintenance, and power for a wide variety of recreational vehicles.

Newest addition to the Wisconsin family is the 30 hp air-cooled model W2-1235 which is suitable for operation on gasoline, liquified petroleum gas, natural gas, and other fuels on special order.

The engine is a 90-degree V-type configuration of L-head design. Continuous 30 hp operation at 3600 rpm engine speed is permissible.

A variety of special stub shaft extensions for pulleys, pumps, generators and other devices is available. The engine has excellent cold-weather starting and is designed for durability with extended maintenance intervals.

The wide choice of fuels and its rugged design make this new 30 hp engine well suited to a broad range of applications: powering construction machinery; oil well pumping units; material and personnel handling and lifting devices; welding and generating sets; pumps; professional turf maintenance equipment and industrial equipment.

Wisconsin also offers a complete line of LPG engines covering the full horsepower range of its standard models. These LPG engines operate on liquified petroleum gas (Propane/Butane) and burn cleaner with less carbon monoxide gas emission. Safety is increased; time between engine overhaul is increased; and better fuel economy is achieved.

For installation either at the factory or by distributors, complete LPG conversion kits are available for most heavy-duty Wisconsin gasoline engines.

LEE A. DELANEY
Chairman, Teledyne Wisconsin Motor

Unique 48-inch diamond blade saw by Target Products is powered by 65 hp Wisconsin V-465D gasoline engine

Newest engine designed and built by Wisconsin is energy-efficient W2-1235 (above) now in volume production (below)

In the 3.5 to 27 horsepower range, Wisconsin has 14 additional models — single-, two-, and V-type four-cylinder — which operate on kerosene or fuel oil of 35 octane or better. These engines are expressly designed for these fuels; they are not merely modified.

Famed for its service-after-sale, Wisconsin has a world-wide network of more than 1800 distributors and service centers in over 90 countries.

In 1971, Teledyne Wisconsin entered into an agreement with Fuji Heavy Industries, Ltd. to have the Japanese industrial firm build a series of compact four-cycle gasoline engines for the American market.

First of the "more power per dollar" engines to be produced were 4.6 hp and 6.5 hp "Robin" models. Since introduction of these engines, which feature aluminum construction, the line has been expanded to nine single-cylinder models of 3.5 hp to 11.0 hp. In addition, there is also available the 16.8 hp opposed twin EY21W engine which is virtually vibration-free.

Wisconsin Robin engines are designed for quick, easy power-mating with a wide variety of American machines and equipment in the industrial, agricultural and recreational fields.

Since their introduction, the Robin engines have established an excellent reputation with users for quality and durability, and are a good 'fit' with the company's line of cast iron engines. Service and warranty features are the same as for all Wisconsin engines.

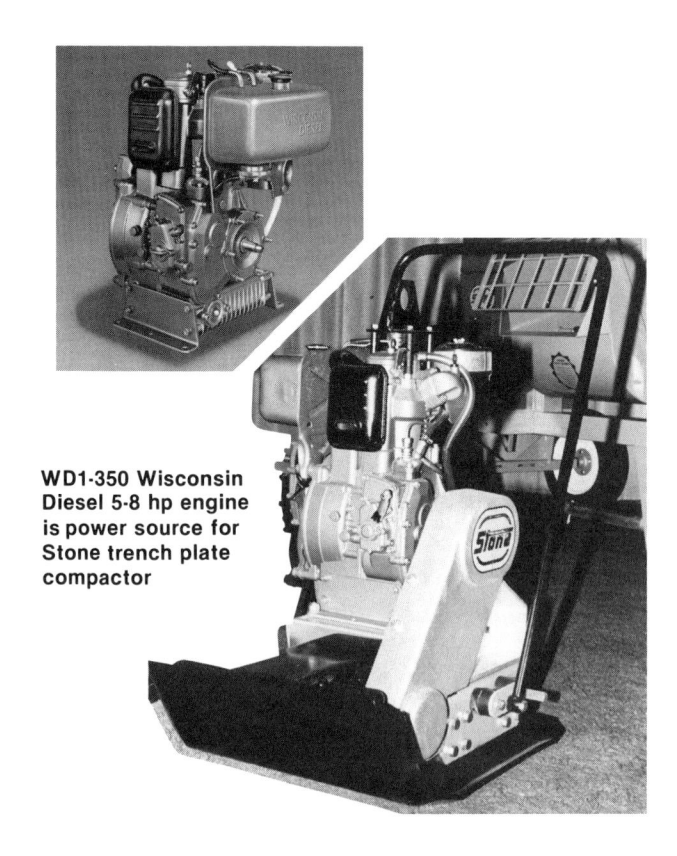

Robin long-life EY18-3W engine, built for Wisconsin by Fuji, powers Yazoo Master Mower

WD1-350 Wisconsin Diesel 5-8 hp engine is power source for Stone trench plate compactor

With world-wide concern for energy conservation, original equipment manufacturers have taken a new look at the economy and efficiency of the diesel engine.

To meet the needs of its customers for a practical power plant alternative, Teledyne Wisconsin in 1978 contracted with Ducati Meccanica S.p.A of Bologna, Italy for marketing and manufacturing rights in the Americas to six single-cylinder and two twin-cylinder diesel engines of from 7 to 21 horsepower.

Suitable for a wide range of heavy-duty industrial and commercial applications, these Wisconsin Diesel engines offer state-of-the-art design including cast iron cylinders and forged crankshafts for long life and reliability, as well as die cast aluminum crankcases for improved power-to-weight ratios and traditional diesel fuel economy.

Teledyne Wisconsin's Milwaukee facilities include three plant buildings and an administrative headquarters. There is over 600,000 square feet of factory and office space at the 40-acre plant site in West Allis.

Management is headed by Lee A. Delaney, Chairman, who joined the company as President in January 1981. Fred Rathert, a former Ryan executive who joined Wisconsin in 1969 was recently advanced from Executive Vice-President to President. (See photo Page 191).

Delaney came to Teledyne Wisconsin Motor from the presidency of Murphy Diesel Co., also of Milwaukee, with which he was first affiliated in 1970. Since graduation from the University of Wisconsin with a degree in mechanical engineering, he has been active in the diesel and gasoline engine industry. He was associated with Allis Chalmers as a research and development engineer, and prior to joining Murphy Diesel was director of marketing for the Waukesha Engine Division.

Acknowledgements

This book is dedicated to Carl Bachle, Jim Ferry and Art Wild, the three veteran Continental Motors executives who "reached back in time to bring to life the pre-Ryan/Teledyne days."

There were, of course, many others whose help was essential in accurately re-creating the eight decades of history of this pioneer engine builder.

Special mention should be made of the contributions of Ralph Dunwoodie, the automotive authority who provided much of the research material covering Continental's first quarter century when automobile assembly companies were the primary market for Continental Red Seal engines.

The contributions of Charles Betts of The Society of Automotive Historians are also acknowledged with thanks. Another automotive researcher, Percy R. Gilbert, furnished valuable material on the automobiles manufactured in the early '30s by Continental Motors. The National Automotive History Collection of the Detroit Public Library was also an invaluable resource and we acknowledge the fine cooperation of Margaret Butzu.

Win Henderson, Ryan Aeronautical Company's on-site advance man when the San Diego firm began its investment in Continental Motors, made available his extremely helpful, comprehensive reports from Muskegon and Detroit, covering the 1962-66 time period.

Extensive but concise background information on Ordnance Corps policy related to tracked vehicles, including the history of American tank procurement during World War II — all of which was based on his own service experience — was provided by Lieut. Gen. Jean E. Engler.

Richard P. Hunnicutt, tank historian and author of definitive histories on the subject, provided useful background material and photos and generously checked portions of the manuscript dealing with tracked military vehicles.

Within the Continental organization, former associates of the author were extremely helpful. Dick Stauss, former Ryan photographer and now graphic arts supervisor at the General Products Division, delved into company records at Muskegon and also provided many of the illustrations.

Don Fairchilds, who went east to head up Continental marketing support activites, provided helpful material on the Aircraft Products Division, which he served as director of communications. The Continental and CAE annual reports compiled by Don Bennett, former Ryan public relations man, during the period when Ryan was acquiring control of CMC, were a valuable, authoritative reference. Angela Rossi, a long-time Continental executive secretary, made available reference copies of still earlier reports to shareholders.

An associate of many years, Paul E. Wilcox, formerly Ryan's chief pilot, recalled his experience as test pilot flying early Continental-powered airplanes at a time when his great-uncle was president of the engine manufacturing company.

Many former Ryan executives who took on new responsibilities at Continental provided useful in-depth interviews. These included Harold Rouse, Ray Phillips, and Fred Rathert, each currently President of a Teledyne Continental Motors company. Similar help came from group executive J. L. (Rich) Richardson.

In addition to chief executives of each of the five companies currently in the Continental group, their staff people have been most helpful. (They know who they are, and my special thanks to each.)

Any author who doesn't mention by name each of the secretaries, typists, researchers, proof-readers, artists and photographers who assist in the production of every book is in trouble — as I now am. I must, however, mention Kim Harris of TechGraphics, who perhaps spent more hours on this effort than the others combined and was solely responsible for the preparation of all 'camera ready' art for the printers.

Acknowledgement, too, should be made of the cooperation extended by the co-publishers, Benjamin F. Schemmer, Editor of Armed Forces Journal, and Ernest J. Gentle, President of Aero Publishers.

Lastly, of course, it was Bill Rutherford, an associate at Ryan Aeronautical Company since 1951 and now Vice President of Teledyne, Inc., who suggested that this history be compiled. I am most appreciative that he suggested I undertake the task. Apprehensive at first, my interest and enthusiasm grew as the many facets of the jig-saw puzzle of re-creating nearly forgotten events fell into place.

William Wagner

December 16, 1982

INDEX

Page numbers in **bold** type
indicate major references

A

Aerojet-General, 202
Aeronca planes, 97, 98, 131, 132, 159
Agricultural (and recreational) Engines (*see Engines*)
Air Launched Cruise Missile (ALCM), 226
Aircraft Engines (*see Engines*)
Aircraft Products Division, 199-202, **211-214**
Aircraft War Production Council, 170
Allis Chalmers, 28
Allison engines and transmission, 74, 101, 102, 199, 216, 218, 220
Altman, Peter, 122, 132, 147, 152
American Locomotive Works, 135
American Motors, 171, 185
American Stock Exchange, 193
Ames Motor Car Company, 13
Angell, Lieut. Chester, 80
Angell, William R.
    (1917-1929) v, 23, 27-29, 31, 33, **35-43**
    (1930-1939) 51, 54, 55, 57, **63-75**, 78-80
    (1940-1945) 85, 86
Angell, William R., Jr. (Bob), 57, 80
Annual Reports (*see Financial Affairs*)
Apperson Brothers, viii
Argyll Single-Sleeve-Valve Engines, **33-36, 39-41**, 52, 53, **64-66**, 70, 72, 73
Armour Institute of Technology, 5
Army Corps of Engineers, 152, 185
Army Ordnance Corps (*see Ordnance Corps*)
Autocar Company (*truck maker*), 7, 12
Autocar Equipment Company, v, 6-8, 38
Automobile Engines (*see Engines*)
Automobile Parts Manufacturers Assn., 142
Automotive Industries (*magazine*), 37, 38
Avco, 155 (*also see Lycoming*)

B

Bachle, Carl F., vi, 35, 38, 40-42, 46
    (1930-39) 51, 53, 54, 57, 65-67, 73, **76-78**, 80, 81
    (1940-45) **86-89**, 91, 93, 95, 101, 106
    (1946-53) **125-127, 138, 140**, 142
    (1954-61) 151, 154, **159-162**, 163, 164
    (1962-82) 180, 181, 182, 184, 193, 206, 223, 232
Badgett, James L., 202
Baker, Berkley, 196
Ballweg, Raymond A., Jr., 194, 197
Banks, Air Commodore Rodwell, 138
Barnes, Maj. Gen. Gladeon M., 124, 125
Barris, Bill, 131
Bath Ironworks, 51
Bayard, Earl, 93
Beall, F. F., 59
Beech Aircraft planes, 120-122, 131, 136, 150, 154, 155, 158, 159, 185, 186, 200-202, 211, 214, 225
Beech, Walter, 43
Bell helicopters, 154, 188
Bennett, Don, 175, 232

Benz, Carl, ix
Bera, Mrs. Frances, 186
Betts, Charles, 232
Bergen, John J., 67, 69
Bigler, Donald G., 202, **211, 213**
Bitely, Michigan, 75
Blackburne, Edward F., 198
Boeing Airplane Co., 96, 154, 211, 226
Boling, Capt. M. L., 159
Bolthouse, A. B., 119
Bolton, L. D., 10
Bonbright, Howard, 23
Bonbright, William P. & Co., 23
Booth, Percy N., 70, 71
Bowman, Capt. James E., 150
Bowman, R. E., 93
Boynge, Russell, 40
Brandana, Bert, 118
Brennand, Bill, 131
Briggs & Stratton Engines, 172
British Aeronautical Research Committee, 40
British Air Ministry, 102, 138
British Continental Motors, Ltd., 33, 64
British Internal Combustion Engine Research Institute (BICERI), 181, 182
British Purchasing Commission, 87, 88
Brookley Air Force Base, 190
Buhl Aircraft, 54, 55
Burkhart, Bill, 159
Burt-McCollum Sleeve Valve Patents, 33, 40
Burt, Peter, 33
Business Week Magazine, 117, 142
Butzu, Margaret, 232

C

Campbell, Colin, 39
Campbell, Wyant and Cannon foundry, 191
Capitalization of Corporations (*see Financial Affairs*)
Capocy, Tom, 124
Carroll, Wes, 97, 131
Carter, President Jimmy, 177
Cass, Lawrence, 93
Cassidy, James, 94
Caterpillar Tractor Co., 161, 181, 191
Centurion (British) Tanks, 216-218
Cessna Aircraft planes, 121, 132, 136, 139, 140, 150, 154, 155, 157, 159, 171, 185, 186, 189, 194, 201, 202, **211-214**, 227
Cessna, Clyde, 43
Chamberlain, P. C., 153
Chapman, Henry B., 96
Checker Cabs and Cars, 31, 124, 157, 178
Chevrolet Motor Co., 85, 88
Chris-Craft Boats, 171
Christmas, Brig. Gen. John K., 76, 77, 90, 124, 125
Chrysler Motors, 36, 88, 90, 91, 124, 134, 135, 162, 199, 216, 219
Civilian Pilot Training Program, 96, 98

Clark Equipment Company, 203
Clark, Gen. Mark W., 98
Clark, Judge George M., 72, 75
Clowar, Mrs. Beda, 173
Colby, Col. Joseph M., 91, 125-127
Combat Cars, 76-78
Compression Ignition (Diesel) Engines (see *Engine Technology*)
Construction (and Industrial) Engines (see *Engines*)
Contex Ignition System, 136
Con-Tex Petroleum Corp., 107, 123

Continental Aviation & Engineering Corp.
  Formation of (1940) 86, 87
  Hyper liquid-cooled engine, 73, 74, 78, 86, 100, 101
  Production, Sales, Research, 102, 103, 106, 121, 122, 131, 137, 160, 169, 172, 176, 193, 194, 196
  Turbine engines, **138-141, 154-157,** 172, 188-190, 194, 203, **223-227**
  (also see Teledyne CAE)
Continental Cars (*1932-1934*) Beacon, Flyer and Ace, 58-63, 68, 72
Continental Clean Air, 75

Continental corporations (also see *Financial Affairs*)
Formation of—
  Continental Aeronautic Corp. *(1939)* 80
  Continental Aircraft Engine Co. *(1929)* 42, 45, 54, 63, 64
  Continental Auto Sales Corp. (1932) 64
  Continental Automobile Co. *(1932)* 59, 62, 64
  Continental Aviation & Engineering Corp. (CAE), 86
  Continental DeVaux Co. *(1932)* 58, 59
  Continental Divco Co. *(1932)* 63, 75
  Continental Gas & Oil Co., 64, 107
  Continental Motor Manufacturing Co. *(1905)* v, 7
  Continental Motors of Canada, Ltd. *(1955)* 153, 191
  Continental Motors Company *(1916)* 17
  Continental Motors Corporation *(1917)* 23
  Continental Motors, Ltd. (British) *(1926)* 33, 64
  Continental Realty Co., 23
  Continental Sales & Service Co., 118, 152, 153
  Continental Wisconsin Corp., 196
  Peninsular Motor Company, 28

Continental Motors Corporation
  Acquisition by Ryan Aeronautical Company, 160-173, 193
  Acquisition by Teledyne, Inc., 195-197
Continental Engine Company, 7
Convair aircraft, 154
Cook, John, 159
Cord, E. L., 40
Corporate Affairs (see *Financial Affairs*)
Cruise Missiles, 226
Cummins Engine Co., 172, 173
Curtis, Mrs. Cornelia O., 6, 16
Curtiss OX-5 Aircraft Engine, 54
Curtiss P-40 pursuit plane, 102
Curtiss-Wright 'Conqueror' Engine, 73
"Cushion-Power" diesel engines, 119, 151
Cwach, Jim, 63

D

Daimler, Gottlieb, ix
Daimler Motor Co., 33
Dallas, Texas, branch plant, 107, 118
Dean Witter & Co., 172, 195
Defense Plant Corp., 90, 91, 100, 102, 123
Delaney, Lee A., 229, 230
de Palma, Ralph, 110
Derr, Emory S., 98
De Sakhnoffsky, Count Alexis, 59
Desert Test Proving Ground, 90
Detroit Diesel engines, 109, 113
Detroit, Michigan, plant, 10, 11, 13, 14, 17
  Sale to Kaiser-Frazer, 137
Detroit Stock Exchange, 67, 68, 79
Detroit Tank Arsenal, 88, 90, 134, 135, 162
DeVaux Automobiles, 58-61, 63
DeVaux-Hall Motors Corp., 58, 62, 63, 85
DeVaux, Norman, 58, 62
Devers, Gen. Jacob L., 90, 125
Dewar, Michael, 87, 88
Diamond T Military Truck, 25
Dickson, A. C., 156
Diesel-Electric Bullet Train, 65
Diesel Engines (see *Engine Technology*)
Diesel fuel policy, 66, 90, 91, 160, 161
Diesel, Rudolf, 159
Directors and Officers (see *Financial Affairs*)
Divco (Detroit Industrial Vehicle Corp.), 63, 64, 68, 70, 75
Dividends, Sales, Profits (see *Financial Affairs*)
Dodge Automobiles, 26, 43, 51
Dominion Motors, Ltd., 58
Douglas Aircraft Company, 193, 211
Drone and Missile Engines (see *Engines*)
DuBois, Clint, 59
Ducati Meccanica of Italy, 230
Dunlap, Howard F., 174, 175, 180, 194
Dunwoodie, Ralph, 232
DuPont, Henry, 40
Durant, Cliff, 40-58
Durant Motors Corp., 28, 29, 36, 39, 58, 59, 85
Durant, William C., 9, 36, 37, 58
Duryea Brothers, viii

E

Erlinger, Arthur A., 111, 197, 198, 203, 204
Eberly, Bessie, 85
Edrington, John L., 93
Eisenhower, Gen. Dwight D., 97, 98
Employment levels, 137, 141
Emtor, Inc., 169, 173, 174
Engler, Jean, 196
Engler, Lt. Gen. Jean E., 76, 90, 91, 125, 134, 162, 232
Engstrom, Thura A. (Thor), 130, 160, 163, 176
Evans Products Corp., 80

ENGINES

ENGINE UTILIZATION

Aircraft Engines
Radial (and V-type), 34, **39-43, 52, 53,** 65, 73, 86, 90, 96, 100-103, 106, 107, 120, 121, 131, 137
Radial, in tanks, **76-78, 87-95,** 137, 163
Opposed, **54-57,** 73, 76, 78, 90, **96-98,** 107, 120, 121, 130-132, 136, **150,** 151, 158, 159, 164, 171, **185, 186,** 194, 200-202, **211-214**
Single-sleeve-valve, 34, 35, 39-41, 53, 73
Liquid-cooled (Hyper), **73, 74,** 78, 86, **100**
Diesel, 222
Turbine, **138-140, 154-157,** 188, 189
in Helicopters, 122, 131, 136, 137, 150, 151, 156, 188

Automotive (Transportation) Engines
(1902-1929) 5-18, **19,** 24-27, 29-36, 38, **43-47**
(1930-1945) 51, 63, 65-67, 74-78, 106, 107
for Continental Cars, **58-63**
(1946-1953) 120, 123, 124, 130, 132, 137, 141
(1954-1975) 151, 157, 158, 164, 172, 178, 186, 187, 194

Industrial, Construction, Agricultural Engines
(1902-1945) **28-32,** 35, 51, 52, 63, 66, 67, 74, 76, 78, **106-111**
(1946-1982) **119-121,** 130-133, 141, 147, 151, 157, 158, 164, 171, **186, 187,** 194, 203, **207-210, 228-230**

Marine Engines
(1902-1945) 5, 8, **32,** 34, 36, **66,** 74, 78, 98, 99, 107, 109, **112, 113**
(1946-1975) 119, 121, 130, 132, 133, 137, 141, 142, 153, 157, 164, 171, 172, 186, 187

Military Engines, Family of, 126-130

Military Truck Engines
24-26, 52, 98, 99, **126-129,** 137, 151, 152, **159, 160,** 164, 171, 172, **183-185,** 194, 198-200, **221,** 222

Military Standard Engines
151, 152, 171, 185, 190, 191

Missile and Drone Engines, 122, **138-140,** 154, 155, **188, 189,** 203, **223-227**

Tank and Tracked Vehicle Engines
Gasoline-powered, 25, **76-78, 87-95, 124-130, 134, 135,** 137, **148, 149, 161-163,** 183
Diesel-powered, **125, 161-163,** 171, **181-183,** 190, 194, 198-200, **215-220**

ENGINE TECHNOLOGY

Diesel (Compression-Ignition) Engines
52, **66,** 67, **81,** 107, 119, 120, 131, 135, 137, 138, 141, 151, **159, 160,** 172, **207-210,** 222, **228-230**
in tanks, **125, 161-163,** 171, **181-183,** 190, 194, 198-200, **215-220**

Fuel Injection, 57, 67, 135
for aircraft engines, **97, 150,** 200, 211, 212, 214
for tank engines, **148, 149,** 161

Geared Engines for aircraft, **150,** 200, 211

Multi-Fuel (Hypercycle) Engines
66, 67, 151, **159-160,** 171, 172, **183-185**

Supercharged (Turbo) Engines
126, 127, 150, 200, 211, 212, 218

Single-Sleeve-Valve Engines
33-36, 39-41, 52, 53, **64-66,** 70, 72, 73

Technical Notes, 18, 19, 32, 46, 47, 81, 138

Turbine (Jet) Engines
122, 131, **138-141, 154-157,** 172, 188-190, 194, 203, 223-227

Variable Compression Ratio (VCR)
181-183, 190, 200, **215-220**

F

Fairchild jet engine, 138, 140
Fairchilds, Don, 201, 232
Farm Lighting Division, 75, 76
Federal Republic of Germany, 183
Federal Securities Act, 68
Fenner & Beane brokerage firm, 86, 105
Ferry, James H., Sr.
(1902-1916) v, 6, 9, 16
(1917-1929) 23, 28
(1930-1939) 51, 70, 75, 78, 79
(1940-1945) 86, **89,** 105
Ferry, James H., Jr., v, vi, 6, 28, 72, 79, 80
(1940-1945) 85-87, 105
(1946-1953) **123,** 141
(1954-1961) 152
(1962-1982) 170, 173, 180, 181, 196, 232
Ferry, Mrs. Mary Shaw, 6, 79, 89

Financial Affairs

Annual Reports (Sales, Profits, Dividends)
(1902-1929) 8, **12, 16,** 23, **26,** 28, 32, **37, 38**
(1930-1945) 51, 52, 68, **106**
(1946-1961) 117, 121, 123, 130, 131, **140, 141,** 147, 154, 157
(1962-1975) 171, 176, 188, **194,** 195

Officers and Directors
(1902-1929) 6, 8, 16, 23, 27, 29, 32
(1930-1939) 51, 63, 70-72, 75, 79
(1946-1961) 118, 152
(1962-1975) 174, 175, 193-197

Stock of Continental Motors and Subsidiaries
(1902-1916) 6-8, 16, 17
(1917-1929) 23-25, 29, 32, 37, 38, 42, 45
(1930-1939) 52, 58, **67-73,** 75, 79
(1940-1945) 86, 87, 105-109
(1946-1953) 117, 121-123, 130, 141
(1962-1975) 169, 170, 176, 193, 195

"Firebee" target drone, (*see Ryan Firebee*)
First Wisconsin National Bank, 108, 111
Fisher, L. P., 40
Fishman, Hal, 202
Flader, Frederic, 138, 155
Flader jet engine, 138
Fokker, Anthony H.G., 34, 39
Forbes, B. C., 58-60, 72
Ford, Henry (and Ford Motor Co.), ix, 7, 9, 13, 36, 38, 43, 59, 76, 124, 135, 152, 156, 185, 203
Ford tank engines, 91, 92
Fornasero, Jim, 85
Four Wheel Drive Co., 110
Francis, Devon, 56

235

Frazer Automobiles, 120, 123, 124
Frazer, Joseph W., 120
Frederick, Walter A., 12, 13, 16, 33, 35, 42, 51, 64, 70, 72
French Air Ministry, 138
Frontenac Automobile, 59
Fuel Injection (*see Engine Technology*)
Fuji Motors of Japan, 158, 171, 204, 230

G

Garland, Texas, plant, 90-92, 102, 118, 123
Gas Turbine (Jet) Engines, (*see Engine Technology*)
Gates, John W., 5
Geared Engines (*see Engine Technology*)
Gebhart, Prof. G. F., 5
General "Aristocrat" Plane, 52
General Aviation Manufacturers Assn. (GAMA), 213
General Dynamics missiles, 225, 226
General Electric, 223
"General Grant" tank, 88, 90
"General Lee" tank, 88
General Motors, 36, 87, 91, 109, 113, 124, 135, 156, 171, 183, 199, 216, 219, 221
General Paint Corp., 172
General Products Division, 198-200, **215-222**
"General Stuart" tank, 88
Gentle, Ernest J., 232
Getty Street Plant, **100-104**, 106, 122, 130, 134, 149, 192
Gilbert, Percy R., 62, 232
Ginn, Earl C., 105, 119, 130, 163
Glascock Body Co., 85
Gluckman, Peter, 159
Godfrey, Arthur, 132
Goodman, B. Kenneth, 174, 175, 193
Gourlie, John C., 37, 38
Graham, Col. James H., 70, 71
Graham-Paige, 63, 120
"Grasshopper" Liaison Planes, 96-98
Gray, John S., 112
Gray Marine Motor Co., 36, 119, 121, 130
   Acquisition of, 109
   History of, 112, 113, 132, 133, 153, 157, 171-177, 186, 187, 193
Gray Motor Co., 112
Guiberson Diesel Engine Co., 66, 90, 91, 102

H

Hackley Union National Bank, 80
Hair, Arthur J., 174
Hall, Col. Elbert J., 58
Hall-Scott Motors Corp., 58
Hanomag Engines, 202, 203
Harinton, Guy J., 129, 130, 173
Harker & Co., 169, 172
"Harpoon" Anti-Ship Missile, 203, 223-227
Harris, Kim, 232
Hart, Mrs. Marion, 186
Hatz industrial engines, 204
Haugdahl, Sig, 111
Hauser, P. N., 141
Havens, R. C. (Bud), 56

Hayes, Bill, 93
Hayes Body Corp., 58, 60, 62, 63
Hayes-Hunt Body Co., 85
Haynes, Elwood G., viii
Health Air Junior Air Conditioner, 75
Hedges, Edison, 133
Heinkel, Dr. Ernst, 138
"Hellcat" M18 tank destroyer, 92-94
Heller, Walter E. & Company, 86
Hendershot, Ralph, 68
Henderson, Winthrop C., 172-180, 191, 193, 197, 232
Herbert, Walter J., 174, 176, 177
Hercules Motor Company, 173, 184, 200, 203
Heron, Samuel D., 57, 73, 74, 102
Herriot, John, 158
Heth, Jim, 159
Higgins, Asst. Secy, Frank H., 162-164
High Mobility/Agility Vehicle (HIMAG), 216, 217
High Mobility Multipurpose Wheeled Vehicle (HMMWV), 221, 222
Hirth Motorren engines, 191, 204
Hollowell, D. H. (Dee), 121, 158, 163, 173, 179, 186
Hoover, President Herbert, 72
Hudson Motor Car Company, 10, 26
Hughes Aircraft, 195
Hughes, Ted, 177
Hulbert, Edward A., 106, 126, 127, 181
Hunnicutt, Richard P., 163, 232
Hunt, J. S.
Hupp, George, 7
Hydropneumatic Suspension System, 216-218, 220, 222
Hydra-Torque engine, 201, 202
Hydro Check Shock Absorber Corp., 43
'Hyper' Aircraft Engine, 73, 74, 78, 86, 87, 100, 101
Hypercycle multi-fuel engine, 151, 159, 160, 183-185

I

Industrial (and Construction) Engines (*see Engines*)
Industrial Products Division, 199, 202, 203, **207-210**
Insley, Robert, 42, 52, 53, 57, 63, 73, 76, 93, 106, 181
Internal Revenue Service, 27
International Harvester Co., 64, 98, 99, 221
Investments in Shares (*see Financial Affairs*)

J

Jackson, Robert C., 169-175, 180, 181, 191, 193, 195-197
Jet Engines (*see Engine Technology*)
John, Charles H., 110
Johnson, C. Wheeler, 118, 163, 176, 179
Jones, Jesse, 72, 88
Jones, Johnny, 96
Jongeward, Woody, 132
Jordan, Edward S. (Ned), 26, 35, 36, 39
Jordan Motor, 26, 35, 36, 39, 51
Judson, Ross W.
   (1902-1916) v, vii, ix, **5-10**, 12, 16, 205, 210
   (1917-1929) 23, 25, 27, 31, 32, 34, 36, 39, 40, 42, **45, 56**
   (1930-1939) **51**, 70, 74
Johnson, Sen. Lyndon B., 148, 149

K

Kaiser, Edgar, 123
Kaiser-Frazer, 63, 120, 123, 124, 137
Kaiser, Henry J., 123
Kalb, Lewis P., 64, 75, 86, 93, 105, 118, 119, 130, 152
Kaman helicopters, 137
Kanitz, Louis J., 28, 43, 58, 63, 72, 210
Keith, Craig, 70, 71
Keller, K. T., 88
Kennedy, Fred J., 108, 141, 152, 170, 174
King Motor Car Co., 25, 112
Kinnucan, James W., 87, 106, 181
Kissinger, Mike, 175
Kline, Harry D., 39
Knight double-sleeve-valve engine, 33, 43
Knox, George, 169, 170, 172, 174, 178, 181, 195, 196
Knudsen, William S., 87, 88
Krohn, Henry, 59
Krueger, Lt. Gen. Walter, 97
Kugler, Alfred E., 198
Kuns, Ray F., 36

L

LaBadie, Rene N. (Ray), 39, 42, 54
Labor Relations, 104, 105, 153, 176, 177
Lakey Foundry and Machine Co., 64, 71, 75, 80, 142, 174, 191
Lakey, W. Earl, 75
LaMeuse Belgian firm, 171
Lanova diesel engines, 119, 151
Lawrence Radiation Laboratory, 105
Lewis, W. E. (Gene), 197, 199, 202
Lexington-Howard "Minuteman", 15
Liberty Aircraft Engine (WWI), 58, 73
Liberty Trucks (WWI), 25
Light, Frank, 174, 175, 193, 196
Limbach, L. M. (Larry), 174, 175, 180, 190, 193, 197
Lindbergh, Charles A., 169, 211
Litrengines, 208-210
Litton Industries, 195
Lockheed Aircraft Corp., 80, 100, 101, 122
"Long Tom" M12 self-propelled gun, 90, 94
Longanecker, John (Bud), 92
Low-emission diesel engine, 199
Lubigraph Company, 73
Lufthansa German Airlines, 202
Luscombe aircraft, 159
Lycoming Engines, 24, 36, 74, 135, 155, 173, 216, 219
Lynde, Maj. Gen. Nelson M. Jr., 160
Lyndon Avenue Plant, Detroit, 147, 152
Lyngaas, Dolores, 192

M

MacGregor, Ian, 87
MAN (Maschinenfabrik Augsburg-Nurnberg), 159, 160
Mansfield, Bill, 182
Marbore Jet Engine, 138-140
Marine Engines (see Engines)
Markin, Morris, 157
Massey-Ferguson, 208
Massey-Harris, 28, 63

Massnick, Al, 160
McDonnell-Douglas aircraft and missiles, 101, 154, 223, 224
Mercedez-Benz Cars, ix
'Merkava' tank, 217
Merlin aircraft engines, 102, 103
Metric industrial engines, 207, 208
Meurer, Dr. S. J., 159, 160
Meyer, Andre, 53
Meyers aircraft, 159
Michaud Ordnance Plant, 134, 135
Michigan Material Corp., 28
Michigan Securities Commission, 24
Michigan Yacht and Power Co., 112
Milbrath, Arthur F., 110, 141
Military Truck Engines (see Engines)
Military Utility Tactical Truck (MUTT), 152
Missile and Drone Engines (see Engines)
Mobile, Alabama, plant, 190, 192, 214
Mock, Mrs. Jerrie, 186
Moon Motor Car Co., 26, 27, 30, 36, 51
Morehouse, Harold A., 57, 73, 74
Motorenfabrik Hatz KG, 204
Motors (see Engines)
Mulford, John W., 113, 142, 153
Mulford, O. J., 112, 113
Multi-Fuel Engines (see Engine Technology)
'Multi-Tool' engine, 132, 133
Murphy Diesel Co., 230
Murphy, Mayor Frank, 73
Murray, James L., (Jim), 180, 193, 196, 198, **223**
Muskegon Chamber of Commerce (and Greater Muskegon Industrial Foundation), 8, 62, 79, 105, 191
Muskegon, Michigan, plants, 8, 9, 31, 32, 102, 103, 192, 207

N

Nader, Ralph, 14
National Advisory Committee for Aeronautics, 43
National Aeronautics and Space Administration (NASA), 213, 222
National Construction Co., 28
National Petroleum Board, 91, 161
National Water Lift Co., 216, 218
Naugdahl, Sig, 110
Navion business plane, 120, 121, 132
Neosho, Missouri, plant, 192, 202
New York Stock Exchange, 67, 68, 70, 72, 79, 169, 195
Nichol, Ira W., 193, 198
Niven, A. M., 33
North American Aviation, 100-103, 120, 121, 154, 195
North Manitou Island, Michigan, 42, 55, 80, 85
Norton, Phil A., 111, 141, **194**, 196, 198
Novi Equipment Co., 158, 172, 175, 177, 178

O

Occidental Hotel, Muskegon, 89
Odom, Capt. William P., 131, 159
Officers and Directors (see Financial Affairs)
Ohlfest, Al, 93
Oil carbureted engines, 67, 119

237

Olds, Ransom E., 12
Ordnance Corps, U.S. Army, 26, 76, 77, 87, 90-92, 94, 95, 124-130, 131, 134, 135, 137, 148, 149, 159, 160-162, 188
Ortiz, Ray (Butch), 190, 199
Othman, Frederick, 12
Owens Yachts, 171
Ownership of Corporations (*see Financial Affairs*)
  Also see Ryan Aeronautical Company
  Also see Teledyne, Inc.

P

Packard Motor Co., 102, 103, 155, 156
"Packette" engines, 136, 151
Panama City, Florida, plant, 190
Parker, Mel, 176
Parkin, Don, 118
Patterson, Allen E. (Pat), 52
Patterson, Robert P., 88
Patton, Gen. George S., 93, 98
Patton tanks, 134, 135
Peek, Dr. Chester L., 57
Peerless Motor Car Corp., 36, 37, 71, 80
Peninsular Motor Company, 28
Perm-O-Flex radio speakers, 75
Peterson, K. Franklin, 10
Phillips, Ramon J. (Ray), 191, 199, 203, **207, 208**, 232
Piasecki helicopters, 122, 137
Piper Aircraft, 55-57, 97, 98, 121, 131, 201, 202, 214
Piper, William T., 55-57, 97
Pond, Lieut. George, 39
Porter, A. W., 70
'Powder Puff Derby', 186
Power and Light Division, 75, 76
Powers, Raymond P., 156, 174, 180, 190-194
Pratt & Whitney Aircraft Engines, 53, 57, 73, 74, 100-102, 106, 137, 223
Product Support Center, Chicago, 191
Profits, Sales, Dividends (*see Financial Affairs*)
Propeller ("Skypower" — by Continental), 122
PSA commuter airline, 202
Purcell, E. E., 93
Purvis, Arthur, 88

Q

Quinn, Lt. Gen. William, W., 184

R

Railroad Engines, 66
Ram Jet Engines, 122, 131
Rathert, Fred, 191, 198, 230, 232
Raven, William G., 177
Raymond, Dr. H. M.
Reconstruction Finance Corp. (RFC), 70, 72, 73, 78, 79, 86, 88, 100, 105, 179
Recreation (and agricultural) Engines, (*see Engines*)
Red Seal Engines, origin of, 26
Reese, Clarence J. (Jack)
  (1930-1939) v, vi, 51, 75, **78-80**
  (1940-1945) **85-89**, 94, 100, 104-109
  (1946-1953) 117-121, 123, **128-130, 141-143**
  (1954-1961) 151, 152, 156-158, **161-164**
  (1962-1975) 169, 170, 173-181, 186, 192, 193, 196

Renault Moteurs, 5-7, 202, 203, 210
Reuther, Walter, 104, 105, 177
Rheinstahl-Hanomag, 202, 203
Ricardo Engineering, 207, 208
Ricardo, Sir Harry R., 73, 207
Richardson, J. Lynn, 173, 174, 178, 180, 192, 193, 196, **198**, 199, 232
Richeson, Will, 172
Riedel, Dick, 131
Rivero, Major Luis, 202
Rockelman, Fred L., 59, 61, 62
Rocketdyne Division (No. Amer. Rockwell), 191
Rockwell International, 191, 193, 202
Roberts, Dr. George A., 195-198
Rolls-Royce Aircraft Engines, 35, 100, 102-104, 106, 154, 158, 171, 184, 185, 213
Rolls-Royce Tank Engines, 163
Rommel, Gen. Erwin, 91
Ronaldson Bros. & Tippett, Ltd., 158, 191, 193, 195
Roosevelt, Mrs. Eleanor, 72
Roosevelt, President Franklin D., 72, 80, 87, 89
Roosevelt, G. Hall, 72, 73
Rosen, Art, 161, 181, 182
Rosenbaum, L. N., 70-72
Rossi, Angela, 232
Rouse, Harold, 175, 192, 194, 198, **215-217**, 220, 232
Rublein, Ed, 118
Rutherford, G. Williams, vi, 140, **174**, 175, 178-181, **191-198**, 232
Ryan Aeronautical Company, 41, 42, 56, 120, 138, 140
  Acquisition of Continental Motors Corp. 169-181, 193
  Acquisition by Teledyne, Inc., 195
Ryan Airlines, Inc., 41
Ryan "Firebee" target drone, 138, 140, 154-155, 189
Ryan Navion plane, 120, 121, 186
Ryan reconnaissance drones, 189, 194, 226
Ryan School of Aeronautics, 54
Ryan, T. Claude, 41, 42, 120, 140, 169, 170, 194, 195

S

Saetta, Alex, 93
Sales Figures (*see Financial Affairs*)
Schemmer, Benjamin F., 232
Schweitzer, Prof. Paul H., 159
Sea Launched Cruise Missile (SLCM), 203, 226
Securities and Exchange Commission, 38, 86, 170
Selden, George S., ix
Seneca, South Carolina plant, 221
Sheaffer, W. A., 133
Sherman, Roger, 6, 58, 63, 70-72, 79
"Sherman" tank, 88-95
Siemens-Halske aircraft engines, 41, 42
Sikorsky helicopters, 154
Simpson, T. M., 63
Single-Sleeve-Valve (*see Engine Technology*)
Singleton, Dr. Henry, 195, 196, 203
Sintz, Claude, 112
Sintz Gas Engine Co., 112
Slusser, Charles, 132
Smith, A. O. Corp., 155
Smith, Lloyd M., 174
Smith, V. M., 40
Societe Turbomeca S.A. (*see Turbomeca*)
Society of Automotive Engineers, 25, 33
Somervell, Gen. Brehon, 90

"Spirit of St. Louis" Ryan Monoplane, 169
Stauss, Richard, 191, 232
Stilwell, Gen. Joseph W., 98, 125
Stock Issues and Stockholders (see Financial Affairs)
Stockholders Protective Committee, 70-72
Stout, William B., 39
Stromberg Carburetor Co., 35
Studebaker-Packard, 156
Studebaker Wagon Company, 8
Stutz Automobile Co., 110
Stutz, Harry, 7
Submarine Engines, 66
Subsonic Cruise Armed Decoy (SCAD), 203
Supercharging (see Engine Technology)
Szydlowski, Josef, 138, 184, 206

T

Tank and Tracked Vehicle Engines (see Engines)
Taxi Aereo Marilia (TAM), 202
Taylor Aircraft, 55-57, 97, 98
Taylor, C. G., 56, 57
Technical Notes (see Engine Technology)
Teledyne, Inc.
   Acquisition of Ryan Aeronautical Company, 195
   Acquisition of Continental Motors Corp., 195-199, 223
Teledyne CAE, 198, 203, **223-227** *(also see Continental Aviation & Engineering Corp.)*
Teledyne Continental Motors, 198
   see Aircraft Products Division
   see General Products Division
   see Industrial Products Division
Teledyne Wisconsin Motor, 198, 203, 204, **228-230**
Temco aircraft, 155
Tiara aircraft engine, 201, 202
Timken-Detroit Axle Co., 26
Timm, Robert, 159
Tinney, Rodney M. (Bob), 186
"Tiny Tim" battery charger, 75, 76, 98
Tobin, Arthur W., v, 5-9, 152
Tobin, Mrs. Ione, 5, 6
Tobin, Benjamin F., Sr.
   (1902-1916) v, 6-10, 16
   (1917-1920) 23, 24, 26, **27**, 51
Tobin, Benjamin F., Jr., 6, 29
   (1930-1939) 51, 70, 75
   (1940-1945) 86, 91, **105**
   (1946-1953) 118, 131, 153
   (1954-1961) 152
Tobin, Benjamin III, 6, 152, 153
Todd, Harold A., 108, 111, 141, 152, 173, 179, 193, 194
Todhunter, Mrs. Margaret, 132
Toledo plant (CAE), 155, 156, 223, 227
"Tomahawk" cruise missile, 225, 226
Truby, Henry T., 5
Truck Engines (Military) (see Engines)
Truman, Pres. Harry S., 134
Trundle Engineering Company, 80
Trundle, Robert C., 152, 156, 174
Turbine Engines (see Engine Technology)
Turbomeca engines, 138, 139, 154-156
Twin Coach Co., 75

U

Unisteel Cylinders, 182, 199, 216
United Automobile Workers (C.I.O.), 104, 105, 176

V

Van Alstyne, David A., Jr., 87, 106, 152, 173
Van Alstyne, Noel & Co., 79, 87, 130
Vandenberg, Gen. Hoyt S., 121
Vandenberg, Senator Arthur H., 58
Vanderbilt Cup Races, 11
Vanderpoel, Robert P., 68
Vandeven, Henry W., 58, 62, 75, 105, 141, 152, 163, 169, 170, 173, 175, 178, 179, 180, 191
Variable Compression Ratio (see Engine Technology)
Variable Speed Training Target (VSTT), 203, 225, 226
Vasco Metals (Vanadium Steel Co.), 195
Verville Aircraft, 52, 54
Vincent, Edward T., 66, 67
Vivian, Leslie L., 86, 105, 108
von Ohain, Hans, 138, 206

W

Waco aircraft, 52-55, 96
Wall Street Journal, 170
Wallace, Alfred W., 36
Wallace, Ltd., 33
Walterboro, S.C. plant, 178, 192
War Assets Administration, 122, 123
War Production Board, 103
Warren, Forrest, 140
"Water Buffalo" landing vehicles, 95
Waters, Leslie, 202
Watson, Luther S., 11
Wells, James W., 175, 194
Westinghouse Electric and Manufacturing Co., 28, 75
Wetzel, Thomas J., 10
Wheeler, L. E., 118
Whitacre, Phil, 175
White Motors, 200
Whitney, Richard, 67
Whittle, Sir Frank, 138, 206
Wilber, H. E., 75
Wilcox, Paul E., 42, 52-56, 232
Williams, Gov. G. Mennen, 121
Williams Turbine Engines, 203, 226
Wild, Arthur W., vi, 41, 42
   (1930-1939) 51, 52, 74, 76
   (1940-1945) **85-87**, 90, 93, 103, 105, 106
   (1946-1953) 122, 123, **127**, 135, **139**, 142
   (1954-1961) 156, 163
   (1962-1975) 169, 170, 173, 175, 176, **179-181**, 193, 196, 197
Willi, Albert B., 103, 106, 129, 130, 135, 163, 173, 180
Willys-Overland Company, 14, 36, 43, 51, 72
Winters, George E., 105, 118, 130
Wisconsin engines, 119, 120, 123, 130, 137, 141, 153, 157, 158, 171, 186, 187, 191, 194, 195, 203, 204, **228-230**
Wisconsin Motor Corp.
   Acquisition of, **107, 108**
   History of, 110, 111, 176, 177, 190, 191, 193, 196

239

Wiseman, William A., 197, 201, 202
Witter, Guy, 195
Wittman, Steve, 131
Woodcock, Leonard, 105, 176, 177
Woodhouse, Bob, 132
Wooldridge, Josh, 178, 196
Worthington, Maj. Gen. F. F., 93
Worthington Pump, 28
Wright Aeronautical Engines, 41, 53, 54, 73, 78, 87, 90, 101, 137
Wright Brothers, 164
Wurtz, E. C., 141

Y

Yellow Cab, 31, 43
Yeoman, George W., 6, 13, 16, 32
Yeoman, Mary Jane, v, 6
Young, Waldo, 61
Youngstown Sheet & Tube Co., 85, 86

Z

Zimmerman, A. H., 23
Zweiner, Wallace, 63